THE ADOPTION RESOURCE BOOK

Courtesy of

ADOPTION DIRECTIONS™

1-800-635-0606

WORK/FAMILY
DIRECTIONS

THE
ADOPTION
RESOURCE BOOK

THIRD EDITION

LOIS GILMAN

HarperPerennial

A Division of HarperCollins*Publishers*

To Ernie, Seth, and Eve

THE ADOPTION RESOURCE BOOK (THIRD EDITION). Copyright © 1984, 1987, 1992 by Lois Gilman. All rights reserved. Printed in the United States of America. No part of this book may be used or reproduced in any manner whatsoever without written permission except in the case of brief quotations embodied in critical articles and reviews. For information address HarperCollins Publishers, Inc., 10 East 53rd Street, New York, NY 10022.

HarperCollins books may be purchased for educational, business, or sales promotional use. For information, please call or write: Special Markets Department, HarperCollins Publishers, Inc., 10 East 53rd Street, New York, NY 10022. Telephone: (212) 207-7528; Fax: (212) 207-7222.

FIRST EDITION

Library of Congress Cataloging-in-Publication Data
Gilman, Lois.
　　The adoption resource book / Lois Gilman.—3rd ed.
　　　　p. cm.
　　Includes bibliographical references and index.
　　ISBN 0-06-271515-1 (hc)—ISBN 0-06-273043-6 (pb)
　　　1. Adoption—United States. 2. Intercountry adoption—United States.
　　3. Adoption agencies—United States—Directories.
　　I. Title.
　　HV875.55.G55　1992　　　　　　　　　　　　　　91-36432
　　362.7'34—dc20

92 93 94 95 96 CC/MB 10 9 8 7 6 5 4 3 2 1

Contents

Preface

"Why are you writing a book about adoption?" This question came up in nearly every interview. Was I a social worker passing on her long experience in the field? Was I a psychologist who counseled children and parents and wanted to promote family health? Was I a lawyer who had handled many a tricky adoption?

No. The answer is really very simple. I'm the mother of two children who are adopted. I am also a journalist and a professional researcher. From the time that my husband and I made our first inquiries about adoption in the seventies, I found myself putting my researching talents to work. As I made my calls and built up my own "adoption file," I wondered: What do others do? How do they get the information they need? When I looked at general books on adoption, I was surprised at how much was missing. I began to feel that there ought to be a clear, accurate guide that anticipates many of the questions and presents much of the information that I—a prospective adoptive parent and now an adoptive parent—had to learn from others piece by piece. I feel that poor information (and sometimes misinformation) too often stands as a barrier between prospective parents and children who need homes. So I wrote *The Adoption Resource Book*.

The first edition of this book appeared in 1984. Since then my children, Seth and Eve, have been growing up. I've shared with them the joy of watching friends adopt. And I've tackled my children's questions about adoption: What is adoption? Why was I adopted? What do you know about my other parents?

As my children have aged, so has this book. Reading it in 1991, I knew that the time had come for a complete overhaul. For this edition the directories and resource sections at the back of the book have been redone to try to reflect the current adoption scene more accurately. While I have retained some of the original chapter headings and content from the 1984 edition, I have rewritten extensively and added a chapter on open adoption. Within chapters I have included much new material. For example, I have explored in greater depth the risks of independent adoption, created a question box that focuses on readiness for special needs adoption, and presented first-person accounts such as that of an adoptive mother who's also a birth mother. I have striven to create a fresh and current book that presents a picture of adoption in the nineties.

My writing on adoption for magazines over the past eight years has also influenced the content and shape of this edition. Ghostwriting the story of two teens' decisions to pursue an open adoption for *YM*, interviewing birth mothers for an article for *Woman's Day*, and describing grandparents' feelings about adoption for *New Choices* opened up new windows for me. In *The Adoption Resource Book* I offer you some glimpses.

The Adoption Resource Book is just the beginning of your learning about adoption. It provides the necessary overview, as well as detailed, specific information. *The Adoption Resource Book* will have fulfilled its purpose if it makes your introduction to adoption just a little bit easier.

Although writing a book ultimately comes down to the relationship between the author and a piece of paper, its creation depends on the help of many people. My thanks to them all.

Scores of adoptive parents have taken the time over the years to talk with me at length about their pre- and post-adoption experiences. Their stories shaped the questions that I have tried to answer, and the scope of the book. Since their stories were told in confidence, I have changed their names and avoided identifying details.

This book has profited from the activities of adoptive parent groups around the country. I have relied on the expertise of staff and volunteers at the North American Council on Adoptable Children, Adoptive Families of America, Families Adopting Children Everywhere, Families for Private Adoption, The Open Door Society of Massachusetts, Latin America Parents Association, Adoptive Parents Committee, and New York Singles Adopting Children. I have also counted on national and local adoption conferences held by these groups and others, as well as information conveyed in newsletters such as *OURS*, *Adoptalk*, and *Adopted Child* to keep me current. Back in 1983 I found the fifty or so parent group newsletters to which I subscribed invaluable. My special thanks go to the groups that responded at that time to my request for a complimentary subscription.

Many people have extended help when it was requested. Among them are: Terry Allor, Kristina A. Backhaus, Maris Blechner, Nancy Boucneau, Virginia Brackett, Deborah Burke, Nancy Carey, Karen Clarke, MariAnne Clarke, Kathy and Tom Coghlan, Kay Donley, Paul Dubroff, Mary Helen Evans, Ann Feldman, Nancy Greene, Donna Haanen, Kenneth J. Hermann, Barbara Holtan, Jim Jenkins, Joyce Kaser, Ernesto Loperena, Phyllis Lowinger, Hope Marindin, Cheryl Markson, Patricia McCormick, AnnaMarie Merrill, Toni Oliver, Reuben Pannor, Marlene Ross, Linda Salzer, Roselle Schubin, Sherry Simas, Peg Soule, Rosemary Stowe, Mary Sullivan, Clyde Tolley, and Vicki Vidak. For my discussion of open adoption, special thanks go to the staff of Lutheran Family Services of Colorado, who allowed me to sit in on their group home study.

Over the years many individuals have served as sounding boards, have read portions of the manuscript, and have offered insightful comments. My thanks to Connie Anderson, Kay Donley, Susan Freivalds, Ellen Fritz, Blanche Gelber, Jim Gritter, Wilfred Hamm, Sara-Jane Hardman, Dr. Jerri Jenista, Sharon Kaplan, Betty Laning, Lois Ruskai Melina, Marlene Piasecki, Susan Pignato, Kathleen Silber, Cheryl Simons, Pat Shirley, and Barbara Tremitiere. At HarperCollins Janet Goldstein and Peternelle van Arsdale have lent their enthusiasm and gently guided me to the best way to tell the story.

Family and friends offered invaluable support. David Heim, Katherine Foran, Eleanor Prescott, Nicholas Garaufis, Jeanne Heymann, Dale Candela, and Susan Stone Wong were always willing to listen to my latest idea or draft of a paragraph, while Dan Carlinsky has offered me his special literary wisdom. At *Time* magazine Jeanne North and Victoria Rainert have encouraged me to pursue my outside interests. Deirdre Laughton has provided a special service, keeping my children happy. As for my family, Lotte Prager and Susan and Brian McCarthy, I know they are always just a telephone call away.

Most of all I thank my three Gilmans. Seth and Eve give me the chance to enjoy both childhood and parenthood simultaneously and, even on the worst of days, make life just a little bit brighter. Since the day in 1967 that Ernest Gilman first served as my editor on the *Columbia Daily Spectator,* he has been my most ardent supporter and my toughest critic. He has slogged through drafts of this manuscript countless times, helped me through computer failures, program snafus, and endless almost-missed deadlines. He has given me the best perspective I could bring to this work: "For love, all love of other sights controls." To him I wish "the good morrow."

Lois Gilman
September 1991

1

Learning About Adoption

Once upon a time there lived a man and woman named James and Martha Brown. They had been married for a long time and were very happy together. Only one thing was missing in their lives. They had no babies of their own, and they had always wanted children to share their home.

So begins *The Chosen Baby,* Valentina P. Wasson's adoption classic for parents to read with their young children. James and Martha, so the story goes, meet with Mrs. White at the adoption agency. She asks them many questions and then visits their home to see where the child would sleep and play. A little baby named Peter is eventually placed in their home. When Mrs. White introduces them to Peter, she says, "Now go into the next room and see the baby. If you find that he is not *just the right baby for you,* tell me, and we will try to find another." But Peter is. An adoptive family is created.

The Chosen Baby, published in 1939 and reissued over the years in updated versions, has been read to three generations of adopted children. A story written about adoption today, however, might be quite different:

- Linda and Edward Tuttle contact Mrs. Andrews at the adoption agency. She tells them that her agency places infants, but that it is the birth mother who selects the future parents of her child. Helen Doe looks at the autobiography that Linda and Edward Tuttle have prepared and chooses them as Peter's adoptive parents. When the baby is born, Helen calls to announce his arrival and invites the Tuttles to visit him at the hospital.

- Linda and Edward Tuttle have three children—two boys (ages ten and eight) and a girl (age fourteen). They have always wanted many children to share their home. They contact Mrs. Andrews at the adoption agency to tell her that they would like to adopt two teenagers. They find John and Suzanne, twelve and eleven, in a photograph book distributed by their state that describes children needing permanent homes.

- Linda and Edward Tuttle have no babies of their own and they want children to share their home. So they place an advertisement in a newspaper in their state: "ADOPTION: Happily married couple wishes to adopt white infant." Helen Doe calls them up about her baby.

- Linda and Edward Tuttle contact Mrs. Andrews at the adoption agency. Her agency places children from Latin America. After she studies their home, she sends their application to an agency in Colombia. A year later Linda and Edward Tuttle travel to Colombia to pick up their infant son, Pedro.

- Linda and Edward Tuttle have been nine-year-old Peter's foster parents for the past three years. They contact Mrs. Andrews at the adoption agency to ask whether they might adopt him.

- Linda Tuttle has always wanted children. But she's forty and single. She contacts Mrs. Andrews about the possibilities of adoption. Linda adopts one-month-old Peter; his mother, a drug addict, had smoked crack during her pregnancy and abandoned him at the hospital.

- Edward Tuttle has always wanted children. But he's forty-five and single. He contacts Mrs. Andrews about the possibilities of adoption. He adopts eight-year-old Peter.
- Linda and Edward Tuttle contact Mrs. Andrews at the adoption agency. She tells them that her agency is not currently taking applications but she will put their name on a waiting list. Five years later Linda and Edward Tuttle are still waiting.

The story of adoptive families is changing. Childless couples are still adopting, but so are couples with birth children, and so are singles. Agencies are still placing babies, but they are also placing older children, sibling groups, and children with physical and mental handicaps. Families are still coming to agencies for help in becoming parents, but they are also seeking to adopt on their own. They are also forming families by adopting children born abroad. And birth parents, once the unseen participants in the adoption story, are playing an active role in the formation of the adoptive family. The portrait of adoption today is a complex one, a composite of many different practices.

In fact the very definition of adoption is no longer as straightforward or as simple as it was once understood to be. Adoption traditionally was seen as an event that culminated when the new parents went to court and vowed, before a judge, to take a child, whose bonds with the birth parents had been legally terminated, as their new son or daughter. The child's past history—the documents that record how the child moved from his or her relationship with the birth family into the relationship with the adoptive parents—was sealed away. The adoptive parents then raised the child as their own, following the model of the family created by birth. To take a child as one's own was understood to mean cutting the child off from his or her genetic past.

Now that view has come under attack. The veil of secrecy that has traditionally surrounded adoption is being lifted.

Adults who were adopted as infants are telling us that growing up as an adopted child is different. They have come back to the agencies and the courts that hold their records and demanded the right to know about those other parents. They have challenged us to look at adoption as a lifelong event, with the court hearing marking the beginning rather than the end. They have told us that we can't obliterate their other parents. Birth parents, who released their children twenty, thirty, and forty years ago, are also returning to the agencies, telling us that the child they surrendered long ago has not been forgotten and that they need to know what happened to their child. And the birth parents of today are voicing the desire to play an active role in the adoption and to maintain some contact with the child and the adoptive parents after the placement has been made. The story of the chosen baby is being rewritten. In its place we have the adoption triad—the birth parent, the adoptive parent, and the adoptee, all with needs and rights that must be acknowledged.

In this new world of adoption no child is unadoptable. Adoption advocates have shown us that a family can be found for the twelve-year-old boy who's spent his life shuttling between foster homes as well as for the cute, cuddly newborn. The notion of who can be parents has expanded to include couples in their fifties, people with physical disabilities, single women and men, homosexual men, and lesbians. Birth parents are encouraged to be the initial architects of the adoption plan for their children, and prospective adoptive parents are now spoken of as the resource for birth parents, not the other way around. As confidentiality gives way to openness, adoption is coming to be seen as a relationship between families, forged out of a mutual interest in a child, that extends for a lifetime.

New adoption practices are emerging. Among them, parent preparation for foster care and adoption in group meetings; the selection of adoptive parents by the birth parents; the encouragement of contact between birth and adoptive parents through meetings, telephone calls, or letters; the disclosure of full information about a child's background and family history to the adoptive parents; continued agency involvement with families after the finalization of an adoption; and the release of detailed information to adult adoptees about their past.

We are also coming to recognize the key roles that grief and loss play in the adoption experience. It is from loss—the birth parents' loss of the child born to them, the adoptees' loss of their birth parents, and the adoptive parents' loss of the child who might have been born to them—that adoption comes about. These losses and the ways they are mourned, the feelings such as shame and guilt that they generate, and the means by which they are resolved, must be confronted as they reverberate over the years.

The Adoption Resource Book tries to answer both the older and the newer questions that adoptive parents have about starting and raising a family. Like most adoption handbooks, it begins with information about how to build a family. As Chapters 2 through 7 make clear, however, there are now many keys that will unlock the door to parenthood. Chapters 8 and 9 detail the paperwork that is part of all adoptions. Chapters 10, 11, and 12 sketch out the needs of parents and children: the preparations parents should make; the weeks, months, and years that go into building a family; the issues involved in raising a family created through adoption. These chapters seek to point out what parents will need to consider rather than to provide definitive answers. Finally, there are state-by-state directories of U.S. and intercountry adoption agencies, a resource list, and a reference list for further information.

Underlying this book are a few basic premises:

• Children have a right to grow up in permanent families. Adoption offers them this opportunity.

- Adoption is a way of building a family. It is no better or worse than any other way. It is different, however. That difference must be acknowledged and dealt with.
- Prospective parents need good, basic, accurate information about adoption.
- Adoptive families need support from others—support that begins when parents first think about adoption and continues throughout the life of the family.
- Adoptive parents must focus on the needs of their children as well as their own needs. Communication and openness are important.
- Adoption is a lifelong experience.

Approaching Adoptive Parenthood

Adopting a child will involve making many decisions. What kind of child? Do you want to adopt through an agency? If not, what other means will you use to make it happen? First, though, you should look at yourself. Is adoptive parenthood or even parenthood itself what you really want? Your own feelings will influence the type of child you seek to adopt and will have a direct impact on the child you raise. Since adoption involves deliberate family planning, as you get started, ask yourself these basic questions:

- How important is it for you to be a parent?
- How important is it for you to have a baby?
- How important is it for you to experience a pregnancy?
- Are you satisfied that you can provide a healthy family life for a child?
- Have you adequately explored avenues other than adoption for parenting?
- If you have a fertility problem, how have you dealt with it? Are you still grieving?

- How do you feel about parenting a child who is not biologically related to you?
- Can you love a child for what he or she is, rather than what you hoped he or she would be?
- Do you have a fantasy child? How does adoption fit with this?
- Do you have the ability to accept a child different from yourself?
- There are risks in adoption, as there are in all life experiences. How willing are you to accept risks?
- What types of risks are you willing to take? How would you feel—and what would you imagine yourself doing—if the child you adopted turned out to have special needs that you hadn't been looking for?
- Your child is going to think about his or her genetic history and relinquishment. Are you prepared to deal with these realities of adoption? How willing are you going to be to explore for answers with your child?
- What are your fears about adoption? Are you worried that you will never be seen as your child's real parent? What else concerns you?
- Where is your spouse/significant other on this? How do other members of your family feel? How important to you are the extended family's feelings?
- Do you have the perseverance to adopt?

Observes adoption consultant Kay Donley: "Families have to understand that with adoption, as with birthing, there is an element of risk that cannot be controlled. You prepare yourself for what is known and what is expected. Then you proceed. That is the way life is lived. People who come to the adoption agency expecting the Good Housekeeping seal of approval on the forehead of a child should think of something else."

THE DECISION TO ADOPT, THE DECISION TO PLACE

Have you ever wanted to ask someone what goes into an adoption decision? Here's what some adoptive parents and birth parents have to say about the decisions they made:[1]

- Ellen Lyons, who with her husband Nick adopted a newborn.

"As we got closer and closer to understanding what our fertility options were—whether we were going to move into *in vitro* fertilization or not, as we got to the point of making the decision of stopping the cycle of Pergonal—I had to open another door. That way I was able to close slowly the infertility door and to open slowly the adoption door. We spent about six months going back and forth. At some point we made the decision we were not going to do *in vitro*. And my husband said to me: 'Do you really want to be pregnant or have a baby?' "

- Abby Elkins, a single woman in her forties who adopted a one-month-old special-needs infant.

"I was getting to be a certain age, and I knew that I really wanted a family. I never thought that I wouldn't have one. It surprised me that I felt a lack of being a parent. My mother's dying made me realize what she had been to me and that I had always expected to be that to someone. I looked at my life. I had been assuming that I had forever. I realized that I wanted to adopt. And I just said that there are children out there who are already made. It didn't seem logical to me to have a biological child. I have this really strong sense that where the child comes from is not important, it's the spirit inside. If this child is put into your care—whether you give birth or adopt—it's your child."

- Johanna Williams, a single lesbian mother in her forties who adopted two four-year-old girls from two different countries in Latin America.

"I decided years before I came out that I wanted to adopt. Then I had to deal with coming out, so it had to be postponed. I thought about adopting for a good ten to fifteen years before I ever did it. Adoption seemed like what I wanted to do; artificial insemination did not.

"I hadn't considered international adoption until I ran into an acquaintance at a gas station who had a child who was clearly Hispanic. So I said, 'My goodness, tell me about this.' And I adopted older children because that's who I wanted to adopt."

- Margaret Alcott, birth mother who placed her infant daughter.

"I'd had two abortions and went through very bad feelings afterward. It was terrible. When I became pregnant with my daughter, I didn't go to a doctor or do anything for six months because I didn't want to be offered the option of an abortion. I thought about keeping the baby, but I knew that the father wasn't going to marry me. I just couldn't see raising the child on my own. It just wouldn't have been fair to the child. I couldn't give a child what a child needed. When the option of a private, open adoption came along, I felt that this was something I could go with. Now I see my child getting fully what she needs."

- Sara Charles, birth mother who placed her infant daughter.

"My boyfriend Matt and I had been dating for four months when I became pregnant the summer after high school graduation. Right from the start, I decided I couldn't have an abortion. I'm Catholic and I knew that I couldn't face myself if I chose that route. I also felt that getting married and raising the baby would create more problems for Matt and me. He was twenty, on leave from college, working and living at home. And college was still in my future. What kind of life could we offer our child? We needed another solution.

"My mom and dad took me to an adoption agency and the people there told me about the difference between traditional and open adoption. It was several months before I finally made up my mind to have an open adoption.

"Picking the family was very important, but it was also very hard and I cried all the time. I loved my baby so much, yet I was going to give her away. But if I kept her, I knew that life would be a struggle. I loved her enough to let her go."

- Matt Thomas, birth father of Sara Charles's infant daughter.

"When Sara told me she was pregnant and that she wouldn't have an abortion, I was startled. Right then I knew that we had to deal with this and that I wouldn't walk away from her.

"Fathering this baby is the toughest problem that I have ever had. As I watched Sara with our daughter in the hospital, I wondered if we should change our minds and keep her. And when the adoptive parents took Danielle home, that was really rough. But the worst day was when we signed the rights over and had no more control over our daughter's life.

"I'm convinced that adoption was the right thing for us. We both felt that we couldn't drop everything and raise a child the way we wished."

Coming to Terms with Your Infertility

According to data collected by the National Center for Health Statistics, one in twelve American women between the ages of fifteen and forty-four—some 4.9 million—had an impaired ability to have children in 1988.[2] Contrary to what you've probably read in the popular press or heard bandied about, the rate of infertility is not increasing, and there is no infertility epidemic. The number of childless women between the ages of twenty-five and forty-four with impaired fertility has gone up, however, because of women's decisions to delay childbearing and because there are more people—the so-called baby boom generation—in that age range. If your inability to produce a child biologically has led you to think about adoption, you will want to be sure that you have dealt with your infertility *before you adopt a child.*

What Do You Know About Infertility?

Infertility specialists estimate that as many as 70 percent of all couples with fertility problems may respond to medical treatment.[3] The past two decades have witnessed many breakthroughs in the treatment of infertility. Powerful drugs can stimulate ovulation, and microsurgery can repair damaged tubes in women. A surgical procedure can tie off a man's varicocele—a testicular varicose vein—and dramatically improve male fertility. Endometriosis may yield to drug therapy or surgery.

We've come a long way from that day in 1978 when the first "test tube baby," Louise Brown, was born. Since then more than 10,000 babies have been conceived through *in vitro* fertilization. Pregnancies are also achieved through GIFT (gamete intrafallopian transfer) and ZIFT (zygote intrafallopian transfer), variations on the *in vitro* process, and egg donations. In addition, each year 30,000 or more infants in the United States are believed to be conceived through artificial insemination by donor (AID), a simple procedure performed at a doctor's office in which the sperm of an anonymous donor is inserted into a woman's vagina near the cervix. For others the choice has been to find a surrogate mother who agrees to be artificially inseminated with the man's sperm, to then carry the pregnancy, and after delivery to relinquish all parental rights to the baby. The permutations and combinations of these new conceptions—whether they be donor insemination, *in vitro* fertilization, embryo transfer, freezing embryos, or surrogate mothers—are many, and the legal and ethical questions they have raised are heatedly debated.

You'll want to do some basic reading about infertility and the new medical technologies. As Dr. Sherman Silber states, "Even for those who have no hope of pregnancy, at least a clear understanding of how their bodies work can prevent needless anxiety about whether or not they have gone far enough in their search."[4] There are many excellent books, listed at the back of this book, that you can consult. Understanding human reproduction and infertility enables you to ask the appropriate questions and to find the realistic answers that you will need in order to come to terms with your medical condition.

If You Adopt a Child, Will You Get Pregnant?

Perhaps you've wistfully thought—or a relative has suggested—that as soon as you adopt, you're bound to achieve a pregnancy. After all, Cousin Irma did. Pregnancy following adoption is one of those adoption myths that refuses to die. Reports Linda Salzer in *Surviving Infertility:* "A number of well-designed, controlled studies have investigated this idea and found no difference in pregnancy rates between those couples who had previously adopted and those who had not."[5]

What Medical Advice Have You Sought?

Both of you will need a full medical workup by a specialist. Fertility problems are equally common in men and women. For the man, that means a physical examination as well as a semen analysis. Sometimes both the man and the woman contribute to the problem. Small changes in both may result in a pregnancy.

Your regular family physician or your gynecologist may be a fine doctor, but he or she may not necessarily be the person most qualified to analyze a fertility problem. Some gynecologists, urologists, or reproductive endocrinologists have developed specialties in infertility. The **American Fertility Society** (2140 Eleventh Avenue South, Birmingham, Alabama 35202-2800; 205-933-8494) can refer you to qualified specialists in your area. The self-help group **Resolve** (1310 Broadway, Somerville, Massachusetts 02144; 617-623-0744), which has local chapters throughout the United States, also provides infertility counseling and referral services. Support groups will make referrals to local physicians, offer lectures and workshops about fertility issues, and give you a chance to talk about your feelings.

If you have a choice of several specialists, try to learn a little about them before you make your decision. Does the doctor have a subspecialty within the field? Does the physician work in a team with other specialists? Is there an infertility counselor (a therapist who will talk with you) on the support staff? Be sure that you find a doctor with whom you feel comfortable and who will permit you to ask questions. Your physician has many infertile patients to consider; you have only one—yourself.

Even after you have found your doctor, you may want to talk with another specialist to confirm a recommended course of treatment, to get a second opinion before surgery, or to help you decide whether it might be time to cease treatment altogether. Before your visit, check with the specialist to be sure that your own physician has forwarded your medical records. It can also be helpful for you to prepare your own medical résumé for the consultant, a summary of your past history, surgery, and drug therapy. Preparing this résumé will force you to evaluate where you are.

What Have You Asked Your Doctor?

Ask *all* the questions that you want answered, and don't be shy about bringing in a list. You'll want a full explanation of any procedures your doctor is advocating, including their risks and success rates. Try to pin the doctor down as to the expected length of any course of treatment. You have a right to know the game plan. If possible, have your spouse present, to give you moral support and to be sure that all issues that concern you are raised.

Have You Acknowledged to Yourself and to Others How Being Infertile Makes You Feel?

If you have been struggling to become pregnant, you've probably felt depressed, overwhelmed, guilty, and cheated. There may be tension in your marriage. You may have harbored thoughts of divorce so that your spouse can find a more fertile partner. You've probably found it painful to be around friends with children. You may find that your sleep is disturbed, that you have nightmares, that you awaken feeling distressed. Says infertility counselor Roselle Schubin: "As a medical problem, infertility is rather unique. You can't get adjusted to it. Every month the question arises—will ovulation occur and will the husband perform sexually? Infertile couples are in an almost constant state of crisis."[6]

Resolving this crisis means not only getting the medical answers that will satisfy you but also coming to terms emotionally with your infertility. The failure to produce a biological child is a major loss and blow to your self-esteem. There are strong feelings that must be acknowledged.

To work through your infertility you must face it openly. You must talk to your spouse and others. Express your feelings. Support groups like Resolve can help you. There are several excellent books that focus on the emotional challenges infertility poses. Since infertility involves loss, you must grieve for the child you never had, for the child who might have been, for your inability to create life. You'll feel angry, upset, guilty, and finally you'll be able to let go. Coming to grips with your infertility may mean giving up the quest and accepting yourself and your family as you are.

How Do You Know That You're Ready to Think About Adoption or Child-Free Living?

There comes a time when people with impaired fertility begin to question whether they should move beyond the medical tests and procedures. Some will decide for child-free living; others will choose to pursue adoption. Each family's timetable is different, and it's not uncommon for one partner to be ready long before the other is. That may be upsetting, but it is quite natural for spouses to reach the decision to adopt at different points in time. "The process of coming to grips with adoption is time-consuming and very emotional," says Linda Salzer. "It can start at a point where people say, 'I will never adopt' or 'I don't want anything to do with it.' There are a lot of people who ultimately adopt who had that kind of viewpoint."

How, then, do people get from point A to point B? Linda Salzer offers the following questions as guideposts:[7]

- Have you exhausted all the medical possibilities that you feel comfortable with or can afford to pursue? You should do as much as you feel physically, emotionally, and financially able to do. That varies with each individual. Some people will try *in vitro* fertilization six times before they say enough; others will say they don't even want to consider hormone treatments.

- Are you feeling now that parenthood is more important, or is pregnancy still a major concern for you?
- Are you upset that infertility seems to have taken over your life? Have you gotten to the point where you are wanting to put this chapter behind you?
- Are you feeling that your present efforts and treatments are hopeless? Observes Salzer: "Many people are able to say that there was a point in their treatment when they moved from hope about each coming cycle to where they said, 'Hey, I'm starting another cycle, but I know that it's not going to work.'"
- Are you upset with the kind of person you've become? Are you tired of having to avoid your friends with children because of the emotional pain it causes you? Are you tired of being depressed and dragged out?
- Are you looking forward to the time when you can stop taking your temperature and can forget about fertility drugs, visits to the doctor, and what the latest infertility research shows?
- Are you feeling the need for some form of closure? Are you thinking to yourself, 'I'll try two more cycles of donor insemination and that's it'?
- Are you finding yourself wanting to talk about alternative means of achieving parenthood?

If you answered yes to many of these questions, chances are that you should evaluate your alternatives. Getting to the next step, says Salzer, "is answering those questions and being able to talk about adoption without bursting into tears. You're starting to feel excited that you will have a family in the not-so-distant future."

There's another key factor in this equation. "Adoption is not a solution to infertility," says social worker Phyllis Lowinger. "It is a solution to the question of parenting."

Getting Information About Adoption

As you contemplate adoption, you will need to explore both resources that will help you build your family and resources that you can turn to for continuing information and support in the years ahead. The **National Adoption Information Clearinghouse** (11426 Rockville Pike, Rockville, MD 20852; 301-231-6510) is a good place to begin, as you can obtain referrals to local agencies and support groups as well as free information sheets. Your initial steps will take you in three directions: (1) making contact with adoptive families and parent groups, (2) checking with social service agencies for general information as well as for details about specific adoption programs, and (3) reading.

Making Contact with Adoptive Families and Parent Groups

Getting to know other adoptive families is a first step in adoption and one you should continue to take as the years pass by. You may know people who have adopted and who will share their experiences with you. Spend time with their families and observe their children. If you are thinking about an intercountry adoption, talk to people about their experiences and observe their children. If you are contemplating an older-child adoption, spend some time around older children. Ask parents what it's like to start a family with a ten-year-old. If you are interested in adopting a child who has a special need, such as a physical, mental, or emotional handicap, try to observe a child with this problem.

There are several hundred parent groups in the United States. Local groups can give you basic information about adoption. The **Open Door Society of Massachusetts** (P.O. Box 1158,

Westboro, Massachusetts 01581; 800-932-3678), for example, is a statewide organization with a membership of 1,500 families and chapters throughout the state. It publishes a newsletter, maintains a library of audio- and videotapes on adoption that members can borrow, sells adoption-related books, and organizes discussion groups. Its annual spring New England Adoption Conference draws some 1,600 people (sample sessions: "After An Open Adoption," "The Infertile Couple Looks at Adoption," "Single Parent Adoption: Is It Right for Me?" and "How Children Think About Adoption").

Some parent groups have developed adoption information courses. **Families Adopting Children Everywhere (FACE)** (P.O. Box 28058, Baltimore, Maryland 21239; 410-488-2656) offers a course on family building through adoption at various locations throughout Maryland and Virginia. The course, which extends over several weeks, uses parents and experts to provide an overview of what's happening in domestic and intercountry adoption. Says Clyde Tolley of FACE: "The course covers the waterfront and provides a general introduction for folks unfamiliar with adoption. It gives them the chance to make decisions about whether they want to adopt, and if they do, which alternatives are going to meet their needs. While there may be books that give an introduction, the experience is not the same as going to a class and participating with adoptive parents, agency people, birth parents, and adult adoptees." The FACE course has served as the prototype for many adoption information courses around the country. If you've got doubts and concerns about adoption, sitting in a class may help clear them up. Observes Peggy Phillips, an adoptive parent who developed a continuing education course for the Northampton County Area Community College in Pennsylvania: "It is much easier to walk out of a class than an adoption agency to which you might be financially committed. This way, you can learn the pros and cons and ask questions you might feel hesitant to broach at an agency for fear you might say something out of line."

The directory at the back of this book gives the addresses of several organizations around the country that can put you in touch with a local parent group. Sometimes, however, it's as simple as checking in your local telephone book under "Adoption." The **North American Council on Adoptable Children (NACAC)** (1821 University Avenue, St. Paul, Minnesota 55104; 612-644-3036) is a nonprofit coalition of individuals and organizations working for the rights of children in the areas of foster care and adoption. As a major national adoption organization, it functions in part as a clearinghouse for adoptive parent support groups around the country. Its state representatives (listed in the first directory of this book under each state) will inform you about local parent groups and agencies. They'll be glad to answer many of your basic questions about your state's adoption practices. As an adoption advocacy group, NACAC also monitors federal child welfare legislation, pushes for better access to adoption services, and holds an annual national conference.

Adoptive Families of America (AFA) (3333 Highway 100 North, Minneapolis, Minnesota 55422; 612-535-4829) is another national parent group that serves as a clearinghouse and has affiliate groups around the country. AFA provides a free, fact-packed adoption information booklet to all who write or call. Like NACAC, it monitors federal legislation and will refer you to local groups. Membership includes a subscription to the excellent, informative bimonthly magazine *OURS.* Adoptive Families of America also stocks an extensive collection of adoption-related books, audiotapes, dolls, and other products that it sells mail-order. And there's an annual conference designed to provide you with basic information about adoption.

The **Committee for Single Adoptive Parents** (P.O. Box 15084, Chevy Chase, Maryland 20815) serves as a clearinghouse for singles seeking information. Membership entitles you to a list of agencies and other contacts (with updates) that singles will want to approach about adoption. The committee can also provide you with the names of single-parent groups as well as other single parents to talk to. *The Handbook for Single Adoptive Parents* (available mail-order from the committee) is an excellent introductory guide to single parenthood offering help on such topics as the mechanics of adoption, managing single parenthood, and coping with challenges. Another specialized support organization is **Stars of David** (2 Wenonah Avenue, Rockaway, New Jersey 07866; 201-627-7752), which is for Jewish adoptive families. Gay men and lesbians can receive help from the **National Center for Lesbian Rights, Adoption & Foster Parenting Project** (1370 Mission Street, San Francisco, California 94103; 415-621-0674).

An excellent way to obtain a quick, general overview is to attend an adoption conference or day-long workshop. **The Adoptive Parents Committee of New York** (80 Eighth Avenue, New York, New York 10011; 212-683-9221), the Open Door Society, and FACE, in addition to NACAC and Adoptive Families of America, are among the groups that hold annual conferences. **Adoptive Families Support Association** (P.O. Box 91247, Cleveland, Ohio 44101-32471; 216-526-3618) sponsors a biennial conference focusing on intercountry adoption, while the biennial conference of **Single Parents Adopting Children Everywhere (SPACE)** (6 Sunshine Avenue, Natick, Massachusetts 01760; 508-655-5426) is devoted to the concerns of single adoptive parents. Check with AFA or NACAC to find out when an adoption conference or workshop is being held in your state.

Checking with Social Service Agencies

Seeking out a parent group is a beginning; so is contacting your public agencies. Your state department of public welfare may be able to supply you with useful information: brochures describing state adoption programs, subsidy programs, fact sheets describing intercountry adoption procedures. Some states now have toll-free telephone numbers that you can call to request information about adoption. (If you write, don't be surprised if it takes two or more months to get a reply. Or it's possible that you may never get a reply.)

You'll also want to start by getting in touch with local agencies, both public and private, to learn about their specific programs. Chapter 2 provides a basic orientation to agencies and how they work. The directories at the back of the book list agencies state by state. Whatever type of adoption you choose to pursue, there's a good chance that you will need an agency's involvement to bring it to fruition. Touching base initially with agencies gives you a better grasp of adoption in the United States and in your state today.

Reading

As a prospective parent you will probably read books that focus on child care and child development. As a prospective adoptive parent, you will also want to read books that touch on some specialized topics related to adoption. References to some of these works are placed at the appropriate points in the text. The section entitled "For Further Reference" at the back of this book surveys current books about adoption. You may want to read some of these now; others may be more relevant in the years ahead. As you start making your adoption plans, you may want to mix your general reading with some personal accounts. Books like Michael Dorris's *The Broken Cord,* Jill Krementz's *How It Feels to be Adopted,* Gail Sheehy's *Spirit of Survival,* Susan T. Viguers's *With Child: One Couple's Journey to Their Adopted Children,* and Joseph Blank's *Nineteen Steps Up the Mountain: The Story of the DeBolt Family* bring the adoption experience up close. Each captures family life and feelings.

The Children Needing Adoption in the United States

Despite reports you may have heard on television or from a neighbor about the lack of infants needing adoption, you'll find that infants are still placed for adoption. Since many people want to adopt healthy infants, some agencies will inform families that they can expect to wait, perhaps for several years, for a healthy, white infant. At agencies where the birth parents choose the adoptive parents, however, you may not be asked to wait, since the agency needs to offer to the birth parents a sizable pool of prospective adoptive parents. (Once you are involved in an agency program, you might still wait for a birth mother to choose you.) There is also often not a wait for black infants. Chapter 2 explains agency adoption programs, while Chapter 5 talks about how open adoptions work.

There is another way that infants enter adoptive families, however. In the majority of states birth parents may bypass agencies and choose to place their babies directly with adoptive parents. Chapter 4 provides a full discussion of independent adoption, while Chapter 2 discusses a hybrid known as identified adoption.

When you inquire at an agency about adoption, you may be told that the children currently waiting for homes are older, or black, or of other minority-group parentage. They may be part of a sibling group. Some may have medical conditions such as cerebral palsy, hydrocephalus, spina bifida, or Down syndrome. Others have emotional handicaps or are developmentally delayed. Some of the older children are physically healthy (though they may have emotional problems) but wait nonetheless because of their ages. There are also younger children, including babies and toddlers, needing adoptive homes; most often their mothers were known to have used alcohol or drugs during their pregnancy, and the children have been deemed "at risk" for future problems. Some infants have also tested positive for the HIV antibody. Most agencies occasionally place healthy white toddlers and young school-age children, but they will have waiting lists for these children. The profile of the black children waiting for adoption, however, is different. There are black children of all ages waiting for homes. Black sibling groups are particularly common. If you are white and thinking about adoption, be aware, however, that many agencies will not place children transracially.

Children who have been waiting for adoptive families for a period of time are often referred to as "waiting children." Children who have disabilities are often referred to as "special-needs" children. The definition of a special-needs or a waiting child may vary state by state. In some states and at some agencies you may find that children who are members of a minority group or who are older are referred to as special-needs children. Chapter 6 discusses waiting children in the United States.

Chapter 7 discusses the children in other countries who wait for homes and who have been placed in American adoptive families.

Making Your Adoption Plan

The chapters that follow survey how you can go about building your adoptive family: working through an agency, working independently, searching for an infant or an older child in the United States, or searching for an infant or an older child abroad.

Your homework begins now. To make your adoption plan you must:

- Pull together as much information as you can, from a variety of sources, sift through it, and evaluate it.
- Determine the kind of child you hope to adopt. Do you imagine yourself the instant parent of an infant, of twins, of a three-year-old and a six-year-old? What feels comfortable? Do you think that a child of a different racial or ethnic heritage will be accepted in your family and community?
- Find a parent group that you can turn to for support and join it.
- Understand how the adoption process works.

- Learn what the various adoption options are in relation to the child you imagine adopting.
- Decide what's of primary importance to you. You'll need to think about waiting times, risks, and your need for confidentiality, for example.
- Determine your financial status: What costs can you assume?
- Assess your flexibility on various adoption issues.

As the next chapter on agencies makes clear, agencies are not alike. Their philosophies may differ radically. How they approach adoption may directly influence how you view adoption and how you create your family. Sometimes it is possible for you to make choices, sometimes not.

Your basic goal now, as you ferret out information, is to seek out supports and build your own adoption network. The friends that you make, the groups that you join, the services that you uncover will stay with you in the years ahead. You're beginning an experience that has no end.

2

Exploring Adoption Through an Agency

Whatever kind of adoption you're thinking about, your road to parenthood will probably take you through, or at least past, an agency. There are different types of agencies that you can contact. Each state has a public agency charged with the care of children in that state. The state agency—frequently identified as the Bureau of Family and Children's Services, the Division of Social Services, the Department of Human Services, or the Department of Public Welfare—oversees the provision of services to children, including foster care and adoption. The state agency usually has local—often county—branches around the state. In addition, cities may have their own departments of social services for children in their care.

Although public agencies are supposed to serve the people, yours may not be able to work with you. Many state agencies today focus on placing waiting children. If you want to adopt a healthy white infant, a public agency may turn you away or offer to put your name on a waiting list. You may be told that you will have to wait several months or years before the agency is ready to take a formal application. A public agency may also be so understaffed that you will need to wait for months or even years before it can work with you. If you wish to adopt a child from overseas, many state agencies will decline to study your family, since their main priority is to help find permanent homes for children currently in their care. Check with your local public agency or your state adoption unit about adoption policies in your state.

States also license private child-placing agencies, which may be nonprofit or for-profit. These agencies have as their clients birth parents considering adoption for their child, prospective adoptive parents, and older children needing adoptive homes. Some have also developed extensive intercountry adoption programs. You will also find that some agencies, while not placing children themselves, will counsel families pursuing an independent adoption, an intercountry adoption, or the adoption of a waiting child in another agency's care.

Some agencies serve members of particular religious denominations; others have no such restrictions. Some private agencies are branches of a national religious or church-sponsored organization. A private agency with a name like "Presbyterian Children's Home and Service Agency" does not necessarily limit its services to Presbyterians or place only Presbyterian children. The name may simply reflect past, rather than current, practice. (Some agencies may have been placing children for fifty years or more.) Some agencies do have a religious standard for service, but it may be broader than a particular denomination. You may find agencies that only work with Christian families or with "evangelical Christians." Other agencies are strictly nondenominational. Don't eliminate any agency from consideration on the basis of its name.

Many agencies do, however, have geographical restrictions. Their area of service, often determined by the licensing authorities of a state, will be limited, and you'll need to determine that fact at the outset.

Certain agencies have also developed specialties. The Family Builder agencies, such as Spaulding for Children in Houston, Texas, Children Unlimited in Columbia, South Carolina, and Project STAR in Pittsburgh, Pennsylvania, are part of a network of nonprofit adoption agencies located around the United States that focus on older, handicapped, and minority children. Since these agencies serve waiting children, they charge no fees to adoptive parents and collaborate with other agencies in accepting referrals of children needing families. Downey Side in Springfield, Massachusetts, and New York, New York, is a licensed adoption agency that concentrates on placing adolescents. Still other agencies, such as Holt International Children's Services in Eugene, Oregon, focus on finding homes for children through intercountry adoption.

The Institute for Black Parenting in Los Angeles serves minority children and families. There are no fees for services, and the staff work evenings and weekends so that prospective adopters don't have to take time off from work. "We follow the philosophy of empowering black families. We guarantee our families a culturally sensitive social worker," says executive director Zena Oglesby, Jr. "We help them complete their paperwork. We make sure that they're getting good treatment on the front end, so that they're available for the thousands of black children who are available." In the first twenty months of the agency's life, 2,500 black families inquired about adoption, 400 families were studied, and 110 children were placed.

There are even agencies that specialize in infant adoption. The Edna Gladney Center, a nationally recognized maternity home in Fort Worth, Texas, placed 239 babies in 1989, while Golden Cradle in Cherry Hill, New Jersey, placed 58 infants.

Requirements

Regulations in every state are made "in the best interests of the child" and seek to protect everyone's rights. Nevertheless, there are no uniform laws of adoption; each state has its own laws and requirements.

All agencies have some requirements for prospective adopters. Some have just the minimum mandated by state law, while others have added criteria of their own. It's not uncommon for an agency to have more stringent requirements for families seeking to adopt healthy infants than for families interested in adopting older or special-needs children.

SOME COMMON REQUIREMENTS

Age
- You may be between twenty-one and sixty years old.
- An agency may be concerned that you be young enough that you can see your child grow to maturity.
- An agency may specify a minimum number of years or a maximum number of years that can separate parents and children.

Marital Status
- Couples may have to be married a certain number of years before they can apply.
- Some agencies may be more concerned about the stability of the relationship than the length of the marriage.
- Previous divorce is often acceptable.
- Singles may be acceptable.

Income
- For infant adoptions, some agencies may require that you meet a specific financial standard.
- Most agencies will ask that you show that you can manage effectively on your income.

Health
- Agencies usually require medical exams and evidence that you are in reasonably good health.
- If you are applying for a younger child, some agencies will require that you provide a fertility report.
- If you are significantly overweight, an agency may question your health and life expectancy.
- If you have a history of substance abuse, an agency may ask for further explanation.

Religion
- Some agencies may require that the child be placed in a home of the same religious background as the birth parents.
- Some agencies may require that you have a religious affiliation and may ask for a recommendation from a pastor.

Family Size
- Some agencies may specify that only childless couples can adopt a healthy infant.
- When placing a healthy infant, some agencies may state that there may be no more than one other child in the home.
- Many agencies will not accept applications from singles for infant adoptions.
- Some agencies may discriminate against large families.

Personal History
- Many agencies will require a criminal history background check by the local, state, or federal authorities.
- Many agencies will require a child abuse background check by local or state authorities.

Residency
- Some agencies may serve only a specific geographic region.

You may discover that an agency, when placing infants, will accept applications only from couples married for several years who can show medical evidence of infertility or of a genetic or medical problem that would make pregnancy inadvisable. The agency may also set an age limit, often specifying that the applicants be no more than thirty-five to forty-five years old. Or the requirements may state that the combined ages of the adopting couple cannot exceed eighty or eighty-five years. Some agencies will require that child care during the first few months after the baby's arrival be provided by one of the adopting parents.

Agencies serving minority, handicapped, or older children often are much more flexible. The Institute for Black Parenting tells prospective adopters in a brochure:

Age requirements are flexible. Married and/or single men and women can adopt. You can be divorced. You don't have to be rich. You don't need money in the bank. The size of your home doesn't matter. You can live in an apartment, and children can share bedrooms. Mothers can work. Arrangements can be made for the care of children. You can have your own children and adopt. The amount of education and kind of job you have makes no difference. You can be of any religious faith.

"We're processing many of the families who were kicked out of the public sector," says executive director Zena Oglesby. "When agencies say 'You're too old,' or 'You're a forty-five-year-old grandmother so you can't raise an infant,' they're screening out much of the black culture. Why wouldn't single parents be considered a major resource when fifty percent of black families are headed by single parents?"

For this agency singles are the "placement of choice" for many children. But other agencies are still wary of singles, who must be prepared to overcome barriers thrown up in their path. One single father who has adopted several handicapped children complained that "my biggest hassles haven't been with my kids but with agencies. Each adoption has been an adversary proceeding, with the agency trying to show why I shouldn't have a child and my having to prove myself."[1] Grumbled another single adoptive parent, "Adoption agencies are the last bastion of the two-parent family."[2]

Singles often find that agencies will not allow them to apply to adopt healthy infants and younger children. Many agencies will tell them bluntly that these children are reserved for two-parent families, and will try to encourage them to consider special-needs children instead. This leads some singles to complain that they are treated as the "dumping ground" for such children. "Singles should not be asked to settle for a child they are not going to be comfortable with," says Ann Feldman of the parent group New York Singles Adopting Children. "They should hold out for the child they want to parent."

The greatest obstacles to adoption are likely to be thrown in the way of single men, maintains Feldman: "Many people are suspicious of their motives. They don't see men as being nurturing and having the need for a parenting relationship. They feel that there has to be another motive for a single man to want to adopt."

People with chronic medical problems or physical handicaps must also be prepared to convince an agency that their condition will not affect their ability to raise a child. "We had a very hard time getting our foot in the door of an agency," recalls Alice Baxter, who had suffered from Hodgkin's disease and was left sterile by the chemotheraphy used to combat it. Five agencies turned her and her husband Ned away despite a doctor's clear explanation of her good medical prognosis. "Hodgkin's has a ninety-five percent cure rate, and I had been disease-free for three years," Alice recalls. "All we got was the standard answer of 'wait five years.'" Alice is also upset that the agencies were unable to view her illness with a more positive attitude. "We felt that the battle against Hodgkin's had strengthened our marriage," says Alice. "We'd been through this, and we knew we could do much for a baby. Yet the agencies treated my history as a turn-off."

As Alice and Ned struggled to find an agency to work with them, their adoption plans changed. "In the process of the search," she says, "we wondered what we were searching for." They saw that their own brush with death, their experience working with the medical establishment, and the strength they drew from each other made them comfortable with the thought of adopting a baby with serious medical problems. Says Alice: "If a child needed parents who could understand her problem and not treat her as if she were different or handicapped, we could do that. We were asking people to take a risk with us, so we decided to take risks too."

With the help of a sixth agency, one that catered to nontraditional clients, Alice and Ned adopted a newborn girl with a major congenital heart defect. Their daughter had one heart operation as an infant and faces another by her third birthday. Yet for Alice and Ned the adoption has brought only joy. "We feel so blessed and enriched by our daughter's first year," says Alice. "We're scared about the next operation, but we know that we've been in that place before."

If you already have several children, don't be surprised if an agency tries to discourage you from adopting or turns you down. Again, you may even be told that you are eligible to apply only for specific children. "After three boys, I wanted a baby girl," says Cynthia Fernandez. She was twenty-eight years old, and yes, she could try again. But she wanted to adopt. "My husband and I went to many agency orientations, but since we are white, they said, 'Don't waste your time, we won't even look at you because you have children.' Finally our local public agency gave us a chance after we said we were willing to take many risks." Two years later, Cynthia became the mother of a baby girl—a newborn who had been abandoned on a New York City stoop on a cold winter day.

David Frater also had to fight to adopt a child. He is a homosexual. In 1983 the *New York Times* reported that Frater had successfully adopted a seventeen-year-old boy in California who had entered his home as a foster child. He had spent two years battling for the finalization of his son's adoption. The laws and policies of each state—and agency—will vary, so that using the "grapevine" and getting to know other gay and lesbian adoptive parents is critical. To explore the possibilities of adoption as well as how to approach an agency, talk first with other homosexuals and lesbians who have successfully adopted. Center Kids (208 West 13 Street, New York, New York 10011; 212-620-7310) in New York City is a special parent support group, and there are others in San Francisco and other major metropolitan areas. You can also contact the National Center for Lesbian Rights in San Francisco.

You shouldn't be discouraged if you're told that one agency

will not consider an application from someone with your particular background. Another agency may be happy to take you on as a client. "It sounds crazy, but we really feel more comfortable with people who have something to draw on—the recovering alcoholic, people who have been through divorce or the death of a child, even people with a criminal history in the past," says Barbara Holtan of Tressler-Lutheran Service Associates in Pennsylvania. Her agency, which specializes in special-needs adoption, placed three siblings with Sam Curran, who's a quadriplegic, and his wife, Sarah. Observes Holtan: "If anybody knows how to get community resources, they do. They know what patience is and what long-term commitment is. We take each person as he comes."

MILITARY FAMILIES AND AGENCIES

For military families the biggest adoption hurdle often comes from the transiency of their military life. A couple may apply to an agency for a child, only to find themselves put on "hold" for an orientation or home study because the military spouse is away from home. Or a couple may wait on a list for service, get near the top, and then find that orders for a change of assignment have come through. At the next stop they have to start from scratch.

Moving around makes it tough to find an agency to perform even the basics. You'll want to do some serious shopping, exploring how each agency's process works. Your goal is to find an agency with a broad search capability that is willing to expedite or tailor its process to meet your particular needs.

Here are some strategies that may help:

- Tell your detailer that you are adopting and address your need to stay in place longer than usual.
- Explore the possibility of tapping into an agency that places in several states or networks with other agencies around the country.
- Try to find an agency that has a good reputation for placing children quickly.
- See if the adoption agency will process you in stages without penalizing you. At Catholic Charities in Richmond, Virginia, says adoption coordinator Barbara Smith, "our big problem with naval families is

that the husband will go out to sea. So we start the home study
and then pick it up as soon as the husband comes back."

- Even when your spouse is away from home, keep him or her involved
in the adoption process. Are there forms that can be completed
while at sea or an autobiography that can be written? Is there other
paperwork, such as fingerprinting, that can be accomplished?

- If orders to move do come through and an adoption seems likely, apply
for a compassionate stay. *Air Force Times* reports that "every
service allows for a delay or change of orders on compassionate
grounds in adoption cases."[3]

- If you are interested in a special-needs child, identify yourself to a
nearby adoption exchange. Some exchanges recruit families on
military bases.

- If you know that you're moving, find out about the adoption resources
in the area you are relocating to *before you even get there.* Perhaps an agency, if it understands your particular circumstances,
will permit you to make an application before you arrive. If not, file
your application as soon as you unpack.

- If you are contemplating an intercountry adoption, present your situation to the foreign source at the outset and see what arrangements
can be worked out with them.

- If you are seeking to adopt an infant, look into the possibilities of
independent adoption (see Chapter 4).

Fees

Most public agencies charge no fee for adoption services.
Private agencies usually do, although they may reduce or waive
their fees when families adopt waiting children. Fees for different programs within an agency often vary.

Some private agencies have a set fee, which might be as high
as $10,000 to $20,000 for an infant adoption. Many agencies
determine their fee on a sliding scale, based on a family's income. Sliding-scale fees often have a set minimum and maximum. You will find that fees vary widely around the country,
ranging from $1,000 in some areas to more than $10,000 in
others. While some states set ceilings on the fees that agencies

can charge, others do not. At some agencies, when you are adopting a healthy infant, you may be asked to pay the birth mother's medical and living expenses in addition to the agency's fee for its services.

The legal fees for the finalization of the adoption in court are usually separate.

Contacting an Agency About a U.S. Adoption

Learning about agencies involves evaluating them and exploring the types of programs they offer. Ideally you should be able to find several local agencies that provide different kinds of services, and then select the one that most closely fits your needs. But that is not the reality of adoption. Depending on the type of child you seek to adopt, you may wait a long time with a local agency. Finding an agency that meets your needs and is able to work with you may take some searching. If you live in a state like Nevada, your choice of a local agency will be limited to the public agency and a handful of private agencies. If you live in a state like New York, your choices are much greater. The state-by-state listing of agencies at the back of this book can help you get started. The state representatives of the North American Council on Adoptable Children (NACAC) and Adoptive Families of America, in addition to the directory, can give you up-to-date information. You can also check with the National Adoption Information Clearinghouse. For a detailed description of the programs, fees, requirements, and procedures of several hundred agencies across the country, see Julia L. Posner's *CWLA's Guide to Adoption Agencies: A National Directory of Adoption Agencies and Adoption Resources.*

Your first telephone call may very likely start and end with the comments "Sorry, we're not taking any applications right now" and "Sorry, we don't have any children to place." There *are* children who need homes, so persevere. Don't be put off by an agency's perfunctory first responses. Observes Susan Frei-valds of Adoptive Families of America, "It sometimes feels as if these first put-offs are part of the screening process."

If you are interested in adopting an infant, particularly a white infant, you may very likely be told that the agency is not taking applications or that it has a long waiting list. Don't give up. Ask questions. When will the agency's waiting list be open? Can you fill out an application now? If not, when? When will an orientation meeting be held? Recalled one adoptive parent who successfully adopted an infant through an agency: "They said to me, 'Don't bother.' I called my agency seven times and they said, 'No babies.' The eighth time they said that they had opened the 'list.' You can't be frightened by the agencies. They are hoping that you'll walk away from them. You have to be persistent to become an adoptive parent."

Agencies may even discourage people who are considering an older child. One hotline for an adoptive parents' group re-ceived calls from people who had been told by a local public agency that there were no older children needing adoption. This agency did not refer callers to the state photolisting book, which included descriptions and photos of waiting children. If you are interested in an older child, insist on coming in to the agency, talking with them, and looking at the state's—not just the agency's—list of waiting children. If you are getting the brush-off from a worker, insist on talking with the adoption supervisor. If the agency informs you that it doesn't serve fami-lies seeking waiting children, ask for a referral to an agency that does. Don't let an agency simply tell you that there are no children.

Be sure that you pin down the workers at an agency about their waiting list. How do they determine who may file an application? Is the waiting list for a child placement or for a home study? As will become clear in later chapters, having a completed home study opens doors to finding children. Unless you are specifically waiting for one of this agency's children, make it clear that you have a strong interest in a home study. It may serve as your passport.

From your telephone inquiries and from the brochures that the adoption agencies provide, you can also get a sense of an agency's "style." Some agencies handle the whole adoption process—walking you through it step by step, prescribing what's to be done when. Others are much more casual, expecting you to take the initiative and to inform yourself about procedures and deadlines, but offering help when called upon. You'll need to screen the agencies just as much as they do you.

Getting Oriented

Most agencies begin the adoption process with an orientation meeting. An agency may hold orientations once a year, once a month, when it has several interested applicants, or when it has social workers free to do home studies. Orientation meetings offer a chance for the agency to provide you with information about adoption, about its policies, and about the whole process. The orientation meeting is also a notorious part of the self-selection process in adoption. People may attend a meeting, walk away discouraged, and decide that they can't adopt.

Consider the very different experiences that one prospective adoptive parent had at two New York City agencies. The group that met at one agency was rather diverse—a few white couples, some Hispanic women, some older black women, and some young black couples. Two social workers from the agency welcomed the group and began listing the agency's requirements. Although New York State had very few requirements for adoption, this agency had many. It had rules about the age gap between parents and children. It had rules that "you cannot share a room with the child if it is over a year old" and a rule that "children of opposite sexes may not share a room," whatever their ages. The social worker did not make clear to the group that these were her agency's rules only—that the same rules might not exist at another agency.

The worker declared that "infants are a rare breed." She then talked about the children served by the agency. Although New York State expects the agency to show prospective adopters a copy of the New York State photolisting books, this worker announced: "I didn't bring the New York State books because it becomes very confusing. I brought a sampling of the children listed. These children happen to be ours." So the group saw photos of perhaps thirty children, not the several hundred typically featured in the state's book.

After the meeting the group examined the photographs and profiles of the children for whom the agency was currently seeking adoptive parents. A young black couple was dismayed to hear "no infants." A Hispanic woman, who really wanted a school-age girl, was concerned that most of the children pictured were boys. If these were all the children needing adoption, she was out of luck. Another woman commented that there were only photographs of thirty children and there were at least thirty people in the room. There clearly were not enough children to go around. A single black woman in her fifties who had a grown son concluded that adopting an eight-year-old was impossible, since the worker had told her that there could be no more than a forty-year age span between parent and child. So most of the group left convinced that the kind of adoption they wanted was out of the question.

Sound familiar? Perhaps you've had the same experience. What would have happened if you stepped into the orientation session of another local agency, which prides itself on its outreach program? This social worker, herself an adoptive parent, informed this group that the agency had a small number of children to place but she considered all of New York State's waiting children hers. To prove her point, she had circulated the photo books before the meeting began. She told the group, "You go through the books and ask to have your home study sent out." She promised that every time families pursuing an adoption met with their social worker, they'd look at the photo books because "every two weeks there are thirty new kids" in the state's photolisting book. There might be 600 new kids featured in the next year.

She tackled the question of infants head on: "What does it mean that you want a baby? Do you want a newborn? A child in diapers?" By her second definition, a two-year-old could still be a baby. She asked another caseworker, the mother of a recently adopted teenager, to talk. The mother said: "My son needs to be the baby. This is a fifteen-year-old who needs to be cuddled and who likes to sit on my lap. He's Swiss cheese, all full of holes that need to be filled up." So much for babyhood and diapers. "Expand your horizons," both workers urged.

During this orientation prospective parents learned about adoption today. But they also learned much more about the spirit they would need to go on, whether with this agency or elsewhere. "If you definitely want to adopt," the first caseworker, told them, "you'll find the way. There's a push. If you want it, you'll do it." Many of the people who attended this meeting would not work with this agency—some wanted infants (and would probably pursue an independent adoption); some wanted to consider an intercountry adoption (and were referred to other local agencies with special programs); others were not ready. All left with a much clearer understanding of the adoption process.

Agencies are not all alike. You must choose with great care. Pat Shirley of the parent group FACE cautions that "the agency that can do your home study the soonest may not be the best choice." Examine the agency and its practices carefully before you commit yourself. What is its philosophy toward adoptive parents, adoptees, and birth parents? Is it contemporary in its thinking? Is its recommended reading list current? What's the last adoption-related book the caseworker read? What national organizations is it affiliated with?

Can you talk with people who've adopted through the agency? Advises Ernesto Loperena of the New York Council on Adoptable Children: "You should always look for other adoptive parents who have been through the experience to find out whether they were able to get good, decent service. Don't just rely on what the agency says." Singles will want to be especially clear on how amenable the agency is to working with them. Be sure to ask other singles who used the agency how long their adoption process took.

If you are hoping to adopt an infant, you'll need to explore the agency's policies toward birth parents and confidentiality. While agencies traditionally have striven to maintain confidentiality through the practice of closed adoption, some—and their numbers have been growing—now foster contact among birth parents, adoptive parents, and adoptees. At some agencies birth parents select the adoptive parents, meet with them before the birth, and exchange full identifying information (last names, first names, addresses). They are encouraged to share the birth experience together and to think about the ongoing relationship—sharing letters and photos, talking by telephone, and visiting during the year. At many agencies, however, birth parents pick the adoptive parents through the review of nonidentifying information, meet with them on a first-name basis only, and communicate with them indirectly after the birth, with the agency typically serving as the intermediary. You'll want to do some reading about open adoption at the outset (see Chapter 5 for a fuller discussion) and ask basic questions: What do you mean by open adoption? How many open adoptions have you done? What kind of information is shared between birth parents and adoptive parents? What do the birth parents decide? What do the adoptive parents decide?

Find out the details about the selection process itself. Do the birth parents choose adoptive parents from *all* adoptive parents working with the agency, or does the agency preselect a handful? You'll find that even the most progressive agencies often exercise some control in this area of the selection process. In the agency's experience, are there any families who tend to wait longer? Why?

If you work with an agency that practices semi-open adoptions, be sure that you explore the agency's policy about opening up your adoption further in the years ahead. Kathleen Silber, coauthor of *Children of Open Adoption,* reports that at one agency "if a letter came through with identifying information, the worker would black it out so that the people could not open up the adoption." You don't want to be caught in a situation where the agency will not allow direct contact even if you desire it.

Try to attend the orientations of several agencies. "It drives me crazy that people will shop for days for a color television, but when it comes to adoption, they just wander into the first door or pick the first name in the phone book," says Jim Gritter of CFCS-Catholic Charities in Traverse City, Michigan. He recommends exploring the workers' own attitudes toward adoption. What would the worker do, for example, if she were pregnant and eighteen? What would the worker do if she were thirty and infertile? Says Gritter: "You're going to have to ask yourself—'Is this person square with me? Can I trust this person to join me in designing this life-altering event? There are going to be some hair-raising times along the way, and I need a rock.' "

The time you take at the outset will not only help you determine whether the agency is right for you, but may help the home study process that follows go more smoothly.

BASIC QUESTIONS TO ASK AN AGENCY

Agencies will ask you many questions during the adoption process. Before you commit yourself to any agency, you, too, should ask some basic questions:

- What are your requirements for adoptive parents?
- Do you have fertility restrictions?
- Do you have religious restrictions?
- Do you have residency restrictions?
- Do you have a minimum income requirement?
- What is the maximum number of children a family may have prior to adoption?
- Will you place a child older than the oldest in the family? Same age as another in the family?
- What are your fees? Any reductions for sibling groups?
- What are your medical requirements for applicants? If a family is applying for an infant, must they present evidence of a fertility problem?
- How many, and what kinds, of legally free children are in your agency's caseload?
- How many children did you place for adoption last year? What were the characteristics of the children placed?
- Does the agency place children in prospective adoptive homes as foster children?
- How do you feel about working in a partnership with another agency to bring about an adoption?
- How many children from outside the agency, outside the county, or outside the state were placed with families studied by your agency?
- Are you presently accepting applications for healthy infants?
- Who can adopt infants at your agency? If I already have a child, will you place an infant with me?
- In infant adoptions, what role do birth parents play in the selection of the adoptive parents? What role do you play?
- Could you briefly describe your home study? Do you offer group home studies? (See Chapter 3 for a full discussion of home studies.)
- What kind of preadoption services do you provide?

- What is the estimated wait between application and start of home study for the waiting child? For the healthy infant?
- How long will it probably take to complete a home study?
- Will you do a home study for an intercountry adoption?
- Will you do a home study for an independent adoption? Will you provide counseling to me or to birth parents?
- Will you do a home study for single applicants? Have you placed children with singles? What type of children have you placed with singles?
- Will you forward copies of a home study to another agency? How often?
- Can I see a copy of the completed home study?
- How long will it probably take your agency to assign a child after a home study is approved? (Ask this if the agency expects to place *its* children with you.)
- What type of background information do you share about individual children? Do you practice "full disclosure"? If so, what does it mean? What do you *not* disclose?
- If the child is in foster care, can the adoptive parents meet with the foster parents? Can adoptive parents visit children in their foster homes?
- What is your policy toward adoption subsidies? Do you encourage families to apply for them? Can families apply for them for their children after the adoption?
- What happens if I turn down a child who is offered to me? What is the agency's policy about future placements?
- What type of contact does your agency encourage between birth parents, adoptive parents, and adoptees?
- Have you opened up any closed adoptions? Would the agency initiate contact and follow through if one of the parties had a specific reason for it to take place? What would be your policy, for example, if we decided we wanted to exchange letters with the birth parents? If we later decided to share full identifying information, would we be allowed to do that?
- What are the services you provide for the *lifetime* of this adoption?
- What types of counseling services and support groups are made available to adoptive parents? To birth parents? To adoptees?
- Do you offer any services to families after the adoption is finalized?
- What is your grievance process if I feel that I am not treated fairly? What kind of recourse do I have?

Inquiring About an Agency's Reputation

When Hannah and Joe Scapiti picked up their newborn son at the adoption agency, they also paid the agency $7,000 to cover various fees and medical expenses. They knew that they would be uneasy during the time after placement that the birth parents could legally change their minds. But that, it turned out, was the easy part of this adoption. Over the next year, their relationship with the agency rapidly soured as they were asked to pay an additional $4,000 for medical bills, but were given no opportunity to examine them or see an itemized listing of expenses. They discovered that basic adoption paperwork had never been completed and were threatened by the agency director. ("I would hate to get the birth mother involved." "Are you refusing to meet with me? After all, I do have custody of your son.") With the help of an attorney they hired to represent their interests, Hannah and Joe eventually completed their son's adoption, but the bitter aftertaste remains. "We put our family's lives in the agency's hands," says Hannah. "Where are the authorities responsible for overseeing agencies?"

I hope your child's adoption will proceed without a hitch, but what happens if it doesn't? Where can you turn? And how can you avoid potential problems by checking into an agency's reputation before you ever sign on?

Start with the licensing agency, sometimes referred to as the regulatory or certification agency, of your state. Advises Beth Furay, a licensing supervisor for Wisconsin: "You can call and ask for information about an agency's track record, whether the agency's been cited for any licensing violations, and whether the licensing office has had any complaints. There is a tremendous volume of information available at the licensing agency that adoptive parents never ask for." Request also a copy of the state's rules governing agencies so that you understand what practices violate your state's laws.

You should also speak with the adoption staff in your state's department of social services (see the state-by-state directory at the back of this book). "A lot of the calls and complaints about agencies really don't have anything to do with whether an agency is violating a statute," says Robert DeNardo, adoption supervisor in the Minnesota Department of Human Services. "But they have a lot to do with poor agency practice—all the way from poor customer relations, instances of staff rudeness, and high-handed behavior." While the department may not have done anything about a particular complaint, staff members will probably share the information they have with you. Complaints can also be filed with your state's attorney general's office, although these are often referred back to the licensing or adoption unit for investigation. If your state or metropolitan area has a Department of Consumer Affairs, you might check to see if it handles complaints.

If you're planning an interstate or intercountry adoption, you can contact the interstate compact administrators in your state's department of public welfare. The compact administrator oversees interstate placements (see Chapter 8) and may have worked with your agency. You can also try speaking with the staff person who handles adoptions at the nearest office of the Immigration and Naturalization Service. Be sure to check also with national and local adoptive parent support groups about the reputations of agencies. The parent group FACE, for example, had so many complaints about a local agency that its board of directors took the unusual step of issuing a warning statement, while Adoptive Families of America has published articles in *OURS* magazine about agencies that have gotten into trouble with their states. "We shared with prospective adopters information about a local agency that started charging all the people on its waiting list for telephone calls made by the agency to Colombia each month," recalls Cheryl Simons of the Latin America Parents Association in New York.

If you plan to use an agency as a springboard to working with another agency elsewhere, you'll want to know about its reputation for networking. Observes Ernesto Loperena: "Some agencies are good at internal or state stuff, but not at interstate. If that's what you're contemplating, you need to find that out up front."

Identified or Designated Adoption

Ellen and Nick Lyons live in Connecticut. When they decided to adopt a baby, they learned that the agencies in their area had long waiting lists for healthy white infants and that Nick's age (forty-six) would probably be a barrier. Several agencies encouraged them to consider an alternative service they provided: identified adoption, also known as "designated adoption." In identified adoption, couples who have "identified" a particular birth parent approach an agency for counseling and home study services. (*Identified adoption* is a misnomer, since adoptive parents and birth parents may not know full identifying information about each other and may even work through an intermediary. Rather, it describes the link between a particular set of birth parents and prospective adoptive parents.)

In identified adoption the prospective adoptive parents, not the agency, "find" the birth parents and put the adoption together with the birth parents. It is a hybrid, combining features characteristic of independent placements with those of agency adoptions. Prospective adoptive parents have the chance to begin the adoption process immediately, rather than wait on an agency list, and exercise greater control over what happens. Identified adoption can play a critical role in states that ban independent adoptions or third-party nonagency involvement, or require a home study by a licensed agency prior to an independent placement. It's also attractive to adoptive parents in states where the law permits the birth parents to change their minds for several weeks or even months after the placement in an independent adoption, but permits a shorter revocation period if an agency handles the adoption.

For birth parents, identified adoption often gives them greater control over the adoption process than might be offered by their local agencies. They have the assurance as well that a licensed agency is involved and that counseling services are available to everyone. While identified adoption is most commonly associated with newborn placements, it can happen in older child adoptions if the agency agrees to the plan.

"The agency becomes more of a facilitator in identified adoption," says Kristina A. Backhaus of Lutheran Child and Family Services of Connecticut. "I'm the person who makes sure that all requirements and regulations are met, while the birth parents and adoptive family make sure the placement fits their needs." If the birth mother resides elsewhere in the state, or in another state, the agency working with the couple may help arrange for the birth mother to receive counseling from another agency and may be involved in coordinating the paperwork of the people at the other end.

In Ellen and Nick's case they attended orientations about identified adoption at several agencies. "It's really important that you have a good fit," says Ellen. "If you choose well, your agency will not only do your home study but will guide you through the morass of state regulations. But you also have to understand the rules, and you've got to handle the negotiations with the birth mother yourself." Nick and she prepared a letter describing their adoption hopes, printed 150 copies, and duplicated photos of themselves with their son Jonathan. But their plans to send the letter out to friends and colleagues around the country never got off the ground. "It was just magic," recalls Ellen. A friend who worked for Planned Parenthood in another state called to say that a very pregnant young woman had come into the office to discuss adoption. A description of Ellen and Nick was hurriedly faxed to her, they talked by phone, then Ellen and Nick met her and her mother (but without exchang-

EXPLORING ADOPTION THROUGH AN AGENCY

ing last names), and two weeks later the baby was born. "The agency provided comfort," says Ellen. "It was tremendously valuable hearing the social worker say, 'I've done three like this.'"

That's not to say there weren't any hassles. The hospital where the baby was born did not permit either the birth mother or Ellen and Nick to visit the infant, and a third party had to carry the baby out of the hospital. For the Lyons the wait was mercifully short, but that's often not the case. Families are often aware of a potential child several months in advance and experience an agonizing wait. Recalls one adoptive parent: "It was torturous. It was like a pregnancy of sorts and the bonding began before birth."

There are other drawbacks to the identified adoption approach. Although every case is different, the costs can be high. It's not unrealistic to expect them to reach $10,000 or even $15,000, since adoptive parents pay agency service fees, medical expenses, and even living expenses (if permitted by state law) for the birth mother during the pregnancy. Identified adoption also has the risks—both financial and emotional—that independent placement adoption incurs. Says Backhaus: "We had one family that had three placements that didn't go through. All three birth mothers initially said that they wanted to go ahead with the adoption, and all three birth mothers changed their minds within forty-eight hours of the birth." Backhaus estimates that as many as half of the families who've worked with her agency on an identified adoption had a potential adoptive placement that didn't work out. And she's clear also about families' financial vulnerability: "We have no way to get the money back. We can't act like a bill collector."

Since many agencies now offer identified or designated adoption as one of their adoption services, you'll want to ask some questions before you sign on. How long has the program existed? How many intrastate and interstate identified adoptions has the agency done? (To get a sense, you can also ask your

state's interstate compact administrator which agencies' paperwork is handled most often and if there have been any problems.) What services does the agency provide? What are the
possible expenses for this type of adoption? Can the agency
break down its fees for you? (For a full breakdown of potential
expenses in an independent adoption, see Chapter 4. If an identified adoption is interstate, potential expenses include two
agency fees, attorneys' fees, medical expenses, living expenses,
and transportation costs.) If a prospective adoption falls
through, is there an additional fee for the next potential placement? How does the agency handle the birth mother's expenses? Is there an escrow account set up? Will the baby need
to be in foster care prior to placement? If it is your preference,
will the agency permit direct-from-hospital placement? What
happens if the adoptive parents decide not to go through with
the placement because the baby is born with a medical problem?

It's critical that you—and the agency—understand state law.
In Connecticut, for example, it's illegal for any money to go
directly from the adoptive family to the birth family or to their
representative. Everything has to go through the agency, and
the agency in turn has to provide an accounting to the court.
There are also regulations governing termination of parental
rights. Observes Backhaus, "I spend the majority of my time
trying to figure out whether certain situations will meet state
regulations and making sure that we're not going to cause a
problem for the birth mother in another state."

Legal Risk Adoption

To move children more quickly into permanent homes, agencies employ another kind of placement—legal risk adoption,
sometimes called "foster/adoption." A family agrees to take a
child—one whose permanent plan is expected to be adoption—
into their home as a foster child, while the sometimes lengthy
legal process goes on.

Hillary was placed with her adoptive parents at two months, but her adoption was not finalized until she was nearly four years old. Explains her adoptive mother:

Hillary's mother was a patient in a mental institution. The mother's condition had been caused by a childhood fall and she had been admitted to the institution by her mother, who had many children and who couldn't handle her daughter's injury. She'd been there for eighteen years and had become pregnant. The agency did not know who the father was. They had to track down the mother's relatives to notify them about the grandchild and to get their release. Even if the agency failed to find the relatives (they had not visited her in the eighteen years), it would still take time.

There was a lot of red tape involved in Hillary's adoption. The agency went through a long search for the mother's family, and over the years there was also a switch in social workers. Although Hillary's mother knew from the day that Hillary arrived that she was likely to stay, "every once in a while we'd see a report on television where a family had to give a child back. And we'd get very nervous."

Legal risk adoptions often involve the placement of younger children, even infants and toddlers, in adoptive families. Children have the chance to get into their permanent homes faster; parents have the chance to raise their children from infancy or toddlerhood. But legal risk adoption brings with it emotional strain. Said one parent about the legal risk experience: "It's living on an emotional roller coaster. One day you're high—she's ours. The next day, reality—another court delay. How do you cope with that reality?"

Since legal risk placements begin as foster care arrangements, birth parents have the right to visit their children in their new homes. There is a real risk that the birth parents will decide not to relinquish the child. It can and does happen.

Bonnie O'Connor became the mother of a two-year-old boy through a legal risk placement. His mother had brought him to the agency saying that she wanted to relinquish her parental rights voluntarily, since she had been separated from his father and the father had recently been killed in an auto accident. Recalls Bonnie: "He fit right into our lives. Days and weeks passed. His birth mother never asked to visit him and she remained firm in her decision." After four months of counseling, his mother set a date with the agency to sign the relinquishment papers. That day arrived, but his mother didn't keep her appointment. "A little later in the day," Bonnie remembers, "she called the social worker and said that she wanted to see her son. She was beginning to doubt whether she could follow through on her decision to surrender him." The visits began, and over the next few weeks she visited frequently. Finally his birth mother took him home. "Having him leave was devastating for us and we missed him tremendously," says Bonnie. "I think about him often and wonder how they are doing." Bonnie and her husband went on to adopt four other children, but the pain of forming an attachment to, and then losing, one child is still there.

Abby Elkins is a single parent who's been raising Jason, now age two, since he was one month old. The agency that placed Jason, a premature infant who had been exposed prenatally to cocaine, felt there was little risk involved in the adoption because his mother had disappeared from the hospital shortly after his cesarean birth and hadn't returned for any medical follow-up. But when Jason was seven weeks old, his mother returned to the hospital to challenge the adoption and claim him. Although the court has never granted the birth mother custody, her parental rights have also not been terminated and the battle drags on. Says Abby: "The longer it goes on, the more crazy it is. I can't believe that this child would be better off with this mother after two years. At the last court hearing she couldn't remember the address of her home. What scares me most is the thought 'What if she gets custody and he's neglected and beaten when he's with her?' "

If your agency offers you a legal risk placement, be sure to elicit as much information as possible. What were the circumstances of the child's abandonment? What kind of risk are you talking about? Risks can be of varying degrees, and some agencies will rank them low to high. What is known of the birth parents or the immediate family? What type of involvement and contact have there been? How many releases have been signed? When is the legal case likely to be presented to the court? Ernesto Loperena warns that "agencies sometimes use the prospective adoptive parents as leverage in court." In situations where the birth mother is involved, says Loperena, "the court tends to lean over backward to make sure that the mother has been given every chance."

How much risk do you feel you can handle? Even with a low-risk situation the court case can take years or something unexpected can happen. Are you willing to live in a state of limbo? Says Loperena: "I caution people about legal risk adoptions. I have seen the emotional ups and downs, the peaks and valleys, that families go through. Although the odds with legal risk adoption may be in your favor, somebody has to be in that percentage of families where the child is reunited with the biological mom."

Foster Parent Adoption

The majority of children who enter foster care will return to their families or relatives after a period of time. Yet many children begin their lives in their adoptive homes as foster children. "There is no longer a hard and fast distinction between foster parents and adoptive parents," says New York social worker Mary Helen Evans, who worked for many years in foster care. "Every foster parent is a potential adoptive parent, and foster parents need to think about adoption before the agency comes to them to discuss adoption." In fact some agencies now process prospective adoptive parents and foster parents together. But foster parents must also be prepared to see children go home to their first family and provide them with the necessary emotional support.

Foster parents are often given the opportunity to adopt a

foster child, particularly if the child has been living in their home for an extended period of time. Agencies will ask the foster parents if they would like to adopt their foster child when he or she is freed for adoption. But foster parents may also be forced to push the agency to make a permanent plan for their foster child or to let them adopt that particular child.

If you are interested in adopting a foster child in your care, talk first with the agency responsible for your child. You should be asking questions right along about the status of the child and the long-range plan for his future. Find out also what rights you have under county or state law. In New York State, for example, foster parents have the right to be considered as the first adoptive parent if the child has been in their home for one year. Foster families in Texas have standing in the court, and they can initiate petitions for termination of parental rights, guardianship, or other needs of the child as perceived by them.

When your caseworker indicates that the agency is thinking of terminating parental rights, be sure to indicate your interest immediately, both verbally *and in writing,* in becoming an adoptive parent. Don't be afraid to be assertive in your request. If you feel that your interest is not being given proper consideration, go up the line beyond your particular agency worker to the supervisor and even the administrator of the agency. If you wish to be included in the court hearings regarding this child, ask whether you have the right. If so, find out if you can be represented by an attorney if you wish.

You'll want to inquire about subsidies for your child and your ability to get them. Sometimes agency workers will try to dissuade foster families from applying for subsidies, suggesting that there are other prospective adopters interested in the child who don't need them. If you feel that your child may be eligible for a subsidy, don't hesitate to ask for it. You'll also want to push for a full disclosure to you of your child's medical and background history. Even though you've had the child living with you for a period of time and know him or her well, there may be aspects of the child's family history that were not shared with you at the time he or she came into your care.

You'll probably want to link up with a local adoptive parent or foster parent support group. Another resource is the **National Foster Parent Association** (226 Kilts Drive, Houston, Texas 77024; 713-467-1850.)

Finally, if you don't want to be considered as the adoptive parent of your foster child, speak up. This needs to be known by your caseworker in planning for the child.

Contacting U.S. Agencies About Intercountry Adoption

Some agencies in the United States have developed intercountry adoption programs. Of these agencies, some place children only with families who reside within a certain geographic area, while others accept applicants from throughout the United States (for a full discussion, see Chapter 7).

An agency may have intercountry adoption programs for several different countries. Each program may have different requirements. South Korea, for example, required that the agency placing the child do both the pre- and postplacement supervision. While an agency like Holt International Children's Services in Eugene, Oregon, might place children from Thailand, for example, in many states by accepting applications from people throughout the United States, it has placed South Korean children only in states where it is licensed. As you learn about agency programs, you are likely to discover that you are ineligible for some agency programs but not others. It sometimes take singles and older couples more time to find the right program. If you don't meet the requirements of your local agency's intercountry program, it just means that you will need to contact an agency outside your immediate area that is able to make a referral through a local agency.

The intercountry adoption directory at the back of this book lists agencies in the United States that have active intercountry adoption programs. Since these programs are constantly changing, you will want to contact parent groups for the most current information. The *Report on Foreign Adoption* (available from the **International Concerns Committee for Children,** 911 Cypress Drive, Boulder, Colorado 80303; 303-494-8333) is a compendium of intercountry adoption information; it lists adoption programs country by country and tries to keep people informed through its annual volume and updates. Adoptive Families of America also compiles a free adoption information booklet that describes many intercountry adoption programs and their requirements.

In most states, whether or not you choose to work with an agency that has an intercountry adoption program, you will need to work with an adoption agency in order to complete an intercountry adoption. The U.S. Immigration and Naturalization Service requires that all individuals who bring a child into the country for the purpose of adoption submit a home study. In some states you may be able to have a certified social worker do your study, but in most you will need to have an agency undertake it. When you approach an agency, explain that you are seeking an intercountry adoption. Often an agency that has a religious requirement for placing its own children can waive this requirement if you make it clear that you need its help in completing an intercountry adoption. Some agencies may have restrictions, however, about the types of foreign sources they will work with, or may require that the agency that will be placing the child make a formal request for their assistance.

3

The Home Study

For all agency adoptions, for all intercountry adoptions, and for most independent adoptions, you will need a preadoptive home study. Although there is no prescribed format that a home study must follow, each state has guidelines on what must be covered.

The home study has traditionally revolved around a series of private meetings between the applicants and an adoption-agency worker. Behind closed doors applicants discuss their lives and explore their feelings about adoption. It can be a time fraught with anxiety because prospective adopters worry that one misstep will lead the worker to decide they are unsuitable parents. Finally the worker produces a written report on the family (the home-study document itself), which becomes the basis for the agency's decision as to whether or not to place a child in the family.

But attitudes and practices have been changing, and the home-study period is no longer seen by most agencies and workers as the place where applicants are screened out. Rather, it is treated as the time to make families aware of the challenges of adoptive parenthood. While some agencies still conduct home studies on an individual basis, many now incorporate the group process into their home studies. Some require that applicants take an adoption information course sponsored by a local parent group as a prerequisite. Others hold a series of group meetings with prospective clients before the social worker meets with people individually. Still others conduct the whole home study in a group setting, but ask participants to do some individual homework assignments.

The home-study process has evolved in this way partly because of the increased interest in placing special-needs and older children. "Families need information to help them make realistic decisions about whether or not adoption is appropriate for them," observes child welfare specialist Thomas D. Morton. "The process has to make maximum use of the family's role in decision-making, and it can only do so if the worker's role changes from that of investigator to educator, from judge to enabler."[1] In the Model Approach to Partnerships in Parenting (MAPP) program, which trains potential foster and adoptive parents together in 10 three-hour sessions, the group examines children's separation and loss experiences and how these impact on placement in a new family. The potential parents think about the strengths they will need to come with—or develop—to help their children cope. "With MAPP you have the opportunity," says adoption expert Toni Oliver, "to try on the foster parent dress or the adoptive parent dress and decide whether you need to make alterations ahead of time." Following the final session there's a home consultation with the family. "Although the agency has the final say," notes Oliver, "applicants are involved in the decision of selecting in or out. There's a greater likelihood that a family will select out than that a family will be turned down."

The group also helps people build a network of support that can be called upon both before and after their child enters their home. Since the discussion focuses on parenting issues, people enter the process with the assumption that there will be a child for them. The business at hand, then, is to decide what kind of child they can parent, what arrangement they will be comfortable with, and how they can get ready for the task.

The written home-study document is also changing. Although the staff check references, visit homes, and write reports of their impressions, a part of the home study is created by the prospective adopters. They contribute autobiographies or statements expressing their beliefs on various subjects and fill out worksheets about the type of children they hope to adopt and their attitudes and expectations. And as adoption has become more open—bringing both birth parents and other agencies into the process—these home-study documents serve as the family's passport to the outside world.

Who Conducts the Home Study?

Within an agency, the person who prepares the home study or who leads the group meeting may be a certified social worker, a caseworker, or even another adoptive parent under the supervision of a social worker. Although home studies have usually been carried on under agency auspices, not all states require that a home study be done by an agency. In some states, and for some types of adoptive placements, you may be able to have a home study prepared by a licensed social worker not affiliated with an agency. If this is possible, you'll want to find out from your state adoption unit what the state's rules and requirements are. Before you sign on with a worker, you'll want to find out about the worker's qualifications, the format of the study, the worker's fees, and how long she expects the study to take. Will the worker be available to you after your child arrives and can she handle postplacement visits and court reports? And on what basis would the worker *not* approve a family for placement of a child?

The Home-Study Process

A question was put across the table to the birth mother attending a group home-study workshop in Denver, Colorado. "If the adoptive parents invited you to a baby shower for the baby, would you come?"

For days Tom and Sheila Hawkins had been mulling the idea over—Tom thought it would be neat to invite the birth mother; Sheila felt it was putting pressure on her—and now he popped the question to Vicky Knight, a young birth mother sharing her experiences of open adoption with a group of prospective adoptive parents. Nothing was off limits in the three day-long group discussions held at Lutheran Family Services. In addition to meeting with birth parents and experienced adoptive parents, the group examined their fears and fantasies of open adoption, the mixed emotions they might feel as they got to know a birth mother, and the painful but exhilarating experience they were likely to share with the birth mother at the time of their baby's birth. There was also a discussion of specifics: how to compose a profile of themselves, how to react if a birth mother called them on the telephone, what questions were important for them to ask the birth mother and her social worker. By week's end Tom and Sheila were confident that open adoption was for them—although they still hadn't resolved the matter of the baby shower—and were eager to proceed.

Meeting at Tressler-Lutheran Service Associates in Pennsylvania, Joan and Michael Arthur, along with several other couples, looked through photolisting books featuring children needing adoption and marked in the books the children who interested them. Over a period of time the group members talked about how children feel when they enter a new home, how it feels to be rejected, how a child already in their home might react to a new sibling, and how each of them would handle questions about adoption. The sessions stressed developing individual self-awareness, building commitment, identifying what is involved in parenting a "challenging child," and finding techniques to work with that child. Experienced adoptive parents and community resource people were also introduced to the group members. "It was," says Joan, "a good parenting course. It was interesting." At the conclusion of the series, Joan and Michael visited a family who had already adopted a child with a profile similar to the one they were hoping to adopt.

At Catholic Social Services in Green Bay, Wisconsin, Kate and Tony Fales participated in group counseling as a "self-education experience." They shared information about their life histories and the people who shaped their lives; their marital relationships; and their childlessness and how it affected them. The couples in the group role-played situations to help them identify with birth parents, adoptive parents, and adoptees. One couple found themselves playing the birth parents who showed up at the adoptive parents' front door many years later asking to meet their child, while Kate and Tony were confronted with a fifteen-year-old who announced that she was going to go live with her "real" parents. Recalls Kate, "The group meetings were a matter of getting you used to accepting an adopted child."

While the specific content of a group home-study process varies agency by agency, there is an emphasis on family preparation and self-awareness. Whether through role-playing, listening to adopters relate their experiences in panel discussions, or getting to know one family in a buddy system, the home studies seek to challenge the adoptive parents before their child ever enters the home.

What happens if your agency or worker prefers to conduct the home study along more traditional lines? In that situation you can expect to have your first meeting with your caseworker as a couple at the agency. Then, typically, the caseworker will meet separately with you and your spouse at the agency office. One or more additional interviews will follow at your home. If you have older children, the caseworker is likely to interview them and may also interview each of them individually. Finally, the case worker will draw up a written report, based on the interviews and documents you submit.

Whether your home study is done in a group setting or on an individual basis, there will be some basic paperwork (see Chapter 8), an extended discussion about adoption, including a look at your motivation for adoption and your attitudes, and a visit to your home. During the home visit the worker is not looking for dust balls under the beds but does want to come away with a picture of the environment the child will be entering. "I will ask people about their reality—how they will fit, for example, into a one-bedroom apartment," acknowledges New York City social worker Phyllis Lowinger, who does private home studies. But Lowinger emphasizes that her main concern is to "make the home study an educational experience."

Whatever the circumstances of the home study, your worker will eventually offer a written evaluation and a summary report to accompany documents that you submit. Adoption expert Kay Donley makes this crucial point: "What everyone has to come to grips with is that the agency and the caseworker have the ultimate responsibility for the choice that's made. They are going to have to deal with the placement of the child." As Lowinger puts it, "My home study has to say that these people are ready to parent a child now."

What's Explored During the Home Study

Whether your study takes place in individual meetings with the caseworker or in group sessions, you can expect to discuss the following:

- Your reasons for adopting a child
- Your strengths and weaknesses
- Your personality: level of patience, flexibility, attitudes toward life, anxiety levels, sense of humor
- Your health
- Your marriage—its strengths and weaknesses; how you handle family disagreements

- The causes of a past divorce, your relationship with your ex-spouse, your relationship with your children from a previous marriage
- Your work: its stability and importance
- Your family plans for working or for staying home with your children—and if you are planning to continue working, your child-care plans
- Your upbringing
- The kind of parenting you had and how you feel about it
- Your housing situation
- Your relationships with family, friends, and neighbors
- Your extended family's feelings about adoption and what support you can draw from them
- How you have handled crises in your life
- How you have resolved a fertility problem, if you have one
- How you handled the loss of a child due to miscarriage, stillbirth, or some other cause, if such has occurred, and your feelings about it
- Your past experiences with children
- Your life-style and how a child will fit in
- Your expectations of adoption and of your new child. How you will feel if your adopted child doesn't live up to your expectations
- How you have handled situations in which your expectations were not met
- What special needs in a child you feel you can handle and what you are willing to consider
- Your awareness of, and willingness to tap, community resources
- How your children, if you have any, will adjust to a new sibling and how you are preparing them for adoption
- How you will handle your child's questions about adoption and birth parents
- Your understanding of, and feelings about, birth parents

- Your preparation for adoption (reading, knowing others, parent group involvement)

If you have a history of previous drug or alcohol use, "you've got to be up front about it," urges Susan Freivalds of Adoptive Families of America. "It's more harmful to you to lie to any agency than to disclose previous chemical use." The agency worker will want to know how long it's been since you overcame the problem and whether you are in a support group today. And the worker will probably probe into your family for any history of drug abuse. The same advice applies if you've been in therapy or had infertility counseling.

If you are single, you will be asked to evaluate what age child you want to consider and what type of child will best fit your situation as a prospective single parent. You can also expect your home study to explore the following:

- Your life-style and a child's impact on it
- Your family and friends—your support system, your extended network, and the alternatives they can provide in the event of your illness or death
- Who will provide the opposite sex-role model for your child
- Your daily plan for the child—how you expect to handle matters from day to day, what arrangements you can make for day care, for after school, for weekends
- Your finances—how you are going to provide for the child over time
- Why you are not married and whether you have had long-term relationships before. You may also be asked about your sexual orientation.
- What would happen in the future if you married, how you think a prospective partner would react to the fact that you are a single adoptive parent, and whether you are worried that adopting will prevent your getting married
- Your work: how flexible it is. Can you take time off from work when the child arrives? When the child is sick?

- How you foresee you and your child handling the special situation of single adoptive parenting. You are going to have to explain to your child—and to the outside world—adoption and why there's only one parent in your family.

The worker will also want to go over the provisions you have made for the care of your child in the event of serious illness, death, or other circumstances that could prevent you from providing care. You'll be asked to discuss your insurance plans and your benefits as well as to name the specific guardians for your child.

Getting References

As part of your home study you will also be asked to submit some references. The agency will want to know how your references feel about your potential parenting ability and whether they perceive you as a mature individual. The people you may be asked to use as references include your family, your employer, your clergyman, your friends, and your neighbors. Each one may have to submit a letter on your behalf, talk by telephone with the social worker, or even come to the agency for an interview. Your references may be cited in your home study by name, and your social worker may quote from the interviews and from letters that were submitted.

Think carefully about the people you will list as your references. Good friends do not necessarily make good references. How do they feel about adoption? How do they feel about your adopting a child? How do they feel about your adopting a particular type of child? Talk with them and explore their feelings and perceptions. Do they think that you will make good parents? Why? Do they think that you are making a mistake? Don't hesitate to give them some pointers as to what you would like them to emphasize about you, and don't be embarrassed to ask your references to read you their letters before they submit them to the agency.

Whom should you choose as references? When the Williamses were applying for their first child, to an agency that specialized in intercountry adoptions, they asked one friend who taught nursery school and with whom they liked to talk about raising children. They also asked a friend who had an interracial marriage and could testify to the Williamses' respect for ethnic differences. Their caseworker also insisted on meeting one of their references. They asked the woman who had introduced them ten years before; she was an experienced journalist, a television producer used to talking with people. Three years later when the Williamses were applying for their second child, they chose a different reference—a neighbor whose son frequently played with their son and who had observed their parenting day in and day out.

Doctors—such as your family physician, infertility specialist, psychologist, or psychiatrist—may also be asked to comment on your application to adopt. Be sure that you talk with them and explain your reasons for adopting. If you're committed to adoption, you don't want your fertility specialist elaborating on all the other tests that he believes you should pursue. Your physician should provide a medical analysis only and understand fully that adoption is your decision.

If you have had psychological or infertility counseling, your therapist may be asked to submit a report stating why you had the counseling and how he evaluates you today. Some Latin American agencies will also request a statement about your mental health. For Latin American adoptions the reference from your doctor should state that you are in good physical *and mental* health and free of all communicable diseases. Physicians and mental health practitioners should also state in references for Latin America who licenses them and should provide their licensing number or a photocopy of their license.

References and other documents submitted to an agency abroad may very likely have to be notarized, verified, and authenticated (see discussion, Chapter 9). To make the process easier, you may want all your references to come from the same state. And you'll want to ask your references to refer to you in any written recommendations by your given name—the one that appears on your birth and marriage certificates—rather than any nicknames. Your primary concern, however, should be that your references are able to talk comfortably about you.

Résumés

For some home studies you may be asked to write up an autobiography or a one-page résumé-like letter that might be shown to birth parents. Your social worker may give you guidance as to content or even provide you with forms. Following is some general advice.

An autobiography or résumé needs to contain some basic information about yourself—your jobs, education, home, community—and your desire to become a parent. But it should be written in an open, appealing manner and convey your personality. Do you play tennis? Do you enjoy movies? Do you have a pet? Do you come from an extended family that gets together frequently? What is important to you in raising a child? How has your desire to parent a child affected you?

The résumé should make a person want to reach out and help you. You will want your readers to feel that they can envision a child's future with you. To round out your profile, you'll probably want to attach an inviting, good color photograph of yourself and, if you have them, your other children and your pets.

The Home Study as Your Ambassador

At a training session of social workers, several families' home studies were offered as sample reading material. The workers then commented on their understanding of each of the families' strengths, weaknesses, resources, and readiness to adopt a special-needs child. After the group had completed its discussion, one worker revealed that she had prepared one of the home studies and that she was dismayed at the conclusions drawn by the group about the family. "That's not at all what the husband and wife are like," she said, "and not what I was trying to convey about them."[2]

As this worker learned, what she wanted to say about the family was not what the other members of the group gleaned from her summary. That's why many adoption experts have urged that families take as active a part as they can in the creation of the home-study document, particularly when it is to be used as their ambassador beyond the agency's doors. Observes adoptive parent Pat Shirley: "Studies seldom say negative things but often give inadequate information, sometimes are written in a superficial or less than readable style. Many children's workers are going to read it and it should make your family as real as possible."[3]

Try to read your completed copy and to review all documents connected to it. At some agencies that is now an accepted part of agency practice. Be sure your home study is clearly, cleanly typed with a good overall appearance. It should be dark enough that it can be successfully photocopied. Any supporting documents such as autobiographies should also be typed. If your home study is going to be mailed out, you don't want the child's worker to ignore your study because it is unreadable.

Examine your home study for typographical or spelling errors. In one home study for an intercountry adoption the social worker spelled *Chile* as "chili" and *Colombia* as "Columbia." Check the chronology of your life (e.g., dates that you attended school, where, what you've done) and other facts carefully. (To ensure accuracy in reporting factual details about your life, you might give your worker a résumé at the beginning of your home study.) If you object to any description of your family, say so. Mary Beth Gart was distressed at the way events in her life were handled. The stillbirth she'd lived through several years earlier was described as "stormy." Her home study dwelled on her childhood and her late father's alcoholism. Her worker reported that she and her husband were motivated to adopt a South Korean child "because they were unable to adopt a white child." She approached the social-work supervisor and asked that the home study be revised. Mary Beth rewrote certain sections, correcting factual errors. The agency took out the objectionable language.

There are other things that you can do to ensure that your home study presents as full a picture of you as possible. Since most agencies will not know your agency and the child's worker may be reluctant to trust another worker's home study, you'll want to:[4]

- Insist that your home-study packet contain multiple copies of photos of you as a family, of your home, and maybe of your activities as a family. It should also contain autobiographies written by you. State your experience with adoptive-parent group meetings and activities.
- Be sure that the entire home-study packet is sent every time you apply for a child. Ask that your worker inspect the packet when it is sent. Offer to pay for copying costs or postage. (If you get the costs you will know whether the entire package has been sent.)
- Include with the package any specific plans for the child's therapy if it will be necessary. Indicate what local resources are available.
- Volunteer to meet with the child's worker in person.

Since the child's agency may not have worked with your agency, ask that your agency include with your home study a brief description of their home-study process and also their plan for follow-up should your family be chosen. Recognize also, writes Pat Shirley, that in a special-needs adoption "your chances for a placement may indeed be lessened when your traditional home study is on the table next to a study done by an agency using the group home study concepts."[5]

If you will be sending your home study to a foreign country, keep in mind the value system of that culture. You may have discussed with your worker that you and your husband lived together before marriage—a practice more accepted in our society than others. Not everything discussed in a home study interview need be written up. One adoption agency found that the mention in a home study of a father's labor-union membership was questioned by a foreign agency, since there labor unions were illegal. What is regarded as an indicator of stability in one culture can be seen as subversive in another.

You may want your worker to focus on the multi-ethnic character of your community, if that is so, and how you can take advantage of its resources. Discuss the opportunities your child will have to meet with other people from his birth country and also how the child will meet with other adoptees. If you come from a small community, explain how you will help maintain the child's cultural and racial identity.

It is up to you, and your agency, to convince a child's adoption worker that you have given a lot of thought and time to the adoption route you are pursuing.

Common Problems and Solutions

If all goes well, you will contact an agency, arrange for a home study to be done, and be satisfied with the result. But sometimes things don't work out as you think they should. What do you do? You have rights. You are a consumer of an agency's services, whether you pay for them directly in a fee or whether they are funded through your tax dollars. The agency and the workers are there to provide you with a service, and you have the right to question those services.[6]

If an Agency Says That It Is Unable to Do a Home Study

- Find out why. If you are told that there are long waiting lists for the type of child you seek, think about broadening the categories of children you will consider.
- Determine whether state law requires the agency to do a home study and if so, within what period of time.
- Sometimes a local agency will not do a home study for an intercountry placement unless it receives a request from a foreign agency, while the foreign agency will not accept an application from you unless it sees your home study. If you are caught in this catch-22, see whether the local agency will accept a letter from the foreign agency indicating its willingness to consider placing a child with you upon its receipt of your home study.
- Find out whether state law permits you to work with a licensed social worker without agency affiliation.

If You Don't Get Along with Your Caseworker

- Discuss your problems with other adoptive parents who have previously worked with the agency or worker. They may have suggestions on how to proceed.
- Discuss your problems with your worker.
- Talk with the adoption supervisor.
- Request a new worker. Your home study may take longer, but it may make a difference in the outcome.

If the Agency Turns Down Your Application for a Child After Your Home Study Is Completed

- Find out why.
- Get the decision in writing.

- Appeal the decision within the agency or beyond. Many states have established appeal procedures.
- If there are specific deficits given, offer a plan to address these deficits in your appeal.
- Don't take the agency's decision as the final answer to your decision to adopt. Some agencies can be more flexible in approving families than others.

4

Searching for a Baby Independently

Pat and Gary Pawling contemplated adoption for several months before attending an adoption orientation class run by a local parent group. When the discussion got around to independent-placement adoption, another couple mentioned that they were running advertisements for a newborn in several newspapers around the state. The two couples chatted about possibly pooling their resources. Nothing more was said. At home Pat started compiling a list of newspapers in which she might run such a personal advertisement. A month later the other couple called her. They'd had two responses to their ads and both birth mothers had already given birth. Were Pat and Gary interested in talking with the birth mother of a day-old boy? They were, and a week later, after contacting an attorney and completing the necessary paperwork, they picked up their new son.

Not all nonrelative, independent (nonagency) placements happen like this, but some do. Most independent placements, in fact, involve a stepparent adopting the child of a spouse, or a relative adopting, for example, a niece or nephew. But private infant adoptions, or "direct adoptions," as nonfamilial independent placements are often called, are also common.

Perhaps the best way to understand independent placement is to contrast it with the more traditional infant agency adoption practice, as the following chart shows. Be aware that as infant agency adoptions become more open, the differences in some practices blur.

AGENCY ADOPTION COMPARED TO INDEPENDENT ADOPTION

Agency Adoption	Independent Adoption
Birth parents surrender child to agency, which then places child with adoptive parents.	Birth parents consent to place child directly with the adoptive parents.
The adoption agency serves as the intermediary between the parties and provides the linkage.	Various intermediaries—attorneys, physicians, counselors, ministers, teachers, friends—may be used to help facilitate the placement.
Birth parents may not know the identity of adoptive parents. They may see résumés describing the family, but only nonidentifying information is shared. Agency may work to ensure anonymity.	Birth parents may know the identity of the adoptive parents. Varying degrees of anonymity maintained.
Birth parents may talk with the adoptive parents, but agency is involved. There may be a meeting, on a first-name-only basis.	Birth parents often have been in contact with the adoptive parents—either by telephone or in person. Contact, which may be on a first-name-only basis, may be frequent.
Infant may be placed in foster care until all the releases have been signed. Then birth parents have no right to the child. If infant is placed in home after birth and before waiting periods have passed, placement is "legal risk adoption."	Infant goes to adoptive parents' home directly from hospital. Birth parents usually surrender child for adoption after the child is residing in the adoptive home. Under state law birth parents may have the right to change their minds about the adoption and reclaim the child.
Agency social worker is involved in the selection of the parents for a specific child. Birth parents may choose from several prescreened families.	Birth parent often does own screening (e.g., through telephone contact) and selects the adoptive parents for her child.

Agency Adoption	Independent Adoption
Adoptive parents have sought out an agency, filed an application, been approved, and followed agency procedures for infant adoption. They wait to be chosen.	Adoptive parents often are actively involved in searching for an infant to adopt. They are active in birth parent recruitment.

The Legality of Independent Adoption

Independent placement is legal in most states, although the laws governing it will vary. Some states impose few or no restrictions on independent placements. Others say that a child must be placed for adoption directly by the birth parent with an adoptive parent; intermediaries are forbidden.

Your state department of social services can tell you exactly what is legal in your state. (The state-by-state directory at the back of this book provides a brief summary. You can also obtain a copy of your state's laws from the National Adoption Information Clearinghouse in Washington, D.C.) In 1991 independent placements were not permitted by state law in Connecticut, Delaware, Massachusetts, Michigan, and North Dakota. If you live in one of these states, find out whether an identified adoption—a cross between agency and private adoption (see Chapter 2)—is possible. If you are considering an independent placement across state lines, you will need to learn what is legal in both states and how the interstate compact, which establishes procedures for the transfer of children from one state to another, will be involved. In all states birth parents cannot relinquish a child to you before birth and usually have the right, for a prescribed period of time after the birth, to change their minds.

No doubt as you ponder independent placement you'll be warned about "gray market" adoptions, "black market" adoptions, and baby brokering. These are terms that people have coined to identify nonagency adoptions. What do these terms imply? A gray market, as the dictionary defines it, is a market using irregular channels of trade or undercover methods not actually or explicitly illicit and dealing chiefly in scarce materials at excessive prices. The implication drawn by some is that nonagency adoptions are gray-market in that they use irregular—that is, nonagency—channels. A black-market adoption, technically speaking, involves an illegal market in which goods are sold in violation of price controls or other restrictions. Huge amounts of money are reportedly passed along in trade for babies. Using an intermediary when one is forbidden by state law would also be a black-market adoption. Baby brokering also suggests schemes and trading in babies.

As adoption practices continue to evolve, it becomes hard to use these terms meaningfully. What about an agency that charges a high fee or advertises for birth parents in the classified section of a newspaper? Agency adoption, like independent adoption, can also involve "brokering" if one recognizes that the agency can "act as an agent for others in negotiating contracts for a fee." Independent placement adoption is just what it says: a nonagency placement that results in an adoption whose circumstances adhere to the rules of the state. Some practices can smell fishy and be illegal whether they are handled by individuals or agencies.

Deciding for Independent Adoption

At age twenty Heather Byrd had tubal surgery and was informed by her gynecologist that birth control was unnecessary because she couldn't get pregnant. Her doctor's assessment was wrong, however, and she became pregnant. "I was very scared as soon as I missed my period, because I knew that I couldn't afford a child and wasn't ready to get married," says Heather. After deciding against an abortion, Heather called local adoption agencies. "I wanted to know the environment my baby was going to, I wanted to know the people, and I wanted them to know me as a human being," says Heather. "I didn't ever want her to think that she came from bad birth parents. I'm not a druggie, I'm not an alcoholic, I'm going to do my best to get by. I wanted her to feel proud of me and I wanted her to feel proud of her father."

At the agencies she contacted, however, the files were closed and there were rules that birth parents could not meet adoptive parents. So Heather spoke with her gynecologist about her dilemma and learned that he'd recently received a letter from a couple hoping to adopt.

"Everything in the letter appealed to me about them," recalls Heather, "except their age—Mike was fifty-seven and Cindy forty-five." She called them up, however, and "as we started talking, it turned out that Cindy had been brought up the way I was and we had similar values. Mike and Cindy were clearly honest, trustworthy, loving people." The couple invited her to their house and while there, Heather asked them the questions she needed answered: What's your background? Any alcoholism? How were you raised? How would you handle my child as a teenager? Are you going to buy her a car when she's sixteen? How will you discipline? Says Heather: "I wanted to pick a family who would give a child choices, a family where a child could make her decisions right or wrong." Despite Mike and Cindy's age, and the fact that they already had grown children, Heather decided these were the right parents for her child.

For Carrie Sullivan, seventeen, unmarried, and living at home with her parents in a rural town, the road to independent adoption was different. Just a few months before, Carrie had given birth to a child. She was now struggling to raise that child while still attending high school. She had thought that she was practicing birth control, but with the method she chose, she found herself pregnant again. First she delayed telling anyone because she was embarrassed. Then she decided that, for her, abortion was out of the question. So when she was several months pregnant with the second baby, she told her minister's wife of her problem. She wanted to release the child for adoption, but was adamant that she did not want to approach the local agency; she did not feel comfortable talking about her situation with strangers, particularly when she felt that they might question how she could become pregnant twice in less than a year.

Said the minister's wife: "Carrie had a fear of interrogation by adults, a fear of sexual questions, a fear that she would have to tell her story to many people. She just wanted one person who would be her advocate, whom she could tell what she wanted and when." The minister's wife became her advocate and her intermediary.

Meanwhile, Earl and Alice Addams, a couple who wanted to adopt, had approached a local agency and placed their name on a waiting list for a home study. Through mutual friends, the minister's wife heard that they had been making inquiries about adoption and had been thinking about the possibilities of an independent adoption, so she contacted them on Carrie's behalf. After Carrie's son was born, Earl and Alice became his parents.

Birth parents may decide to place their children for adoption independently because they want more control over the process. They may feel it is important to select the adoptive parents, to talk with them, and even to meet with them. Many agencies now permit these practices, but others don't. Financial need may also play a role in birth mothers' seeking out independent placement. Many agencies cannot pay medical bills or other expenses, although they may direct a woman to public assistance and other forms of aid. Many states, however, will permit adoptive parents to pay for reasonable expenses in an independent placement. A birth mother may also be reluctant to approach an agency for counseling, fearing that the social worker will be passing judgment on her. She may fear too much probing—and be reluctant to name the birth father. Or she may have gone for an interview at an agency and been turned off.

Adoptive parents may seek out an independent placement because there are long waiting lists with local agencies or too many agency restrictions (age, fertility history, length of marriage, and religion are common barriers). Or there may be no suitable agencies in their area. Some adopters may feel strongly that they want to have more information about their child and the birth parents than their local agencies have been willing to provide. Others may want a more open—or closed—adoption than their local agencies permit. Ron and Dorothy Sanders chose an independent placement adoption because they wanted to adopt a newborn directly from the hospital, while their local agencies insisted on a period of foster care. Jack and Wendy Wilson adopted their first child through an agency and had planned to put their name on the waiting list for a second, but pursued an independent opportunity instead after a colleague of Jack's happened to hear about a pregnant teen interested in a private adoption. Despite what you may read in the press or hear bandied about, most people who adopt independently are not forced to do so because of their rejection by an agency but rather choose to because they believe it is most appropriate for them.

Independent adoption is also attractive because it often brings results fast. Bonnie Gradstein, Marc Gradstein, and Dr. Robert H. Glass, who conducted a study of private adoption in California and reported their findings in the journal *Fertility and Sterility,* found that all but 2 of 105 infants had been placed in their adoptive homes within a year of their parents' starting to look.[1]

Finally, if you want to have direct contact with a birth mother, such an arrangement is quite common in independent adoptions. In fact, some states have laws mandating direct contact between birth parents and adoptive parents. For a more complete sense of open adoption's potential in independent placement, see Chapter 5.

Getting Prepared

If independent placement interests you, your first step will be to understand what is permitted. Here are some basic questions to ask your state social service department:

- Who can legally place children for adoption?
- Must you meet directly with the birth parents?
- Can you use an intermediary if you don't wish to meet with the birth parents directly?
- What type of parental releases and/or consents must you obtain?
- What are the waiting periods required for the releases?
- What are the rights of the putative father? (Once you identify a particular child, be sure to ask who the putative father is, where he is now, and whether he's agreed to the adoption plan.)
- Does the state require that adoptive parents and birth parents be of the same religion? Can religious restrictions be waived?
- Does the state require a home study before placement? If so, who can do it?
- Does the state require a fingerprint check or a criminal background check before placement?
- Does the state have a residency requirement?
- What expenses related to the adoption can you legally pay for?

If you are adopting in another state, you will need to contact that state's department of social services to find out what is legal there. You must consider the standards of the interstate compact. And if you are considering adopting a child of Native American ancestry, be sure that you understand the regulations of the Indian Child Welfare Act of 1978. This federal law protects the rights of Indian children, families, and tribes. It stipulates that *in all foster care, preadoptive and adoptive placements, preference is given, unless there is good cause to the contrary, to placing a child with a member of the child's extended family, other members of the child's tribe, an Indian foster or adoptive family, and an Indian-operated institution.* Placements with non-Indian families are considered a last resort. Even if the birth parents are not living on the reservation, and even if they have said that they want you to become the parents, the tribe has the right to intervene in court proceedings and make its own decision. There have been major custody battles around this issue; when the tribes have opposed the placements, the courts have made adoptive parents relinquish their children.

You may also want to explore whether an independent adoption or an identified adoption through an agency (see Chapter 2) best suits your situation. Some states permit birth mothers several weeks or months to change their minds when they place a child independently but have a much shorter revocation period when an agency is involved.

As you gather information, you'll want to hook up with an adoptive-parent support group. The **Adoptive Parents Committee** (80 Eighth Avenue, New York, New York 10011; 212-683-9221) and **Families for Private Adoption** (P.O. Box 6375, Washington, D.C. 20015; 202-722-0338) are two groups whose members have successfully adopted independently. You can obtain from them written materials or attend workshops that stress independent placement as a legal, viable adoption alternative. **Families for Private Adoption** has produced an excellent handbook, *Successful Private Adoption.* Although some of it is geared specifically for Maryland, Virginia, and District of Columbia residents, much of it is of general interest. Check also with your local chapter of **Resolve.** It's also helpful to do some reading about independent adoption. See the directory at the back of this book for suggestions.

Meanwhile, you still have more questions to ask and answer for yourself:

- Do you want to have contact with the birth parents?
- What do you mean by contact? Face-to-face? Letters? Photographs? Telephone calls?
- Do you want to use an intermediary?
- How much anonymity do you want?
- What questions do you want to ask the birth parents?
- Are there aspects of the birth parents' medical history that concern you, such as smoking, drinking, possible drug use?
- What type of counseling have you had? Do you want the birth parents to have had counseling?
- What medical risks are you willing to assume?
- Will you accept a child born with a birth defect?
- What is the state of your savings?
- Can you afford to pay the legitimate pregnancy-related expenses?
- Can you afford the expenses of a cesarean section if it occurs?
- Are you willing to travel to pick up your child?
- Are you willing to live for several months in another state if that is necessary?
- Are you willing to bring the birth mother to your state to give birth to her child?
- If you bring a birth mother to your state, what facilities and costs are involved in providing shelter and maintenance for her?
- Whom will you turn to for legal advice?
- Whom will you turn to for both obstetric and pediatric medical advice?
- How much risk and uncertainty are you willing to live with?

The Risks of Independent Adoption

"Hope wants the baby back!"

On a sultry summer evening Jeanne and Harvey Hammer got the telephone call every adoptive parent dreads. The sixteen-year-old birth mother of their seven-week-old daughter Rebecca had changed her mind about adoption. "I was hysterical, I was sobbing, I couldn't believe it," says Jeanne, her voice breaking as she remembers the events of a year past. "I was Rebecca's mother," she says softly. For seven weeks she'd loved and cuddled her, but her state's adoption statutes give birth mothers ninety days to revoke their consent. Jeanne and Harvey tried to fight—they got the local court to hold a hearing—but the judge told them that the birth mother had an ironclad right to her child. "It was over. I packed a diaper bag full of clothes and formula and put Rebecca's baptismal cap in there with a note," recalls Jeanne. At their attorney's house they returned the baby to Hope.

"This was so horrible to go through," says Jeanne. "I was devastated. I would wake up in the night crying. I knew that I had to grieve, to experience the despair and sorrow." Then there was the anger: "We had this feeling that we got stiffed, that we'd spent thousands of dollars and didn't have a child." Jeanne and Harvey worried how they would ever adopt again when they had just spent so much of their savings. "And we had to grapple with this angry feeling that Hope had used us."

It took months before Jeanne and Harvey felt strong enough to consider adoption again. When her sister met a young woman interested in adoption, Jeanne insisted that the birth mother go for counseling, that the adoption be handled by an agency, and that the young woman also be represented by an attorney. "I believe in private adoption, but for my own peace of mind the second time around," says Jeanne, "I insisted on an

identified adoption with the birth mother receiving counseling
at the agency. I couldn't go through ninety days of wondering
whether we'd get a phone call demanding the baby back." This
time the adoption went without a hitch, and Jeanne was even
present for their baby's birth. Still, there are the strong memories of Rebecca. "We lost our first daughter," she says. "I wonder and worry about her. We had two children; now we only
have one."

What befell Jeanne and Harvey is rare, but independent
placements do sometimes unravel. The possibility of disappointment with independent adoption begins early. You may
hear of a woman in her third month of pregnancy who is thinking about surrendering a child for adoption. Recalls one adoptive mother: "Before Sarah's adoption came through, we had
other leads; they always seemed like sure things, and then they
would fall apart." You will have to wait out the pregnancy
realizing that the birth mother may indeed change her mind
either before or after the child is born. Recalls adoptive mother
Audrey: "The baby was born. We had the crib sitting by the
bed. We gave her a name: Caroline. We had a baby shower."
All that remained was for Audrey and her husband to travel to
the distant city to pick their daughter up. On the day that the
baby was to be released from the hospital, they flew into town.
"When we got into the lawyer's office, we knew by his face that
the mother had changed her mind. It was like a miscarriage—
very painful." Remembers another woman about the failed
placement of an infant boy: "It was devastating. He was ours.
He was ripped out of our arms even though we didn't get him."[2]

Even after your child is placed in your home, depending on
your state's law, the birth parents may have the right to change
their minds for a specified period of time. If the birth parents
have received proper counseling and their decision was made
without duress, this is unlikely to happen. But, as Jeanne and
Harvey discovered, it can. Can you live with that uncertainty?

There is also a financial risk. You may pay for medical bills, counseling, or other legally permissible bills, but you won't necessarily get your money back if the adoption fails to go through. Bob and Adrienne Bauer had an adoption crumble after they had flown cross-country to pick up the baby. By that time their out-of-pocket expenses exceeded $4,500, including the $2,000 they spent for their airfare and hotel bill, $1,200 for legal fees, and $1,300 on the birth mother's expenses for rent and food prior to the birth. Sometimes you can ask the birth mother for repayment of her costs, but the chances are mighty slim.

Even a successful independent placement can be complicated and emotionally trying. Mike and Eve's situation illustrates how involved some private adoptions become. Someone from another state told them about a birth mother interested in adoption. Checking with a local attorney in the state where the birth mother resided and with attorneys in his home state who advised him on the general legality of the situation, Mike learned that he and his wife would have to be residents of the state where the birth mother lived in order to adopt. They would have to set up an apartment and live there. This state's preadoption requirements involved a home study before the child could enter their home. Their costs would include an attorney's fees, medical expenses, and living costs in two states. Mike would continue working and commute by air on weekends to his new home.

They decided to take the chance. They did their preadoption paperwork and had their home study done. Eve sat in their new home waiting for the baby to be born. Then things got even more complicated. The birth mother, a young frightened teenager, gave birth under an assumed name, left the baby with a friend, and ran away. At that point, says Eve, "we were getting ourselves psychologically prepared to pack up and cut our losses." The birth mother returned, however, and had additional counseling. She eventually surrendered the baby. Several months after Mike and Eve had traveled to the new state, they

84 THE ADOPTION RESOURCE BOOK

returned home with their new son. Would they do it again? Yes, and no. "We wouldn't be separated for almost four months. For our second child, we'd probably not go out of state like that." But, continues Eve, "for William, we were willing to do almost anything."

Just how much risk and uncertainty you are comfortable with should be carefully weighed.

Seeking Legal Advice

As you pursue an independent placement adoption, you will need to consult with an attorney. Chapter 8 provides general information about interviewing attorneys. To find attorneys with expertise in independent adoptions, check with adoptive parents, adoptive parent groups, your local and state bar associations, and the **American Academy of Adoption Attorneys** (P.O. Box 33053, Washington, D.C. 20033-0053). Be sure that you find out from your state social service agency what role the attorney is allowed to play in the adoption.

Explore with your attorney what role he expects to play in the independent placement process. Following are some questions to ask:

- What matchmaking role—if any—does the attorney play?
- Will he interview the birth parents on your behalf? If he is not available to talk to birth parents, who in his office does?
- Who provides counseling of the birth parents? When does it take place? Is this something that might be ongoing, or does it stop once the baby is placed?
- Will the attorney take charge of the medical arrangements?
- Will he represent you in court?
- Who will represent the birth parents in court? (Some courts do not permit one lawyer to represent both you and the birth parents, since there may be a conflict of interest.)
- How does he handle the rights of the putative father?

- How many independent adoptions and agency adoptions has the attorney handled? How recently?
- How many interstate adoptions has he handled?
- What are his fees and what do they cover? Is there a retainer?
- How will funds be disbursed to the birth parents? Will an escrow account be set up?
- If you want to, can you participate actively in the process and reduce the lawyer's time and fees? What would you do?
- Should there be a written agreement with the attorney, before the child arrives, as to what services he will provide?
- What does the attorney know about open adoption? Has he attended any workshops or conferences that focused on open adoption? What are his views? How current and well read is he in his thinking?
- How does the lawyer feel about contact between adoptive parents and birth parents? Is contact between adoptive parents and birth parents encouraged before the birth? After? How does the attorney feel, for example, about letter writing? About direct contact? What role is he willing to play before and after?
- If there is no direct contact between the adoptive parents and the birth parents, who might handle a question that arises in five years? Is the attorney staffed for this? How are requests handled now?
- What kind of records does the lawyer maintain? What happens if his practice closes? Where is the information going to go?
- Do *you* feel comfortable with the lawyer who is about to share the intimate procedure of family building? Do you trust him?

Be sure that you check the lawyer's reputation among his colleagues and other adoptive parents. Has the court ever questioned the independent adoptions he's handled? If so, why? You can also check with your interstate compact administrator and attorney general's office. If you have any doubts at any point, get other legal opinions.

While it's tempting to use a sympathetic friend, relative, or the attorney who handled your latest real estate deal, beware. One couple lost their baby in part because of their lawyer friend's inexperience. The father of their just-arrived baby learned after the fact of the placement of the infant and insisted on his right to the child. Their attorney had not demanded that the father be located and his feelings about relinquishment be obtained before the baby entered their home. "An adoption is something you want to do absolutely right," observed one attorney with an expertise in private adoptions, "because it's not the sort of case you want to have to win before the court of appeals." Observes Pat Shirley of FACE: "Many horror stories we hear center around well-meaning but inexperienced lawyers not understanding the complex processes."

Spreading the Word

In her Christmas cards, Fay Alfred wrote: "We're trying desperately to adopt and if you hear of anything, let me know." Shortly after Christmas, she got a call from a physician for whom she had once worked who had moved out of state. He had a patient who had just given birth to a baby boy. Were they still interested in adopting? She was, and she did the necessary paperwork to travel across the country to pick up her son. Five months later, Fay got a call from her obstetrician, who told her he knew of a baby. Not right now, Fay said, but thanks and keep me in mind for the future. And two years after those cards went out, Fay's sister's obstetrician called from another state to ask whether they were still interested in an independent adoption.

Spreading the word—telling others that you are interested in adopting a child and are willing to adopt independently—is a crucial first step—and possibly the only step you may have to take in pursuing an independent placement. If you want to adopt, you must talk about it. That means telling your parents, your aunts and uncles, your cousins, your neighbors, your friends, and whomever else you can think of. "I called everybody that I knew," recalled Roberta Rolfe, whose daughter arrived several months after her inquiries began. "I promised myself that I'd make one telephone call a day. At parties I'd walk up to people, complete strangers sometimes, and say, 'Hello, my name is Roberta Rolfe and my husband and I want to adopt a baby. Do you know of anyone who wants to put up a baby for adoption?'" (She'd hand them her business card with the handwritten message "Hoping to Adopt.") When Roberta accompanied her husband on a business trip to Louisiana, she picked up the telephone and called the local department of social services to inquire about adoption. "It was an obsession. There was nothing more important than this," says Roberta. "I was monomaniacal."

Was Roberta crazy? No. The more people that she told, the greater the likelihood that someone might know someone. Beyond family, friends, neighbors, and colleagues at work, reach out to other people within your community. Go through your address book, your parents' address books, your sister's address book. Are there some old college chums who might help? Adoption counselors particularly recommend that you contact nurse-midwives, physicians, social workers, birth control counselors and other health professionals, clergymen, teachers and high school principals, and even beauticians. These are often the people who might come into contact with pregnant women. Establish as extensive a network as you can; indeed, if state laws and finances permit, explore the possibility of contacting people in another state.

How should you go about letting people know? Some adoptive parents use the telephone; others send out letters, while still others try to talk to people in person. Encourage the people you contact to talk with others about your desire to adopt.

Keep track of all your contacts. Get a notebook and record

details about everyone you approached and exactly what they were told and what they told you. Follow up on as many leads as possible—and be prepared to retrace your steps at a later point.

There are also more formal ways to alert others to your needs. Some prospective adopters have done mass mailings of letters to obstetricians, pediatricians, and family practitioners whose names have been taken from phone books and medical directories (including the membership directory of the American College of Obstetricians and Gynecologists). There are even adoption services around the country that sell preaddressed mailing labels.[3] Other counselors have suggested contacting abortion clinics, right-to-life groups, Planned Parenthood centers, and free health clinics.

Some people have tried sending out detailed autobiographies or résumés along with their letters. The autobiography or résumé should include a phone number where you can be reached—collect! You might also give the names of other contacts (for example, your attorney). Round out your profile with a snapshot of yourself.

You might also want to print business cards (e.g., "Adoption—a gift of love. Call us collect anytime. We can offer you a choice.") that you hand out and post on bulletin boards in supermarkets, laundromats, restaurants, and other public places. Some families have gone one step further, creating adoption signboards that sit atop their cars as they drive around!

Placing advertisements in newspapers is one technique that adoptive parents have increasingly utilized. Just as agencies have found that newspaper features about a particular waiting child will elicit a response from potential adopters, prospective adoptive parents have found that placing an advertisement in the personal section of the classifieds alerts birth parents to their desire to parent a child. The ads convey their concerns:

ADOPTION, NOT ABORTION: Let us adopt your baby. We are a young, happily married couple who wish to adopt a white infant into our home. If you can help us, our gratitude goes to you. Expenses paid.

ADOPT: Childless couple will be wonderful parents and give terrific life to newborn. Answer our prayers.

ADOPT: Happily married couple, will provide love, finest education, country home for baby, confidential, expenses paid.

ADOPTION: If you are considering adoption, I am a single man, financially secure, who will be a caring and devoted parent. You will always have a place in this child's life. Please call collect so we can talk. Confidential. Expenses paid as legal.

In states where newspaper advertising is legal (see the state-by-state directory at the back of the book), the ads have become so widespread that birth parents seeking an independent placement will often start there. "I had seen the personals for a long time," says one birth mother who interviewed fourteen couples before making her decision. "There were always a lot of ads in the newspaper, and they caught my eye. I felt awkward with the first couple I spoke with, but then I felt better." She found the couple she wanted: married with other children.

How does the advertising process work? You begin by locating newspapers that accept this type of classified ad—the *Gale Directory of Publications* and *The Editor & Publisher Yearbook* are two directories found in library reference rooms that describe publications nationwide. Consider also college newspapers and limited circulation papers such as the *Pennysaver* or the *Thrifty Nickel*. While you could list your home telephone in the advertisement, many adopters arrange for a second telephone line and an unlisted telephone number specifically for adoption inquiries. As part of your preparation process, you'll also want to work up a brief questionnaire—covering the birth parents' age, due date, ethnic background, marital status, medical history, religion, financial situation, and reasons for choosing an adoptive placement—that you can keep by the telephone and fill in as you talk. You'll want to talk with your attorney in advance to discuss the legal requirements.

When the ads appear, you'll receive responses either directly from the birth mother or from an intermediary, such as her sister or a friend, speaking for her. You may talk several times and may then refer her to your attorney, if state law permits, to make the arrangements. It's quite possible that you'll meet or maintain a telephone relationship for several months.

Don't be surprised if your ad is not the only one appearing in a particular newspaper. You may want to make your ad as personal as possible. Try to put yourself in the place of the birth parent who will be reading the newspaper. Don't pinch pennies when writing these ads. They speak for you. Be aware also that you may need to run your ad for several months in several newspapers. *The costs can mount into the hundreds or thousands of dollars if you spread your net wide over an extended period of time.* "The advertising became addictive," recalled Bob Bauer, whose expenses rose into the thousands. "My wife and I felt uncomfortable if a week or two went by and we hadn't run an ad." You may also receive many calls and talk with many people who never follow up. You may get crank calls and offers from people to "sell" you their baby. Recalls Laura Stanton: "One lady called who had a six-month-old girl and she wanted $15,000 just for herself. I had a truck driver who called me and said that his route was through New York and he wanted to drop the baby on my doorstep. It just went on and on."

Naomi and Nicholas Adler placed ads in weeklies that covered an entire county in several states and changed the ads and newspapers frequently. They limited their advertising expenses to $200 a month. Recalls Naomi: "It was absolutely horrible to sit by the telephone. It was horrible when it didn't ring and when it did." Finally, four months after they placed their first ad, the call they were dreaming about came, and two months later they were parents of a little girl. Says Naomi: "We'd tried word of mouth and didn't come up with anything.

Advertising gave us the chance to reach pregnant women directly and also gave us the chance to weed out situations that we didn't think were legitimate. We knew what was happening. We were talking with the birth mother. We were really secure that we weren't going to have any surprises along the way." Naomi and Nicholas learned of their daughter's birth from her mother. Naomi now looks back with enthusiasm: "The whole experience was so exciting. It's so hard to believe that it really happens all the time."

Be sure that you find out whether it is legal to place an ad for an adoption in a state. Check also with the state department of social services, a knowledgeable adoption attorney, and parent groups. You may also have to search around for a newspaper that is willing to take your ad. Remember also that newspaper advertising is controversial and open to abuses such as the growth of expensive and unreliable adoption advertising services. For a fuller description of the process, giving step-by-step instructions, take a look at *The Private Adoption Handbook*, which is listed in the Resources section at the back of this book.

The Cost of an Independent Adoption

Costs for independent adoptions often range between $6,000 and $18,000. It's difficult to come up with more exact or typical figures, however, because each adoption is different. If the birth mother is living at home and has health insurance coverage under her parents' policy, then the expenses of the adoption will be much less than if the birth mother has no health insurance and delivers the child by cesarean section. If the birth mother travels to your state to give birth and resides there before delivery for a month or more, the cost will be higher. The difference to you can be as much as $5,000.

Consider the cases of four Maryland couples, all of whom adopted infants born in the state[4]. The first family's adoption expenses came to $6,496, including $412 for advertising for five weeks in three in-state newspapers, $2,668 in legal fees (for their attorney and the birth mother's), and $3,094 for medical expenses. The second couple spent $9,140, including $2,968 on legal fees, $3,305 on medical expenses, $228 on newspaper advertising, $130 for telephone installation, and $2,384 for pregnancy-related expenses that included lodging the birth mother for twenty-two days in a hotel prior to the birth. The third couple's expenses of $12,300 included $8,641 in legal fees (for their attorney, the birth mother's, and the birth father's), $2,155 in medical expenses, $524 for newspaper advertising, $423 for travel, and $400 for a home study. As for the fourth couple, their first adoption ($3,959) fell through when the birth mother revoked her consent after the baby was in their home (there were no medical expenses, as the birth mother and baby were covered by Medicaid). A second adoption ($1,045) came apart when the birth mother changed her mind before the birth. Their successful adoption cost $10,315, for a grand total of $15,319.

What do you imagine the expenses would have been for any of these couples if the birth mother, who had no medical insurance, needed to be hospitalized for ten days and the adoptive parents were expected to pay her bills? Recalls an attorney about one such adoption: "The birth mother became ill after delivery with an infection. There were bills for ambulance services, the hospitalization, the obstetrical fee, surgery, and psychological counseling. We had bills for absolutely everything. We had affidavits explaining the bills."

Given the variables, a cardinal rule for assessing costs in an independent placement must be that all expenses be reasonably documented—there should be receipts for all expenditures. Attorneys should be paid for the professional legal services they perform. Physicians should be paid for the professional medical services they render. Social workers or clergy should be compensated for any professional counseling services they perform. *You should not be paying an attorney or anyone else a "finder's fee."*

WARNING: You should not be paying for the birth mother's college tuition, the down payment for her house (or her parents' house), a vacation in Europe, or "designer" maternity clothes. You may be asked to cover such expenses, *but these expenses are not considered reasonable expenses.* When you finalize the adoption in court, you may be asked to submit a sworn accounting of all payments made, or your actual receipts, and the judge may look very carefully at all expenses incurred.

INDEPENDENT ADOPTION EXPENSES

Your General Adoption Expenses
- Home study fee (home study often required before placement)
- Medical exams
- Fees for documents (e.g., birth and marriage certificates)
- Photocopying fees
- Court costs for completion of the adoption
- Long-distance telephone calls (these mount rapidly if the adoption is interstate)
- Your attorney's fees

Birth Parents' Adoption Expenses
- Birth mother's hospital and doctor bills
- Birth mother's lab fees, vitamins, tests, drug bills
- Counseling for the birth parents
- Birth parents' attorneys' fees

Infant's Adoption Expenses
- Infant's hospital-nursery and pediatric bills
- Infant's drug bills

Other Possible Expenses
- Birth mother's lodging and maintenance expenses for one or several months (if permitted by state law)
- Birth mother's or birth father's travel expenses for the surrender of the child (if permitted by state law)
- Putative father's pregnancy-related expenses
- Your travel, including airfare and car rental, and accommodation costs to meet birth parents or to bring baby home
- Postage for mailing out your résumé

- Advertising expenses in several newspapers for several months
- Installation of a separate phone for your adoption search

Getting Background and Medical Information

Adopted children have many questions about their birth parents. To help you get the information your child will need, you'll want to create some forms (much as an agency does) that you can have your child's birth parents and their families fill out. Explain that you will keep this information confidential, but will share it with your child in the future. Let the birth parents know you will also provide pertinent medical details to physicians. Request some photographs as well. Here are some of the topics you'll want to cover:[6]

- General description (age, height, weight, bone structure, eye and hair color, blood type, birth date and place)
- General medical (vision, dental history including orthodonture, medical problems corrected as a child. Create a checklist that includes medical conditions such as arthritis, cancer, high blood pressure, heart disease, diabetes, birth defects, acne, overweight, allergies, anemia, epilepsy, alcoholism—even trick knees. Ask the family to indicate if anyone has suffered from the condition and if so, to give some details). Did the birth mother use drugs or alcohol during the pregnancy? What about the birth father?
- Education (school history, learning disabilities, particular problems, particular talents)
- Family (parents, siblings, grandparents). Get general descriptions of them and details about their medical histories, their schooling. Has anyone in the family died prematurely? If so, why? Is there any family history of chronic disease? Is there any history in the family of substance abuse?
- Talents, interests, hobbies, sports abilities (the birth parents' and their families')

- Ethnic background
- Personality of birth parents and their families
- Why the birth parents have chosen adoption and what they wish you to share about themselves with their child

Things to Watch Out For

I wanted a baby. After years of marriage and wanting to have a child, you're willing to do anything. That puts many couples into dangerous situations. You're afraid to turn away any situation whether it's legal or black market or anything in between. It takes a tremendous amount of courage to say no when your gut feeling says that this is the wrong thing to do. I want to warn other couples who are desperate to have children to go very cautiously in their pursuit. There are a lot of people out there who are playing on your desperation. Never become that desperate to fall into the hands of those characters. There's a baby out there.

Those words were spoken by a woman who thought that an adoption service, which promised to find her a baby, was the solution. She sent the man running the service thousands of dollars to advertise for a child for her. Nothing ever happened, and the service eventually was closed down for violating state law.

If you decide to pursue an independent placement adoption, you should proceed cautiously at all times. Be on the alert for:

- *Parental consent.* No one should be pressured into releasing a child for adoption. Be sure that the parent has made the decision without duress. Be sure that you obtain the father's release. If there is no father's release, you may be asked to locate him. The rights of unwed fathers vary state by state, but the courts have begun to recognize their claims and so must you.
- *Attorney expertise.* Be sure that your attorney is experienced in adoption law, particularly for independent adoption and for the county where you will be adopting your child.
- *Pressure from intermediaries.* Don't let anyone tell you that

this is a once-in-a-lifetime situation. Private adoptions happen all the time.

- *Costs.* Examine these carefully. Are you being asked to put down money to place your name on an intermediary's waiting list? Are you being asked to advance large sums to a birth parent prior to placement? If you are being asked to put money into escrow, what is it for? Are you receiving an itemized bill for expenses?

- *Health.* Arrange to have the infant assessed by your pediatrician or by another physician of your choice. Get as extensive medical records about the birth parents and the child as you can. Don't hesitate to ask questions and to have the basic medical tests performed. Don't assume that "routine newborn care" has been completed unless you have the records that document it.

- *Counseling.* Be sure that the birth parents have adequate counseling and, again, that their decision is not made under pressure from you or anyone else.

Remember, in an independent adoption, you are relying on yourself, rather than an adoption agency, to ensure that your child's placement proceeds legally and successfully.

5

Understanding Open Adoption

In September 1989, Joan Smith got married. As the guests milled around, Joan beckoned young Michael Blair to her side and asked the photographer to snap a picture of her and the child. "This is the little guy I had six years ago," she said. "And this"—pointing to a smiling couple standing nearby—"is his mother Sharon and his father Ralph."

For Joan, Michael, Ralph, and Sharon this was just another chapter in the story that began in March 1983 when Joan, eighteen years old, unmarried and living at home with her parents, released her infant son, Michael, at birth for adoption. She had selected Ralph and Sharon Blair as the family that she felt matched her own after reading applicants' autobiographies shared with her by the agency's social worker. She saw her son at the foster home prior to his placement and also met with Ralph and Sharon. Joan was determined to do an open adoption because she feared that "I would be wondering every time that I saw a child on the street whether he was my son. I told my counselor that I wouldn't give up my child without knowing the parents. I wanted to know who he was throughout his life."

Joan hasn't had to wonder. The families, who live several hundred miles apart, typically get together in the summer and around Christmas, with Sharon sending photographs in between. Joan's known by her first name, while Michael and his brother call Joan's parents Grandma and Grandpa. "In this family," says Sharon, "several older couples have that title, but the kids know that they're Joan's parents." The kids also know who Joan is. Sharon's overheard Michael telling a little friend "about Joan who carried me in her belly," and laughs remembering how Michael informed Joan at the wedding that "that man who put me in your belly came to visit me this year." While Joan has lost contact with her son's birth father, the Blairs have spent some time with him.

Both Joan and the Blairs are pleased with how the open adoption has worked out. "If I don't talk to Joan or see her in a year's time," says Sharon, "I miss it. It's really a loss. And Michael will say, 'We haven't seen Joan for a long time.' The need is there." Says Joan: "I'm happy with what I have, but the adoption is not going to be forgotten. I'm glad to get pictures of Michael, to see him, to talk to him, to know he chipped his teeth, and that he likes sweets like I do. I think it would have driven me wild not knowing."

Yet this is not shared parenting. For Joan, "Michael's like a friend's child whom I really care for. I don't look at him as though he's my son, although I will identify him as my son. I catch my breath sometimes just watching him—realizing that I have a school-age child now." Sharon is equally clear about the relationship between the two families: "Joan has nothing to say about the way we raise him. She doesn't know every time Michael falls and hurts himself." Open adoption is "like sharing your life with a friend," says Sharon. "I wouldn't ask my friend where she'd send my kids to school, and I wouldn't think of asking Joan. But if there's something special that happens, our friends would know—and Joan's a friend—so she would know."

In open adoptions birth parents and adoptive parents meet one another, share identifying information, and communicate directly over the years. They may get together often, occasionally, or not at all, as the individuals determine what is best for them.[1] With two daughters adopted eight and four years ago, Donna and Bill King have met members of their daughters' birth families at the time of their placement, exchanged names and addresses, and have corresponded faithfully with them ever since. But as far as Donna is concerned, that's as far as she wants the relationship to go right now. "I don't think we've even talked about getting together," says Donna. "I don't know if I'd be in favor of it at the age my daughters are now. That would blow their minds. My husband and I aren't comfortable with either of them meeting their birth parents until they're seventeen or eighteen."

Claudia and Bob Bender feel similarly. They met with the birth mother and her family a week before their son Joel was born. They paced the floor of the hospital waiting room with Joel's birth grandmother and ate dinner at her house afterward. Since then they have written and talked by telephone. "At this point everybody agrees that face-to-face contact is something we're not going to be doing for a while," says Bob. "I think there are a lot of unanswered issues. Maybe that's being a little conservative, but I think there are some risks for Joel. I know a lot of people don't feel that way, but I'm not altogether persuaded. At this point I'm not willing to take the risk."

Open adoption, which is sometimes referred to as "cooperative adoption,"[2] is based on the assumption that people are capable of choosing each other and staying in touch directly, trusting each other enough to sustain a relationship and work together cooperatively to advance the best interests of the child. It assumes that adoptees are entitled to a full knowledge of their birth heritage and that birth parents have much to offer their children. As a corollary, open adoption advocates are now saying that birth and adoptive families must view each other as members of an extended family. Says James Gritter, a social worker at CFCS-Catholic Charities in Traverse City, Michigan, one of the pioneering agencies in open adoption: "Early on we viewed open adoption as connections, as people having a natural interest in one another. It has evolved to a very interesting relationship—really like relatives."

There are many "open" adoptions in the United States that stop far short of the criteria some advocates now propose. These adoptions might best be described as "semi-open" adoptions or even just "open placements." In many instances, while the birth parents and adoptive parents do meet, only their first names may be revealed, but no other identifying information. Any subsequent communication is carried on through an intermediary. Sometimes there will be no contact between the parents after the baby's birth. When you talk with adoption agencies about their "open adoption" program, be sure you find out exactly what their expectations are. An agency that proclaims it has "newborn infants available by open adoption placement" but then notes "no identifying information revealed" is serving up something other than an open adoption in the full sense of the term. If you are arranging a private adoption, be sure to clarify with the birth parents what their ideas and expectations of open adoption are. If there are intermediaries involved, you'll need to explore their opinions about open adoption and make sure that they are clear about what you and the birth parents have in mind.

Keep in mind that open adoption is not just for infant placements. Older children may stay in touch with their birth families, and this can be important for their adjustment and growth. "Now that David sees his birth mother on a regular basis," reported one adoptive parent, "he sees that she is very different from the person he remembered. He has stated many times that he is no longer afraid for her because she can now take care of herself." This birth mother has also let her son know that she is happy with the adoption: "David's birth mother gave him a very clear message that we are his parents and this was the plan she had made for him. Her role has been that of an interested person who cares about him very much, but who is not and never again will be his parent."[3]

As you explore the world of open adoption, you will find yourself entering into newly charted territory. There are ever-growing numbers of birth parents, adoptive parents, and adoptees creating new family relationships. And there is an ever-expanding literature—*Cooperative Adoption, Dear Birthmother, Children of Open Adoption, Adoption Without Fear, To Love and Let Go, An Open Adoption,* and *Open Adoption: A Caring Option*—to point the way. (You will find a discussion of these and other works in the reference section at the back of this book.) But the children of open adoption still have their growing up to do. As Becky Miller, a committed adoptive parent who has appeared on open adoption panels, put it: "We all wonder how the kids will view the situation in ten or fifteen years. Will they think that this is strange? Whether you are the adoptive parent or the birth parent, you hope that your child understands and accepts how this all came about."

This chapter, drawing on interviews with birth and adoptive parents who have chosen open adoption and the experts who have developed the programs, seeks to help you understand what open adoption is all about today. While the following pages explore basic questions and answers, they can only provide a brief distillation of a complicated subject. You will want to dip into the readings and other materials cited at the back of this book and find adoptive parent and expert support in the larger community.

The Advantages and Drawbacks of Open Adoption

When Katherine was six years old, she wanted to know how long her birth mother was in labor. Her questions regarding this matter became a point of intense fixation. This had to do with the building frustration of not receiving an answer since her mom did not have the information. In an effort to dissipate the mounting feeling, it was decided that Katherine could write to her birth mother and ask for the missing information. . . .

When the answer arrived it was dramatic to witness how the

information was absorbed and the whole matter became "no big deal." It is amazing to behold such a transformation of emotional energy when an answer becomes available![4]

"For the adoptee, open adoption provides answers to his normal questions," observe Kathleen Silber and Patricia Martinez Dorner in *Children of Open Adoption*. "He can get immediate answers when questions arise and can go on with other developmental tasks without getting stuck on adoption issues."[5] When communication lines are open, the adoptee is also guaranteed continued access to genetic information. "In addition, with open communication within the family, the adoptee does not have to feel that he is being disloyal to his adoptive parents by being curious or asking questions about the birth parents," write Silber and Dorner. "He is allowed to care about both sets of parents without feeling guilty."[6] With the birth parent only a letter or a telephone call away, there's also less reason to fantasize about his other parents. They are real people whose likes and dislikes he knows. As for his adoptive parents, he has a "sense of belonging," since he is aware that his birth parents chose them for him.

For the adoptive parent, open adoption starts with a feeling of empowerment. Consider this adoptive mother's account:

> There were about 15 people in my sister's house—Erin's [the birth mother's] friends, our friends. It was an incredible experience. Each person held Heather [the baby] while she or he talked about what this situation meant to them. . . . Bernardo [the birth father] was the last one to talk. Then he and Erin brought Heather over to us. He said "Aquí les entregamos nuestra hija." [We bring you our daughter.] Erin said, as they handed Heather to us, "We give you your daughter."[7]

Observes Becky Miller: "There is an entitlement for the adoptive parents because the birth parents have given you permission to love this child. The birth parents wanted us at the hospital when our children were born. That's definitely real entitlement."

Knowing the birth parents also mitigates any fears adoptive parents might have concerning the birth parents and makes it easier for adoptive parents to explain adoption issues to their children. "You've met a couple of very nice people who just happened to get into trouble like anybody could have," says Donna King. "You can face your children a lot easier when they ask because you've met these people and you're comfortable with them. You don't have to make up any stories about who they were and how they are."

For birth parents, open adoption brings a greater sense of control. While they will still grieve for their loss, they will know that they have made a plan for their child and that they will not be cut off from direct knowledge of their child's well-being. As birth mother Sara Charles put it, "I feel good to see my baby with a happy smile, with people who have time for her and who are letting me share in that joy."[8]

Open adoption advocates talk about the "honesty" of this kind of adoption, with no secrets or sealed records involved. The unknown, say advocates, compounds children's fears that something wrong with them must have led their birth parents to abandon them. And secrets hinder the building of their self-esteem and sense of control. Maintains Kathleen Silber: "Open adoption makes adoption very concrete. It's so much more understandable."

Yet open adoption is also complex and there is still plenty of pain. "I can't explain how much I hurt," recalls Sara Charles. "My whole heart broke. When the adoptive parents walked out of my hospital room with Danielle, I just started bawling. It was just a big loss." Two years later, talking about the adoption can still bring tears to Sara's eyes and a lump in her throat. With an open adoption, this pain is witnessed up close by the adoptive parents. "We've seen what a tremendous sacrifice giving up a baby is for a birth parent and how tough the decision is," observes Becky Miller, the adoptive mother of Sara's child. "Both joy and grief come out of this type of situation. We have tremendous joy over being able to parent, but we also experience and feel the pain that birth parents go through."

There may be strains after the placement as adoptive parents and birth parents discover the differences between their expectations and reality. "Everybody's feelings change a little bit after the baby is born," says Silber. "The birth mother may have thought she didn't want a lot of contact while she was pregnant but once the baby is born, she will want more contact than she thought. Everybody makes this agreement not knowing how it feels to give up a baby, or how it feels to parent a baby." At the Independent Adoption Center in Pleasant Hill, California, where Silber works, birth and adoptive parents meet with a mediator after the placement to express their feelings and discuss, once again, how they see the relationship developing over time.

There may be additional strains if family and friends do not understand or are not supportive. It's possible that a relationship could develop between the birth grandparents, rather than the birth parents, and the adoptive family. While this may bring great joy to them, some adoptive grandparents may resent these other grandparents. Observes Marlene Piasecki of the Golden Cradle in Cherry Hill, New Jersey: "In some families who've waited a long time to have a child, the two grandmothers want to be supreme. They don't want another grandmother in the picture."

Some adoptive grandparents may also be plagued by doubts and insecurities. At the time of their son Jonathan's adoption, Marlene and Eric Wilson were sure that his parents, Gregory and Dorothy, were enthusiastic supporters of the open adoption. After all, the special adoption telephone that birth mothers called in to had been installed in the senior Wilsons' home (Marlene worked long hours, while Dorothy was at home), and Dorothy had talked with several birth mothers. The two families had discussed adoption frequently—even watching some TV broadcasts about open adoption together. Eric's parents knew that Eric and Marlene had met Jonathan's birth mother at the time of the placement and continued the relationship through letter writing. Three years later, however, when Marlene announced that Jonathan was going to meet his birth mother on an upcoming trip, Eric's parents were horrified. "You're not going to see her?" said a panicked Dorothy. "I have a lot invested in this child." Since then Marlene is convinced that her in-laws have emotionally pulled back from their grandchild, fearing that the continued contact through telephone calls, letters, and occasional visits will lead to a situation where they will eventually lose him to his birth mother.

Other families will react differently. Recalls Donna King: "My parents were terrified when they first heard about open adoption. They didn't like it at all. They were concerned that the birth mothers would come back and take the babies, since they knew where the babies were." Eight years later she says, "They understand open adoption a little better now and think it's kind of neat."

In the long term, there is also the possibility that, as the birth parents' lives take on new shape, they will be inconsistent in their contact, or even drop out of their children's lives. This has led to emotional distress for the children as they wonder why their birth parents have chosen to stop communicating with them. (For a fuller discussion, see the section "The Children of Open Adoption" later in this chapter.)

Open Adoption: Your Fears and the Facts

If you are contemplating an open adoption, you probably have many questions. Here are the questions people frequently ask at the beginning and what the experts have to say:

- *How likely is it that the birth parents will change their minds after the baby is born and we have taken custody?*

In any adoption where the baby goes directly from the hospital to the adoptive parents' home there is the potential risk that the birth parents will change their minds during the time before they legally terminate their parental rights. "That is the period of highest vulnerability for the adoptive family," admits Gritter. "Good counseling doesn't mean that somebody is fixed in an adoption decision. At our agency we may go a year without that happening, and then we'll have four straight cases. It ranges between 10 and 20 percent of the placements."

Putting a child into temporary foster care until the birth parents' decision is legally irrevocable is an option that some agencies will offer to adoptive parents. Others feel that this denies adoptive parents the chance to build a relationship with the child from the outset and moves the child unnecessarily. And foster care also displeases birth parents.

So there's a risk that the adoption will unravel after the baby is born or in your home. If you already have an adopted child in your home, you'll also need to think about the potential impact on your older child if the birth parent reclaims the baby. To get a sense of how families feel, take a look at *Adoption Without Fear.* In this book, edited by Gritter, seventeen couples describe their experiences. Several of them had one or more disrupted placements.

- *Will the birth parents show up at our door uninvited if we share our name and address?*

"I've never known a birth mother to show up uninvited," says Silber. "Birth parents have spent considerable time and effort to arrange for their children to have a stable, loving environment and do not want to jeopardize this." In fact, birth parents and their families are likely to be very concerned not to intrude into the adoptive family's life. "I still feel stupid if I call the adoptive parents," one birth mother confided to a group of prospective adoptive parents at an agency orientation. "I don't want to seem like I'm barging into their lives." Sara Charles is equally clear about her respect for the adoptive parents' privacy: "I'd love to see Danielle all the time, but I don't want to be a problem. Every family needs time alone."

- *Do adoptive parents have any control over the experience? What if you're chosen by a birth parent that you don't like?*

Typically, with an agency or private placement, it's a mutual choosing. If you feel uncomfortable, you should be able to say no. The birth parents may select a particular family, but then there should be a meeting where you get acquainted. The placement should not proceed unless both sides agree to it and are satisfied with the plan.

Sara Charles describes the interviewing process she and her boyfriend Matt followed: "We selected four couples to interview. They were all very nice, but something just didn't click with the first two. The third couple was Becky and Bill. We sat around for hours talking and drinking pop. As we left, Matt said 'They're it!' and I knew he was right."

Just as birth parents take their time and often interview several adoptive parents before making their decision, you should also feel free to meet with several birth parents. If your initial talks or meeting with a birth parent leave you feeling uncomfortable, take the risk and say no. After all, you are making a commitment for a lifetime.

- *Is this shared parenting? Aren't the adoptive parents really just glorified baby-sitters?*

No matter how open the adoption is, it isn't shared parenting. If a birth mother envisions coparenting, then adoption isn't the choice for her, and her counselors should be helping her find a way to raise the baby. The birth parents are not parenting their child or participating in child-rearing decisions. As in other adoptions, there is a complete and irrevocable legal transfer of parental rights and responsibilities by the birth parents.

"Open adoption isn't shared parenting," says Becky Miller. "Danielle is with us around the clock. She has bonded to us and knows us as Mommy and Daddy. But there's nothing wrong with having more people—Sara, her birth father Matt, and their families—love Danielle."

- *If children have an open relationship with their birth parents, will they be confused as to who their parents are? Won't they see their birth parents as their "real" parents? Could adoptive parents lose their parental relationship with their children?*

Silber maintains that "it's the adults who are confused and freak out about the concept of open adoption, not the kids. Children know who Mommy is: she's the woman who's there every day. When children need mothering, when they fall down and skin their knee, they run to Mommy. They can clearly understand who's Mom and who's the birth mother. No matter how open the adoption is, from the child's point of view he doesn't have two mothers."

Your child will acknowledge his birth mother or birth father just as he will other adult relatives or close family friends who visit during the year. Think of it this way: He doesn't become confused as to their roles in the family just because they say they love him and shower him with kisses and gifts. Even when birth parents or birth grandparents visit regularly, children see them as their parents present them—as other caring relatives or friends. Reports Professor Harold Grotevant of the University of Minnesota, who is conducting an ongoing study of open adoption, "There doesn't seem to be confusion in the family as to who is the parent."[9]

It's important, however, to tell your child that this is the birth mother and that he grew in her womb. From the time you first start talking about adoption, you'll want to present your child with the truth. You'll also want to refer to the birth parents by their first names. (They are not "aunts" or "uncles.") And, as your child grows, you'll need to further explain the relationship, filling in the details and discussing it more than once. (For a fuller discussion about talking with children about adoption, see Chapter 12.)

- *Does having an open adoption automatically mean that you're going to have a visiting relationship?*

Silber maintains that "people meet initially, but then they decide how much contact they want on an ongoing basis. A lot of open adoptions include visits, but a lot don't. Some families keep in touch through letters and pictures." Sharon Kaplan, coauthor of *Cooperative Adoption* and executive director of Parenting Resources in Tustin, California, emphasizes that "open adoption was created for children. They should have the opportunity to have their heritage and their linkages preserved. The adults involved don't have a right to say that they don't want to stay in touch. It's the right of the child to have that preserved."

As your child grows, he will better be able to express his own feelings about open adoption and how contact is maintained. He may be content knowing that you write or talk with his birth parents from time to time. Or he may ask that he have the chance to see them.

- *If you set up an arrangement one way, does that mean it will stay that way over time?*

No relationship is static. Open adoptions evolve as people change. Often the contact is most frequent during the first year after the baby's birth. As the birth mother gets on with her life, perhaps finishing school, getting married, and having other children, the frequency of contact might be less than it was at the beginning.

But it can work the other way. Professor Grotevant reports that in adoptions where the relationship was less open at the start, there seems to be a pattern of moving toward more openness over the years.

- *If you already have an adopted child whom you adopted through a closed adoption, is it going to be difficult to explain to your first child what's happening with your second child?*

If you adopt two children, even in a closed adoption, each one is going to be different and there will be different explanations for each child. So it will be with your open adoption. Silber reports that in the situations she's observed where one adoption is closed and the other is open, the birth mother in the open adoption often becomes the "family" birth mother, acknowledging both children and bringing presents to both of them.

Since the literature on raising children in open adoptions is scanty, we must depend in part on what birth and adoptive families report. Sharon Blair says that "whenever we see Joan, she treats Michael and his brother Mark just the same. It's nice because Mark isn't the outcast." Remarks one birth mother about the other adopted child in her daughter's family: "I love him too. He's just as special as the rest of them are."

Is Open Adoption for You?

"There's just not one way to do an open adoption," observes Professor Grotevant. "This is not an all-or-nothing situation." As you come to understand the philosophy of open adoption, you've got to assess your own readiness and comfort level. You'll want to read some of the basic literature (see the synopses in the reference section at the back of this book). It's also helpful to find some adoptive parents with whom you can talk about their ongoing experiences. Check whether a local parent group holds an adoption conference or workshop featuring panels on open adoption or discussion groups with birth parents. Attend the general orientations of local agencies or organizations claiming to do open adoptions and listen to what they have to say. Then ask yourself some basic questions. You may discover that you're comfortable with the idea of an open placement but not with a fully open adoption.

• *How have you resolved your infertility?*

Having a relationship with birth parents and their families openly acknowledges that somebody else gave birth to your child. If acknowledging the difference between parenting a child who was born to you and parenting a child by adoption makes you uncomfortable, then you are going to have trouble with openness. Observes one adoptive parent: "Open adoption touches upon that matrix of feelings that adoptive parents have toward their children and toward birth parents. It really puts everybody on the line. Are you going to admit that you are an adoptive parent? It's the attitudes toward birth parents and toward adoption that are the real issue in open adoption—not the mechanics."

• *How do you define your family? Who can be in your family? Can you perceive the birth family as part of your family?*

These are questions Sharon Kaplan likes to pose to families. She asks them to think about their relationship to their spouse's family when they married. While you may not have been enamored of your in-laws, you probably worked at integrating them and their extended family into your new family. Chances are that you and your spouse didn't flip a coin at the wedding, says Kaplan, to decide which family could stay and which had to go. You found a way to link up both families for the sake of your spouse and, later, your children. Are you prepared to find a way to bring the birth parents into your family?

• *Can you make space in your life, in terms of time and energy, for other people?*

"Some people are very private and focused on their own small nuclear families," says Kaplan. "They are not going to be comfortable with an open adoption. The families I see moving into open adoption expect to share their kids with a lot of people and feel that the more love, and the more relatives, the better." Families involved with open adoption often say that their children are on loan to them and that their job is to be the best possible parents as their kids are growing up.

Even if these are your feelings, keep in mind that you're going to have to put time and energy into the relationship. Observed Sharon Harrigan in an article in *OURS* magazine on the problems families may face in an open adoption: "Several adoptive mothers in my group noted that they barely have time to write and send pictures to members of *their* families, much less their children's birth families. For one mom with four children, sending letters and pictures was almost a full time job!"[10]

• *Do you secretly believe that if you do the open adoption "right" at the beginning, then the birth parents will go away and leave your family alone?*

"That's a question I often ask people," says Kaplan, "and they often say to me, 'You're right. My secret thought is that if I'm very open and loving and show the birth parents what a good parent I'm going to be, when they're comfortable with me, they'll go away.'"

Families should not agree to any form of openness just to have a placement. The worst thing is for adopting parents to say "Yes, I would do anything" and then after finalization to say no.

Emphasizes Gritter: "Don't do something for the sake of expediency that really works against your grain."

• *What about the members of your extended family? How are they going to feel about open adoption?*

Maybe you've decided that you are comfortable meeting and communicating over the years. But you're not so sure you want your parents or other relatives to know the details of the arrangement. If so, you're perpetuating the secrecy that open adoption seeks to avert, and you're putting yourself and your child in a very uncomfortable situation.

It's not uncommon, however, for family members to be wary of open adoption and to have all the questions and concerns you initially had. Educating them about open adoption, and encouraging them to express their feelings, is important.

• *How flexible are you?*

Open adoption experts believe that adoptive parents must be able to improvise. Think about what you imagine an open adoption will be like and what your comfort level will be. Then keep in mind that whatever you decide, it may well change. You may decide you want to be relatively closed and that's what the birth parents want, but five years later you or the birth parents may try to initiate some contact with each other. Or your child will express an interest in meeting his birth parents. While you may make important decisions and commitments now, this relationship will not be static. You've got to deal with the fact that quite likely there will be more openness than you've anticipated.

Getting Involved in an Open Adoption

If you participate in an agency's open adoption program, its counselors should help you define the issues that need to be discussed, provide guidance in communicating with birth parents, and be present at the meeting or meetings you initially have with each other. If you are pursuing an independent adoption, a counselor of your mutual choosing can provide similar assistance. You can get referrals to counselors and agencies with expertise in open adoption from the **National Federation for Open Adoption Education** (c/o the Independent Adoption Center, 391 Taylor Boulevard, Pleasant Hill, California 94523; 415-827-2229). Says Silber: "It really helps to have an objective third party. It's important to have somebody facilitate discussion and help both sides." Keep in mind that the first meeting or telephone call between you and a birth parent is like a blind date: You don't know what to expect and you're all very nervous. Emphasizes one birth mother, "We are scared of being rejected too."

How does the process unfold? At CFCS-Catholic Charities in Traverse City, Michigan, where open adoptions are the norm, the birth parents select the adoptive parents by examining portfolios containing everything from autobiographies and photographs to the family's financial profile. After the birth parents choose the prospective adoptive parents who interest them, there's a meeting to make sure that the families feel compatible. "Then we'll check with them afterward to make sure that they both want to press on," says Jim Gritter. Finally, the agency holds what's referred to as a "vision merging session" in which the families focus on their visions of adoption and how they foresee it working out over time. (You'll find that vision merging sessions are common at many of the agencies and organizations encouraging open adoptions.) The intention is to tap into the families' mutual value systems and to get down to specifics. The families discuss what will be happening around the time of the baby's birth, and what they envision in the days, weeks, and months afterward. "All the things that are predictable will be ironed out in advance," says Gritter. "What is crucial is that the families have a sense that they're working together and that they have problem-solving skills to figure things out on their own." At the Independent Adoption Center families even talk about who's going to call whom first after the baby goes to the adoptive parents' home. Emphasizes Silber, "This way everybody knows what to expect."

Whether or not you're involved in a formal open adoption program with prescribed steps and procedures, there are many issues that need to be discussed by you and the birth family. Among the subjects you'll want to explore are:[11]

- What's the relationship going to be like during the rest of the pregnancy? Will you be in touch before the birth? Will you get together?
- Will you be called when the birth mother goes into labor?
- Where will you be during the birth? In the delivery room? In the waiting room? Not in the hospital at all?
- If you're in the delivery room, who's going to hold the baby first?
- How much contact will there be in the hospital?
- Who's going to feed the baby?
- Where is the baby going to be in the hospital? In the nursery? In the birth mother's room?
- Who's going to name the baby? Are you going to name the child? Does the birth mother want to participate in that? How do you feel about it?
- If the baby's a male, will there be a circumcision?
- Where is the baby going after release from the hospital? To your home? To foster care? (At some agencies this is referred to as "cradle care.")
- What's going to be the pattern of contact? Are you going to be in touch by letter? By telephone? By visiting? Will the contact go through the agency or will you communicate directly? How frequent will this be?

- What's going to be the pattern of visiting?
- What's going to be the relationship with other members of the birth family? Will you be in touch with them?
- If one of the birth parents changes his or her mind about the adoption, how is that going to be handled? Who will contact whom?
- What about your will? Who will be the child's guardian? Who else in the adoptive family is convinced that this open adoption is a good one?
- If something needs to be discussed in the future, how will this be handled? Who's going to be there to help you negotiate any major disputes? What happens if some serious problem develops—for example, if the birth parent or a member of the extended family tries to intrude or one of you doesn't keep up your part of the bargain? Who will negotiate a solution? Where will you turn for help? And who will pay for the counseling?

It's important to talk about these details in advance so that you minimize the number of potentially awkward moments later on. You want to avoid creating situations where someone feels hurt or disappointed. One birth mother recalls the discomfort she felt at the hospital when "everybody in the room was crying except for the adoptive parents, who had the biggest smile on their faces." Another birth mother says she was unsettled by the adoptive parents' taking video pictures of the new baby in her hospital room. Says Silber, "All these kinds of details are important to talk about first, before you get into the emotional experience of the hospital."

You'll also want to consider the possibility of formally getting together for another planning session with the birth family and an uninvolved third party a few weeks or months after your child's placement. At the Independent Adoption Center, a prebirth and postbirth agreement are even drawn up. Involving a third party, who might even be a divorce or mediation counselor in your community rather than an adoption worker, makes it easier for people to express their feelings at a time when everyone is concerned about not upsetting the other. After the birth you'll be talking about how you see the relationship developing over time, how you feel about your ongoing contact, and what's happening with other family members. "We actually talk about all these things pre-birth," observes Silber, "but postbirth it's for real, and families are able to look at it more clearly than when it was more abstract."

If you're creating an open adoption independently, you'll want to be sure that any intermediaries you involve, such as attorneys, physicians, clergy, or counselors, have an understanding of—and commitment to—open adoption. Just as you've explored your feelings about open adoption, you'll want to ask them about theirs. You might even ask them some of the questions raised in this chapter. Chapter 4 provides questions to ask attorneys, including those when an open adoption is planned. If there is an adoption agency or an educational organization in your or the birth parents' community that runs workshops on open adoption, you may want to see whether you can attend their sessions without fully participating in their agency program. And you might explore their willingness to provide counseling to you and the birth parents.

The Children of Open Adoption

"Kids are growing up with open adoption as a big ho-hum. They just seem to be more relaxed and are not seeming to struggle with the issue of adoption in quite the same way. Everything is right there. They can touch it, talk about it, and ask questions about it." That's the assessment of Sharon Kaplan, whose work at Parenting Resources in Tustin, California, has brought her in contact with more than 700 families who are now involved in ongoing open relationships. Her views are

shared by Kathleen Silber: "The children of open adoption find
the experience to be 'no big deal.' "[12]

That said, it's clear from talking to the advocates that the lives
of the children of open adoption are not problem-free. One
significant problem seems to be inconsistent contact or a drop-
off in contact by birth mothers as the years pass. As they finish
school, move, marry, and start raising their own families, birth
mothers' contact with their children frequently lessens or even
ceases. For the adopted child that's painful: Accustomed to
visits, telephone calls, or just letters, the kids feel hurt, sad, and
mad when that abates. "We keep seeing more and more that
kids are upset," says Silber. "They've been used to having a
certain relationship with a birth mother, even if it's just hearing
from her once a year. When the child stops hearing from her
for two years, the child perceives this as a rejection—'I was
given up once and now she's rejected me again.' It's a double
whammy."

It's therefore important for the adults choosing to create an
open adoption to understand its long-range emotional impact
on the child. Even if your child's birth parents stop writing or
calling you after four or five years, you've got to continue to be
in contact with them—even if it's just a brief note—for your
child's sake. At a later point your child will be able to make his
own decisions about the nature of the ongoing relationship.

The issue of sibling relationships also seems to be causing
children and parents some concern and bafflement. Birth parents who later have other children are faced with the task of
explaining to these children why they chose not to parent their
siblings or half-siblings. Joan Smith recently gave birth to a baby
girl and confesses she's stymied: "I'm really apprehensive about
my daughter growing up and having to tell her that she has an
older brother, Michael. That seems weird to me. I'm worrying
about the reaction: What's she going to say and how is she going
to react to it? I just don't know how I'll bring it up to my
daughter." For the kids themselves there's the need to find the

language and the way to describe the siblings in their birth family and their adoptive family. Do they count the siblings in their birth family when they tick off the number of brothers and sisters they have? Do they share with their friends the fact that they have siblings who don't live with them? Observes Kaplan: "Kids are trying to figure out how they all fit and what to call each other. It appears to be a question they are chewing on. Because of divorce and remarriage, however, lots of other school-age children are also troubling over the fact of siblings in other homes. This is not an issue that's unique to families built by open adoption."

Like other adoptees, the children of open adoption must also answer the questions posed to them by their friends and the larger community. There will be a reaction when the children start talking about those significant others in their lives. Curiosity and expressions of amazement are to be expected. Your own initial questions will be voiced by others. So will some negative opinions. It's even possible, as some families discovered, that there will be instances where families of children with closed adoptions, fearful of opening up Pandora's box, try to prevent their children associating with the children of open adoption.

"Open adoption is an exquisitely difficult form of family building," concludes Sharon Kaplan. "It is not an easy answer." It is complex and has its own share of pain. It is by no means a magic elixir that cures all the ills of adoption. "There are all these new experiences that you couldn't prepare yourself for," observes adoptive parent Merilee Scilla, whose daughter's fully open adoption dates back to 1983. "If I sit here and worry— open, closed, knowing my daughter's birth mother, not knowing my son's—I could probably go crazy."

This chapter and the growing literature that describes open adoption seek to provide you with glimpses of what might be. During this decade, as the children of open adoption become adults and start to tell their own story, we will all know more.

6

Searching for a Waiting Child in the United States

Tens of thousands of American children wait each year for an adoptive family. As you'll discover, there *are* babies and younger children to adopt. Some of these children have potential health risks because of their perinatal exposure to drugs or alcohol. They are children like Michael, who was described in a photolisting book as an alert three-month-old infant who was on an apnea monitor to measure his breathing and heart rate due to his prenatal exposure to cocaine. There are also healthy minority children of all ages needing adoptive families. And there are siblings such as Jonathan, nine, and Carolyn, seven, whose mother abandoned them and whose father is in prison. In the past five years the youngsters have been in four foster homes. Says the therapist working with them: "Jonathan is small for his age, loving, and cuddly. Although Carolyn is younger, she bosses her brother around, is demanding, and throws temper tantrums."

Adoption workers tend to identify youngsters as "waiting" or "special-needs" if they are:

- School-age, white, and over the age of eleven
- Children of color, especially if they are over the age of four

- Part of a sibling group, particularly if they are school-age or in a group of three or more
- Known to have intellectual, physical, or emotional disabilities—ranging from hyperactivity, dyslexia, autism, mental retardation, and Down syndrome to hearing impairments, blindness, cerebral palsy, and spina bifida
- Known to have suffered physical or sexual abuse in their birth families
- Born to drug-involved mothers. Infants are considered "at risk" if the mother has used drugs during her pregnancy or if there are traces of a drug such as cocaine in the baby's urine or in the blood in the mother's umbilical cord. Some infants will show residual effects from their mother's prenatal use of drugs after their birth and will exhibit a range of developmental difficulties or delays as they mature.
- Born to alcohol-involved mothers. Children whose mothers drank during their pregnancy may have alcohol-related birth defects. A child who is identified as suffering from fetal alcohol syndrome (FAS) is often small, has certain distinct facial characteristics, and some level of mental retardation. Children with fetal alcohol effects (FAE) have some of the characteristics of FAS, tend to be very active, and have difficulty completing a task before moving to the next.
- Found to test positively during infancy for the HIV antibody. Babies born to HIV-infected mothers, according to the Centers for Disease Control, have a 30 percent chance of being infected with HIV, but you will not know if the child is actually infected with the AIDS virus for fifteen to eighteen months after birth.

To learn more about waiting children and special-needs adoption, get in touch with the **National Adoption Information Clearinghouse** in Rockville, Maryland. Its staff can provide you with basic fact sheets and refer you to local agencies. The **Na-**

tional Resource Center for Special Needs Adoption (16250 Northland Drive, Suite 120, Southfield, Michigan 48075; 313-443-7080) can also direct you to reading materials and local resources, as can **AASK America** (657 Mission Street, San Francisco, California 94105; 800-447-5400).

Is Special-Needs Adoption for You?

"Our daughter Sharon started life as a twenty-six-week-old preemie hooked up to a respirator. She was severely damaged at birth, with all sorts of medical complications, and the doctors didn't think she'd ever walk. She's almost three now, and the specialists working with her say she can enter a regular nursery school."

Those are the words of Sharon's dad, Charles Waters. He beams with pride at her accomplishments—"It's a lot of fun to see her do things we never thought she'd be able to do"—but he's also realistic about the time and commitment this adoption has demanded. For the first two years of Sharon's life, Charles and his wife took time off from work at least twice a week for the medical appointments and physical therapy Sharon required. Life at home was also trying. "Sharon was not an easy kid to live with," he admits. "With special-needs adoption you've got to be willing to put up with a lot."

When you approach an agency about special-needs adoption, you're going to be given extensive information and also asked to assess yourself—and your family—quite candidly. You'll need to look at how you deal with problems and problem solving, at how the adoption will affect you and your family, and at how comfortable you will be tapping into school and community resources. For there's no doubt that these children present special parenting challenges, and the agency worker will want you to think about how you will face them.

"Love is not enough," insists Peggy Soule, executive director of the national photolisting service *The CAP Book.* "You have to be open to accepting help and assistance." Observes adoption expert Kay Donley, "Special-needs adoption requires honest, caring people who work hard at understanding themselves, at how they relate to people, and how they relate to a child."

If you are considering adopting an infant who is known to have been perinatally drug-exposed, you'll need to weigh your ability to deal with risks and unknowns. These infants, often of low birth weight, may be irritable or lethargic and may have poor sucking abilities that hinder feeding, irregular sleeping habits, and rigid muscle tone. Adoptive parents report that some of these babies object to being held, refuse eye contact, and cry all the time. While not all drug-exposed children are damaged, researchers report that some such preschoolers are hyperactive, experience sudden mood swings, are slow in learning to talk, and have difficulty relating to people. They may also be overwhelmed by stimuli such as noise or toys in their environment, are easily frustrated, appear "disorganized," and have trouble concentrating.

Life with a drug-exposed infant can be rough on a day-to-day basis. The birth mother of Linda Seijo's daughter used both alcohol and cocaine throughout her pregnancy, leaving her baby with the effects of both. "It was not uncommon during infancy for my daughter to wake crying seven times a night, sometimes unconsolably," reported Linda. "I held her as she screamed and tried to push me away." Observed another mother, "Do you know what it's like to hold a child you love and have her bite you?"[1] Says Barbara Holtan of Tressler-Lutheran Service Associates in York, Pennsylvania: "It's a grueling job of parenting."

It's also important to realize that researchers do not fully understand the nature of the neurological damage these children may have suffered and cannot say what the long-term effects will be. Janie Gore Golan of Adoption Resource Consultants in Richardson, Texas, tells the story about a child whose birth mother stopped using drugs in her second month, when she found out that she was pregnant. At birth the baby appeared fine and was placed by an agency for adoption. When the child was a year and a half old, however, he started showing signs of cerebral palsy. Gore Golan, who is involved in a longitudinal study of prenatally drug-exposed adopted children, maintains: "We don't know what the facts are. We don't have the complete picture." Observes MaryAnne Clarke of the National Adoption Center: "You have children with the potential for significant problems and disabilities that haven't manifested themselves yet. Families have to be willing to accept the worst, even if it doesn't happen, to be realistic and honest as to what they can accept."

If you are considering an infant who is at risk of developing AIDS, then you must be prepared for the possibility that your child could die. And you've got to be able to put up with the fears that others have of these children. Joy and Jim Jenkins decided to pursue the adoption of a local "AIDS baby" abandoned at their local hospital because, as Joy says, "everybody needs love. I couldn't bear the thought of any child being abandoned with no one to call Mom or Dad. I didn't give AIDS a second thought." But, as she and Jim discovered, others did. When they discussed their decision with their family physician, "He stepped back, glared at us, and in a very strong voice, tinged with anger, shouted, 'You two are crazy. Don't you know this goddamned baby is going to die?'" After the Jenkinses brought their son home, they had trouble finding a medical practice comfortable with handling an AIDS baby. "The physician's nurse asked me to place the baby on the table to measure him, and she tossed me the tape to do it," recalls Joyce, who is also a nurse. "This being done, she handed me the thermometer to take his temperature. Then she remarked that she needed his blood pressure and slid over the cuff and pump for me to perform this job." Joyce, having had enough, dressed her son and walked out of the office.[2] The Jenkinses went on to form the **Children with AIDS Project of America** in Phoenix, Arizona

(P.O. Box 83131, Phoenix, Arizona 85071-3131; 800-866-AIDS),
which seeks to link infants with individuals who will provide
loving permanent homes.

ARE YOU READY FOR A SPECIAL-NEEDS ADOPTION?

As you think about special-needs adoption, here are some of the questions you'll want to consider:

- What life experiences have you had that prove your ability to deal with problems and to survive crises?
- What have you experienced that you've been able to manage? What was hard? How will that be useful to you?
- Has there been a problematic member in the family? How do you feel about the way the family dealt with the person? How would you go about handling a problematic family member?
- How do you respond to problems, and how do you solve problems?
- How do you feel about unknowns? Do they drive you crazy?
- What's the difference in the problem solving between yourself and your spouse?
- How do you handle rejection signals? Do you get hurt? Do they devastate you? When they occur, do you feel you have to end the relationship? To be a successful parent of an emotionally disturbed child, for example, you'll need to override rejection signals.
- How do you measure success? Is it in terms of steady progress or achieving a goal? If your child had a problem with stealing, for example, what would you consider success—when he stops stealing or when he steals less? Can you accept a partial success?
- What's your time frame? Some people can tolerate delays and wait for things to happen; others can't. The progress of developmentally delayed children may be measured in tiny increments over an extended period of time. So too with children who are emotionally disabled. Says therapist Claudia Jewett Jarratt: "If you've got a child who's had five years of instability in his life, for example, you've got to give him 'equal time' to turn around. Think in terms of five years—not one year."
- How do you feel about challenges? Are you open to them?
- Are you flexible enough to change your expectations if things don't improve?
- How do you handle disappointment?
- Do you have a sense of humor? How do you use humor to defuse

situations? Do you use it with yourself? Can you step back from
a situation? Can you use humor in a nondestructive way?

- Are you comfortable with counseling and therapy? Would you be embarrassed to ask for it? How would you feel if the school suggested
to you that your child needed help?

- How would you feel if your child had a physical handicap and people
stared at you? Would you be embarrassed? "When my adopted
FAS daughter was an infant, I would get looks that told me, 'What
kind of mother are you? Look at that scrawny, pale, sickly baby,' "
recalls one mother.

- Do certain physical attributes turn you off? What are your gut reactions
to various physical deformities? (If you feel uncomfortable around
people with facial deformities, for example, then a child with a cleft
palate would not be ideal.)

- How would you feel if your child acted out in public? What would be
your reaction if your child's teacher called and said that your child
had been stealing other children's lunch money?

- How would you feel if you learned that your child had been sexually
abused in a previous home? "The majority of the kids in the foster
care system today have been exposed to sexual abuse," maintains Joan McNamara, coeditor of *Adopting the Sexually Abused
Child.* "These are hurt, traumatized children, and the work you do
in a family is going to be more important than that of any therapist.
It's going to be made real by the continuity, safety and warmth of
a family."

- How comfortable will you be talking about sexuality and sexual abuse?
Is there a history of sexual abuse in your past? If so, how was the
experience resolved?

- How does your family feel about this adoption? How do the children
already in your family feel? Will they be embarrassed, resentful,
annoyed, ashamed? What about other relatives?

- What's your support system and extended network like? How will your
neighbors feel? How about your school? Is your family doctor
going to support you if you adopt a physically, emotionally, or
mentally handicapped child? Is the physician going to tell you that
you're crazy for doing this?

- What's your life-style? What children best fit into it? (If your family
relishes skiing in the winter and hiking in the summer, for example,
you might find it hard to accommodate a physically handicapped
child. If you're a very social or church-oriented family, you might
find it tough to deal with a child who acts out in public. What
happens the first time your child swears in public?)

- How flexible is your work schedule? Can you find the time for doctors' appointments, therapy, even hospital stays?
- How will you handle this adoption financially? Although the agency may be able to help you get a subsidy, what are your resources?
- How persistent are you? How do you feel about having to search for appropriate medical and educational resources for your child? Do you have any idea about how to go about identifying them?
- What's your community like? Are there top-notch medical facilities available to you if they're needed? Are there services locally that can support your child's special need?
- What *can* you cope with and what *can't* you?

Getting the Adoption Process Under Way

Your first—and last—step in pursuing the adoption of a waiting or special-needs child might just be to contact your local public or private agencies. But what if nearby agencies say they do not have any children needing adoption, or that they can't help you? Chapter 4 showed how people looking for infants can go outside the agency system to try to locate a child. Families seeking to adopt older or special-needs children need not go outside of the agency system, but they may also have to search—using local, state, and national programs created to serve waiting children.

Today there are local, state, regional, and national adoption exchanges that can act as "matching services," registering children and sometimes prospective adoptive families in order to make links. Many of these adoption exchanges have created photolisting books that describe waiting children. These books, resembling the multiple-listing books used by real estate brokers, provide capsule portraits of children. Some exchanges also bring children to life through videotapes. "The families see a child's personality," observed Marilyn Panichi of the Adoption Information Center of Illinois. "They get an alive, complete, vibrant picture of a child." To get the word out about their waiting families, some exchanges also circulate "family albums" with photos and descriptions of people hoping to adopt special-needs children.

Exchanges also employ other recruitment devices, such as weekly newspaper columns or regular television newscasts that feature waiting children. In Boston, adoption parties bring together social workers, prospective adoptive parents, experienced adoptive parents, and waiting children in informal settings. A trip to the zoo, for example, featured a picnic lunch, a tour, and a chance for interested people to mingle, share information, and become more familiar with adoption. At one event, eight children were linked with new families. Although the children come to the event, there is no pressure for families to accept a child. Events such as this give children the chance to meet adults—and offer you the chance to find that special child.

State Adoption Exchanges

Many states operate some form of adoption exchange where agencies—both public and private—can list waiting children and, in some instances, waiting families (see the directory at the back of this book for a state-by-state list). If an agency has a child needing to be placed in an adoptive home, but no suitable family, it can register that child with the exchange. Some states even mandate by law that agencies *must* register their children with a state adoption exchange if they fail to find an adoptive home within a specified period of time. The exchanges do not have children in their custody. Rather, they take referrals and try to facilitate placements. Both services are free of charge.

The Massachusetts Adoption Resource Exchange (MARE) is typical of a full-service exchange. Its programs include adoption information, referral (trying to match a referred child to one of the exchange's registered waiting families), photolisting (the *MARE Manual*), and recruitment (the *Boston Sunday Globe* column "Sunday's Child" and WBZ's television news segment, "Wednesday's Child"), exchange meetings, and adoption parties. At any given time some 250 children and some 200 families are listed with MARE. MARE responds annually to thousands of inquiries. All the children matched have special physical, emotional, or intellectual needs. The average age of all children registered with the exchange is between seven and eight, while on the average minority children are somewhat younger.

The photolisting book, the *MARE Manual*, accounts for approximately 40 percent of the matches. It features children from Massachusetts, Connecticut, Maine, Rhode Island, and Vermont. The photolisting provides a profile of the child through a detailed biography and a photograph (see Figure 1). Updated monthly and usually containing write-ups of almost all the registered children, the manual is circulated to adoption agencies, community centers, public libraries, and parent groups—places where interested people might go for information. If a person sees a child featured in the *MARE Manual*, he or she can contact the MARE office and be put directly in touch with the child's social worker if that child is still waiting. If a child is "placed" or "on hold," then the telephone number of the worker is not given out.

As a person seeking a special-needs child, you should contact one or more exchanges. If waiting families are permitted to register with your exchange, then do so yourself or ask your worker to register you. Try to list yourself with other states' exchanges, particularly those nearby. Consult as many photolisting books as possible (see the state-by-state directory at the back of this book) at frequent intervals. Find out whether your local parent group or a local agency has the photolisting books of other states' exchanges. (Some parent groups or agencies, particularly those with an interest in placing special-needs children, subscribe to out-of-state listing services.) You may not want to look at every exchange's books, but it's recommended that you look at the books of neighboring states, or states that have a large number of children in foster care. Remember, however, that the children listed in these books will be those for

Walter, who previously appeared on pgs. 139
& 140, is an attractive 12 year old boy of
Black parentage. He is of small build with
a medium brown complexion, large dark brown
eyes, and dark brown hair.

Walter has an appealing smile and is very friendly
and outgoing. If one were to describe Walter
in one word, it would be "energetic". He is
very sociable and loves to please. He especially
enjoys showing off his skills with sports and
academics. His hobbies are watching television,
reading and sports of all kinds, he also likes
to pose for pictures and is a natural model.

At a very early age, Walter suffered major
losses and rejection; "As well as being affected
by lead paint poisoning which has left him
moderately retarded". He functions intellectually
and emotionally like an eight year old child.
He attends a special class which includes speech
therapy in a public school. He gets along very
well with his teachers and peers and is very
much at ease with strangers.

Walter has no behavioral problems, and despite his past physical and emotional traumas,
he is now felt to be in good health.

Walter has been in the same foster home for the past seven years. It has been a positive
experience for him since the family has provided him with much love, care and attention.

The agency is looking for a small family for him
and would prefer a two parent Black home able
and willing to devote their time and love. Walter
will need a lengthy period of visiting before
moving into his new home.

Walter is a loving and lovable child with much
potential and should be able to live independantly
as an adult.

He is legally free for adoption.

Figure One   Sample photolisting from *MARE Manual.*

whom an agency has not been successful in finding a home locally.

Using a photolisting book, even for out-of-state children, can result in a successful adoption. Carol and Bob Wilson had been consulting their state photolisting book and those of several other states for several months. They saw the photos of the children who would be theirs—a brother and sister with developmental and physical handicaps (including congenital cataracts that severely limited the children's sight)—in the photolisting book of the Texas Adoption Resource Exchange. It took seven months and many interstate telephone calls, and they had to contend with the reluctance of the children's social worker's belief to place them out of state. But says Carol, "persistence paid off." The caseworker confided to her afterward that the biggest selling point—what broke down her resistance to an interstate placement—were the letters Carol sent expressing the family's sincere wish to adopt the children. All the other families under consideration had provided only factual information. "Our file was more personal," Carol says, "and that's what made the difference." That and the willingness to use a photolisting book, and the persistence to follow through.

Regional Exchanges

Regional exchanges take referrals of children from several states and circulate information about adoption. Very often the children listed with the regional exchanges have special problems that have made their placement more difficult. Agencies contact a regional exchange to seek a wider exposure for such children and to recruit families. Like the state adoption exchanges, regional exchanges usually register waiting children and families and distribute a regional photolisting book. They run recruitment programs and provide technical information to social service agencies.

You may want to contact your nearest regional exchange or

the other regional exchanges around the country. A list of them follows.

Adoption Center of Delaware Valley
1218 Chestnut Street
Philadelphia, Pennsylvania 19107 (215-925-0200)
(Serves Delaware, New Jersey, and Pennsylvania)

Maine-Vermont Exchange
Maine Department of Social Services
Bureau of Social Services
221 State Street
Augusta, Maine 04333 (207-289-5060)
(Serves Maine, Vermont, and New Hampshire)

Northwest Adoption Exchange
909 N.E. 43rd Street
Seattle, Washington 98105 (206-632-1480)
(Serves Alaska, Idaho, Oregon, Utah, and Washington)

Rocky Mountain Adoption Exchange
925 South Niagara Street
Denver, Colorado 80224 (303-333-0845)
(Serves Colorado, Nevada, New Mexico, South Dakota,
Utah, and Wyoming)

Southeastern Exchange of the United States (SEEUS)
P.O. Box 6647
Columbia, South Carolina 29260-6647 (803-782-0882)
(Serves Alabama, Florida, Georgia, Kentucky,
Mississippi, North Carolina, South Carolina, and
Tennessee)

Three Rivers Adoption Council
307 Fourth Avenue
Pittsburgh, Pennsylvania 15222 (412-471-8722)
(Serves Ohio, Pennsylvania, and West Virginia)

National Adoption Exchanges

June, a seven-year-old black child with Down syndrome, was living in Georgia awaiting adoption. She was registered with the state exchange, featured in the state photolisting book, shown on an Atlanta television show, and named child of the month in a local newspaper. All this was done to try to find an adoptive family for her. Finally, her social worker registered her with *The CAP Book*, a national photolisting service in Rochester, New York.

Bertha, a single black woman in her fifties, was searching for a child to adopt in upstate New York. She looked through *The CAP Book* and saw June's photograph. She called her social worker; her social worker called June's social worker; Bertha's home study went to Georgia; and June's biographical information came to New York. June and Bertha's search was over; a new adoptive family had been formed.

The CAP Book registers children from throughout the United States who need wider exposure. Workers must be willing to place the children across state lines. This photolisting book, updated biweekly, contains hundreds of children. Both adoption social workers and families can contact the staff of *The CAP Book*, who serve as a clearinghouse and direct people to the appropriate agency and caseworker. All the children featured in *The CAP Book* are hard to place. Check your local adoptive parent group or specialized agency for the book. For further information, you can also contact **The CAP Book, Inc.** (700 Exchange Street, Rochester, New York 14608; 716-232-5110).

The **National Adoption Center** (1218 Chestnut Street, Philadelphia, Pennsylvania 19107; 215-925-0200), which provides information and referral services, operates a telecommunications network that lists waiting children and families and links agencies around the country. This computer system can be accessed by adoption workers around the country whose agencies participate in the network. Using the telecommunications network, a social worker in Tallahassee, Florida, who is seeking an adoptive family for a ten-year-old boy with mental retardation can plug into the computer system and turn up interested families in Albany, New York; Boise, Idaho; or Albuquerque, New Mexico. With that information the worker can then contact the families or their agency worker directly. Families with completed home studies can ask their worker to register them with the network or take the initiative and register themselves directly.

Michael and Pam, a black couple stationed in Germany, used the electronic bulletin board after their efforts to adopt a young black child had been unsuccessful because of their posting overseas. They contacted the National Adoption Center, and their interest was listed on the electronic bulletin. A social worker in Wisconsin saw that message and got in touch: The agency had a ten-month-old child waiting for an adoptive family.

Although the staff at the National Adoption Center will answer questions about adoption and refer you to local resources, remember that their telecommunications network is designed to serve those seeking to adopt waiting children. Be sure to look at several state or regional adoption exchange books so that you will know the type of children awaiting placement.

Some Specialized Referral Programs

In addition to state, regional, and national exchanges, there are also some specialized exchanges and programs with which you may be able to link up:

Down Syndrome Adoption Exchange
56 Midchester Avenue
White Plains, New York 10606 (914-428-1236)
   A voluntary adoption exchange providing services to birth parents, adoptive parents, and agencies. Accepts listings from agencies of children needing placement. Families seeking to adopt children can also list themselves. Can also help birth parents seeking to place a Down syndrome infant with an agency or independently.

Native American Adoption Resource Exchange
c/o Council of Three Rivers American Indian Center
200 Charles Street
Pittsburgh, Pennsylvania 15238 (412-782-4457)
   Serves Native American children by providing recruitment and referral of adoptive Native American families. Families can apply for registration with the

exchange if one or both parents are Native American. You will be expected to provide documented evidence of Indian ancestry (for example, your enrollment number, census number, certificate of degree of Indian blood, or a letter from your tribe on tribal stationery). Be sure your home study also mentions the name of your tribe and your cultural life-style.

Transracial Adoption

In the 1960s, black children were increasingly placed for adoption in white homes. That policy came under attack in the 1970s, and today most agencies will not place black or other minority children in white homes. Notes Harvard law professor Elizabeth Bartholet: "The available evidence indicates that today most public and private adoption agencies are governed by powerful race matching policies. . . . There is very general agreement among adoption agency policymakers that children should be placed inracially (if possible) and transracially only if necessary, or as a last resort." Yet, as you look through the exchange books or inquire at your local agency, you'll discover that many of the children waiting for homes are members of a minority group.

Transracial placements still occur, but when white families inquire they must be prepared to encounter many hurdles and questions. If you are white and are interested in a child of black parentage, consider whether your family and your community can provide the appropriate resources for the particular child you hope to parent. Evaluate carefully how you will meet your child's special needs and how you will provide positive role models.

If you feel strongly about a transracial adoption, however, then you should persevere. Says the white mother of a black girl: "To me, a choice for a permanent parent is by far preferable to a long wait for a child in foster care. I believe that there's more damage that can be done in the wait than in the issue of race."

There are some specific steps that families can take. If you see a child listed over time—and you apply and don't hear back—start to keep track. Ask how many weeks or months the agency intends to wait before it will consider a family of another background. Find out what the bottom line is. "If you go back three months later," observes Peggy Soule of *The CAP Book,* "and the child is still there, you can start making a hassle. You will force the agency to place. The child will not be placed with you, but you'll get the agency to make a placement." You might also file a civil rights complaint against the agency under the Federal Civil Rights Act of 1964. For advice contact the **National Coalition to End Racism in America's Child Care System** (22075 Koths, Taylor, Michigan 48180; 313-295-0257) and your local chapter of the American Civil Liberties Union. If you're the foster parent of a transracially placed child and now hope to adopt that child, you can also turn to these organizations for help.

As to the adoption of Native American children, this falls under the jurisdiction of the Indian Child Welfare Act. This legislation requires that the extended family of an Indian child be given first priority for adoption, followed by a member of the child's tribe, and then a member of another tribe. An agency that seeks to place a Native American child in a non–Native American home may in fact be violating federal law.

The Frustrations of Working with Exchanges and Photolistings

We first started looking at the Books (with an eye toward a two to three member sibling group around ten years of age) during the time we attended Parent Preparation Classes. By the time we received the letter from the agency certifying us as "perfect" prospective adoptive parents we already had selected a sibling group here we wanted to adopt. Several nervous weeks later we were told that unexpectedly relatives had come into the picture and those children were no longer up for adoption. But, "please try again."

We did. This time we chose two boys from another state's book we thought would fit into our home. It was several days later when we discovered that, unknown to the agency in our state, the boys were already in the process of being adopted. So, "please try again."

A week or so later one of the social workers from the agency called to say that she had just received a new exchange book, and that there were three siblings she felt were definitely suitable. We asked that she call about them rather than write, thus cutting down on the suspenseful waiting time. Within an hour she called back with the information that just the week before the children had appeared on *Wednesday's Child* in another state. They too were already on their way through the adoption process.

Shortly thereafter we chose two children from another state. The news from their social worker, "please try again."

Several days later our social worker told us that another state had gotten information on us through the regional exchange and had sent a computer match-up of two brothers they believed would be suitable for us. These children were in no way anything like the sort of children my husband and I felt that we could deal with. The social worker came back to us with that information and then urged us to "please try again."[4]

When Alice wrote about her experience, she had been trying to adopt for a year. Shortly after that, she and her husband gave up. They were not a young couple—they were people in their late forties, and her husband had grown children from a previous marriage. They got tired of trying and decided to get on with other things in their life.

Alice's litany of woe is unfortunately not that unusual. Many people hoping to parent waiting children report that their search is unending despite the fact that they've seen children listed for adoption and that, like Alice, they have been willing to consider a wider range of children. "I would sit at our public library for four to five hours poring through photolisting books," recalls Cathy Beaver, who was hoping to adopt three siblings under the age of six. "I would walk out of there in tears. At one time I gave our social worker twelve choices, and the responses all came back 'hold' or 'placed.' " Parent-group newsletters are full of stories like Cathy's. People report that when they inquire about a specific child they are told that the child is on "hold." Yet months later these people report that they still see the child's photo appearing in an exchange book.

You may find that social workers are reluctant to place children out of the county or out of the state—despite the fact that no adoptive family has yet been found locally. Stories like the one told by Ernesto Loperena of the New York Council of Adoptable Children are not uncommon. A black family in New Mexico was interested in a sibling group of three in New York City. While the agency in New York that had custody of the children was interested in this family, the local New Mexico social service department turned down their request for a home study because the children were out-of-state. After Loperena's intervention, a home study was done, but then the New York state agency had second thoughts, expressing concern about moving the kids cross-country. "We've cut distance by fax machines, telephone, and jet airplaces," observes Loperena, "but we still think of New Mexico as a different kind of world." It was only after more arm twisting that this adoption proceeded.

There is also the suspicion that social workers are "collecting" home studies, poring through as many as sixty before beginning to make a decision. Alice even found, when she inquired about one child in another state, that the social worker had only listed the child for adoption because the state had mandated it; the worker had no plans for placement and was surprised—and not very interested—when Alice contacted her. Be aware also that only a small percentage of the children legally free for adoption may be listed with an exchange or photolisted. In states where listing is mandated by law, the number will be higher than where listing is voluntary.

Exchange books and television appeals that heighten a child's visibility are clearly important tools in placement and recruitment. But, as people seeking to adopt will tell you, they're hard on families. Reporting on the impact of a local Connecticut television program, "Thursday's Child," the Connecticut Adoption Resource Exchange noted that for three black brothers, ages six, five, and three, it received forty-six calls; and for an eighteen-month-old girl of mixed parentage with developmental delays it got thirty-two calls. In both cases one of the responding families became the children's adoptive parents.[5] The television program worked, but if you, as a family, set your heart on one particular child, you were likely to be disappointed. These types of recruitment programs are good for children, but they are often very hard for "waiting families."

Some Tips on Searching for That Waiting Child

- Be sure that you understand who is a waiting child or a special-needs child. You may be searching for a child who is not likely to appear in the exchanges.
- Consider how flexible you are. See how much you can broaden your scope. Evaluate what behaviors or disabilities you can handle in a child.
- Decide if you are comfortable with a legal risk adoption, in which the youngster enters your home as a foster child. If you are, say so.
- Be sure that you are listed with all local exchanges and informal exchanges available for your area.
- List yourself with the state exchange, if possible.
- List yourself with the regional exchange, if possible.
- When your home study is complete, you may want to contact the National Adoption Center.
- Be sure your home study is as complete as possible.
- Check your state photolisting book (and others that you decide to consult) frequently and try to respond to *as many* listings as possible. Don't feel shy about requesting information on more than one child listed in the book. Let your agency know promptly about your interests.
- If you see a child who interests you in a photolisting book, either you or your worker should call, rather than write, to

get some initial information about the child. If your worker has a problem making out-of-state telephone calls, see what special arrangements can be worked out.

- If you're still interested in a child after the initial phone call, follow up immediately by sending out your home study.
- Don't wait to hear about one child before you inquire about another.
- Note the date when you talk with your worker, and follow up—your worker can get busy. Keep track also of when you contacted the child's agency and be prepared to follow up.
- Encourage your worker to lobby on your behalf.
- Keep track of which children you inquired about, when you made the inquiry, whom you talked with, and what was done. Follow up.
- When you are rejected for a particular child, ask why.
- Don't set your heart on one particular child you've seen featured. Chances are you will be successful in adopting a child like the one who attracted your attention rather than that particular child.
- If you are having trouble adopting a child who appeared in a photolisting book or a listing service, notify the exchange or listing service that you are having problems. They can often help expedite the process.
- If you are hoping to adopt a younger special-needs child, spread the word also in the independent adoption grapevine. Tell people you are interested in the direct placement of an infant with significant medical problems or whose birth parents have a medical history that might be considered high risk.

Be persistent. People who seek to adopt independently must work hard to spread the word, and you will probably need to do the same if you are looking for a special-needs child. You know there are children who need you. It may just take some time to make the connection.

Pursuing an Intercountry Adoption

Intercountry adoption involves the placement for adoption in the United States of children born abroad. In the 1980s the number of adoptees coming from abroad surged, rising from 4,868 children in 1981 to a high of 10,097 children in 1987, according to figures kept by the Immigration and Naturalization Service. South Korea alone accounted for half of those placements; in 1987, for example, 5,910 of the adoptees entering the United States were Korean. By 1990 the foreign adoption picture had altered; the total number had dropped to 7,088 and the number of South Korean adoptions had shrunk to 2,603. But foreign adoptions were still taking place from other Asian countries, including the Philippines (423), India (361), Thailand (111), and mainland China (28), and from Central and South America, including Colombia (628), Peru (441), Chile (300), and Guatemala (263). There was also a stampede to adopt from Romania—90 adoptions were reported for 1990 and 616 adoptions were counted by the INS between October 1990 and May 1991—as international attention focused on the children languishing in orphanages. Experts predict that foreign adoption will undergo more change during the 1990s: We're likely to see a continued drop in adoptions from South Korea, more intercountry placements from Latin America, Eastern Europe,

Russia and the other republics that once comprised the Soviet Union, and China, as well as the implementation of some standardized international intercountry adoption laws.[1]

This chapter describes the mechanics of intercountry placement. Although I will often focus on how the process works, keep in mind always the reason why people concerned with children both here and abroad have supported intercountry placements. "Every child in the world needs a family," observed a priest working at a Chilean orphanage. For him and many others, intercountry adoption is a way to find "families for children, *not* children for families."

There are some very basic matters that will affect your life as a family and your future child's life, and should therefore influence your decision regarding intercountry adoption. Holt International Children's Services in Oregon devised a series of questions and comments that you should seriously evaluate as you consider intercountry adoption:[2]

1. What are your ideas about race? What characteristics do you think Asian, Indian, Latin American, etc. people have? Do you expect your child to have these characteristics? The children become Americanized; therefore try to visualize that cute little baby growing up into a child—a teenager—an adult—a parent. Think about grandchildren.

2. How do you feel about getting lots of public attention, stares, etc.? Possibly your adopted child will get too much attention and other children will tend to feel left out.

3. You will become an interracial family. Do you raise your child to have the same identity as you or your other children? How do you help him develop his own identity? Should his name reflect his national origin? What relationship will the name have to the sense of "Who am I"? Imagine a child you know and love being sent overseas to be adopted. How would you want him raised? As an American in a foreign country? A native in that country?

4. How can you learn to know what it's like being nonwhite and growing up in a white society if you don't know this from your own experience? You will have to find out how to teach or educate yourself to become sensitive to your child's world.

5. Your family will now be interracial for generations. Adoption of a child of another race or country is not just a question of an appealing little baby. How do you feel about interracial marriage? How does your family feel about interracial marriage? How do you feel when people assume that you are married to an Asian person?

In addition to your qualities and abilities as parents, it is important for you to understand your motivation for this kind of adoption. Do you feel you are doing a good deed for a poor, homeless child, who will perhaps be more grateful to you when he is older than if he were your birth child? This is poor motivation and not very realistic.

If your primary orientation is to help the child become absorbed into your culture at the expense of his own, then transracial adoption is not for you. You must have an attitude of respect for the country and culture of the child.

DO YOU HAVE THE CAPACITY TO IDENTIFY WITH THIS CHILD, to see the world from his point of view and to lovingly supply his physical, mental and spiritual needs? Do you want to learn more about the child's culture and heritage? If you do, then you can consider further the idea of intercountry adoption.

Consider the conversation that one mother had with a stranger about her daughter:

He: "What is it?"
She: "She's a little girl—my daughter."
He: "No, I mean, what is it?"
She: "She's a child."
He: "No, where's she from?"
She: "She's from Korea."
He: "You mean your husband's a Chink?"
She: "No, she's adopted from Korea."
He: "Couldn't you just make a baby like normal people?"[3]

You'll be asked: What do you know about her parents? What's her real name? How much did it cost? ("I've heard that there's a lot of international baby buying.") Several people are likely to nominate you, in front of your child, for sainthood for rescuing the poor waif. They'll also tell her how lucky she is that you adopted her. Someday you may have the experience that another parent of a young Korean adoptee had:[4]

> The usual questions continued throughout the dinner (in a restaurant filled with senior citizens)—"Where are the children from?" "Are they related?" "They speak English so well." "Don't you love their eyes." As we prepared to leave, I took my daughter to the bathroom. She burst into tears—and I assumed that she hit her head on the door. When I asked what happened, she sobbed "I'm not hurt in my head, I'm hurt in my feelings—why don't people leave us alone?" I said—because you are cute children, who happen to look different. She said—"I don't want to look different, I want to look like you, Mommy."

These issues are ones that will confront you as the parent of a child adopted from abroad. Many of the questions will be discussed in later chapters of this book. All of them should be explored by you *before* you adopt a child from another country.

How Intercountry Adoption Works

In the United States, you may work with a local agency that places children directly from abroad, with a nonlocal agency that has an intercountry adoption program and networks with local agencies, or with a facilitator. For some countries, you may work directly with a contact abroad in what is known as a direct or parent-initiated adoption (you will still need to have someone, either a licensed social worker or an agency, do a home study of your family). Your child may be placed by a national department of social services, a government orphanage, a local orphanage, maternity homes, private foundations, or other social welfare organizations in the foreign country. Depending on the laws of a country, judges, doctors, lawyers, social workers, and other people interested in child welfare may be involved in arranging intercountry adoptions. If you have relatives, friends, business associates, or church contacts in a foreign country, they may be able to help you arrange an independent intercountry adoption.

The fact that you choose to work with an agency in the United States does not necessarily mean that your U.S. agency's intercountry adoption program will be with an agency or orphanage in the foreign country of your choice. *Some U.S. agencies work with attorneys and other individuals in a foreign country as well as with orphanages and other agencies.* Be sure that the U.S. agencies you contact tell you exactly with whom they work abroad. You might also want to get in touch with the **Joint Council on International Children's Services from North America** (their mailing address changes frequently; for a current address, check with Adoptive Families of America). Joint Council has established standards and guidelines for intercountry adoptions and promotes services consistent with these goals. Many intercountry adoption agencies belong to the organization, as do some parent groups.

To get a clearer sense of how intercountry adoption works, let's follow four families and see how their children's adoptions proceeded.

Agency Placements

Gena and Duane Moss adopted an infant girl from South Korea through a local U.S. agency working with a social welfare agency in South Korea. The local agency's worker met with them and conducted a home study. After the local agency approved Gena and Duane as prospective adoptive parents, it forwarded the home study and other documents to its counterpart in South Korea. A year later Gena and Duane's worker called them into her office and showed them photographs of a five-month-old Korean girl. She also shared with them whatever records, particularly medical information, the Korean agency had provided. Gena and Duane were delighted and accepted the referral. They filled in some agency papers, including a statement that they would accept financial responsibility for the child, and processed their I-600 form with the Immigration and Naturalization Service (see Chapter 9). They then waited while the South Korean agency did its share of processing forms (for example, obtaining the baby's Korean passport). Two months later their worker called to tell them that their daughter would be arriving on a flight later that week, brought by a volunteer escort. (With the number of adoptions from South Korea dropping, many families now travel to pick up their children.)

Dana and Bill McCarthy adopted an infant boy from the Philippines with the help of a local agency, an agency in another state, and the Philippine government. They applied to the agency in another state because it had an intercountry Philippine adoption program and would take applications from out-of-state people. Bill and Dana arranged for a local agency to do their home study and serve as the "receiving" agency. This local agency agreed to provide postplacement supervision of the child and work with the family toward finalization of the adoption when the child arrived.

When their home study was completed, the local agency sent it to the out-of-state agency with the international adoption program. This agency also approved them as adoptive parents. This agency, working with its counterpart abroad, handled the arrangements in the foreign country: finding an adoptable child, arranging for court procedures, arranging for the child's passport, escorting the child to the United States.

About a year after Bill and Dana submitted their application to this agency, their local agency received a child referral. This information was sent to them from the out-of-state agency via the interstate compact officer. All written communication, in fact, between the two U.S. agencies went through the interstate compact officer. Bill and Dana also filed papers with the Immigration and Naturalization Service and waited for their child to be escorted to the United States. Their child was brought to the United States by the agency with the intercountry program. Bill and Dana traveled to an airport near the placing agency, which served as a central arrival point for children coming from abroad.

Facilitated Placements

Denise Warren, who is a single parent, decided that she wanted to adopt a preschool girl. With the encouragement of a nearby parent support group, she contacted a social worker in the United States who worked with an attorney in Guatemala. Her social worker advised her about state and federal adoption laws. Through the parent group, she was referred to several local agencies that would be willing to do a home study for her. When the home study was completed, she brought her materials to the social worker, who checked them for thoroughness and accuracy. He forwarded them to his associate in Guatemala.

Several months later, the Guatemalan attorney, who knew people at children's homes and who often had young women approach him directly about relinquishing children for adoption, located a baby girl at a children's home. The Guatemalan attorney sent a description of the baby to the social worker, who contacted Denise and showed the referral information to her. Denise also processed papers through INS. Shortly after, the Guatemalan attorney notified her that the preliminary paperwork was complete and that she could come to Guatemala to pick up her daughter. She took a flight later that week, and then spent about a week there doing additional paperwork. The U.S. social worker had served as a "facilitator" or an "intermediary" in this adoption.

Direct Placements

Lisa and Brian Slovinsky chose to apply directly, without the help of a U.S. adoption agency or a facilitator, to an orphanage in Colombia that placed newborn infants. They like to travel and decided that they wanted to spend time in their child's birth country. They got the name and address of the orphanage from an adoptive parent support group.

First they sent a letter to the orphanage, indicating their reasons for wanting to adopt a Colombian child and requesting an application. When they had obtained all the required U.S. documents (including a home study, done by a local agency), they submitted the package to the orphanage. A few weeks later they received a letter of acceptance from the orphanage informing them that their names had been put on a waiting list. A year later, the orphanage director called to ask if they would be interested in adopting a month-old baby boy. They agreed to the placement, and spent the next week doing paperwork in the United States. Then it was down to Bogotá.

In Colombia, on the recommendation of their adoptive parents group, they stayed with a family that rents rooms to adoptive parents. This family knew the entire adoption process and served as their tour guides and translators. Lisa spent a month in Colombia processing her papers through the Colombian court system, and then flew home with her son.

As it turned out, this was just the first chapter of Lisa and Brian's adoption story. They kept in touch with the orphanage, sending monthly letters and photos of their son. Two years later they wrote to ask about adopting a second baby; four months later they were en route to pick up their second son. Since then, Lisa's brother and sister-in-law have also adopted through the orphanage. Reports Lisa: "Our whole family went down with them for a week. The orphanage director fussed over our kids, and the two boys spent time at the orphanage. That really reinforced their feelings about Colombia and adoption."

The Children

Hee Ra, infant girl, Korean, left at birth in the hospital where she was born.

Alfredo, infant boy, Colombian, relinquished at birth by his mother at a maternity home.

Sharpla, infant boy, Indian, abandoned at birth weighing just three pounds.

José and Margarita, brother and sister, age five and six, living in an orphanage in Costa Rica.

Sompit, age three, female, living since infancy in an orphanage in Thailand.

These are just a few of the children who have been adopted in the United States. These children have found parents, but there are more like them still waiting to be adopted. The children needing permanent homes range in age from infancy up to their teens. They may be orphaned, abandoned, or have a parent or relatives who cannot care for them because of poverty or other conditions. Some may have lost or been separated from their families because of war. Older children may have spent time living on the streets or may have spent all or most of their lives in orphanages. In some countries, agencies may attempt to place the infants in foster care, but that is not the general rule. *All* children who come to the United States for adoption must meet the federal requirements for the designation "orphan" under federal immigration law (see Chapter 9).

If you are contemplating an intercountry adoption, try to seek out people who have adopted children from abroad. Attend parent-group meetings, particularly ones where some of the children will be present. If that is not possible, be sure to look at photographs of these children.

As in the United States, there are also waiting children and special-needs children abroad. In another country children may be considered hard to place solely because of their age—and in some countries or in some circumstances, that may be a pre-school-age girl or boy. Young children may be considered hard to place if they are part of a sibling group or have a correctable handicap such as a cleft palate. Here are some of the children that agencies that specialize in intercountry adoption have listed as "waiting":

Roshan, five-year-old girl, Indian, has cerebral palsy, attending a special school, affectionate, friendly.

Paulo, five-year-old biracial blind boy, Brazilian, independent, a lot of poise, not born blind but there was an accident.

Juanita, Maria, Fernando, Costa Rican, three siblings, two girls and a boy, ages ten, eight, and seven, who come from a neglect situation.

Pia, seven-year-old girl, Thailand.

The waiting children generally needing adoptive families are school-age boys and girls, older sibling groups of two, sibling groups of three or more, and children of any age with significant medical needs. The medical needs that you might find include orthopedic problems, heart defects, blood disorders, cerebral palsy, major vision limitations, hearing limitations, seizure disorders, severe malnutrition, burns, significant developmental delays, and emotional problems.

Some agencies have intercountry programs devoted to the placement of special-needs children. If a special-needs child interests you, and your local agency does not have an active program, several agencies have nationally recognized programs for waiting children and will often work with other agencies around the country. You might contact the Children's Home Society of Minnesota in St. Paul, Minnesota; WACAP in Seattle, Washington; Americans for International Aid and Adoption in Birmingham, Michigan; and Holt International Children's Services in Eugene, Oregon.

You can also consult the Adoption Listing Service of the **International Concerns Committee for Children (ICCC)** in Boulder, Colorado. Each month ICCC sends out information sheets that feature photos and descriptions of waiting children who are Asian, Latin American, Indian, African, or black, as well as the name of the agency or organization to contact for information about each child. You'll see listed infants and preschoolers with correctable or noncorrectable medical conditions, and school-age children, some of whom also have known physical, emotional, or developmental problems. Although a few of the children are already in the United States, having experienced a disrupted adoption after their arrival, the majority wait in their birth countries. Several hundred children are listed.

Requirements

For an intercountry adoption, you will need to meet the requirements of your state government, the federal government, and the foreign country. Chapter 9, which discusses the special paperwork of intercountry adoptions, explores this at greater length. If you are considering a direct adoption, find out whether your state permits independent placements from abroad and what preadoption requirements must be met.

Each foreign country, or possibly an individual district within the country, usually has its own laws about guardianship and adoption. These laws may govern such matters as the length of your marriage, your age, previous divorce, residency, and whether intercountry adoption is permitted. If you are thirty and married for two years, you might be eligible to adopt in one country but not in another. There may be special requirements pertaining to such matters as your religious affiliation or your need to establish a residency abroad. To find out about the laws and procedures for a specific country (if you are not working with a U.S. agency), you can contact the country's consulate in the United States. Remember that agencies within the foreign country may also have their own requirements for prospective adoptive parents. The Instituto Colombiano de Bienestar Familiar in Colombia, the national organization that oversees the country's adoption program, has required, for example, that applicants for newborns to two-year-olds be between twenty-five and thirty-five years old, while people seeking to adopt children ages seven and a half to twelve may be as old as fifty.

Some U.S. agencies with intercountry adoption programs also have special requirements. The most common, of course, is a geographic requirement—that is, an agency will work only within a specific area or state. Other common requirements involve age, marital status, and religion.

The ability to travel abroad is not necessarily expected of you for an intercountry adoption. Some countries require that you appear before a court or a social welfare agency before they will place one of their children in your family; others do not. Families adopting from Latin America often must travel abroad. If you are planning to do a direct adoption, it is advisable for you to travel to see the child.

The Costs of an Intercountry Adoption

Intercountry adoptions are costly, ranging from a minimum of $6,000 to upward of $16,000. Some agencies may charge less when you adopt a sibling group or a special-needs child; others do not. Expenses will vary depending on how many agencies are involved, whether you must travel to the country, and how long you must stay there.

The chart "Intercountry Adoption Expenses" tries to outline some of the basic costs that you can anticipate with an intercountry adoption. Expenses will differ by country and by program. Not all fees are due at once, and if there is an agency involved, there is likely to be a schedule for payment over a period of time. "If any agency says that it must be paid ahead of time, look elsewhere," urges AnnaMarie Merrill of the ICCC.

INTERCOUNTRY ADOPTION EXPENSES

General Adoption Expenses
- Home-study fee (home study required by Immigration and source of adoption in foreign country and foreign court)
- Medical exams
- Fees for documents (e.g., birth and marriage certificates)
- Photocopying fees
- Immigration and Naturalization Service fees
- Notarization fees required for some documents
- Postage or express mail fees
- Document-translation fees (often required for Latin America)
- Document verification and authentication fees (often required for Latin America)
- Long-distance telephone calls and other communication expenses
- Child's airfare from the foreign country (also possibly escort's)
- Agency fees in the United States or in the foreign country
- Child care fees in the foreign country (e.g., for foster care)
- Attorney and other court fees in the United States or abroad (possibly both pre- and postplacement expenses)

Additional Adoption Expenses if You Travel to a Country
- Round-trip airfare for those who travel
- Lodging expenses
- Meals
- Taxi and other transportation fees (you may have to take another plane if your child is in a distant city)
- Donation to orphanage (if recommended)

The Risks of Intercountry Adoption

All adoptions have risks. Let's explore some of the special issues that arise with intercountry placements.

Health Concerns

When Sarah's infant daughter, Evelyn, came off the plane after her daylong journey from South Korea, she was sick, not with a life-threatening illness but with the kinds of maladies that you may find in children coming from abroad. She had an ear infection, an upper respiratory infection, marks on her arms from an earlier bout with scabies, a few infected sores, and head lice. She went straight from the airport to the pediatrician. The infections cleared up with a course of antibiotics. Her transformation was quite something—within a week you'd hardly have recognized her.

The problems Evelyn and other adoptees sometimes bring with them—acute infectious diseases such as otitis media and upper respiratory infections, sores, scabies, lice, parasites, deficient immunizations, lactose intolerance—are medical difficulties that are easily remedied. Some children may also be undernourished, have a low resistance to infection, or be anemic. In fact, the Minneapolis-based International Adoption Clinic, which specializes in the particular needs of intercountry adoptees, found undiagnosed—and curable—problems in two of every three children seen at the clinic.[5] "There are very few problems that are long-term," assures Sandy Iverson, a nurse-practitioner at the clinic. Even so, you'll want to make sure that your child has a complete medical evaluation (see Chapter 10) after her jet lag and immediate medical problems have cleared up. Says University of Michigan pediatrician Jerri Ann Jenista, who has written about the health needs of adopted children, "We recommend an early 'quickie' visit to take care of ear infections and lice, followed by a calmer, more thorough visit after two to four weeks to do everything else."

Low birth weight and small stature in comparison to American children are not uncommon among foreign-born adoptees. If you are worried about a child's reported measurements, ask the people caring for the child abroad to provide your doctor with growth statistics for the child from at least two points in time, preferably a month or more apart. You're interested in learning if a child is "continuing to grow," rather than how she stacks up on a growth chart.

Developmental delays, in comparison to American children, may also be apparent. However, the six-month-old Korean baby who doesn't roll over may have been held for the first six months and not had the chance to get down on the floor and explore. To put your concerns in perspective, ask how this child compares to others in the same environment. Do the caretakers see the child as "delayed" by their standards? "Many of the 'problems' people fret about can be explained by cultural differences and not medical shortcomings," says Iverson.

Older children are likely to have rotten teeth that must be filled or pulled, and may be small for their age. They may arrive with few or no medical records. You may find that the age estimates given for older children by the agency have little to do with a child's actual chronological age. Agency staff may have guessed the child's age when he was placed in their care. Bone, dental, or endocrinological tests performed on children here may reveal that a child is older or younger than the agency and the adopting parent believed. It may, however, take months of nutritional rehabilitation before the age discrepancies are apparent.

If you are adopting a child from South Korea, Thailand, India, the Philippines, Taiwan, or Vietnam, you're likely to be asked during your home-study process if you will consider a child who is a hepatitis B virus carrier. The illness, once called "serum hepatitis," is highly endemic in Eastern Asia and moderately endemic in Central and South America. A child may become a carrier at birth from an infected mother or later from child-to-child transmission, from blood transfusions, or injections using inadequately sterilized needles. The hepatitis B profile—blood tests that your child's physician can order—will reveal whether a child is a carrier. (Many intercountry adoption agencies also test children in their birth countries.) Infection can be prevented, however, by a vaccination, so that children in some countries are now being immunized. Children who are hepatitis B carriers may *not* have symptoms but *can* transmit the disease to family members. (If your child is a carrier, your family should be vaccinated.) Carrier children are also at risk of future liver disease.

If your child is a carrier, you'll need to be concerned eventually with situations in which intimate contact arise, such as blood-to-blood exchanges or sexual intercourse, since hepatitis B is transmitted through blood and other body fluids. To learn more about hepatitis B, contact the Centers for Disease Control (Hepatitis Branch, Division of Viral Diseases, Atlanta, Georgia 30333; 404-321-2340) or the International Adoption Clinic (University of Minnesota Hospital, Harvard Street at East River Road, Minneapolis, Minnesota; 612-626-6777).

As for AIDS, the Immigration and Naturalization Service requires that a physician approved by the U.S. Embassy abroad do a general physical exam prior to visa approval. In areas where the HIV virus has been recognized as being endemic, such as Romania, Haiti, or Uganda, a physician might ask that a child have an HIV-antibodies blood test. "An HIV test is *not* routine for orphan visas," reports Dr. Jenista of the University of Michigan. Parents cannot count on their child having one. Keep in mind also that tests on infants are not diagnostic (see Chapter 6), and that you will not know whether a child is actually infected with the AIDS virus until fifteen to eighteen months after a child's birth. To assess the risk, ask yourself: What do you know about the prevalence of the disease in the country itself? (The regional office of the World Health Organization in Washington, D.C., and the Centers for Disease Control can give you data for individual countries on the number of reported AIDS cases.) Have you been given a profile of the birth parents and any information about possible high-risk behaviors? From what you know about the country and your child's birth parents and situation, you should be able to make some determination about the likelihood of infection. Now put this information into perspective: *You* reside in a country where there are thousands of AIDS cases annually. Have you submitted your test results to adoption personnel in the foreign country? If you make a big issue about HIV testing, particularly if your child resides in a low-incidence country, don't be surprised if the agency starts asking you questions.

Changes in Government Policy

There are other types of risks—war, change in government, changes in adoption laws, changes in agency policy. Negative media coverage about adoption may lead to a country's temporarily or permanently stopping intercountry placements. When foreign agencies are swamped with applications, they may temporarily stop their intake. Or U.S. agencies may stop placing from a particular country or agency for a variety of reasons, including long delays.

Adoption Scams

While the majority of intercountry adoptions proceed without difficulty, there are some sticky situations that people pursuing intercountry adoptions find themselves in. Carol and Bob Trotter decided to work with a woman in the United States who facilitated Mexican adoptions. After the facilitator "assigned" them a baby girl, they were told to send $5,200 to Mexico. First they heard nothing from Mexico about the money; then word came back that Mexico had received $4,100, not $5,200. No one seemed to know what had happened to the rest.

There was still no indication as to when the Trotters might pick up their baby. They were led to believe that it would be a matter of weeks, but the weeks soon stretched into six months. Then the facilitator called and offered them another baby girl. Recalls Carol: "We asked what happened to the baby we'd named Karen Jo. We were told that the baby's mother had neglected to sign a paper and she'd disappeared."

With a feeling close to desperation, Carol and Bob said yes to the second baby offered them. But there was another catch: "We were told that the baby had been ill and that if we wanted her, we had to send an additional $1,600 to pay the hospital bill." They hesitated; the call to travel to Mexico never came. Carol and her husband subsequently sued the facilitator to try to regain their original outlay of $5,200.

Barbara Adams also hooked up with a facilitator. She liked the woman's voice on the telephone and felt that she was reliable because "she had adopted children from Mexico." Since Barbara was told that the lawyer in Mexico placed newborns, "I went out and bought a crib and newborn clothing." There were the usual promises—a baby by Christmas, then in the spring, finally the fall. There was even the day when she was told that her baby was expected to be born momentarily and she sat by the telephone all day. Finally, after months had passed, she and her husband decided to meet this woman, who lived in another state. A face-to-face meeting with the woman led Barbara to feel that "this was crazy" and she and her husband returned home and contacted a local agency that placed South Korean infants. A year later they welcomed their daughter home, and in subsequent years adopted two more children through the agency.

Carol lost $5,200. Barbara spent nine months on an emotional roller coaster. Carol's and Barbara's stories, unfortunately, are not unique. Several U.S. families lost $2,500 each when the Chilean attorney to whom they'd entrusted their money and papers fled Chile without honoring his promise to locate adoptable babies for them. Recalls one of those prospective parents: "We were calling down to the office once a week. It was just promises, promises. I had gone through losing a baby and that just topped it off. We were just completely drained—financially and emotionally—by the whole experience."

Problems sometimes arise for people who pursue independent placement adoptions here and can plague people who use facilitators for adoptions abroad. The risks may increase if you try to do an adoption yourself abroad, particularly if you use a lawyer or other source *not proved to be reliable to you or others*. Even reputable foreign attorneys may run afoul of the law when they try to meet the insatiable demand from abroad (coming from couples in Canada, Western Europe, and Israel as well as the United States). The attorneys may cut corners in an effort to help. The scams that Americans find themselves enmeshed in, reported an Immigration and Naturalization Service examiner, have included stand-in mothers (where women sell their babies to a midwife and then another woman claims she is the mother), forged documents (two babies have the same name and documents), and baby smuggling. An official in the Bureau of Consular Affairs at the Department of State reported that consular officers continue to hear about problems with people taking money: "Either taking too much money and eventually delivering a child or stringing people along, sending pictures of a child, and not delivering."

Minimizing the Risks of Intercountry Adoption

Working with a U.S. agency that has a relationship with a foreign agency, or applying directly to a national orphanage or well-known private agency abroad, minimizes risks. Says Betty Laning of ICCC: "By using licensed agencies, adoptive parents have some leverage should something go wrong with an adoption program. Parents stand a chance of getting some of their money back if no child is forthcoming. With facilitators or lawyers in a foreign country, there may be no refunds and no way to proceed legally to force a refund." If you are working with a facilitator or with an attorney in a foreign country, proceed cautiously.

All may indeed go smoothly, but there can be difficulties. To minimize the chances of an intercountry adoption going sour, examine all sources very carefully. Check with your local adoptive parent group or a group in the United States whose members have successfully adopted from your desired country. Contact the Citizens Consular Services at the Department of State (202-647-3444) and the U.S. consular officer in the U.S. Embassy abroad. They may be able to provide you with a list of reputable attorneys and the consular officer abroad may be able to report on any complaints the embassy has received. To be blunt, look at references just as you'd do before you would hire someone to work for you. Don't let your heart rule your head. If at any time you feel uncomfortable with the position you find yourself in, don't hesitate to bail out.

To help you minimize the risks, here are some questions to keep in mind:

- How long has the resource been in existence? How long has the particular program been in existence?
- How many children have been placed by the resource or the program?
- Are there written materials that describe the intercountry adoption programs?
- What experiences have other families had in working with the child-placing resource?
- What legal right does the resource have to place children?
- What information is the resource willing to reveal to you?
- What is not being disclosed?
- How much money overall is required?
- How much money is required initially?
- How much money is required before you get the child's papers?
- How much money is required before you see the child?
- What written agreements are there? What do they stipulate?
- What happens if there is a problem with the adoption after the child has been assigned to you (e.g., the birth family changes its mind; the child is ill)? Will there be another assignment? Will there be additional fees? Will you get a refund?

- If you decide against intercountry adoption, what provisions are there for the return of your money?
- Has it ever been suggested that you can bypass federal or state immigration requirements?
- Has it ever been suggested that if you are unhappy with the child, you can still bring the child into the country and then the agency/person will find another family for the child?
- What type of information is being offered you about the child? What type of medical history is available? Are there details about the family available? Can you see photographs of the child?
- Is the child-placing resource trying to answer your additional questions about the child?
- What has been promised to you about the adoption?
- Has it ever been suggested to you that you put your name on the child's original birth certificate so that there would be no need for an adoption?

Getting Information About Your Child

The day will finally come when you will receive a telephone call or a photo and a description of a child. Don't be surprised if the information you receive is scanty rather than thorough. It is possible you will receive little background information about your child and few medical records. If you want to adopt a child about whom you can receive an extensive medical and personal history with detailed information about birth parents, then intercountry adoption is most likely not for you.

You should feel free, however, to ask for more information. If you are concerned about a medical history, ask for it. The foreign agency, orphanage, or social welfare organization may not be able to give you much in the way of family medical background, but should be able to provide detailed information about your child's health since coming into care. You'll want to get specific growth measurements such as height, weight, and head circumference, and ask such questions as "Is the child alert?" and "Is the child learning new things?" If your child's placement is being handled by an attorney, social worker, or other helping professional, this person may well have met one of the birth parents or another relative and can ask for medical and genetic information as well as provide more general descriptions of the birth parents.

If you have been sent a medical report, share it with a pediatrician or family physician (see Chapter 10). If your doctor has questions, don't hesitate to refer them to your local agency or foreign resource. If your doctor feels that additional simple tests are needed, ask for them.

Most children won't be ill, but if there's a problem, it's best for your child if the condition is detected as soon as possible. The **International Association for Medical Assistance to Travelers (IAMAT)** (417 Centre Street, Lewiston, New York 14092; 716-754-4883) publishes a directory listing medical centers around the world. The center abroad can give you a list of approved doctors—internists and other specialists. IAMAT physicians will provide a medical report if you need it, make referrals for you, and report to your own physician. Other resources include parent groups, the International Adoption Clinic in Minnesota, and its counterpart in Boston at the New England Medical Center (750 Washington Street, Box 286, Boston, Massachusetts 02111; 617-956-7285). You might also ask the director of the orphanage or the lawyer who is helping you abroad for the name of the physician who cares for *her* children and offer to pay for this physician to see *your* child.

Where to Turn for Information about Intercountry Adoption

People you know who have adopted recently from a foreign country, people who have lived in another country, and people who have family or friends abroad can often serve as beginning sources of information about foreign adoption. This is particularly true if you are thinking about an adoption from a country where there are no organized intercountry adoption programs with the United States. But there are many other excellent resources to whom you can turn. As you get started, you'll want to:

- *Check with adoptive parent groups.* Parent groups are crucial to successful intercountry adoptions, since members can offer both support and up-to-date information. The National Adoption Information Clearinghouse in Washington, D.C., has a state-by-state list of adoptive parent groups. Adoptive Families of America offers a wealth of resource materials in its magazine *OURS* and can put you in touch with a local parent group whose members have done intercountry adoptions. The **Latin America Parents Association (LAPA)** distributes information about adoption and document preparation to people seeking to adopt children from Latin America. The organization has prepared detailed fact sheets about various Latin American countries, covering such topics as local orphanages and attorneys, the specific paperwork required, and where to stay while traveling abroad. Chapters also hold cultural, social, and informational meetings during the year. For further information contact LAPA's New York chapter (P.O. Box 339, Brooklyn, New York 11238; 718-236-8689).

  If you expect to work with a U.S. agency, you may also find that there is a local adoptive parent group directly linked to it.

- *Contact the foreign country's embassy or consulates located in the United States.* You'll find offices in Washington and New York City and sometimes in other locations around the United States. In one day's telephoning, I found that I'd gathered quite a bit of information from the consulates, including lists of agencies abroad and descriptions of procedures to follow. You may also use the consulate to process your paper-work.

- *Check with the Citizens Consular Services office of the Department of State in Washington, D.C.* By calling their hotline (202-647-3444) you can request detailed fact sheets about adoption in specific countries, such as "Adopting a Colombian Orphan," "Adopting a Child in Honduras," and "International Adoptions—The Philippines." There are also country-by-country lists of recommended attorneys. Call during working hours, and you can speak with consular officers who can tell you about any recent adoption scams that have come to their attention or particular problems. There are also twenty-four-hour hotlines with recorded travel advisories (202-647-5225).

- *Contact the U.S. Embassy abroad, particularly if you are planning on a parent-initiated intercountry adoption.* The consular officer may send you information about various organizations. If there have been complaints about adoption attorneys or facilitators, the officer may tell you.

- *Write the national agency concerned with the welfare of children in a particular country.* (The country's consulate here can give you that information, and so might your public library.) The foreign agency may send you information or an application, or it may send you a list of other organizations to write to.

- *Get in touch with family, friends, friends of friends, and business associates abroad.* They may offer information and emotional support if you travel abroad. If you are considering a parent-initiated intercountry adoption, they may be able to refer you to an orphanage, an agency, an attorney, or other helping professional in adoption. They may even know birth parents seeking to make arrangements. Be sure that your contacts understand what is legal and accepted adoption practice. In one country paying a mother's medical expenses may be considered desirable, while in another country it may be seen as buying a baby and scandalous.

- *Read some personal accounts of intercountry adoption to get a sense of the process, including the feelings of parents and children as they form a family.* Gail Sheehy's *Spirit of Survival* and Carolyn Koons's *Tony: Our Journey Together* describe the experiences of single parents with older children. Sheehy chronicles the life of her daughter Phat Mohm in Cambodia and New York; Koons's story, which has strong religious overtones, unfolds in Mexico and California. The focus in Susan T. Viguers's *With Child: One Couple's Journey to Their Adopted Children* is on infant adoptions and tells of success in adopting in Colombia as well as independently in the United States. The parent group FACE compiled the adoption stories of member families in *They Became Part of Us* (available through FACE). *OURS* magazine is chock-full of personal testimonies of intercountry adoption.

- *Contact U.S. adoption agencies about their intercountry programs.* The resource directory at the back of this book lists many of the U.S. agencies that have developed intercountry adoption programs. Remember that some agencies will have nationwide programs while others will only place children within a particular geographic region. An invaluable resource for information about intercountry adoption is ICCC's *Report on Foreign Adoption.* Jean Nelson-Erichsen and Heino R. Erichsen's *How to Adopt from Central and South America* (available through Los Ninos International Adoption Center in Texas) provides detailed information about Latin American adoptions. For an agency's perspective on Latin American adoptions, take a look at James A. Pahz's *Adopting from Latin America.*

Working with a U.S. Agency Program

Whether you write or call an agency, be sure to request information about all its programs. Agency workers sometimes frown on phone calls—they say that talking takes their time away from working on their programs. But many people feel they learn more from the telephone contact. (If you call, keep in mind the agency's location and be aware of time zones.) Ask for an application. If you are told that the agency is not taking applications, ask when intake will be open. Remember that the situation in intercountry adoption can change quickly, so try again within a few months. An agency may open a new program or expand its waiting list. If you are willing to be a pioneer in a new program, indicate your interest. If you are willing to consider a special-needs child, say so and ask for information.

If you write to a U.S. agency to inquire about intercountry adoption, make your letter brief and send a self-addressed stamped envelope. Include some basic biographical information, but leave your letter vague enough that the agency sends you as much information as possible. The more specific you are about yourself and your wishes, the more likely it is that you will inadvertently shut doors. (For a letter to an agency abroad you will be using a different approach; see the discussion "Getting the Process Under Way" later in this chapter.)

As you consider the information provided by the agency, ask some questions: How long have the agency and the particular program been operating? What are its programs and its "sources"? Have you been given the names of the "sources" in the foreign country? How are the arrangements described to you? What is your responsibility in completing the adoption and what is the agency's? How many children have been placed to date? How many children does the agency expect to place this year? How many people are on the waiting list? Reports Cheryl Simons of LAPA: "We've known of agencies that have done four adoptions but had a waiting list of several hundred families." Look into program fees carefully, as these can vary widely in intercountry adoptions. And remember that your licensed adoption agency in the United States may not necessarily be working with a licensed agency in the foreign country.

You'll also want to have the agency delineate its policy if there's a problem abroad. Some agencies practice what is known as "linked adoption." Under this arrangement, according to James Pahz of Children's Hope in Michigan, the agency introduces the adopters to the overseas child-finding source, prepares the clients' documents, and submits the proper documentation. But "the agency does not assume responsibility for the success or failure of that portion of the adoption process which occurs overseas."[6] Clients sign a "statement of understanding" indicating that the agency is not to be held accountable for parts of the adoption process over which it has little or no control. If the foreign adoption resource is an attorney, for example, adoptive parents pay him directly and the U.S. agency has no responsibility if the attorney fails to provide service. Says Pahz, "You have to be somewhat of a gambler and be willing to assume those risks."

Searching Independently for a Child Abroad

Why do people choose a direct intercountry adoption over a U.S. agency's intercountry adoption program? Some people do so because they want a child of a particular nationality and there is no agency placing those children. Others have family or friends who make a connection for them. Still others feel that they want to do the adoption themselves—and that includes finding their own child abroad. Others feel strongly that in a country like Colombia, where there is a well-established social service system and a well-trod path involving intercountry adoption, there is no need to pay a U.S. agency an "overseas handling fee." Some feel that, since families may have to do most of the paperwork—that is, the verification, authentication, and notarization—why not do everything? Finally, there are some organizations abroad, such as the Casa de la Madre y El Niño in Bogotá, Colombia, that prefer to work directly with the adopting couple. You should realize, however, that the number of U.S. intercountry adoption *agency* programs has expanded. Don't be surprised to discover that the orphanage or social welfare organization that you've chosen to work with independently abroad has also established ties with several U.S. agencies. You may even find out that the organization gives preference to its institutional connections.

A direct overseas adoption is not for everyone who is thinking about an intercountry adoption. As you gather information, you'll want to ask yourself:

- Is it important to have someone help you through the adoption process step by step?
- How much of the legwork are you willing to do yourself? There may be a parent group to which you can turn, but you will not be working with an established program in the United States.
- How much uncertainty can you live with? With any intercountry adoption, things may not go as you would like. With a direct adoption, delays or snafus may arise.
- What is the state of your finances? If there are unanticipated expenses, can you absorb them? With an agency's intercountry adoption program, there are fees that you can anticipate. (If you must travel to a foreign country—whether under an agency intercountry adoption program or for a direct adoption—there may be additional unanticipated expenses.)
- How do you feel about traveling abroad?
- How do you feel about spending time in another country, perhaps as much as two or three months?
- How do you feel about spending time abroad alone, without your spouse and possibly without contact with another English-speaking person?
- How self-reliant are you?
- What foreign languages do you speak? You may have to deal with attorneys, bureaucrats, and other officials in a foreign country. How do you plan to communicate with them?
- What risks are you prepared to assume?

Some of the questions listed apply to any intercountry adoption—whether independent or through a U.S. agency program. With a direct adoption, however, more of the burden of bringing the adoption to fruition lies with you.

Consider the experience of Robert and Carolyn Lange, who arranged an adoption through business associates in a Latin American country where intercountry adoptions are rare. They flew to a remote, mountainous section of the country, half a day's distance from the capital. The next day, with a two-week-old infant in their arms, they found that the local passport office had been closed down by armed guards because officials had been selling passports illegally. Recalls Carolyn, "We tried to reach our attorney back in the capital for advice, but the telephones weren't working. We took a chance and flew back to the capital with our new baby, but without the passport."

There were more hitches: The mother's release for adoption didn't state that the baby was allowed to leave the country. Their attorney had to contact a lawyer in the baby's hometown to obtain a new declaration from the birth mother. Meanwhile, back in the capital, the Langes had to be interviewed by a court-appointed social worker in their hotel room and then wait for the worker to write up his report to the judge who then ruled on the placement. The baby had a bad case of diaper rash, so they went to see a local doctor. "Through all of this," says Carolyn, "the people were wonderful to us." When the Langes finally departed—having postponed their flight plans many times—the staff at the airline reservations office threw a party and gave them little gifts. Ironically, it was the Americans they dealt with, particularly the consular officer at the embassy, who were the most "uncooperative" and even hostile.

Five months later the Langes returned with the baby to the country's capital to appear before the judge for a postplacement visit. "Going back to court was scary," recalls Carolyn. "We were concerned that the judge might find something in the postplacement reports she didn't like and take the baby away from us."

"Flying without a net" is how Carolyn describes their adoption experience. "We learned as we went. The support system that people get from an agency—and that buffer—wasn't there. If something went wrong, we were the ones who found out."

Getting the Process Under Way

If you decide to pursue a direct intercountry adoption, most likely you will begin by sending out some letters to people abroad to learn more about intercountry adoption and to request an application. If at all possible, as a courtesy, write in the language of the person to whom you are addressing the letter; your contact may not have access to a translator. Any letters that you send should be accompanied by return postage and international reply coupons available at your local post office.

Make your letter warm and friendly, not businesslike. It should be "from the heart" and you should use personal, not business, stationery. You are writing to people. Let them know who you are. The impression you create in your introductory letter is critical. This is a time when you can permit your feelings to come through. Says one adoptive parent, who spent time working at a Colombian orphanage: "The letters that the women in the orphanage read to me were flowery ones, with statements like 'We wanted a baby all our lives and just found out that we will have to adopt' or 'We have a house and we are anxious to paint the nursery.' The women would say, 'Oh! we want to help them.' "

So what do you say? Describe yourself, your occupation, and your interest in children, and how long you have wanted to adopt. Mention the status of your home study and ask for more information about their program. If your extended family supports your adoption decision, say so. If you know people with foreign-born adopted children and they have been influential in your decision-making, say so. If you are acquainted with people who have worked with the agency, let them know. You might want to include a photograph of yourself, your family, and your house. You'll also want to mention anything about yourself that might pose a potential problem—previous divorce or stepchildren, for example. Advises Cheryl Simons of LAPA: "The letter should be a very complete picture of yourself and your situation in the world. Any information that you feel dumb about including should be in that first letter. There's no point in getting started if you are going to be rejected later."

Should you state a preference for a particular kind of child? Many agencies are truly offended if you say that you want a child "who is as light as possible" or "who looks like me." If you feel that this is something you must emphasize, consider again why you are pursuing an intercountry adoption. If you want only a boy or only a girl, be prepared to explain why. You can sketch out some parameters, but be flexible. If you are writing to an attorney, or another individual, be sure that your letter does say that you are seeking a "legal, ethical adoption."

Should you contact more than one agency? For initial letters of inquiry you can. Policies may have changed or intake may be temporarily closed in some agencies. At the beginning you are gathering information. Singles particularly may find that they have to search around for the appropriate place to apply. If you are working with one of the well-known, established agencies, most parent groups advise that one application should suffice. You may want to keep two going if there is something unusual about yourself—you are older, you have stepchildren—or if one of your applications is to an agency that has not been involved in intercountry adoptions for a long period of time, what parent groups often refer to as a "new source."

You'll have to make the decision about what's appropriate. If you do apply to more than one agency, *be sure to notify the other agency immediately when you are offered a child.* After all, an orphanage may close its waiting list to others while you're on it.

Once you receive a reply to your inquiries and the direct adoption process gets under way, there are still more things that you are going to have to work out:

- What legal steps must you take to realize the placement of a child?
- Who will be doing your legal work abroad?
- Exactly what paperwork will you be required to do?
- What are the expected costs? Try to get a breakdown of probable expenses—lawyers' fees, court costs, foster care, orphanage or agency donation, medical care.
- What expenses, if any, must be paid "up front"? (This is particularly relevant if you will be working with an attorney.)
- When are fees to be paid?
- What references can the person provide (if he or she is not known to you)? Has this person ever helped with a U.S. intercountry adoption before?
- How long is the whole process likely to take?

Be sure your contact overseas understands exactly what documents you will need in order to bring your child legally into the United States. Your contact may know the requirements for a legal adoption in his country; you may have to tell him what is required for U.S. immigration. You will also want to get a listing of *all* services and *all* fees *in writing*.

There may be a significant time lapse between when you first approach people about intercountry adoption and when you finally become a parent. During that time you will want to keep in touch. Don't feel shy about sending letters about your continuing interest and plans for the future. It's important to remind the people abroad that you're eagerly waiting. You might also ask if there are phone hours during which you can talk to them.

Traveling Abroad

With many intercountry placements, families are asked to travel abroad—to finalize the adoption, to work out the guardianship, or to bring their child home. Everybody's travel experience is different, but there are some general guidelines that you can keep in mind:

- Contact a parent group before you go, in order to learn about places to stay, things to take with you, local transportation, and the like. You may be referred to local hotels, taxi drivers, and families who cater to the needs of adoptive parents.
- Contact the foreign embassy or foreign tourist office for information about the country. Ask your travel agent for material.
- Contact the Citizens Consular Services of the Department of State in Washington, D.C., to check if there are any travel advisories for the country you are visiting. Obtain a copy of its publication *Your Trip Abroad* (available through the U.S. Government Printing Office).
- Contact the international travelers hotline of the Centers for Disease Control in Atlanta, Georgia (404-332-4559). You can get details about vaccination requirements and recommendations, reports on disease outbreak abroad, and order a copy of the excellent booklet *Health Information for International Travel.*
- Make sure that *your own* immunizations are up to date. Advises Dr. Jenista, "All the childhood illnesses prevented by vaccine in this country are endemic in the countries you are likely to visit."[7] That means you need to discuss with your physician whether you've had the routine childhood immunizations for polio, measles, mumps, rubella, diphtheria, whooping cough, and tetanus, and any recommended boosters.

If you are going to be around children or eating question-able food or water, you might also want to consult with your doctor about getting a shot of gamma-globulin as partial pro-tection against hepatitis A. Special vaccines such as cholera, typhoid, or yellow fever are usually not required for tourist travel.

- Read some guidebooks about the country you will be visiting.
- Consult with your doctor about whether you should bring along some diarrhea-prevention preparations. You might also discuss whether to take along anti-scabies or anti-lice medi-cines.[8]
- When you're in the country, take the time to see the sights. Show an interest in the country's customs. Take photographs of the country and also of the people involved in your child's adoption. And purchase some mementos that are characteris-tic of the culture. Your child will enjoy looking at these, and talking about them, as she grows up.
- Try to learn a little of the language. Don't feel hesitant about using a dictionary and pointing to words. People appreciate your making the attempt to communicate, even if your at-tempts aren't perfect.
- Bring donations to the orphanages—clothing, medical sup-plies, formula, toys. Your local parent group can probably give you supplies to carry with you. If advisable, give a finan-cial donation.
- Work at building bonds—spend time at the orphanage, vol-unteer to help. You'll probably want to bring small gifts to the people who have helped you with the adoption.
- Don't complain.

You represent adoptive parents, and the image you project speaks for us all. Be prepared to feel homesick, confused, and lonely. You're likely to be very excited, but you also can feel terribly unsettled. It probably won't feel like a vacation. When you're staying in a hotel or other accommodation, there's nothing romantic about having to boil baby bottles in a hot pot rather than in a fancy sterilizer. Says one parent who traveled to Medellín, Colombia: "Staying in a country club [which is where families adopting through one agency were housed], the American couples were operating in a social vacuum without supports. No family, no friends." Whatever your situation, she says: "You must understand that you are a *guest* in another country and understand their ways of doing things. They are giving you a precious gift."

A precious gift—that is what your child adopted from abroad is. A gift from one country and one culture to another. Your travel to your child's country is the beginning of your learning about his land. Respect the people and their culture. Dress and act appropriately for *their* culture, not yours. From now on, your child's country is yours.

8

Paperwork

Paperwork and adoption go hand in hand. Whether you are
adopting a child in this country or abroad, you will at some point
have to amass documents: birth and marriage certificates, financial statements, the birth parents' releases. With intercountry adoption, the paperwork expands, since you must meet the
requirements of a foreign country, the U.S. government, and
your state government. This chapter focuses on the basic paperwork. Chapter 9 looks at the special paperwork of an intercountry adoption.

Documents You Can Expect to Need for an Adoption

When a U.S. or foreign agency sends you an application for
adoption, or when a foreign country requests information, you
will be asked to submit documents about yourself. At some
point you can expect to show the following:

- Certified copy of your birth certificate
- Certified copy of your marriage certificate
- Certified copy of any divorce decree
- Certified copy of the death certificate of any deceased former
  spouse

- Medical statement from physician about your health (agency may provide forms). You may also be asked to submit a statement about your mental health.
- Medical statement about infertility (if applicable)
- Notarized financial statements, including letters from your bank describing your accounts, an accountant's report, a statement of liability and assets, and a notarized copy of your most recent federal income tax return.
- Verification of your employment stating salary, position, length of employment, and stability of your position.
- Letters of reference from friends or colleagues

You may also be asked to provide:

- A criminal history and child abuse background check from local, state, or federal authorities
- A certified copy of your children's birth certificates
- Brief autobiographies, including life experiences
- Photographs of yourself, your children, your home

If you are a naturalized citizen, you will be asked to show proof of your naturalization. Do *not* photocopy naturalization papers—this is illegal. Some states may also require a check for a police record or may send your name to a central registry that lists people who have been accused of child abuse.

As you begin thinking about adoption, you should begin actively working on your documentation. Certified copies of birth, marriage, death, and divorce certificates can take time to obtain, since they must be gotten from the state in which the event took place. Since these documents certify a past event, they usually do not have to be updated, so you can and should obtain several copies of each document at one time. One family ordered five copies of the relevant documents and were able to use them for two adoptions. The extra money spent may save months in paperwork. (If you are planning an intercountry adoption, find out whether the foreign country must have copies that have been recently certified. Some countries require this; others do not.) You should also try to figure out in advance how many certified copies of each document you are likely to need for any given adoption. (The Immigration and Naturalization Service will accept photocopies of documents if an Immigration officer compares them to the originals and certifies them as duplicates.)

Obtaining Birth and Marriage Records

The chart that follows lists where you can get information about certified copies of birth and marriage certificates. Call first to find out about the procedures for obtaining certified copies and what the fees are. In some states certified copies of marriage licenses must be obtained from local courts.[1]

BIRTH/MARRIAGE RECORDS

Alabama
Center for Health Statistics, Department of Public Health, 434 Monroe Street, Montgomery 36130-1701; 205-242-5033

Alaska
Bureau of Vital Statistics, Dept. of Health and Social Services, P.O. Box H-02G, Juneau 99811-0675; 907-465-3391

Arizona
Vital Records Section, Department of Health Services, P.O. Box 3887, Phoenix 85030; 602-542-1080

Arkansas
Division of Vital Records, Department of Health, 4815 West Markham Street, Little Rock 72201; 501-661-2336

California
Vital Statistics Section, Department of Health Services, 304 S Street, Box 730241, Sacramento 94244-0241; 916-445-2684

Colorado

Vital Records Section, Department of Health, 4210 East 11th Avenue, Denver 80220; 303-320-8474

Connecticut

Vital Records, Department of Health Services, 150 Washington Street, Hartford 06106; 203-566-2334

Delaware

Office of Vital Statistics, Division of Public Health, P.O. Box 637, Dover 19903; 302-736-4721

District of Columbia

Vital Records Branch, Room 3009, 425 I Street N.W., Washington, D.C. 20001; 202-727-9281

Florida

Vital Records Section, Department of Health and Rehabilitative Services, P.O. Box 210, Jacksonville 32231; 904-359-6900

Georgia

Vital Records Unit, Department of Human Resources, 47 Trinity Avenue S.W., Room 217-H, Atlanta 30334; 404-656-4900

Hawaii

Office of Health Status Monitoring, Department of Health, P.O. Box 3378, Honolulu 96801; 808-548-5819

Idaho

Vital Statistics Unit, Department of Health and Welfare, 450 West State Street, Statehouse Mail, Boise 83720-9990; 208-334-5988

Illinois

Division of Vital Records, Department of Public Health, 605 West Jefferson Street, Springfield 62702-5079; 217-782-6553

Indiana

Vital Records, State Board of Health, 1330 West Michigan Street, P.O. Box 1964, Indianapolis 46206-1964; 317-633-0274

Iowa

Vital Records Section, Department of Public Health, Lucas Office Building, 321 East 12 Street, Des Moines 50319; 515-281-5871

Kansas
Office of Vital Statistics, Department of Health and Environment, 900 Jackson Street, Topeka 66612-1290; 913-296-1400

Kentucky
Office of Vital Statistics, Department for Health Services, 275 East Main Street, Frankfort 40621; 502-564-4212

Louisiana
Vital Records Registry, Office of Public Health, 325 Loyola Avenue, New Orleans 70112; 504-568-2561

Maine
Office of Vital Records, Human Services Building, Station 11, State House, Augusta 04333; 207-289-3184

Maryland
Division of Vital Records, Department of Health and Mental Hygiene, 4201 Patterson Avenue, P.O. Box 68760, Baltimore 21215-0020; 301-225-5988

Massachusetts
Registry of Vital Records and Statistics, 150 Tremont Street, Room B-3, Boston 02111; 617-727-7388

Michigan
Office of the State Registrar and Center for Health Statistics, Department of Public Health, 3423 North Logan Street, Lansing 48909; 517-335-8655

Minnesota
Section of Vital Statistics, Department of Health, 717 Delaware Street S.E., P.O. Box 9441, Minneapolis 55440; 612-623-5121

Mississippi
Vital Records, State Department of Health, 2423 North State Street, Jackson 39216; 601-960-7981

Missouri
Bureau of Vital Records, Department of Health, 1730 East Elm, P.O. Box 570, Jefferson City 65102; 314-751-6387

Montana
Bureau of Records and Statistics, Department of Health and Environmental Sciences, Helena 59620; 406-444-2614

Nebraska

Bureau of Vital Statistics, Department of Health, 301 Centennial Mall South, P.O. Box 95007, Lincoln 68509-5007; 402-471-2871

Nevada

Division of Health—Vital Statistics, Capitol Complex, 505 East King Street, Carson City 89710; 702-885-4480

New Hampshire

Bureau of Vital Records, Health and Human Services Building, 6 Hazen Drive, Concord 03301; 603-271-4654

New Jersey

Bureau of Vital Statistics, Department of Health, South Warren and Market Streets, CN 370, Trenton 08625; 609-292-4087

New Mexico

Vital Statistics, New Mexico Health Services Division, 1190 St. Francis Drive, Santa Fe 87503; 505-827-2338

New York

Vital Records Section, Department of Health, Empire State Plaza, Tower Building, Albany 12237-0023; 518-474-3075

For New York City: Bureau of Vital Records, Department of Health of New York City, 125 Worth Street, New York 10013; 212-619-4530; marriage records through city clerk's office in borough where license was issued.

North Carolina

Vital Records Section, Division of Epidemiology, Department of Environment, Health, and Natural Resources, 225 North McDowell Street, P.O. Box 27687, Raleigh 27611-7687; 919-733-3526

North Dakota

Division of Vital Records, State Capitol, 600 East Boulevard Avenue, Bismarck 58505; 701-224-2360

Ohio

Division of Vital Statistics, Department of Health, G-20 Ohio Department Building, 65 South Front Street, Columbus 43266-0333; 614-466-2531

Oklahoma

Vital Records Section, Department of Health, 1000 Northeast 10th Street, P.O. Box 53551, Oklahoma City 73152; 405-271-4040

Oregon
   Vital Statistics Section, Health Division, P.O. Box 116, Portland 97207; 503-229-5710

Pennsylvania
   Division of Vital Records, Department of Health, Central Building, 101 South Mercer Street, P.O. Box 1528, New Castle 16103; 412-656-3147

Puerto Rico
   Demographic Registry, Department of Health, P.O. Box 11854; Fernandez Juncos Station, San Juan 00910; 809-728-7980

Rhode Island
   Division of Vital Records, Department of Health, Cannon Building, 3 Capitol Hill, Providence 02908-5097; 401-277-2811

South Carolina
   Office of Vital Records and Public Health Statistics, Department of Health and Environmental Control, 2600 Bull Street, Columbia 29201; 803-734-4830

South Dakota
   Vital Records, Center for Health Policy and Statistics, Department of Health, 523 East Capitol Street, Pierre 57501; 605-773-3355

Tennessee
   Vital Records, Department of Health and Environment, Cordell Hull Building, Nashville 37219-5402; 615-741-1763

Texas
   Bureau of Vital Statistics, Department of Health, 1100 West 49th Street, Austin 78756-3191; 512-458-7111

Utah
   Bureau of Vital Records, Department of Health, 288 North 1460 West, P.O. Box 16700, Salt Lake City 84116-0700; 801-538-6105

Vermont
   Vital Records Section, Department of Health, Box 70, 60 Main Street, Burlington 05402; 802-863-7275

Virginia
   Division of Vital Records, Health Department, P.O. Box 1000, Richmond 23208-1000; 804-786-6228

Washington
> Vital Records, 1112 South Quince, P.O. Box 9709, ET-11, Olympia 98504-9709; 206-753-5936

West Virginia
> Vital Registration Office, Division of Health, State Capitol Complex Building 3, Charleston 25305; 304-348-2931

Wisconsin
> Vital Records, 1 West Wilson Street, P.O. Box 309, Madison 53701; 608-266-1371

Wyoming
> Vital Records Services, Hathaway Building, Cheyenne 82002; 307-777-7591

You may also want to arrange for your physical examination as soon as possible. Some agencies may insist that the physical examination forms be submitted before a home study can begin, and it may be difficult to see your physician immediately. As you begin your adoption inquiries, find out about an agency's medical exam requirements—particularly about lab tests, such as the tuberculin test, the blood test for syphilis, and an electrocardiogram. You can often have the physical done and then, within a few weeks or months, ask your physician to fill in the form. Be sure to find out how current the examination must be.

Consents

Before an adoption can be approved by a court of law, certain consents must be obtained. The child will be asked to consent to the adoption if he is legally old enough to do so. (This will vary state by state, but the age of legal consent is typically at least twelve years.) The consent of the birth parents—both mother and father—is expected. If the parents are dead or have abandoned the child or lost their custody judicially, then the consent of the guardian, next of kin, court-appointed "friend," or an authorized agency will be used. If you are adopting a child through an agency, the agency will be sure that the necessary surrenders are obtained. The agency will then be authorized to consent to the adoption. If you are adopting a child independently, you or your attorney must make sure that the necessary surrenders are obtained. Be sure that if a father is known (whether or not he is actually married to the birth mother), you obtain his consent. If you cannot readily locate him, the court in some states may ask you to show that you made an effort to find him. In some states that may mean searching for him by placing an advertisement in a newspaper. States may also have regulations stating the length of time that must elapse between a child's birth and the parents' relinquishment. There may also be provisions stating the length of time in which a parental release is revocable.

Medical Consent Forms

If you are adopting a child independently, before you take custody of the child, have the birth mother sign a medical consent form stating that you can legally provide medical treatment for the child. Adoption agencies normally provide you with their consent for treatment.

The Interstate Compact

Sometimes families will identify a child in another state whom they would like to adopt. These adoptions are carried out under the Interstate Compact on the Placement of Children. The compact is a uniform law enacted by all the states, the District of Columbia, and the U.S. Virgin Islands. It establishes procedures for the transfer of children and fixes specific responsibilities for those involved in the placement of the child. At each step of the adoption process, your documents, and a prospective child's, are passed through the state's interstate compact administrator. The interstate compact is designed to protect children and parents to make sure that everyone knows what is happening. Any interstate placement, whether done through an agency or independently, must follow compact procedure. Failure to comply violates the law and could result in your child being ordered returned to the first state.

For a fuller explanation of procedures, contact the administrator in your state's social services or public welfare office. You might also want to request a copy of the *Guide to the Interstate Compact on the Placement of Children,* available from your state's social services or public welfare office or from the **American Public Welfare Association** (810 First Street, Washington, D.C. 20002; 202-682-0100).

Finalizing an Adoption

Since a legal adoption is a procedure that establishes a relationship of parent and child between people who are not biologically related, you will have to go to court to finalize an adoption. This may be in your state of residence, your child's place of prior residence, or even the agency's place of business operation, depending on state laws. If you are involved in an intercountry adoption, you may be adopting your child abroad.

Some states require a waiting period before you may petition the court to initiate formal adoption proceedings. In other states, you may be able to file your court papers immediately but must still wait a period of time before finalizing the adoption. The process usually begins when you submit to the court a petition for adoption. This petition, signed by the people seeking to adopt, sets out information about them, the child, and the biological parents. It asks the court to approve the adoption, and may also include your request for an official change of your child's name. Along with the petition, you are usually asked to provide birth certificates, documents concerning guardianships, statements of the consent or termination of rights by the biological parents, the (older) child's statement of consent to the adoption, and the agency's consent to the adoption. The court may require that the consents (of birth parents, agencies, etc.) be submitted with the petition for adoption or at a hearing.

The court usually requires an investigation and the investigator's report before approving an adoption. If a child is placed through an agency, the agency will probably already have done its own postplacement follow-up. If a child has been adopted independently, the court will probably arrange for a study of your home.

The court usually holds a hearing. It may be in a closed courtroom or in the judge's chambers, and you may or may not be present. After the hearing, the court, having approved the adoption, issues an order or decree. The nature of the decree depends on state law. It may be a final decree or an interlocutory decree (a temporary one stipulating that at a later date— perhaps six months or a year—the court will again consider the application). Practices may vary by locality and by state. Which court actually considers your petition will also depend on local statute. It may be the probate court, district court, family court, superior court, or even the county court.

Getting Legal Help

Attorneys usually handle the court paperwork. In selecting an attorney to handle an adoption, ask around and do some comparison shopping. Be sure to:

- Find an attorney who is experienced with adoption law. The more adoption cases an attorney handles, the more familiar the attorney should be with the forms, the courts, and the local clerks.
- Ask parent groups, the local chapter of the American Bar Association, the **American Academy of Adoption Attorneys** (P.O. Box 33053, Washington, D.C. 20033-0053), and the clerks at the courts that handle adoptions in your community for recommendations.

- Ask your adoption agency for recommendations. The agency's lawyer is not necessarily the best suited to handle your case, however. The agency's attorney may have an arrangement to handle adoptions for a set fee. You may find an equally competent attorney who charges less. The agency's attorney, because he also handles all agency legal matters, may be very busy, and finalizing adoptions may be a low priority on his agenda.

- Ascertain what the fees include. Are you billed for the time spent, or is there a set fee for every adoption? Watch out for hidden fees. One attorney, when asked to break down his fees, said that he charged $200 to file a child's naturalization papers. You can do this yourself.

- Inquire about not only an attorney's fees but also how long it will take for him to get to the paperwork. Courts may be backed up, but if an attorney's caseload is too heavy, there may be delays because he or she simply does not have time to work on your case.

- Check into an attorney's reputation. Some adoption attorneys may not be well regarded by the court because of the poor quality of their paperwork or their questionable legal practices.

Should you use an attorney to handle your child's adoption? Some jurisdictions may permit you to file your own adoption papers, particularly the papers for finalization. Be sure to consult with other adoptive parents who have finalized their children's adoptions, with your local parent group (which may have sample completed forms for your area or state), and with your agency.[2]

Before you consider doing your own adoption, however, think it over carefully. Says Blanche Gelber, an experienced adoption attorney in New York City, "No two of my adoptions have been the same, and despite all my experience, the variations on the theme seem unpredictable and endless." Independent adoptions, particularly, are complex and often very intricate. Gelber points out that each judge may have his own beliefs and ways of approaching adoption. One judge might have a pattern of questioning independent adoptions, while another might be more favorably disposed.

Consider the experience of three families in Virginia. The Tellers used the forms that an attorney—whose child had also been adopted from Chile—had obtained from the local court and had successfully used. They essentially filled in the blanks. Their son's adoption went through the local court without a hitch. However, in passing on the "sample" papers to a third family—who also had a Chilean child but lived in another jurisdiction—things went awry. This family's judge was adamant in his insistence that the family provide evidence of having tried to obtain the putative father's consent. So they hired an attorney both in the United States and in Chile and advertised for the putative father.

These three families, living just ten miles apart but in different counties of a state, had different adoption experiences. If you will be following in the steps of someone else, particularly on a road *well trod* and with your agency's support, then adopting without an attorney may be a viable alternative.

If you are pursuing an independent adoption, you'll have some special questions to ask an attorney. These are explored in Chapter 4.

The Sealed Record

With the issuance of the final order of adoption, the adoption proceeding is completed and the case is legally closed. The legal practice has been to keep the adoption records confidential. In the past they have been available in most states for inspection by court order only. In most states the child's original birth certificate and the other documents collected for the adoption petition are placed in sealed court files. Agency records are not necessarily sealed, but some agencies do not release the information. Access to this basic information can thus be very limited, even to adult adoptees.

In some states, however, adoptees can now receive "nonidentifying" information about their birth parents. They can request identifying information (name of child before placement, birth parents' names, most recent address of birth parents), but this information will not be released until the state receives statements of consent from the birth parents (in some states the consent of the adoptive parents is also required). To keep track, some states maintain a central adoption registry—a file of birth parents' and adoptees' consents or denials to release information. When all the necessary parties have consented, then the state discloses the names and addresses to everyone. In still other states no registries exist, and no information is disclosed. Under federal law a foreign-born adoptee can obtain the records that were filed with the Immigration and Naturalization Service.

Chapters 10 and 12 discuss at length the importance of getting information about a child. Keep in mind that any information you turn over to the court may indeed be sealed and no longer be accessible. If you are concerned about sharing with your child information about his background, keep a copy of whatever information you have received and push your agency or contact to share information with you.

Obtaining a New Birth Certificate

It is customary, upon the adoption of a child, for the state to issue a new birth certificate or an amended birth certificate giving the new name of the adopted child. The certificate will usually give your child's name, will list you as parents, and may give the child's birthplace and other details. The new birth certificate will not reveal any information about the child's birth parents, nor does it usually state that the child is adopted.

Your attorney may handle this routinely as part of the adoption process. If you are not using an attorney, check with your state office of vital records. It is always a good idea to order more than one certified copy of the new birth certificate, as your child may need the birth certificate when entering school, when obtaining a driver's license, and when marrying. (For details about birth certificates for children adopted abroad, see Chapter 9.)

9

The Special Paperwork of an Intercountry Adoption

The amount of paperwork increases with an intercountry adoption. Even if you will be working with an agency, you must be well informed, well organized, determined, and willing to assemble what in advance may seem like an awesome array of personal documents. It can be done and has been done by thousands of people. The paperwork is extensive because you are meeting the requirements of a foreign country, the federal government, and your state system.

Meeting the Immigration Requirements of the Federal Government

Everyone bringing a child into the United States for the purposes of adoption must file an I-600 petition—a "Petition to Classify Orphan as an Immediate Relative." This petition is filed with the Immigration and Naturalization Service, which has offices throughout the United States. When you file the I-600 with the INS, you will need to submit a variety of supporting documents and pay a filing fee by check or money order. The I-600 form also states that you must meet certain federal requirements:

- The term *orphan* under the immigration laws means an alien child who is under the age of sixteen years at the time the visa petition on his behalf is filed and both of whose parents have died or disappeared or abandoned or deserted the orphan, or the child has become separated or lost from both parents. Under the INS definition an orphan may also have one parent. If the child has one parent, that parent must be incapable of providing for the child's care and must have in writing irrevocably released the child for emigration and adoption.
- To enter the United States, the orphan either must have been adopted abroad or must be coming to the United States for adoption by a U.S. citizen and spouse jointly, or by an unmarried U.S. citizen at least twenty-five years of age. Your spouse does not have to be a U.S. citizen.

In sum, the child must be under sixteen years of age; both parents must have died or disappeared, or, if there is one known parent, that parent will have had to release the orphan irrevocably. *If there are two known parents, then the child does not qualify as an orphan under the I-600.*

The I-600 also states that you must meet state preadoption requirements, and that if the child has not been adopted abroad, you must certify that he will be adopted in the United States.

There is no way around filing an I-600. Children brought in for medical procedures are brought in on different visas. If you try to bring a child into the country on a temporary visitor's visa, then you are asking for trouble.

Processing Through the Immigration and Naturalization Service

Long before your child arrives in the United States—even before a particular child may be assigned to you—the paperwork for adoption begins. As outlined in the previous chapter on paperwork, you should begin gathering your documents in advance so that your application can proceed. Accompanying the I-600 will be the documents that describe you and your child.

The I-600 requires that you submit the following for yourself:

- Proof of U.S. citizenship of the petitioner
- Proof of marriage (and proof of any previous divorce)
- Home study favorably recommending adoption
- Fingerprints (Form FD-258)

To speed the INS paperwork process, you may begin with the "Application for Advance Processing of Orphan Petition" (I-600A) with the INS *before you have identified a specific child*—that is, you present your documents, the I-600A, and a nonrefundable filing fee. Thus INS can run a fingerprint check on you (your fingerprint cards are sent to the FBI) and look at your documents. *You can even file the I-600A before your home study is completed.* (The home study must be submitted to the INS within one year of the filing date of your application.)

You can have your fingerprints taken at your local police station or at an INS office. INS personnel often recommend that you use their own service because fingerprints provided by local police are often smudged and illegible. Remember that a fingerprint check processed by the INS can take as much as forty to sixty days and that a smudged fingerprint may need to be redone, causing additional delays. The INS recommends that you submit two sets to them, just in case one of the sets turns out to be illegible. An INS spokesman indicated that the INS, when submitting your fingerprints to the FBI, can ask the FBI to "expedite" the check; when this happens, the FBI will turn around the request within forty-eight hours.

Sometimes fingerprint checks will reveal a record of a previous arrest. Convictions for drunk driving, trespassing, participating in an antiwar demonstration—even if they are years past—will show up. When this occurs, you will have to submit additional documentation to the INS to clear the record. It's recommended that to avoid this delay you reveal this information in advance to your social worker so that your home study can indicate knowledge of this as well as a statement that you are approved for parenting an adopted child.

If the INS approves your I-600A application, you will receive a "notice of favorable determination." When you obtain your child's documents, you file an I-600, and the I-600 is processed. You do not need to resubmit with the I-600 the material that was presented to the INS for the I-600A. Nor do you need to pay an additional fee, unless your application is more than a year old.

Advance processing can shorten your wait. Nothing is more frustrating than to get a child referral and know that your child is ready to emigrate, but be held up because your documents are not in order. To expedite matters further, you can, in fact, request in writing when you file your I-600A that the INS cable *your preapproval* to the U.S. consulate in your child's country.

For an I-600 application, you will also be showing your child's documents to the INS for approval. If your child's documents are in a foreign language, you must provide a translation in English. For the child that you are planning to adopt you must show:

- Proof of age of the orphan (e.g., birth certificate)
- A certified copy of the adoption decree, together with a certified translation, if the orphan has been legally adopted abroad
- Death certificates of the child's parents, if relevant
- Evidence that the sole or surviving parent is not able to provide for the child's care and has in writing irrevocably released the child for emigration and adoption
- Evidence that the child has been unconditionally abandoned to an orphanage, if the child has been placed in an orphanage by his parent or parents

- Evidence that your state's preadoption requirements have been met if you will be adopting the child in the United States

If you are adopting more than one child, you will need to file a separate I-600 for each child.

Once the INS has approved the I-600 application, an official can notify the embassy in the country where the child is located that he or she has permission to enter the United States. If you are traveling abroad to complete the adoption there, you can submit the completed I-600 to an INS service office abroad or to the U.S. Embassy in your child's birth country. If you file the I-600 in the United States, the local INS office will cable the visa petition approval to the embassy. Ask for confirmation from the INS. If you are not going to be traveling to pick up your child, you will want to follow up with the agencies to be sure that the visa approval was received. After your child has had a medical exam, the U.S. Embassy can issue a visa permitting the child to enter the United States on a permanent basis.

The wait for your child after you file the I-600 will vary. With an agency adoption, such as an adoption from South Korea, you can expect to file the I-600 as soon as you receive the child's documents and then possibly wait for a month or more before the agency completes the paperwork in South Korea. If you will be adopting your child abroad, the submission of the I-600 may come at the end of your wait, when your child is already with you, and you and your child may enter the United States shortly afterward.

Meeting State Preadoption Requirements

To meet preadoption requirements, some states may demand that you submit certain documents—for example, your home study, your child's birth certificate, the release for adoption, and a police report or fingerprint check—to them before they will approve the child's entry. Not all states have preadoption requirements, but be sure to inquire with your state's department of social services and the state's interstate compact administrator what requirements you must meet and what procedures you must follow.

If your child will be entering the United States with a final adoption decree, then you do not need to meet state preadoption requirements.

Notarization, Verification, Authentication

If you are adopting from Latin America, you are likely to be told that some of your documents must be notarized, verified, and authenticated at the consulate. A document that is notarized bears the seal of a notary public, who attests that the signature of the person on the document is valid. The county clerk of the county in which the notary is registered or the secretary of state for the state in which the notary resides verifies that the notary's seal and signature are valid. (Birth and marriage certificates are certified copies, so they do not usually require this step.) Your notarized and verified documents, with translations if required, then go to the consulate. The consul of the country to which you are applying to adopt then attests to the authenticity of your documents and letters by his seal and signature. Some countries may require that everything you submit—your references, your birth certificates, your home study, your doctor's report—be notarized, verified, and authenticated. (Some countries will also require an additional step before authentication takes place—that the U.S. Department of State must also certify the notarized and verified documents.) Costs can mount to several hundred dollars, so you'll want to have this procedure done when you are sure of your adoption plans. Be sure you call ahead to the consulate in advance to ask about hours and costs (cash payment may be expected) and to make an appointment if necessary. You may have to leave the documents and have them returned to you by mail.

Translations

Your documents may have to be translated into a foreign language. Your child's documents will have to be translated into English. If you are working with an agency, it may have the translations done. If you are asked to arrange this yourself, be sure to use a competent, experienced translator, preferably someone working in his or her native language. Your translator will need to provide you with a statement of competency bearing an official raised seal. The statement might read: "I, _____, hereby certify that the above is a complete and accurate translation of the original and that I am competent in both English and _____ to render such a translation."

Getting Help

As you do the paperwork for an intercountry adoption, it's useful to talk to people who have recently completed the process. They can give you tips about who to see at the INS, what process to follow, and how long things will take. Many parent groups have often written up the local INS or foreign consulate procedures.

Legwork

As the volume of paperwork grows with intercountry adoption, so too does the time it takes to process the papers. If you live near the offices of the INS, or indeed within any reasonable distance, it often pays to do your paperwork in person. Be sure to call ahead to find out opening and closing hours, lunch hours, and the days when the people you need to see will be on vacation or out of the office. Most families carry as many of their documents as possible by hand. They may spend one day at their state's secretary of state's office getting documents verified (if that is required by the foreign country), another at the foreign consulate getting the papers authenticated, and still another filing papers with the INS. One family found that the only time they mailed in their documents—for their son's U.S. citizenship—they received a notice from their local INS office four months later stating that the letter had just been opened and their application assigned a file number. If you must mail your documents to your state government, for example, send them certified, return receipt requested. You can also use an express mail service. (When using express mail services to communicate abroad, ask your local parent group, agency, or facilitator for a specific recommendation, as some services have a better track record handling foreign correspondence than others.) If there is a specific person who will be handling your documents, such as the interstate placement officer, you may want to follow up your letter with a telephone call a week later. Be sure to send a self-addressed stamped envelope for the documents' return.

Getting in Touch with the Immigration and Naturalization Service

It's often frustrating trying to contact the INS. Phones are constantly busy, and the staff does not have the time to answer questions. To obtain forms by mail, check your telephone directory (under "U.S. Government") to see if there is a special phone number designed to handle document requests.

The INS has also prepared a helpful booklet, *The Immigration of Adopted and Prospective Adoptive Children.* You can obtain a copy from the INS (Director, Outreach Program, U.S. Immigration and Naturalization Service, 425 I Street, Washington, D.C. 20536).

The offices in the following list can give you information about immigration. Addresses marked with an asterisk (*) are the INS district offices.[1]

ADDRESSES FOR IMMIGRATION INFORMATION

Alabama
See Georgia

Alaska
New Federal Building, 701 C Street, Anchorage 99513; 907-343-7820*

Arizona
Federal Building, 230 North First Avenue, Phoenix 85025; 602-379-3122*
Federal Building, 300 West Congress, Tucson 85701-1386

Arkansas
See Louisiana

California
Federal Building, U.S. Courthouse, 1130 O Street, Fresno 93721; 209-487-5091
300 North Los Angeles Street, Los Angeles 90012; 213-894-2119*
880 Front Street, San Diego 92188; 619-557-5570*
Appraisers Building, 630 Sansome Street, San Francisco 94111; 415-705-4411*
280 South First Street, San Jose 95113; 408-291-7876

Colorado
1787 Federal Office Building, 1961 Stout Street, Denver 80294-1799; 303-371-3041*

Connecticut
Ribicoff Federal Building, 450 Main Street, Hartford 06103; 203-240-3171*

Delaware
See Pennsylvania

District of Columbia
4420 North Fairfax Drive, Arlington 22203; 703-307-1501*

Florida
400 West Bay Street, Jacksonville 32201; 904-791-2624
7880 Biscayne Boulevard, Miami 33138; 305-536-5741*
5509 Gray Street, Tampa 33609; 813-228-2131

Georgia
Federal Annex Building, 77 Forsyth Street S.W., Atlanta 30303; 404-331-5158*

Hawaii
  595 Ala Moana Boulevard, P.O. Box 461, Honolulu 96809; 808-541-1379*

Idaho
  See Montana

Illinois
  Dirksen Federal Office Building, 219 South Dearborn Street, Chicago 60604;
  312-353-7334*

Indiana
  46 East Ohio Street, Indianapolis 46204; 317-331-6009
  51 West 80 Place, Georgetown Plaza, Merrillville 46410

Iowa
  See Nebraska

Kansas
  See Missouri

Kentucky
  U.S. Courthouse Building, West 6th & Broadway, Louisville 40202; 502-582-
  6375

Louisiana
  Postal Service Building, 701 Loyola Avenue, New Orleans 70113; 504-589-
  6533*

Maine
  739 Warren Avenue, Portland 04103; 207-780-3352*

Maryland
  E. A. Garmatz Federal Building, 101 West Lombard Street, Baltimore 21201;
  301-962-2065*

Massachusetts
  J.F.K. Federal Building, Government Center, Boston 02203; 617-565-3879*

Michigan
  Federal Building, 333 Mt. Elliott Street, Detroit 48207; 313-226-3240*

Minnesota
  923 New P.O. Building, 180 East Kellogg Boulevard, St. Paul 55101; 612-854-
  7754*

Mississippi
   See Louisiana

Missouri
   9747 North Conant Avenue, Kansas City 64153; 816-891-0603*
   200 North Tucker Boulevard, St. Louis 63101; 314-539-2532

Montana
   Federal Building, 301 South Park, Helena 59626-0036; 406-499-5288*

Nebraska
   3736 South 132nd Street, Omaha 68144; 402-697-9155*

Nevada
   Federal Building, U.S. Courthouse, 300 Las Vegas Boulevard South, Las
   Vegas 89101; 702-384-3696
   712 Mill Street, Reno 89502; 702-784-5427

New Hampshire
   See Massachusetts

New Jersey
   Federal Building, 970 Broad Street, Newark 07102; 201-645-4400*

New Mexico
   Federal Building, 517 Gold Avenue S.W., Albuquerque 87103; 505-766-2378

New York
   U.S. Post Office and Courthouse, 445 Broadway, Albany 12207; 518-472-
   4621
   68 Court Street, Buffalo 14202; 716-849-6760*
   26 Federal Plaza, New York 10278; 212-206-6500*

North Carolina
   6 Woodlawn Green, Charlotte 29403; 704-523-1704

North Dakota
   See Minnesota

Ohio
   U.S. Post Office & Courthouse, 100 East 5th Street, Cincinnati 45201; 513-
   684-3781
   Anthony J. Celebreeze Federal Building, 1240 East 9th Street, Cleveland
   44199; 216-522-4770*

Oklahoma
   Federal Building, 4149 Rloh Line Boulevard, Oklahoma City 73102; 405-231-4121

Oregon
   Federal Office Building, 511 N.W. Broadway, Portland 97209; 503-326-3006*

Pennsylvania
   1600 Callowhill Street, Philadelphia 19103; 215-597-3961*
   Federal Building, 1000 Liberty Avenue, Pittsburgh 15222; 412-644-3356

Rhode Island
   Federal Building, U.S. Post Office, Exchange Terrace, Providence 02903

South Carolina
   Federal Building, 334 Meeting Street, Charleston 28210

South Dakota
   See Minnesota

Tennessee
   Federal Building, 167 North Main Street, Memphis 38103; 901-544-3301

Texas
   Federal Building, 1100 Commerce Street, Dallas 75242; 214-655-5384*
   700 East San Antonio, El Paso 79984; 915-532-0273*
   2102 Teege Avenue, Harlingen 78550; 512-425-7333*
   509 North Belt, Houston 77004; 713-847-7900*
   Federal Building, 727 East Durango, San Antonio 78206; 512-229-6350*

Utah
   230 West 400 South Street, Salt Lake City 84101; 801-524-5771

Vermont
   Federal Building, St. Albans 05478; 802-951-6658

Virginia
   4420 North Fairfax Drive, Arlington 22203; 703-307-1501*
   Norfolk Federal Building, 200 Granby Mall, Norfolk 23510; 804-441-3081

Washington
   815 Airport Way South, Seattle 98134; 206-442-5956*
   691 U.S. Courthouse Building, Spokane 99201; 509-353-2129

West Virginia
   See Pennsylvania

Wisconsin
   Federal Building, 517 East Wisconsin Avenue, Milwaukee 53202

Wyoming
   See Colorado

Passports

If you will be traveling to pick up your child, you will need a valid passport. You can apply for a passport at a regional passport agency of the U.S. Department of State, at federal or state courts, or at some U.S. post offices. With the application you must present proof of U.S. citizenship such as a certified copy of your birth certificate, a prior passport, or your naturalization certificate. You will also need two recent identical photographs of a specified size, evidence of your identity such as your driver's license, and a fee. If you are applying for a passport for the first time, you must apply in person. For further details, you can call the recorded message of the Department of State, Office of Passport Services (202-647-0518).

Since passports for adults are now valid for ten years, apply for your passport as soon as you can. Some Latin American agencies will ask for your passport number on their applications, and the foreign consulate may ask to see your passport when you present your documents. Even if you do not plan on traveling abroad, you should have a valid passport so you can travel if you need to.

You may also need a visa to travel. Check with the foreign consulate, the airline that you will be traveling on, or the Office of Citizen's Consular Services of the Department of State (202-647-3444).

The child you adopt will also need a passport issued by his birth country to travel to the United States. If you are adopting through an intercountry program, your agency will most likely make these arrangements. If you are adopting independently, you may have to make these arrangements when you go abroad.

Paperwork Abroad

As part of the intercountry adoption process, you will be submitting basic documents, including your home study, to a foreign source. This usually precedes the assignment of a particular child. If you are working with a U.S. agency, the staff may handle all communications abroad. If you are adopting independently, you may be doing all your own paperwork. If you are working independently with a foreign agency or attorney, you may be asked to send a power of attorney giving them permission to act on your behalf in the adoption proceedings. This power of attorney will probably have to be notarized and verified.

You will need to meet the adoption requirements of your particular resource (foreign agencies have requirements) and also of the foreign country. A country or an agency may have requirements pertaining to age, length of marriage, religion, residency, and divorce or marriage. *If you do not meet the foreign country's or foreign agency's requirements, you cannot adopt even if you satisfy all your state and federal requirements.* Chapter 7 discusses how to get information about the laws and procedures in a specific country.

If you will be traveling to pick up your child, you may have to appear before foreign authorities and do some paperwork at that time abroad. You can also expect to visit the U.S. Embassy to obtain your child's visa. You may be asked to do such things as submit affidavits to a department of welfare or documents to the court, obtain statements from a physician about your child's health, or file an application for your child's passport. Your agency or attorney abroad may do this, or you may have to do this yourself.

Keeping Track

You will want to devise a method to keep track of all the documentation you need to accumulate (see Figure 2, for example). Be sure to keep copies of all correspondence and all documents.

Remember that you are preparing *at least* three sets of documents: one for the agency or person who is handling the placement of your child, one for the Immigration and Naturalization Service, and one for yourself (a duplicate set that you can use if necessary).

Alien Registration

When your child immigrates to the United States, he or she enters as an alien, not as an American citizen. You will receive from the INS an alien registration card. This card should be carefully safeguarded along with other important papers. Until your child becomes a U.S. citizen, whenever you move, you must notify the INS of the change of address.

Readoption

If your child has been legally adopted abroad, the adoption is valid. Still, most adoption authorities recommend as an additional safeguard that you readopt your child in the United States under the laws of your state. This will also give you readily available evidence of the validity of your child's adoption. Some states may not permit readoption, so check locally to see if this can be done.

If your child left his or her country of birth under a guardianship, not a final adoption, then you *must* adopt in the United States (see the discussion in Chapter 8 on finalizing an adoption).

| | Request | | | | | |
	Sent	Rec'd	U.S. Agency	Foreign Agency	INS	State (Preadopt)
Application: 1. 2. 3. 4.						
Documents **Birth Certificates** No. Needed Husband Wife						
Marriage Certificate No. needed						
Divorce Record						
Death Certificate						
Medical Reports Husband Wife						
Bank References Savings Checking						
Employer's Reference Husband Wife						
Income Tax Form						
Home Study Date started: Date completed:						
References 1. 2. 3.						
Form I-600A			✕	✕		
Fingerprint Cards (2 for each of you)			✕	✕		
Form I-600			✕	✕		
Passports, Visas Husband Wife			✕	✕	✕	
Your Future Child's Documents Proof of Age Parental or Agency Release Medical Report Background Information: Others:	✕	✕		✕	✕	

Figure Two   Checklist of documents.

Conferring U.S. Citizenship on Your Child

If you adopted your child abroad, you can apply to the INS to make him or her a citizen immediately. Otherwise, as soon as your child has been legally adopted in the United States, you can take this step.

There are two procedures that can be used to confer citizenship on an adopted child. One is the long-standing method in which you submit to the INS an "Application to File Petition for Naturalization in Behalf of Child" (Form N-402). The application must be accompanied by a fee and special photographs taken within thirty days of the filing of the petition.

At a later date you are called for a hearing before an Immigration officer. Bring your child's birth certificate, a certified copy of the child's adoption decree (if your child was adopted abroad, be sure that you have the adoption decree translated and that you have your translator's statement of competence), your various documents (birth, marriage, divorce certificates), the alien registration card, your child's passport, and your child. Even if the INS fails to tell you to bring your documents, do so.

Only one parent needs to file the naturalization petition (Form N-402). If there is a family emergency—or illness—only the parent who filed the petition must attend the hearing and naturalization. With this first method, however, be prepared for a wait.

Sometime after your meeting with the Immigration official, you will be summoned to the "swearing in" naturalization ceremony. It is for all new citizens, not just adoptees. The amount of fanfare surrounding the ceremony, which is typically held in a courtroom, will vary by locale (in some areas of the country the local Daughters of the American Revolution distribute souvenir American flags at the ceremony's conclusion). Sometime after the naturalization, the INS will send you a naturalization certificate for your child.

There is also a faster, less complicated alternative procedure for conferring citizenship on adopted children. *If you and your spouse are both U.S. citizens,* you can file—by mail if you choose—an "Application for Certificate of Citizenship in Behalf of an Adopted Child" (Form N-643). Along with your application you submit your supporting documents. A hearing is not required, so that the only time you set foot in an INS office is when you pick up your child's certificate of citizenship. At that time you take the oath of allegiance on behalf of your child.

Must a young child be present for either procedure? It is the parent, rather than the young child, who takes the oath of allegiance. Most parents want their children present, but it is apparently not mandatory.

Once your child becomes a U.S. citizen, you will also want to check with your adoption agency or with the foreign consulate to find out whether your child holds dual citizenship. If that's the case, you will probably want to complete the paperwork to nullify the other citizenship. It's unlikely, but an adopted child who has not become a U.S. citizen or whose citizenship has not been renounced could be required to serve in his birth country's armed forces.

Obtaining a Birth Certificate for a Child Adopted Abroad

If you have adopted a child abroad, some states will permit you to apply for a state birth certificate without readoption, while others will insist on readoption. Some states will issue a birth certificate for foreign-born adoptees upon their U.S. citizenship; others permit parents to submit a copy of the child's translated birth certificate and a translated copy of the child's final adoption decree. Check with your state's vital records office (see Chapter 8). The policy of issuing birth certificates to foreign-born adoptees has been changing, so even if you have previously inquired and were told that your state does not issue a certificate, it is wise to keep calling at periodic intervals.

Some states will issue a foreign-born child a birth certificate that is the same as the birth certificate issued to all people born in the state. Other states issue "certificates of foreign birth."

The Immigration and Naturalization Service will issue a certification of birth data to foreign-born children under twenty-one years old who have been admitted to the United States for permanent residence. The INS can provide this certificate before naturalization. Check with the INS for details on how to obtain it.

Follow-up Contact Abroad

Once your child's adoption has been completed, there's a strong desire to "get on with living" and put the past behind you. That feeling may extend to failing to keep in contact with the people who helped in your child's birth country. You may not be legally required to keep in touch with the agency or court, but intercountry adoption advocates urge you to do so. Send cards on your child's birthday or at holidays. You may also want to send packages of clothing, small donations of money, and, of course, photographs that show your child's development. The judges and social workers in foreign countries who are involved in intercountry adoption are concerned about the welfare of those children who have left. Send letters not only the first year, but for the next five or ten years so that others can see that your child is loved and cherished. It's good for you, good for your child, and good for intercountry relations. A judge or an agency who never hears about the outcome of intercountry adoptions might just decide to stop approving placements to the United States.

10

Preparing for Your Child

The wait—all adoptive parents have to go through it—
whether for a few days, a few weeks, a few months, or years.
Waiting is a critical part of adoption: Children wait for homes;
parents wait for children. When you've done all that paperwork, when you've done all the preliminaries that you need to
do in order to make your adoption happen, you may still have
some waiting to do.

Keep busy. If you're working, keep working. If you plan to
take time off for parenting, wait until your child is ready to
enter your home; don't quit your job or start your leave in
anticipation of your new status. Do other things that you'd
planned: Don't defer a vacation or other project "because the
adoption call might come." Let your life continue.

Get involved in your adoptive parent group. Others have
been through the waiting and they may help. "Looking back,
the waiting period was just a few months," observed one
adoptive parent, "but those months were the longest, most
stressful, emotionally turbulent months of my life." For this
parent, the monthly meetings of New York Singles Adopting
Children were critical: "Seeing the children helped to rein-
force that 'it will happen.' Those who had been through the
wait could understand as no others could. I met others whose

wait began around the time of mine, so we went through it together. And, when the placements came, we shared each other's joy."[1]

The waiting period should be the time when you sit down and read about child care and adoption. Think about the future. How do you see yourself as a parent? What do you think your life will be like once your child arrives? What roles will your spouse, other children, family, and friends play in the upcoming adoption? How will your relationships with them change? What do you expect of your new child? "Waiting parents," says Claudia Jewett, "are wise to discuss openly their dreams and fears and plans for their coming child."[2]

Consider those first days and weeks after your child arrives. If you are working, will you be taking time off? If so, how much? Do you want help at the beginning from a spouse, parent, or friend? What kinds of support will you require? When?

This chapter outlines some of the things you will want to get done in preparation for your role as an adoptive parent. You may want to change insurance policies and wills, arrange for a leave of absence from work, meet with a prospective doctor for your child, and possibly with a dentist. If you are adopting an infant, you may want to set up your child's room and do some shopping. If you are adopting an older child, you may want to do some fix-up yourself and leave some things to do with your child. Time is likely to be in short supply once your child arrives.

Leaves of Absence and Adoption Benefits

Carole Fezar wanted to take an unpaid maternity leave to spend time with her infant daughter—a common request among working mothers. But unlike most mothers, Carole had to file a grievance with her union to get that opportunity. For Carole had adopted her daughter. A federal arbitrator ruled that she was entitled to her leave. He said:

It is apparent that the term *maternity* does not singularly embrace conception and childbearing but rather that it encompasses the duties and responsibilities of motherhood. The very fact that maternity leave can cover a period of time up to one year in duration serves to establish the fact that it sets a major portion of the time for child-rearing. It must follow then that the adoption of an infant child requires the same care, the same responsibility as would be with an infant born to a natural mother.[3]

The number of employers offering adoption leaves and benefits has been growing. In fact, many states have passed legislation mandating employers to provide adoption leave. Female and male workers in Kentucky, for example, were guaranteed up to six weeks leave of absence for the adoption of a child under the age of seven in 1990, while state employees in North Dakota were allowed four months leave for the adoption of a child. Laws concerning family leave, which includes adoption leave, have undergone rapid change: Thirty states considered new legislation in 1989.[4] Keep in mind, however, that adoption leaves are almost always *unpaid* leaves of absence, while maternity leaves, which are subject to the federal Pregnancy Discrimination Act of 1978, typically provide some disability benefits, including financial compensation, for time off.

Recognizing the strains placed on a family's budget when they adopt a child, some employers are also now offering adoption benefits. In a 1990 study of work and family benefits, the independent consulting firm Hewitt Associates found that 12% of 837 major U.S. employers provided their employees with some form of adoption assistance. Noted Hewitt Associates: "The most compelling reason for an employer to offer adoption benefits is equity. Through adoption assistance an employer can provide comparable benefits to employees who become parents either by adoption or by birth."[5]

Fifty-six of the seventy-seven employers studied by the U.S. General Accounting Office in 1989 offered their workers some financial assistance for adoption expenses.[6] At the majority of the companies employees could request reimbursement for their agency, legal, and medical fees, as well as for temporary foster care expenses. A few employers provided lump-sum payments instead. Benefits, usually paid out after the adoption is finalized, ranged from $200 to $4,000. At Wendy's International, whose founder is an adoptee, employees were entitled to up to six weeks of paid adoption leave in 1990 and could also apply for financial assistance up to $4,000 (up to $6,000 for special-needs children). U.S. military personnel are eligible for reimbursement of up to $12,000 per child for reasonable expenses. There are restrictions, however, including the provision that the adoption be arranged by a public or nonprofit, voluntary agency. For details, contact the National Military Family Association (6000 Stevenson Avenue, Alexandria, VA 22304; 703-823-6632).

If you are a working parent waiting to adopt a child, then you will want to explore your employer's leave and benefit policies. Start by looking at your employer's human resources booklets outlining benefits and then talk with one of your company's human resources counselors. Be sure that you get the policy outlined to you *in writing* and that you understand it fully. Since state laws governing family leave have been changing, you may want to check with your state department of labor whether your employer is in full compliance with current law. The **Women's Legal Defense Fund** (2000 P Street N.W., Washington, D.C.; 202-887-0364), which has been tracking legislation nationwide, and **Catalyst** (250 Park Avenue South, New York, New York 10003; 212-777-8900), which has surveyed corporate adoption policies over the years, may also be helpful. In your research, you will need to find out:

• Does your employer grant adoption leave? If so, to whom and under what circumstances? Are both men and women eligible? Are there any restrictions? If you are adopting an infant who is not a newborn, can you take a leave? If you are adopting an older child, can you take an adoption leave? Some employers do not offer benefits to parents of children who are more than six months old.

- Is your employer's adoption leave a formal policy or has it been granted informally, on a person-by-person basis?
- What are the specific provisions of the adoption leave?
- Are there differences between your employer's maternity leave, adoption leave, and family leave? If so, exactly what are they?
- How many weeks of adoption leave are you entitled to?
- Are you entitled to *paid* weeks of adoption leave? If so, how many?
- How far in advance must you request an adoption leave?
- Are you guaranteed your job—or a similar job—when you return?
- How are your health insurance, disability, and other plans in which you participate affected while you are on leave? Who pays for them?
- Is there a restriction on the number of adoption leaves, or the frequency of leaves, that you can take?
- Does your company offer adoption benefits? Adoption benefits are often distinct from the specific provisions of the leave policies.
- How does the benefit package work? Is there reimbursement for specific, itemized expenses? If so, what's covered? Or is there a dollar ceiling set for each adoption, regardless of your actual expenses? Are the benefits available for all adoptions or just certain types of adoptions? Are the expenses incurred in an independent adoption, for example, eligible for reimbursement?
- When are you eligible to apply for reimbursement under your company's benefit package? Many plans do not reimburse you until after your child's adoption is *finalized* in court.

If your company does not offer an adoption leave, Marcie Schorr Hirsch, co-author of *Managing Your Maternity Leave,* suggests that you start by asking your boss to support your request for a leave, and then talk with your employer's department of human resources. It helps to be aware of what's common within your industry. You might also, as Carole Fezar did, ask your labor union to back your individual request. Enterprising adoptive parents have also gotten their unions to include an adoption assistance program as part of the union's contract negotiations. If you negotiate for yourself a leave policy, be sure to get all the terms of the leave *in writing.*

You'll also need to decide when to inform your employer about your adoption plans and your interest in taking a leave. When you discuss your plans, you may find that your employer has some difficulty dealing with the timing of an adoption leave. If you're a male planning on taking an adoption leave, that may also take some additional explaining. Employers and benefits managers are used to having people tell them that "my baby is due on March fifth and I want to leave work two weeks before that." Employers usually can deal with medical complications that suddenly force a woman to leave work earlier than she had planned. It's much more difficult to grasp the reality of adoption: that people don't know when the blessed event will take place, that families will not have much notice, that working parents can't give much notice. Your employer may be stymied by a statement like "We don't know when the agency will contact us." You may also have difficulty getting people to understand that you won't have time for a while to come back to the office to take care of things unexpectedly left hanging. You'll need to explain to them that you're going to be swamped at home for a while. You may not be exhausted from the birth of your child, but that's only a small part of new parenthood. Adjusting to a new child—whether by birth or adoption—will require your full attention.

Health Insurance

Before your child enters your home, you should be sure that you have proper medical coverage. Some agencies may require a statement about the exact coverage that you have. If you are adopting a child with special needs, be sure you understand the details of any health coverage or subsidy that the child will receive. *In all cases you want to be sure that your child will be covered upon "placement," upon "arriving" in your home, or from the time that you are responsible for care—rather than upon finalization.*

Check with your health insurance company or health maintenance organization to find out about your plan's coverage for dependents and *get it in writing.* Some plans cover foster children; others do not. One may state that it covers *"legally adopted"* children, while another begins "coverage for an adopted child on the day you begin legal proceedings for the adoption of the child," and a third provides "coverage from the time the child is placed in the custody of the adoptive parents." Most plans will not cover costs incurred in the hospital for the care of a newborn. Find out what you must do to get your child covered under your policy. Be sure to explain that the child is not adopted at the time he enters your home but that you are fully responsible for the child's well-being. If your health insurance carrier will not cover your child upon birth or upon arrival in your home, you will need to take out additional coverage through your insurance company, or else contact other insurance carriers to arrange for separate coverage for your child. (An insurance broker or your agency or adoptive parent group may be able to help you find a company. A sympathetic employer might put pressure on your insurance carrier or health maintenance organization to change its policy so that coverage is available.) Find out also whether the policy covers preexisting conditions, both diagnosed and undiagnosed, and get a letter from the insurance company verifying your coverage.

If you have individual coverage under a group plan (sometimes spouses are covered individually by their employers), you'll need to convert to *family* health insurance coverage. This is particularly important if you are a single parent, because you will need to have a family policy in order to cover your child. Check also whether there is any waiting period before coverage begins.

You might also want to find out who holds the guardianship of your child in the period between placement and finalization. If the state or your agency is the guardian, your child may qualify for Medicaid until your health insurance policy takes over. Says Dr. Jerri Jenista of the University of Michigan Medical Center, "Private agencies and international agencies may not realize or take advantage of this." Children with severe disabilities—even if they are foreign-born and not yet U.S. citizens—may also be eligible for Medicaid and other assistance through the Supplemental Security Income (SSI) program if specific criteria are met.

While states may prohibit insurance companies from discriminating against adoption—stipulating that adopted children be treated on the same basis as other dependents—there are many loopholes in insurance coverage, and differential treatment frequently occurs. In the past few years, under pressure from adoption advocates, state laws and insurance practices have been changing. To find out the situation in your state and whether your health care provider is in compliance, check with your state's insurance commissioner, your elected state representatives, and adoption advocacy groups.

Wills

If you don't have a will, you'll want to write one to be sure that from the time your child arrives in your home he's provided for. Your will gives you a chance to name the executor of your estate as well as the guardian of your child and your child's property. In naming guardians, you will need to explore with them their feelings about adoption and about raising an adopted child. Just as seriously as you prepared for adoption, you will want to talk at length with the people who might end up raising your child.

You'll need to look closely at your will to be sure that it protects your child. Wills and trusts sometimes include terms like *issue, heirs of the body, born to, next of kin,* and *descendants,* which are not always legally understood to include adopted as well as biological children. To protect your child, you should insert a clause stating that all biological and adopted children are to be considered equally as heirs and beneficiaries. One family's wills state that "whenever the terms *child, children* or *descendants* are used or are relevant under this will and in the disposition of my estate, adopted children shall be considered and treated in all respects the same as natural children." A clause such as this protects your adopted child, but not necessarily during the period before you've been to court to obtain the final order of adoption. Some attorneys recommend that to protect your children fully, you should state their names (both the names under which they are currently known and any other names they have had in the past). If you do that, however, update your will whenever you add a child to your family.

You may want to ask relatives, such as grandparents, who may be making bequests in their wills to your *descendants* or *issue* to insert similar clauses to ensure that all your children inherit equally.

Life Insurance

Life insurance policies may also use terms such as *descendants* or *issue* or *heirs of the body,* so be sure that you are covering your adopted children. It is also recommended that you advise your insurance company in writing (keeping a copy) that you have adopted children and request confirmation that the policy applies to them. Also check into the provisions of your pension plan and any company death benefits.

Some adoptive parents have also taken out life insurance policies for their children. "When our son was an infant," Laura said, "we took out a ten-thousand-dollar life insurance policy. We had adopted our child from abroad and had used up our savings. We felt that if something were to happen to our child, we would not otherwise have the financial resources to undertake a second adoption. We felt funny taking out the policy, but we did it."

Finances

All states have developed some adoption subsidies (sometimes referred to as "adoption assistance"). Subsidies are based on the special needs of children and help hard-to-place children find families. The subsidy provides the financial base for a family so that the adoption of a special-needs child will not result in expenses beyond the reach of many adoptive parents. If you're considering a child for whom a subsidy may be possible, you'll want to find out:

- What children are eligible for subsidy?
- Are there monthly cash stipends for the child?
- Are there payments for specific medical, surgical, psychiatric, or other costs?
- How long is the subsidy designed to last? A subsidy may be paid for a specific period of time or it may continue until a child reaches maturity.
- Are there one-time, nonrecurring expenses, such as legal fees, that will be paid?
- How do you apply for subsidy?
- Can the subsidy go with the child if you move to another

state? What must you do? Some states participate in the Interstate Compact on Adoption and Medical Assistance. For details, check with the American Public Welfare Association in Washington, D.C.

• Is the state requiring that adoptive parents submit financial information about themselves as a "means" test?

• Would subsidy be available after the fact if you can identify that there was a preexisting condition?

Subsidies, which may come from federal or state money, vary state by state: Some states have restricted programs; others, more inclusive programs. Contact your state's department of social services to learn about your state's subsidy program. If you are considering adopting an out-of-state child, check with the social services department of the state where your potential child resides. You can also ask your agency or parent group for help.

Once your child enters your home, you should be able to declare him or her as a dependent on your federal income tax return, and there may be other deductions for which you qualify. Contact the IRS, an accountant, or another qualified person for help. Some states have also permitted income tax deductions for adoption. These deductions have sometimes included the medical and hospital costs of the birth mother or the child welfare agency and legal fees for adoption expenses. Check with your state's department of revenue to learn whether your state permits any deductions.

Getting Medical Advice and Arranging for Medical Care

You'll want to line up a pediatrician or family physician before your child arrives. If you are considering a child with a special need or a child who will be coming from abroad, you may want to consult a physician before you apply for a specific child or at the time you receive a child referral. Says Peggy Soule of *The CAP Book:* "Be sure to let your physician tell you the *facts* about specific diseases or handicaps. The doctor should tell you what to expect but should not put his own value judgment on whether or not you should adopt. That is your decision. Too often because the doctor would not adopt a child with the specific handicap you are considering, she will advise the family not to do it."

Ask other physicians, family members, co-workers, and particularly parents whose children may have the same needs as your prospective child about their experiences with local physicians. When selecting a physician, take the time to have a sit-down discussion about your child. (Some doctors will talk with families on the telephone, but many will not.) A meeting at a doctor's office may mean that you will have to pay him for his time, but it's well worth it. If you are a new parent, you're going to want to find out about his practice. Among your questions: What are the office hours? How are phone calls handled? When you call in, will you speak with the doctor or the nurse? Are there special "call-in" hours? What happens when your child is sick? Who will treat your child at night or on weekends? If the doctor is part of a medical group, will you normally see your doctor? When do you meet the associates? If you are a working parent, how does the doctor feel about someone other than you bringing your child for checkups or sick-child visits?

Try to visit during office hours so you can also meet other parents and children and observe the routines. How long are patients kept waiting? How are sick and well children handled? You can also discreetly ask the parents in the waiting room about their experiences.

But you'll also have some more adoption-specific questions:

- Does the doctor see other adopted patients in his practice?
- Has the doctor treated foreign-born adoptees? Your physician should be able to accept, for example, that a child

adopted from abroad might not have reached the developmental milestones or the weight and height that American children of the same age have.

- How does the physician feel about adoption? What has been the doctor's experience with adoption? One family learned their pediatrician's opinion about adoption when he discovered a heart murmur in their newborn and recommended that the family not keep the baby.
- Is the doctor willing to read articles or medical materials that you bring in, especially those that concern the special medical concerns of adopted children?
- How many patients in the doctor's practice have been in foster care?
- What is the physician's expertise with the special needs that your child presents? What is the physician's attitude?
- What does the doctor know about prenatal substance abuse and its effect on children?
- What is your physician's policy about Medicaid? A 1989 study published in *Pediatrics* found that many pediatricians limited their participation. Reported the authors: "Only 56% of pediatricians allowed comparable access to their practices for both Medicaid and private patients." If you will be receiving a subsidy for your child and if it involves Medicaid, be sure your physician will accept it.
- How does the physician feel about receiving incomplete medical records? There may be a lot that is unknown about children who have been in foster care in the United States and about children born abroad. Adoptive parents report that U.S. doctors are often very uncomfortable working with children who do not have a complete medical history.
- Will the physician share what is in the medical records with you?
- How much support do you expect to receive from this physician?

Raise issues that concern you. You may want to discuss child care, child-rearing, circumcision, even your plans for feeding. Linda Elway had told her pediatrician about the uncertainty of her child's arrival from South Korea and had raised the possibility that her daughter might arrive on a Saturday. Would the doctor see her? Sure, he said. But when she called her physician on a weekend night to tell him that her daughter would be arriving the next day and that the agency had requested that the baby be seen because of a rash, she found out differently. She recalls: "The pediatrician refused, saying that he did not have office hours and that he didn't trust an agency's opinion about whether a child should be seen. This agency had brought thousands of South Korean children to the United States and had called us long distance to urge us to make medical arrangements. Here was a pediatrician doubting our word. We switched pediatricians."

If you are adopting a child from abroad, you will want to be sure that your child's doctor does a few basic tests on your child when he arrives. If you are working with a U.S. agency that has an intercountry adoption program, your agency will probably tell you what tests they require. You will want to ask that your child's physician do a:[7]

- Hepatitis B profile, to include hepatitis B surface antigen and antibodies to hepatitis B surface and core antigens
- Mantoux test for tuberculosis. (Be aware that in some countries children are vaccinated at birth against tuberculosis—the BCG vaccine—and may test positively.) Notes Dr. Jenista: "This is the 'blister under the skin test,' not the four-prong tine quick test."
- Complete blood count
- Stool examination to check for ova and parasites
- Stool culture for bacterial causes for diarrhea
- Blood test for syphilis

- Urinalysis and urine culture
- Vision and hearing screening

You might also want to provide your physician with some specialized adoption literature. Many U.S. agencies have prepared fact sheets about the health and care of the children they are placing. The staff at the International Adoption Clinic at the University of Minnesota will provide you with reprints of their articles and will consult by mail or telephone. You can also consult with its counterpart in Boston at the New England Medical Center (750 Washington Street, Box 286, Boston, Massachusetts 02111; 617-956-7285). You can also contact Dr. Jerri Jenista at the University of Michigan Medical Center in Ann Arbor, who has written extensively about the health concerns of adopted children. The American Academy of Pediatrics (P.O. Box 927, Elk Grove Village, Illinois 60009; 800-433-9016) has produced a policy statement, "Initial Medical Evaluation of an Adopted Child," that you might share with your doctor. And you might suggest that your physician consult the American Academy of Pediatrics' recommendations for internationally adopted children as listed in the 1991 "Red Book" (the Report of the Committee on Infectious Diseases). You'll also find a discussion of health-care issues in Lois Ruskai Melina's *Raising Adopted Children* and articles she coauthored with her husband, Dr. Carl M. Melina.[8]

If you are adopting a child who is not an infant, you will probably want to take your child to a dentist within a few weeks of his arrival. Indeed, since older foreign-born children often have extensive tooth decay, you may want to talk with a dentist in advance.

Getting Background Information About Your Child

Whether you are adopting through an agency either here or abroad, a birth parent, or an intermediary, try to get *as much information* about your child as you can. Don't shy away from asking questions, fearing that you might rock the boat and upset the adoption. Ask about the birth parents' names and ages, ethnic group, religion, education, occupation, personality, temperament, medical and psychiatric history, and intellectual capacity. Find out the circumstances of the birth parents prior to your child's birth (Were they married? Is the birth father known? Was the birth mother raped?) and the reasons for the relinquishment. What can you learn about the birth grandparents? What were their feelings and their involvement in the adoption decision?

Try to get as much medical information about the birth parents—and their family—as possible. While it may be awkward, ask about drinking and drug habits. (Did she ever drink during her pregnancy? Has she, or a family member, ever been in Alcoholics Anonymous?) Be aware that if you're told that "when the birth mother found out she was pregnant, she stopped drinking or taking drugs," it's also a signal that for a period of time, perhaps as many as two or three months, the birth mother *was* involved in substance abuse.

Push your worker or intermediary for any personal descriptions (e.g., "She enjoys singing"). There are also the little details in a birth parent's life that you might want to inquire about. When did the mother get her first menstrual period? Does she bite her nails? When did she cut her first tooth? When did she first talk? Has she had a weight problem? If you had a child by birth, you might have asked your parents some of these questions about yourself as you tried to think about what family traits your child has inherited. So ask your child's birth parents for him. If you're wondering how your child might look when he grows up, then requesting photographs—or meeting—can offer clues. At the very least, get a good physical description, including eyes, hair color, height, weight, body build, voice, gait, posture, and special characteristics.

If you adopt your child as a newborn, then you should have

detailed information from his very first hours. But if your child is older, whether it be two weeks old or ten years old, you'll want to know the experiences of this child from birth on, and there is a line of questioning to pursue. Was the child born in a hospital? How long was the child in the hospital? Who did the child live with after leaving the hospital? How long did the child live with them? What was the child like as a small baby? Are there pictures that can be shared? Were there other places the child lived? When? Why? With whom? Who have been the important people in this child's life? Why? If the child was separated from these people, why? Are there people who have information about this child that will be crucial to you and your family? Says adoption consultant Kay Donley, "It's important for children to understand how many places they lived until they came to live with their mom and dad."

Get the information in writing. Don't trust your memory. Take detailed notes during any meetings or telephone conversations, and be sure to save your notes. You might want to bring a tape recorder to meetings so that everything is preserved. Make sure that your worker also shares any notes she makes of her conversations with you.

If you are adopting a child from abroad, you may find the names of birth parents or other relatives on your child's documents. Be sure to keep copies of all documents for your child and that you get *full* translations of them. Keep any attorneys' letters, health reports, even medical bills that you may have been sent. And politely push your agency or intermediary for any further information they can provide; let the agency or intermediary know that you are asking for this information for your child's well-being, not because of your anxiety. It's a lot easier to get the information during the adoption process than five, ten, or fifteen years later when your child is pushing for answers to many questions.

If you are adopting a U.S. special-needs or older child, your agency should tell you the reason the child came into foster care and provide copies of your child's health history records, school records, mental health records (psychological and social evaluations), and any residential setting records. You should be informed of the number of placements the child has had, of any sexual abuse experiences the child has been a victim of, and of any unusual traumas, such as death or divorce. Get as much detail as possible about the child's experiences in foster care. What have been the foster parents' impressions of this child? Ask the worker: Is there information in this child's history that would indicate high risk for future developments that could be problematic? While you may worry that your worker will interpret your question as showing reluctance to take the child, you need to know the facts.

You'll also want to find out what possessions belong to your child. Are there photographs, mementos, toys, or other items that have traveled with him during his childhood? What about clothing? Ascertain what belongs to him—and make sure that it makes the move with him when he enters your family.

Insist on full disclosure—that all available information about your child be shared with you. Then, urges Ernesto Loperena of the New York Council on Adoptable Children, "double-check any information the agency provides. Have your own physician do a physical workup. Have your own child psychologist do an analysis." These independent evaluations may turn up other facts that could lay the groundwork for Medicaid or subsidy.

Be prepared that a child's condition may have been misdiagnosed—hence the labels attached to a child may not adequately reflect his situation. Children who are identified as retarded or as slow learners may just be reflecting the lack of stimulation that existed in their previous environment. Paula Fox describes what she learned when she took her son, identified as a slow learner and a behavior problem, for a full medical checkup:

He had a sixty percent hearing loss because of a fibrous tumor in one ear that had gone undetected in his fourteen foster homes. He was an underachiever because he couldn't hear. He's actually quite bright and taught himself to lip-read, which is why the tumor went undetected for so long.

You may also find that a worker tries to gloss over a problem or not disclose full information if she feels that it could jeopardize a child's placement. Because of the issue of confidentiality, agencies are often reluctant to reveal whether a child has been abused. Jewett, in *Adopting the Older Child,* notes:

One of our daughters came to us from a foster home that was being suddenly closed because it had been determined that the children there had been exposed to sexual abuse. Hesitant to share this information, our daughter's worker deliberately omitted mentioning the abuse to our agency or to us. This information would have made no difference in our willingness to adopt our child, but it would have saved us valuable time and lessened our concern at her seemingly unreasonable terror of men and of bedtime.[9]

For an older child Jewett suggests that prospective adoptive parents ask:[10]

- Why is this child not living with his biological parents?
- What has the child been told about his first family? What was his last contact with them?
- How old was the child when he came into care? Where has he lived? If he has lived in more than one other family, what were the reasons he moved?
- How is the child's physical and emotional health? What is his history—shots, allergies, dental care?
- How well does the child's worker know him? How long has she been assigned to him?
- How does this child feel about himself? How does he respond to other people?
- How does this child handle failure, anger, anxiety, fears, happiness, success, pain, disappointment, sadness, affection, discipline, daily routines?

- Does this child understand about adoption? About foster care?
- How has this child said good-bye to people left behind? How has this child left other families?
- How has this child said hello to new people? How has this child entered other families?
- Why was this child picked for me?

Preparing for an Infant

When Susan McGovern learned that she was pregnant, she began eight months of planning and reading about infants before her baby arrived. Closer to her due date, she and her husband took a class in prepared childbirth. Although the classes focused on the childbirth experience, the last session included a film about an infant's first three months. The instructor gave her a checklist of things to pack for the hospital and things to have at home for the new baby. Susan took a class at the hospital to prepare herself for breast-feeding. After her daughter was born, she was kept busy in the hospital with a series of classes: the feeding of infants, general child care (e.g., how to diaper a baby, how to bathe a baby), and infant development. When she took her daughter home at four days, she felt shaky but informed about her new role.

Prospective adoptive parents often find themselves less well informed and feeling adrift. Fran Elman had read some books about child care but lacked much experience. She enrolled in an infant care course at her local American Red Cross, but withdrew the first day when she found that everyone else was eight months pregnant. "Too awkward," she recalls. So, she says, "When I traveled to Chile to pick up my baby, I knew very little about babies. I'll never forget my first diapering of her—alone on an airplane, not too sure which end went where. Nor did I know how much formula she should take, how frequently to feed her, and how to burp her." Amanda Khan has another story that she likes to tell about her adoption experience: "I didn't know what a bunting or a layette was. When we were expecting Jonah, we bought newborn-sized clothing. Since he was seven weeks old when we brought him home, he outgrew it all in a week."

Recognizing that prospective adoptive parents need to be better informed, there are now special "expectant adoptive parent classes." While some programs focus more on providing hard-core information and hands-on experience, others meld together such topics as basic infant care, infant development, CPR, and choosing baby toys and baby clothes with adjustment to parenting and adoptive parenting. Observes adoptive parent Mickey Lutz, whose classes have been attended by more than 1,500 adoptive families in the northern Virginia area: "This is the first place that people think of themselves as *expectant* adoptive parents. Here, joining others in a similar situation, they feel safe. They don't worry about jinxing the process. The classes focus them on something positive and cement the adoption in their minds."

To find a class in your community, start by checking with adoptive parent or infertility support groups and adoption agencies. In some communities you'll find these specialized classes offered through continuing education programs at community colleges, Y's and other community centers, and local hospitals. If you're interested in helping to start a class, look at Carol Hallenbeck's curriculum guide, *Our Child: Preparation for Parenting in Adoption—Instructor's Guide* (available through Our Child Press, 800 Maple Glen Lane, Wayne, Pennsylvania 19087).

If you have friends with infants, spend some time with them. Volunteer to baby-sit for a day or evening so that you can get some hands-on experience. Take a look at some of the books about infant care and select a few to own. You can also write to the magazine *American Baby* (Cahners Publishing, 475 Park Avenue South, New York, New York 10016; 800-678-1208) to request a six-month complimentary subscription. Expectant and new adoptive parents are eligible for this free offer.

You might also want to explore the possibility of breast-feeding your baby. Even if your new baby is two months old, experts say that it's possible to get him to nurse. While breast-feeding will probably not satisfy your infant's total nutritional needs, it offers the chance to enrich the parent-child relationship through this special physical relationship.[11] Although women can stimulate the breast to produce some milk, most have to supplement their milk through the use of nursing supplementers such as Lact-Aid® or Supplementary Nutrition System. These bottlelike devices hang from around the mother's neck, hold the formula, and feed the infant through very fine flexible tubes. When a baby sucks at the breast, he takes the tube in addition to his mother's nipple into his mouth and gets his nourishment through the tube. If you are interested in breast-feeding, you'll want to learn as much as you can about it before your baby arrives and obtain the necessary equipment from the manufacturers. For further information, contact the lactation consultant at your local hospital and **La Leche League International** (9616 Minneapolis Avenue, Franklin Park, Illinois 60131; 312-455-7730). La Leche has pamphlets about breast-feeding an adopted infant and can put you in touch with a local leader who will work with you toward your goal.

If your baby is known to have been exposed to cocaine, alcohol, or other drugs prenatally, you'll want to do some reading about the possible effects of these substances on infants and the special needs these children may have. These infants, who are often born prematurely with low birth weights, may be irritable, startle easily, sleep poorly, have a high-pitched cry, and have difficulty feeding and sucking. For the baby who is easily overstimulated by loud noises, bright lights, and excessive manipulation, as perinatally crack-exposed infants sometimes are, swaddling in a blanket and offering a pacifier can be calming. Rocking or jiggling and singing at once can be too much, as can walkers and jumpers. Gentle rocking in an up-and-down motion is advised. Roughhouse play must also be toned down, with slow, gentle swinging through the air replacing rapid movements through space.[12] You also need to be aware of early distress signals—yawns, sneezes, hiccoughs, motor agitation, color changes, frowns, and eye aversions. If you notice these, your baby needs time out and even help in calming down. For further information and referral to local specialists, contact the **National Association for Perinatal Addiction Research and Education** (11 East Hubbard Street, Chicago, Illinois 60611; 312-329-2512).

Preparing for a Child from Abroad

As you prepare for your foreign-born child, "know your child by his culture," says Cheryl Markson, director of Friends of Children of Various Nations, a Colorado agency that has specialized in intercountry adoption. Find out about the child-care practices in his culture, and try to use them to ease him into your home. Do some reading about the country; you might also want to listen to music of the country to get an idea of how the language sounds. If you know people from his birth country, ask them what they found strange when they first came to the United States. Talk about differences in cultural patterns between the two countries. Ask about family relationships and how they differ. Ask other adoptive parents and older foreign-born adoptees about their experiences. Reports Cheri Register in *Are Those Kids Yours?*, "Soon Hee Truman remembers her surprise when her new family walked into the house with their shoes on." For Silvia Kowalski, who was twelve years old when she was adopted from Colombia, the shock came from seeing her mother undressed. "I thought she was totally disrespectful to *me.* The Hispanic culture is very private, and that was the ultimate to me."[13]

If your child has been used to physical closeness with adults, even sleeping with them at night, then he is likely to be petrified of sleeping alone in a bed or crib. Korean infants or toddlers are usually carried on their mothers' backs; if your child has been with a foster mother, carrying your child in a backpack may provide a soothing and familiar manner of locomotion.

If your child has been in an institution, then you need to learn about orphanage life. He may not have received much individual attention and may never have been alone. All his days and nights may have been spent in the company of other children. His activities there may have been so tightly regulated that he is not adept at making decisions, knowing how to use free time, or playing independently with toys. "Children are spoon-fed and dressed beyond the age in which children born into families learn these skills," note the editors of the *Report on Foreign Adoption*. "Just imagine trying to re-button 20 little smocks or clean up after the attempts of 20 children to feed themselves." Many children also will not have had anything they could call their own and therefore have no concept of personal possessions—either theirs or yours. The world of the orphanage child may have been orderly, circumscribed, and governed by rules and routines.

Your child may be fearful. If your infant has been in a foster home where no man was present, he may be scared of men. Even if he's been around men, the differences in appearance from what he's used to, including full beard, may frighten him. The physical size of adults, which may be radically different from those in his previous environment, may be upsetting. He may be scared of pets, particularly dogs, since in some cultures they are used as guards or run wild in the streets. And, of course, he will have to cope with dietary changes. You can help him by having familiar foods on hand. It's worth keeping in mind that some children from Asia and Latin America will have a lactose intolerance or sensitivity, and that infants from these areas may need soy-based formulas. This is something you should discuss with your child's doctor.

If you are adopting an older child (toddler and up), learn some basic words and phrases in your child's language so you can communicate with her in both her language and yours. While you're waiting, you might enroll in a foreign language course offered at a local college or community center or by a company like Berlitz. You could also check local public libraries, bookstores, or adoptive-parent support groups for foreign language audio- or videocassette tapes that you might obtain and listen to at home.

You might also want to line up an interpreter who can help explain things in the early weeks. One parent whose Korean-born daughters have served as translators for other adoptees says that they were able to "answer children's questions, relay parents' questions and messages, and help clear up misconceptions. One child, for instance, wanted the two boys 'visiting' her new home to go to their own house and was surprised to learn that they were her brothers."

Be sure, however, that you let your translator know exactly what you want communicated. Says Markson: "You don't want your translator to tell your child that 'you must behave or they'll send you back.' And you do want your translator to tell your child that 'it's okay to cry.' You must *educate* your interpreter."

Ask your agency and people in your parent group for help. Some agencies and parent groups offer workshops that focus on preparing. Other parents may be able to share tips with you about specific child-rearing customs that will ease your child's transition. You should also inquire whether it's possible to correspond with the foster parents caring for your child or the caretakers at the orphanage. Not only can they give you detailed information about your child's daily routines, but their correspondence—and perhaps photographs—will also help your child at a later point fit together the various pieces of his life. And, if your child is old enough to flip through it, you'll want to send a book of photographs depicting yourself, your family, and your community.

Cheri Register's *Are Those Kids Yours?: American Families with Children Adopted from Other Countries* explores how the emotional bonds between parent and child are "sealed, maintained and tested in families formed across racial and cultural boundaries." The book utilizes the author's experience as the adoptive parent of two Korean children and that of other adoptive parents and older foreign-born adoptees to discuss how families come together and deal with the questions of race and identity. The reference directory at the back of this book lists this and other books, such as Frances M. Koh's *Oriental Children in American Homes: How Do they Adjust?*, Hyun Sook Han's *Understanding My Child's Korean Origins,* and Jean Nelson-Erichsen and Heino R. Erichsen's *Gamines: How to Adopt from Latin America.* Adoptive parents have also reported that personal accounts of adoption experiences helped them prepare.

Preparing for an Older Child

As you prepare for the arrival of your child, particularly an older child, you've got to try to put yourself in his place. It is important that you keep in mind the environment that he came from and the environment he will be entering. Think about the impact that moving has had on you and on other families that you know. How might a child react to change? What can you do to ease the transition?

"Parents have to be prepared to deal with the child who should not be happy to come to their house," observed one therapist. "They're glad that these people have said that they'll be their parents, but they're not glad to be adopted."[14] For kids who have not known permanence, adoption is just another move. In fact, since adoption is described as a "forever family," a youngster may feel that he is permanently trapped. Says the therapist: "You need to be in touch with what your kid's expectations are."

How are children helped to make the move? As part of the adoption preparation process, your child may have created a "life book," which tells the story of his life through pictures, drawings, and other materials. His social worker will have used this to help him talk about his life. Children's life books, writes Claudia Jewett, may "include pictures and comments about foods that they love and hate; people that they love and hate; things that make them feel good and bad; some of the things that they are afraid of." The book will "express feelings, so that the child is less concerned about what his new parents will think of the things he considers unacceptable about himself, less fearful that his new parents wouldn't want him if they knew what he was like inside."[15]

What are some of the steps you will want to take as you get ready for your child?

Read Some Adoptive Parenting and Child Development Books

Claudia Jewett's *Adopting the Older Child* has served as a primer for adoptive parents for many years. It's a balanced, insightful book—based on case studies—that will help direct your thinking. So can her *Helping Children Cope with Separation and Loss* (Harvard, Mass.: Harvard Common Press, 1982), which deals with the child's response to grief when he loses a family member, whether through death, divorce, or separation from his birth family. You might also want to look at Jean Illsley Clarke, *Self-Esteem: A Family Affair* (San Francisco: Harper & Row, 1978), Wilfred Hamm, Thomas Morton, and Laurie Flynn's *Self-Awareness, Self-Selection and Success: A Parent Preparation Guidebook for Special Needs Adoption* (Washington, D.C.: NACAC, 1985); and Linda Dunn, ed., *Adopting Children with Special Needs: A Sequel.* Dunn's book is a collection of stories of different family experiences. The writings of Vera Fahlberg *(Helping Children When They Must Move, Attach-*

ment and Separation, Residential Treatment—A Tapestry of Many Therapies) also cover older and special-needs adoption. For a quick immersion in adoptive parenting issues, see Lois Ruskai Melina's *Raising Adopted Children* and Judith Schaffer and Christina Lindstrom's *How to Raise an Adopted Child.*

If you're interested in the child's perspective on adoption, look at Jill Krementz's *How It Feels to Be Adopted.* The children Krementz interviewed share their fears and fantasies and discuss their relationships with their adoptive parents, their siblings, and their birth parents. While some of the children were placed as infants, several were older. Maxine Rosenberg's *Growing Up Adopted* offers the insights of eight children and six adults, while John Y. Powell's *Whose Child Am I? Adults' Recollections of Being Adopted* features the memories of adults who were adopted as older children. His interviewees reflect on the strengths and perils of older-child placement. These and other books are listed in the reference directory at the back of this book.

Be sure you also do some reading about child development. You want to understand a child's behavior at the age of your future child—how he thinks, acts, feels—and the common developmental landmarks. Some of your child's behavior may be typical of his or her age group rather than a response to the move to your home.

You will also want to look at material that discusses sexual abuse in children. Bernard and Joan McNamara's series of pamphlets and books on adoption and the sexually abused child can provide you with an overview, as they discuss both the impact of sexual abuse on adopted children and offer helpful tips and information. For a quick overview, try Joan McNamara's pamphlet *Tangled Feelings* (available through the SAFE-TEAM Project on Child Sexual Abuse and Adoption, Family Resources, 1521 Foxhollow Road, Greensboro, North Carolina 27410; 919-852-5357) and the fact sheet prepared by the **National Adoption Information Clearinghouse.** For more in-depth discussions, see Joan and Bernard H. McNamara's *The SAFE-TEAM Curriculum: Preparation and Support for Families Adopting Sexually Abused Children* and *Adoption and the Sexually Abused Child,* which is an anthology of articles they edited, and *The Adoptive Family: The Healing Resource for the Sexually Abused Child* by Chrisan Hooper and Deborah H. Minshew.

Line Up Postplacement Support

Building a family is hard work. You and your child may need help initially—and in the long run. Your parent group, where you can talk with families who have adopted older children, will be an invaluable resource. You may also want to turn to a therapist for help. Insists adoption expert Barbara Tremitiere, "You can't drop these kids in cold."

Larry Jones, a parent whose four-year-old son almost started a fire in their house, describes how he and his wife floundered. "We planted our own seeds of failure," he recalls, "because we didn't understand what was going on. We'd been told that our son had a deprived background. What we found was that the things that we accept as part of our everyday life (how to eat at a table, how to interact with others, how to take a bath), he hadn't been taught." He and his wife were embarrassed to talk to their social worker about their problems—"I was scared that people would think I was a rotten father." The relationship deteriorated. "It was like drowning in molasses. You couldn't move fast enough to get out. There was no one to throw a rope."

Two and a half years after their son was placed with them, Larry and his wife relinquished their adopted son. That was in 1974. Looking back, Larry says: "Now Jamie would be no problem. In foster care [which they've done since 1974] we've had thirteen different children. We've had children who've been physically and sexually abused, children who've been physically and emotionally handicapped. We've learned a great deal about how children work and how children think. We adopted one of our foster children, a girl with spina bifida. Today I spend a good deal of time talking and sharing with others."

The **National Resource Center for Special Needs Adoption** in Michigan is designed to improve the availability and quality of adoption and postadoption services for children with special needs and their families. The center's primary focus lies in the training of agency workers and providing support services to agencies, parent groups, and other organizations, rather than helping individual families directly. It does, however, distribute resource material, and staff members can refer you to agencies, therapists, and other mental health professionals in your community with an expertise in adoption. You'll also want to check with the **National Adoption Center** in Pennsylvania and the **National Adoption Information Clearinghouse** in Rockville, Maryland.

Observe Other Children

If you have never parented an older child, observe children about the age of your expected child to familiarize yourself with their interests and behavior. Perhaps you could volunteer at your local school, community center, or scout troop.

If you are adopting a child who is developmentally delayed or physically challenged, you'll want to get to know children of the same age who present similar challenges. By locating the local foundation or organization that works with these children, you can attend functions where you can observe the children and talk with their parents about their experiences.

If Possible, Visit with Your Child

When an agency places an older U.S. child, the prospective parents and the child may meet, perhaps a few times or over an extended period of time, before the child moves. First visits might revolve around outings to a park, zoo, or other neutral surrounding. It's helpful to visit your child at his foster home, where he may feel more at ease and where you can observe his environment and have the chance to talk with his foster parents. Children may also spend time in your home, including weekend sleepovers.

There is no prescribed way or specific length of time that visiting will take place before the child is placed in your home. The circumstances vary with the individual child. Don't feel pressured to assent to a child's move to your home until you feel you're ready. (You'll have to ask yourself: How do I know that *I'm* ready?) Take the time you and your child need.

Think About How Your Household Operates

If this will be your first child or your first older child, consider your household and the rules that you will want observed. When is bedtime? What about homework? What about television? What household chores will he be asked to perform? Keep in mind that your child's understanding of tasks may be different than yours. You'll need to give clear messages about your expectations. When you tell a child to "clean your room," you may mean that you expect him to pick up the trash from the floor and make his bed. In your child's previous home that may have meant to wash down the walls.

Visit the School Where Your Child Will Be Going and Talk with the Staff

Since school will play an important role in your child's life, you should begin working with the school before his arrival. What is your child's educational background? Will the child attend your neighborhood school, or do you need to look further? Does the school you are considering offer special services that you can tap? Do you anticipate that your child will need an after-school tutor to provide additional support?

Try to visit the school to see what it is like. Can you meet with the principal and the guidance counselor to learn about the school and to acquaint them with your child's situation? Is there a special education coordinator or an English as a second language (ESL) teacher whom you should meet? Keep in mind that under U.S. Public Law 94-142, all children with handicapping conditions, including mental, physical, sensory, emotional, or speech and language difficulties, are entitled to a free appropriate public education. The school system must provide it or alternatively pay an external agency for services.

What can you learn about the teachers at the appropriate grade? Can you observe them in their classrooms? Have you talked with some parents with children in the school to learn about their experiences? From the staff and parents, find out how you can have some input into your child's classroom placement.

When you share background information about your child with the staff, make it clear to them this is for their eyes only and must be treated as a professional confidence. If your child has been sexually abused, you'll want to share this, although you don't need to go into the details. Imagine what could happen to your family if you didn't disclose this information, and your child were to say "My daddy sleeps with me." She's referring to the dad she left behind, but school personnel, knowing nothing about her past, will assume she's describing the present.

Prepare a Book of Photographs That Features Your Family, Your Home, and Your Neighborhood

All children appreciate photographs to look at, but this is particularly important if your child will be coming from abroad or if you will be unable to visit. Sending photos and letters before your child enters your home gives him an introduction to you and helps to familiarize him with his new surroundings. He can thumb through them as much as he wants, just as you are probably looking at his photograph and spinning dreams based on it. Your book might say: "This is the mom in the family. She likes to do X, Y, and Z. She likes a child who does X, Y, and Z. Here is the dinner table, and here is where you will sit." Says Claudia Jewett Jarratt, "Kids look at these books and try to find a place for themselves in the family." For foreign-born children, you'll also want to include photographs of things that might be "strange" to them: the car seat, the four-poster bed, stairs, the bathtub, snow on the ground. Reports one adoptive mother, "Seat belts horrified my older kids."

If several weeks or months will elapse before your child arrives, you will want to continue the contact, just as your agency is probably sending you updates. If you are adopting a toddler or young child, ask your agency if you can send a toy or other item that he can bring with him as a transitional object.

Fashion a Cover Story for Your Child and Yourself

From your child's first day in your home, he and you will be asked by playmates, neighbors, friends, teachers, and others in your community about himself and his past history. Rather than have him and you flounder, or even betray personal information that should not be shared, you'll want to prepare a "cover story," a bland, all-purpose summary that is offered to the world.

You'll want to imagine the potential questions—"Where did you come from?" or "Why couldn't you live with your parents?" or "Tell me what you *know* about him"—and review the appropriate information that can be shared. It's helpful to make a list of the likely questions, who might ask them, and the possible situations where they will come up (e.g., introducing your child to a neighbor, the first day of school, meeting new relatives). Then prepare some simple responses: "My name is John Doe. I used to live in Miami, but I'm living here now because my family had problems. I'm being adopted because I couldn't live with my other family anymore." Finally, role-play the questions and answers. You'll also want to teach your child how to deflect people's questions: "So, where are *you* from?" "I'm sorry, but you'll have to ask my mom that question." Says Kay Donley, "Every child entering a new living situation needs this preparation."

Adopting older children is very complex, and I've just sketched out a few of the many issues. Adoption experts believe that successful adoptions are more likely to occur when parents and children are realistically prepared. Do your homework.

Naming Your Child

Bestowing a name on a child is one of the fundamental ways parents claim children as theirs. For adoptive parents, however, the matter of naming a child can be problematic. If they've had a relationship with the birth mother, as is the case with so many infant adoptions today, should she have a say in naming the child? If so, what? "Jennifer, Jane, and I each shared several ideas before we collectively settled on Aaron Alex," reports Carl Tonn in *Adoption Without Fear*. "The naming process symbolized our determination to work together in Aaron's behalf." The adoptive parents of David Christopher Thomas gave him his first name, but it was his birth mother Chris who chose Christopher, saying that she wanted to leave him a part of herself.[16]

If you're involved in an open adoption, you'll want to work out an arrangement with the birth parents that is comfortable for all of you (for a further discussion, see Chapter 5). Nothing could be worse for your child than the situation that arose in the Baby M surrogacy case, where Mary Beth Whitehead insisted on calling her daughter Sara, while Bill and Betsy Stern used the name Melissa.

What do you do if your child already has a name by which he's identified and that he recognizes? Mused one parent:

When my son arrived from India at age three-and-a-half, he was wearing what was probably his first pair of shoes—used, too small, and with no socks they were rubbing his toes raw. But he would not give them up. Only through much hand waving could I convince him that the removal of his shoes was temporary, and only then did he part with them in order to take a bath. They had to be returned to his feet immediately following—over the sleepers with the built-in feet—and then into bed with him. How little and simple were his possessions! The other item he was attached to was the bag (you know, the one on the airplane for emergency use) he was carrying with two pennies in it. His shoes, the bag, and pennies, and, yes, his name, were his only possessions—his security. And I wanted to change his name. The shoes he gave up for brand new ones. The bag was eventually set down and lost in the shuffle. But the name? Something he had for three-and-a-half-years? How would I? How could I take that?[17]

By the time children are school-age, most parents realize that a name change would be hard—that names are very much tied up with a child's sense of self. Keep in mind that children, even before their first birthday, know their first names and respond to them. What type of confusion will occur if you change the name? Observes Lois Melina: "A preschooler may have a partic-ularly difficult time adjusting to a new first name. A young child's identity is so closely tied to her first name that changing it during the preschool years can cause a child to think she is not really the same person, or that one name goes with being a good person and one name with being a bad person. A name change can make it more difficult for the child to integrate her past life into her present."[18] Cautions Dr. Vera Fahlberg, who has written extensively about children and attachment, "Adopted children have enough issues to deal with without having to understand what it means to have their names changed."[19]

You, as a parent, may feel strongly the need to give your child a name that you—rather than a birth parent, a social worker, or someone else—chose. After all, you've waited for the day when you could confer a name upon *your* child. You may feel that it helps build attachments. Your family may have a naming tradition. You will have to weigh your needs with your child's.

You may want to consider renaming a child, however, if there is already a child in the family with that name. Parents of foreign-born children sometimes change their child's name when it is difficult to say or spell, retaining the child's original first or last name as a middle name. Rachel and David Abrams changed the name of their Colombian infant from Jesus to Joshua, because, says Rachel, "We are Jewish and he would have had difficulty being accepted in a Jewish community today with that name." If your child has an unusual name—one that might lead to teasing or ridicule from his peers—he might welcome a nickname or an additional middle name that he might choose to use at a later point.

If you do decide to change your child's name, then consider picking a name that's similar to the original. You'll also want to ease your child into the name change gradually, using the new name as well as his original given name in conversation.

You will probably want to call your child by your family last name from the day that he is placed in your house. (While it's not unusual for mothers and fathers to have different last names today, their children usually carry their joint last names or one of the parents' surnames as their surnames.) You may have to battle with your child's school, however, to recognize this name change before the adoption is finalized. Adoptive parent Gloria Peterson brings the point home most vividly: "One of our children was not riding the school bus for weeks. I was at work when our son arrived home on foot and was unaware of the situation. When it was discovered, the answer was that his bus pass was in his old name and he simply refused to show it to anyone and so he walked."[20]

Even here, however, there are two sides. One therapist has pointed out that youngsters who have bounced around from one situation to another have one thing that traveled with them—their name. Their reaction to adoption may be: "And now you even have to give up your last name."[21]

Preparing Family and Friends

If you have older children, you began preparing them at the time of the home study. You've talked about adoption and the type of child you're hoping to adopt. If you are adopting an infant, then you'll need to help your children understand what infants are like. A young child will have to learn to share his parents and toys.

If you are adopting an older child, make your children aware that the new sibling may seem less than overjoyed at joining their family. Indicate that there are likely to be rocky times ahead and that the new child's behavior may be different from what they expect. They should realize that the child may hoard, hit, or act like he doesn't like them. Says Cheryl Markson: "Prepare the siblings for the worst, just as if you were bringing home a new baby and wanted to educate your child in advance." There are also some children's novels that focus on the foster care experience and the feelings of children moving to a new home. These books are listed in the reference directory at the back. Your children might want to read one of them before their new sibling arrives. Keep in mind that your children will be faced with a difficult transition. They may be resentful and jealous and feel that the new sibling is receiving preferential treatment.

If you are traveling abroad to pick up your child, you may want to bring your other children along with you. The trip will give them a chance to see their sibling's birth country and to forge their own special bonds. "When the orphanage directress went to get the baby, she took our three-year-old son with her," recalls Lisa Slovinsky. "To this day Michael still remembers that he was the first one to see his brother." Lisa also feels that the trip "helped give Michael a perspective" and "now he writes letters to the orphanage when I do."

Adoptive grandparents also need preparation and a chance to vent their feelings. Even the most eager grandparents-to-be, like prospective adoptive parents, have their own grieving to do over the lost biological grandchild. "I was disappointed to a degree that my son and his wife didn't have their natural child," admits Jerry, whose son Tom and daughter-in-law Kathy adopted a newborn independently. "But the adoption was to be a fact, and I was very much in favor of it." Mary, whose son adopted two school-age children from Chile, admits that she felt a tinge of regret that the family's bloodline would not be carried on: "But it wasn't a big point. If you can't have the next generation one way, you're very happy that you can have it another."[22]

Prospective grandparents also have to deal with their own lack of knowledge about adoption and their particular prejudices. Learning about Kathy and Tom's plans to advertise for a baby, her father Ed's reaction was, "What is this? You put an ad in the newspaper? What about the kooks?" Ed also admits to having "reservations about the child's medical history. I worried about AIDS, that maybe the mother didn't know who the father was, and everything else that can affect the baby's health."

There are other feelings that grandparents-to-be may leave unspoken to their children. After Tom and Kathy started speaking with a pregnant woman about an independent adoption, the prospective grandparents feared that the adoption might fall through. "That was the hardest part," recalls Tom's mother Jean. "I worried that the mother would change her mind, which would break Kathy's and Tom's heart." Kathy's mother Pam found the days just after the baby's birth particularly trying: "Tom and Kathy were so many miles away, living in a hotel with a brand-new baby. It was scary." A possible open adoption makes grandmother Shirley nervous: One fell through when the birth mother reclaimed the baby after several months. She knows that this is rare, but says "it was like a death in the family, and I don't want this to happen to my daughter again."

Lois Melina, in her books *Raising Adopted Children* and *Making Sense of Adoption,* offers some helpful suggestions for preparing the extended family. She recommends introducing the idea of adoption gradually, rather than springing it on them, and being sure to provide ways for the family to get information. You might, for example, invite prospective grandparents, aunts, or uncles to join you at a meeting of an adoptive parents group, give them a subscription to an adoption newsletter, or arrange for them to talk with experienced adoptive grandparents by telephone. Perhaps your local adoptive parent group could hold a special workshop or panel discussion for adoptive grandparents. Just how critical that can be was underscored by one prospective grandparent, who announced at a workshop of the Adoptive Parents Committee in New York: "I've been so in the dark. This is the first time my daughter has shared with me her adoption plans."

Family and friends will also welcome some reading material. You could give them Pat Holmes's *Supporting an Adoption* (available from Our Child Press), which gives a quick run-through of the adoption process and postplacement, or Linda Bothun's *When Friends Ask About Adoption* (available through Adoptive Families of America), a question-and-answer booklet designed to help parents of nonadopted children answer their questions.

If you are still coming to terms with your infertility, take a look at Linda Salzer's *Surviving Infertility* and Gay Becker's *Healing the Infertile Family.* You might also find helpful Pat Johnston's *Understanding: A Guide to Impaired Fertility for Family and Friends* (Fort Wayne, Indiana: Perspectives Press, 1983). As you prepare everyone for the adoption, however, think carefully about revealing to others the background information that you have about your child—this is information for you and your child (for a full discussion, see Chapter 12). As you enthusiastically share details about the adoption process, exercise some caution. Ask yourself: What facts are "private" and belong to just my child and I?

PREPARING FOR YOUR CHILD

It is to be hoped that the family member or friend who worried about "not knowing what you'll get" or perhaps expressed concern about "diseased children from abroad" when initially talking about adoption later changes his mind. Counsels Melina: "Forgive relatives for any insensitive remarks they made while they got used to the idea of adoption. Adoptive parents forget that there was a time when they, too, may have had doubts about adoption, told racist jokes, or thought there was no choice but to conceive a child."[23] The day may come when you'll get a letter saying: "We are counting the days when we will come to you and hold the darling in our arms. We keep looking at the picture all the time."

11

Adjustments

What's it like to become a parent through adoption? In our society, with its emphasis on the early bonding of parents and infants—via birthing rooms, soft music, and nonviolent births—adoptive parents are often reluctant to discuss what they felt when their families were formed. They will acknowledge that the process is different, but how it differs and how they worked at forming a family are often very private topics. People who have adopted older children may be more open about acknowledging that they didn't feel instant love and that the bonds between parents and child will have to grow over time. Families with newly adopted infants or toddlers may be less open about how they felt in those early weeks or months.

The outsider is often left to believe that "love" and "rapport" magically occurred. Perhaps you've even heard an adoptive parent say, "Everything has been golden." Or you've seen a television report on intercountry adoption that featured an airport lounge festooned with banners and balloons and smiling adoptive parents cooing over their newly arrived babies. This is the silk from which adoption mythology is spun.

But there are other tales to be told, where things do not go as well as expected:

I was ready to pack our bags and leave. That was my first reaction to the baby we had traveled so far to adopt. Here we were in Santiago, Chile, tired, anxious, no sleep in two days, and faced with a screaming, sweaty, red-in-the-face, quite unpleasant, almost 7-month-old little boy. The only thing that prevented me from leaving was having to face friends and relatives upon our return home.

The weeks before our trip were filled with excitement. There was furniture to buy, wallpaper to hang, curtains to sew. I made tons of stuffed animals, interviewed doctors, and bit my nails. I also spent many hours drooling over the pictures.

Throughout this time people continually asked, "Aren't you nervous?" My answer was, "Well, a little," but in truth, I felt pretty calm. I only fell apart when we were introduced to our son—a tired, screaming, ugly baby.

I was unprepared for negative feelings towards the baby we longed for. I had spent two years reading wonderful stories in adoption newsletters about parents meeting their children for the first time. Perhaps some of these stories did describe negative encounters, but I must have selectively ignored them. Nobody wrote about wanting to leave the kid behind, or wanting to throw up!

Needless to say, my trip to Santiago was not very enjoyable. I saw no sights, unfortunately for our son bought no souvenirs, got no sleep and easily lost five to seven pounds in four days. The plane trip home, though uneventful for the baby, was a very anxious time for me. I was only able to relax when we landed in Miami.[1]

In the weeks that followed, as the baby drank his bottle, played with his toys, and smiled at his new parents, the "happy, smiley and full of fun" baby that this mother had fantasized about emerged, and the bond between parent and child developed. "I'm *so* glad that I didn't pack and leave without him," she finally enthused.

But the story she tells—of an adoptive parent facing a scene quite unlike any she'd imagined, of experiencing negative feelings toward her new child, of wanting to bail out—is one that must be confronted. This chapter looks at how parents and children experience the coming together into an adoptive family. For adoptions, like marriages, need time for the ties to cement, and the transition can be difficult and stressful.

Coming Together

Parents awaiting the birth of a baby often fantasize about their child-to-be, talk with family and friends about their impending parenthood, and engage in nesting behaviors such as preparing their infant's room and buying clothes. When the baby arrives, there's a flurry of activity, with grandparents, siblings, and friends dropping in to offer congratulations and support.

For adoptive parents the experience may be quite different. While Chapter 10 discusses the preparations prospective adoptive parents can make, many do much less. Before their child's arrival, not knowing when, where, or whether the adoption will occur, adoptive parents may be reluctant to plan and fantasize. "It's hard to picture nothing in your mind," observed Kate Burch about her difficulty in imagining the Chilean siblings that she hoped to adopt. "Maybe they'd be two girls, maybe two boys, maybe the children would be five and six, maybe eight and ten. We just didn't have any idea, and we couldn't imagine anything." Parents involved in an independent adoption may avoid dreaming at all, fearing that the placement might fall through. Recalls one mother who adopted independently, "Part of me wanted to be really excited and part of me wanted to hold back." Expectant adoptive parents may also delay sharing their adoption plans with family and friends, and when they do, they may receive less than wholehearted support. Observes psychologist David Brodzinsky, "Unlike nonadoptive parents, whose parental status is warmly welcomed by all, adoptive parents frequently must justify to others why they have made their particular decision."[2] Lacking also are traditional rituals, such as baby showers, to celebrate the impending arrival. Familiar steps of validation and attachment that families follow before a child's arrival are thus absent or short-circuited in adoptive families.

When the child finally arrives, the circumstances of the child's entry into the family are often less than idyllic. Linda's daughter arrived from South Korea the day after her husband returned from a week-long hospitalization. After waiting for three months, they were notified on a Tuesday that the baby would be brought to the United States on Saturday. "The timing was terrible; the baby wasn't well, wouldn't sleep, and cried every time my husband tried to touch her," recalls Linda. For Betty, a single mother who traveled to South America to pick up her daughter, it is the airport scene on her return that sticks out in her mind: "We entered the country covered with shit. She had diarrhea. At the airport, all I wanted to do was get out of there, go with my parents, go to a hotel room and take off my clothes. I didn't want to stand around an airport and celebrate. I needed to get to a private place." And for Carol, whose daughter arrived from South Korea when she was fifteen months old, it was the first night at home: "She was very weak and had pneumonia, impetigo, scabies, and herpes in her mouth and in her throat. She couldn't even crawl. The first night she had to be held in my lap the whole time. We were shocked."

How these children looked and reacted to their new surroundings must surely have influenced these mothers' feelings. It can be hard to fall in love instantly with a child who is smelly, weak, covered with sores, and generally unappealing. Illness can have a dual effect: It fosters togetherness between parent and child, but it also creates strain because of the demands and the worries put on the parents. An anxious stay in a foreign country, where the parent or parents are alone, without supports, coping with a new culture and the intricacies of a foreign legal system, not to mention the rigors of the journey itself, may also increase the stress of the initial adjustment.

Barbara Berg's account of the adoption of her newborn daughter in *Nothing to Cry About* gives us a sense of the equally difficult conditions under which independent placements can occur. Berg and her husband learned about the possibility of adopting their daughter Alison at the moment of her birth and just a few days later flew out to California to pick her up. It was to be a joyous occasion, and in her book Berg tells us about her strong and immediate feelings of attachment. We also know about her own lack of preparation. We have a sense of the stress of the time and the place—caring for their daughter in a hotel room, waiting impatiently for papers to be processed in New York so that they can return home. She writes:

> All of a sudden I felt very insecure. I was three thousand miles away from home, in a city where I hardly knew a soul. No doctor, no refrigerator, no way of sterilizing with a newborn baby totally dependent upon me. For the first time since Alison was born, I worried about how well I'd manage. Other women "in waiting" worried about how well they'd cope with formula and schedules and croup. I hadn't. I had only worried about whether or not I'd have anyone to worry about. Now that I did, I worried about what everyone else worried about.[3]

As the child moves into the family, parent and child interact. Now is the time for the new parents to get acquainted with their child, to love, cherish, and nurture their new son or daughter. Yet newly adopted children may not want the closeness that the parent offers. Christine describes her first months with her eighteen-month-old daughter: "I was not prepared for the anger. She wasn't able to accept comforting for four months. She'd wake up at night and be frightened. I'd pick her up and she'd stiffen and I'd have to wait until she'd worn herself out crying."

This behavior puts a distance between parent and child and can form a part of the bonding process as it goes on. For many parents, closeness and distancing interplay—the parents wanting to make the attachment; the stress of the new parenting role and the child's actions making it difficult and exhausting. The adoptive mother of two Korean sisters, ages two and four, tells this story about the first few months:

Sleeping: What's that? Why is Kendra inconsolably sobbing NIK-O-YAH for three hours? A call to our Korean friend at 11 P.M. fails to resolve this tiny question. Oh, she wants to sleep with her little picture book we had sent to her in Korea. How could we be so stupid? But, at least Kendra, aged four, liked to sleep. With Lisa, aged two, nothing worked. She screamed, raged, rolled all over until one night, in desperation, I spanked her legs. INSTANT silence. So, that's what they must do in Korea. Well, it may work for a few nights but forget it. One night, we let her follow me around the house. I walked in a circle for 45 minutes from 10 o'clock to nearly 11. Was she tired? Of course not.[4]

This mother's tale raises another basic issue in adoptive parenthood. How does it feel to take on the instant role of mother or father? Despite having read all the parenting books you could find, you are now confronted with your child—not the hypothetical child—whose habits, likes, and dislikes you barely know.

All parents must come to terms with their child. The parents of newborns can follow some basic advice: If the baby's wet, change him; if he's hungry, feed him. Parents who adopt non-newborns may grope around for other answers. One adoptive mother describes how it felt to take on her new role:

He was two years old when he arrived from South Korea. The day after he came, we were in a restaurant. I got ready to order breakfast for my two kids—Carol, my two-year-old birth daughter, and John, my new son. I knew what to order for Carol, but I had no idea what to order for him. I felt terribly inadequate. Since he spoke Korean, there was no way to communicate with him. Because I had become his "mother," I felt that there was something inborn that I should have had, but I didn't have it.

Mothers of infants can have these same feelings. "When I started to talk with other mothers about my son," says Paula, "I felt terribly unsure of myself. My son and I had a lot to learn about each other."

The First Days

The questions always come up: When you bring your child to
your house, who should be with you? Should you celebrate?
Should you take your child around to meet family, neighbors,
and friends immediately? Or should you stay at home for a
while just to acclimate yourselves?

This is a time of transition. Your family may profit from some
private time. If you are adopting an infant and feel that you'd
like a more experienced hand around, such as a grandparent,
then go ahead. But an older child may appreciate the time to
become acquainted with you and your house before being
asked to relate to the larger family network or to the neighbors.
There is, after all, a lifetime ahead.

People should understand that this is a time when you may
need to be alone. While your child is settling in, you may not
want to feel obliged to entertain company.

Postadoption Stress

Before Adam came I had read everything I could get my hands on
about cerebral palsy. I was prepared for his not walking and his
speech difficulties. However, reading about a disability and living
with a child on a daily basis who has that disability are two different
things. All of a sudden I was overwhelmed with it all—not overwhelmed with joy and happiness; instead I was overwhelmed with
fear and guilt and tremendous feelings of failure. The last thing in
the world I felt like celebrating was "Mother's Day" when I was
feeling so inadequate as a mother (or anything else for that matter).[5]

That's not the way it's supposed to be. Or is it? Most people
have heard about postpartum depression, but postadoption
blues? You're feeling depressed, irritable, fatigued, tense,
inadequate, and overwhelmed. Everything seems up in the air,
in turmoil. And why not?

Your family is changing. It's disorganized. New relationships are being established. The waiting and the tension surrounding the wait are gone. Now you wonder when things will ever settle back to normal. But what is normal? Not the way it used to be. A new family constellation is emerging, but you don't yet know how it will work. You're unsure of yourself and your child.

The family has to set up new routines and find ways to establish authority and control. Your new child keeps "testing" you to see how things work in your home. He's got to figure out how the hours and days are organized in your family, what's off limits and what's not, who disciplines, who nurtures, and which of his actions will be punished. Your other children are jealous of the new sibling and act up, testing to see where they fit into the new scheme of things. Life is exhausting.

If you experience feelings of incompetence, don't let them get you down or cause embarrassment. Try to view these feelings as simply a sign that you've got learning to do: While you can prepare in advance for a child in some ways, most of the learning process really begins when your child is in your home.

If you've adopted an infant, you may find that holding your new baby suddenly makes you confront, once again, your infertility and your feelings of biological loss. You may think about the birth child you never had and how life might have been different. If you've lost a child, as one mother did when an independent adoption fell through, your new baby could trigger feelings about that other child. Recalled Janet: "Getting Caroline has brought Michael to the front of my mind. I wonder where he is now."

Recognize what is happening. Seek out supports. Be sure to leave some time for yourself. Do what you feel you can; leave what can wait until tomorrow.

Children Talk About Their Feelings

In *Mothers and Their Adopted Children—The Bonding Process,* Dorothy W. Smith and Laurie Nehls Sherwen asked thirty-three older children about their bonding experiences. They found that many of the children had not fantasized about their mothers in advance. Several of the Asian children, however, had fantasized that their mothers would look like them. Said one: "I felt sad. She was not my Korean mommy."[6] They then had to cope with the gap between their fantasy and the reality of their parents' appearance.

The happiness that parents often feel on a child's arrival was not shared by many of the children. They reported feeling scared, shy, mad, sad, and strange: "I cried all night."[7] Armando Jordan, who was separated from his mother in Colombia when he was nine years old and later placed with an American couple, told Cheri Register: "I asked them how far away I was from home, and they told me it was miles and miles and miles away and it was over the ocean. I yelled out, 'Why did you let them do that to me?' "[8]

For some children there is the fear instead that the long-awaited adoption might fall through. "I guess the hardest thing for me in the first year was when I had to go back to the agency for follow-up visits," Melinda confides in *How It Feels to Be Adopted*. "I was always terrified that I would see my other mother there and she would want to take me home with her again. That's because when I was in foster care we had monthly visits—my mother and I—in the playroom at the agency."[9] Renee, who by age eight and a half had lived in eight different foster families in just three and a half years, expresses similar concerns in *Growing Up Adopted*: "When I first came to Mommy's house, I felt sure she would also give me up like the other families I had stayed with. When I told her this, she said to me, 'This family is it!' Deep down I'm starting to believe her. . . . Once we sign the adoption papers, I'll feel better."[10]

Even Infants Have Adjustments to Make

> When I held my nine-month-old daughter for the first time at the agency, she burst into tears and wouldn't let me hold her. She stopped crying when her foster mother picked her up.
>
> For our next visit, her foster mother brought her to our house. She didn't want to be held. She let herself be on the floor. She still cried almost the whole time.
>
> So for the next visit to our house, her ten-year-old foster sister brought her. She still cried every time I picked her up.

Amanda reacted just as you would expect an infant to react to strangers. She cried. But these strangers were her new adoptive parents. After placement she did form a strong attachment to her new mother. In fact, for the next two years she had major difficulty separating from her mother, and she slept fitfully, frequently tossing and turning, crying in her sleep, waking up and wanting to be held. "We did not sleep through the night," reported JoAnn, "until she was past two." Her pediatrician suggested it might be teething. When her teeth came in, he gave the explanation that many one-year-olds had trouble sleeping. JoAnn feels, however, that Amanda was grieving for her foster mother.

Consider the experiences of the parents of Jane, who was born in South Korea and joined her new family when she was four months old:

> At first her parents were delighted that she did not cry or appear frightened. They became concerned, however, when she failed to respond to them or to anything around her. She neither laughed nor cried for several weeks. Alert and watchful, she indicated awareness by stiffening up when she was moved or spoken to. After about two months she smiled at her brother, Joe, then two years old. Shortly thereafter she began to respond to her mother, but it was about a year before she responded to her father. This withdrawal and isolation concerned and frustrated her parents and caused tensions between them.[11]

Her mother feels that the disruption in her care—and the need to adjust to new patterns of child care—caused deep feelings of insecurity which continued for several years. She feels that she underestimated the adjustment needs of her daughter "because of the myth of the adaptability of infants." She had expected her baby "to be happy and to trust" her. Instead, her first year was "unsettled and difficult."

The burgeoning field of infant studies is revealing that infants perceive a lot at very young ages. Works such as T. Berry Brazelton's *Infants and Mothers: Differences in Development; The First Twelve Months of Life,* edited by Frank Caplan; and Stanley I. Greenspan and Nancy Thorndike Greenspan's *First Feelings: Milestones in the Emotional Development of Your Baby and Child* chronicle the stages of infant development. We learn how infants develop a sense of their identity separate from that of their parents, and along with that, fears of strangers and separation; how, as they develop physically, they explore their environment but periodically come back to their caretaker for nurturance and support. "A parent should expect rejection or withdrawal as part of the infant's adjustment to the new situation," says Brazelton.[12] The adjustment period may stretch for "weeks or months."

Adopted infants can be expected to grieve. They have suffered a major dislocation in their lives. They have left behind familiar sights, sounds, smells, and people, as well as established sleeping and eating patterns. They cannot verbalize their feelings but they can vocalize them and act them out. They may cry; they may withdraw; they may refuse to smile. Glum infants who sleep almost all the time, who wake up for short periods to eat and play, and who never really laugh and smile are in mourning for the life they left behind. They are reacting normally to the changes that are going on in their lives. As a parent you will need to help them work through their grieving.

Adjustments and the Foreign-Born Adoptee

Foreign-born children must cope with moving from one country and one culture to another. Asian children travel through many time zones to get to their new homes and may have sleeping problems because, for them, days and nights are reversed. The child's schedule may straighten out in a week, but his sleep may remain troubled. Infants who have been carried on adults' backs may have a tendency to catnap rather than to lie down to nap as American babies do. If the child has been malnourished, then food and eating may be very important. Recalls one mother:

> There was a period of time after he came from South Korea when our two-year-old son would wake up at night and hold his stomach and talk about the ghost in his stomach. He also typically hid food. We'd find rotten oranges around the house. And he guarded his food. We'd had him for a couple of months when one night he dove onto the table to prevent us from taking his plate away. Kind of a flashback. Talk about two grown-ups dancing around the kitchen showing him that there was food all over.

This child's preoccupation with food lasted many years, and seven years later, his mother was still careful to pack a snack whenever he went out.

Children may cling to one parent and reject the other. Often the parent who traveled abroad to pick up the child will be the person to whom the attachment is formed. But the opposite may also take place: A child whose first contact was with the adoptive mother might choose, nevertheless, to attach to the father, because of the painful memory of the loss of the birth or foster mother. One parent is then left in the "odd man out" position, while the other is the round-the-clock caretaker. Either way, it hurts, exhausts, and causes tension.

If your child grew up in an orphanage, he may have difficulty making decisions, recognizing his feelings, and showing emotions. Observes adoptive parent Barbara Holtan: "Knowing pleasure from pain, knowing sensation, and knowing how to make a choice, are acquired, learned. . . . Gazing at that tall, lanky eleven-year-old and realizing that he needs to master two-year-old skills is difficult for us. For the orphanage child, these attributes may not only have been untaught but positively frowned upon."[13] Holtan's son, Seth, who came from an or-phanage at age seven, had to be helped to distinguish what was "fun" and what was not. Recounts Holtan:

> Every night at dinner time, each of us was expected to tell three good things that had happened to him or her that day. When it was his turn, Seth was silent for many nights running. He truly had no idea how to separate the good from the not-so-good. Gradually as we identified things ranging from "Amy gave me two stickers at school" to "I made a base hit at baseball practice," Seth began to make the connection that life has categories.
>
> The kaleidoscope of life began to take form, to show patterns for him. When, at last, at his turn he mumbled, "I liked lunch today," we were jubilant. We did the same things for the bad things that had happened and decisions we had made during the day.[14]

Cheryl Markson of the Denver adoption agency Friends of Children of Various Nations points out that the foreign-born child may also communicate more in physical terms. Since lan-guage creates a barrier, the child will have to show you through his actions how he feels. One older child tried to run away several times in the first days after he arrived from South Korea—a graphic statement about how unhappy he felt.

The Adjustment of the Older Child

In 1974 Laurie Flynn and her husband adopted two teenag-ers, ages fourteen and twelve. The teenagers came with a his-tory of many foster homes and needed love and security. Writ-ing about her experiences in an article entitled "Why Would Anyone Adopt a Teenager?" Flynn notes: "We knew they would resist much closeness for quite a while. After all, they had no reason to trust adults. The traditional concept of family held little meaning to them."[15]

During the next few years, her son experimented with drugs and alcohol, ran away from home repeatedly, and was arrested for theft and vandalism. He was eventually ordered by the juvenile court to a residential treatment facility. Her daughter also had a difficult time adjusting to the family. "Sometimes she withdrew," writes Flynn, "and wouldn't speak to us for days at a time." Flynn balances her description by saying that they also had many "great times"—taking their son to his first real restaurant, throwing the first party for their daughter, having family picnics and camping trips. Affection did develop and "once in a while, they would open up a little and share some of their deepest feelings. And slowly and gradually, trust and caring grew between us."

The "adoption of the older child is a lot like marriage," Flynn writes. "If we are lucky, maybe the child will choose to change. But the changes belong to him, not to us. What matters most is that he have the chance to learn and grow through what we have to offer. To be effective parents, we must learn to accept risks and approach them as challenges. That essentially is how we made it with our teenagers."

Children who move into adoptive families need to work through their experience of separation. Whether they are separated from their foster parents, birth parents, or a caretaker in an orphanage, they will have to come to terms with what has happened to them before they can fully make new attachments. They will need help to open up, to talk about and share their feelings. The process of recovery from the separation, and then forging new links, will be gradual and can take years.

Experts liken the child's grieving and attachment process to the experience that we have when a loved one dies.[16] The adjustment process may begin with an attempt to deny that this has happened. Or it may start with what is called the "honeymoon" period. The child and the parents are on their best behavior. Things are calm. This is the time when parents are likely to report that the child made a rapid adjustment into the family.

However, the calm is deceptive. You might compare it to your response to an extended vacation. At some point the exhilaration wears off. You feel frightened, overwhelmed, tired. You say to yourself: "I want to be where I can relax, where I can understand my world." You long for the familiar. In the child you may begin to see two responses: withdrawal and rage. These are normal reactions to a new situation.

Be it two weeks or two months after the child enters the home, the "testing" period will begin. The child will show his anger, often violently, and stop being obedient. He will exhibit a range of behaviors, both good and bad, and see how the parents react and deal with the behavior. It is not uncommon for children to have behavioral problems, acting out through temper tantrums, running away, stealing, lying, or setting fires. The children are testing you, seeing how much you will tolerate before you will throw up your hands and say "Enough!" as others have done in the past, and throw them out. During this "testing time" the children are trying to fit themselves into the family, figuring out what the rules and routines in the household are and how they affect them. They need to learn what you expect of them, to be told that "hitting your brother is unacceptable" and "running away from home is not how we solve problems."

Children will also regress. Their behavior will tell you, "I need attention; I am insatiable." They may have eating and sleeping problems. They may wet the bed or soil themselves. They may have difficulty separating and will have fears. Bedtime may be particularly trying.

Adoptive parents often report that their children want to go through the stages of their childhood that they may have missed. One parent reports: "When I put my eight-year-old daughter to sleep at night, she wanted to try to nurse on my lap. She needed to sit on my lap and cuddle. She needed this so badly."

According to Claudia Jewett, an older child entering a family can act several different ages at one time. Parents may find it difficult to respond to the child because they may not recognize what age a child is being at any given moment. She writes: "It's almost as if your kid has to crawl back into the womb and act through all of the time that you haven't shared together. So if you get an eight year old, he's going to go through parts of being 1, 2, 3, 4, 5, 6, and 7 with you." The child may act like a four-year-old for one week, for example—but, writes Jewett, "you're going to have that week, if that's what it takes him."[17]

Some parents are upset by such behavior. But it is part of the child's need for parenting—to relive pieces of his life. One mother who refused to cuddle her ten-year-old daughter at the time reflects now, "I should have given her the comfort that she missed from that part of her life." Adjustment and bonding take place as parent and child interact.

Life usually settles down. But over the years the parent may find that certain events may trigger a child's behavior and the family may go through a mini-adjustment process again. It's not uncommon for children to experience "prefinalization jitters"; old and new behaviors surface as they deal with guilt about abandoning others from their past or worry that they may not be able to fulfill the expectations of their new parents. Adolescence is another predictable crisis period.

Much is involved in the integration of older or special-needs children into a family. Parents and children may have to deal with issues of health, school, siblings, change of birth order, and the acceptance of the family and community. I have only touched on a few of these issues in this book. The reading you should be doing and the contact you have with adoptive parents will help you identify others. By the time your child enters your home, you should have made extensive preparations, including identifying support services in your community. Claudia Jewett says: "Parents often come out feeling that the older child's adoption has been one of the most significant experiences of their lives. They talk about a sense of enormous personal growth, of satisfaction at having sought a meaningful challenge and met it, and of the privilege of having shared something of lasting value with another human being. Most are convinced that the rewards of their adoptions were well worth the hard times, and that they wouldn't have missed out on their experiences for anything."[18]

Helping the Child Who Has Experienced Sexual Abuse

Many of the children in foster care in the United States have been the victims of sexual abuse. They may have been abused in their original homes—even placed in foster care because of a reported incidence of sexual or physical abuse—or they may have experienced abuse while in foster care, either by an older child or an adult. Older children adopted from abroad may also have had sexual experiences. In some circumstances sexual interaction may have been a culturally acceptable way of life for children who have spent time on the streets, in orphanages, and in prisons (where some societies will keep older children). Foreign-born adoptees may also have been abused while in foster care.

"Abused children are hurt and traumatized children, and require resources of security, stability, and support beyond the love and attention that adoptive parents are going to give them," says Joan McNamara of Family Resources in Greensboro, North Carolina. "Parents need to become comfortable talking with their children about past issues of sexual abuse and present issues of family rules, roles, and routines. They've got to educate their children about personal safety, sexuality, and sexual abuse. That is very difficult."

As a parent, you must deal with your child's reality. A few suggestions:

- Try to get in advance whatever information you can about your child's sexual history. Be aware that caseworkers may not know or that they may not record this information in a child's record. Children are often reluctant to disclose past incidents of abuse, fearing they'll get in trouble if they admit this "badness" in themselves, or feel guilty that they allowed this to happen to them. If their "telling" resulted in their removal from their family, they may also feel that their placement was their punishment. It's not unusual for children to be in a home for several months or years before they reveal this secret. Hard as it may be for parents to hear the sordid details, the telling itself is a sign that the child trusts his new parents sufficiently to unearth the past.

- Talk with other adoptive parents about their experiences. Belonging to a parent support group and having your child involved with group activities are important for the healing process. You'll also want to do some reading about sexual abuse and provide your child with therapy. Your adoptive parent group and the **National Resource Center for Special Needs Adoption** should be able to help you find a therapist who's versed in both adoption and sexual abuse issues.

- Know some of the common signs of sexual abuse in children. They may be fearful of adults, suffer from nightmares, be afraid of the dark, and have difficulty sleeping. Their sexual knowledge may be advanced for their age; they may act seductively toward adults or peers and even imitate some of the abusive behavior they've been taught. Some children dislike being touched; others tend to be clingy. Some masturbate excessively and in inappropriate places.

- Be aware of how sexually abused children may behave. Feeling they are "damaged" and low in self-esteem, these children may be untrusting and find it hard to establish a relationship with others. They may have a range of defensive behaviors that are hard to breach. Abused children may also lash out and be abusive to others, including friends and adoptive siblings; they may try to involve others in inappropriate

sexual behavior. They may also withdraw, either physically or
emotionally, experience mood swings, and have fits of anger,
with the adoptive parent the target.

- Give your child guidance as to how grown-ups and children
are expected to act. Your child needs to understand that rules
are made to keep children safe, not to punish them.

- Recognize that your child will need help in sorting out what
abuse, sex, love, caring, and intimacy mean. Your child may
have a distorted perception of how parents act toward children. Your child will need to learn to differentiate between
"good touch" and "bad touch." While you'll want to hold
your child's hand, bestow kisses and pats on the shoulder, and
put her on your lap, she may resist or stiffen. Saying what you
are doing—"I like being close" and "You feel good to be
near"—helps. Brushing a child's hair, applying nail polish, or
helping her hold a tennis racket are other, less physically
threatening ways to come close. Both you and your child will
need to find the means to express feelings.

- Talk with the other children in your household about their
new sibling. Help them understand that this is a hurt child
whose mixed-up feelings sometimes lead to inappropriate
behaviors. Your children should understand that if they see
inappropriate sexual behavior, or are asked to touch—or are
touched—in an inappropriate way, they should say no and
inform you of what transpired. Make clear that they won't be
punished for telling; you can't help their sibling unless you
know. You'll also want to discuss the situation with members
of your extended family and other adults who may have considerable contact with the child. "Privacy is fine," advises
Joan McNamara, "but there should be no more secrets."

Postadoption Support

The adjustment process may take months, but it can also take
years. Just because a family "finalizes" an adoption in court

doesn't mean that the adjustment process is ended. Children's and families' timetables are different than those of agencies and courts. As the following chapter also makes clear, there are special issues that adoptive families must deal with. Building a family by adoption is different from building a family by birth, and adoptive families must meet adoption-related issues head-on. Often you will handle them within your own family. At other times, however, you may want to turn to others for support and guidance.

What types of situations prompt people to seek help? Perhaps there's a recalcitrant teenage girl, an only child who's acting up in school and whose teacher or counselor thinks the problem is adoption-related. Or a continual struggle between father and son. Or a mother who's unnerved when her child says, "You're not my real mother. Leave me alone." Or a parent who does not feel "bonded" to the child—even if the family relationship is long-standing. Or a child who says, "What am I doing in this family?" Observes Judith Schaffer, coauthor of *How to Raise an Adopted Child:* "There's a temptation to wonder: Is this adoption-related? There are all kinds of doubts." With those doubts is the need to talk and to share.

You may have joined a parent group before you ever identified your child. Now that your child is in your house, the temptation may be strong to let your membership lapse as your family settles in. Don't. Parent groups are not for plucking information from and discarding once you achieve the goal of a child. A parent group gives you the chance to talk with people who've had similar experiences, to share with them your knowledge and to draw upon them for support. Groups with an intercountry focus often sponsor cultural events for families. You can also raise the questions that vex you. And your child can get to know and interact with other adopted children.

If you are experiencing any adjustment problems, a parent group can be indispensable. Some groups have developed a buddy system, pairing experienced adoptive families with new families so that the buddy family provides insight and moral support. Others provide respite families who, when a family is experiencing difficulty with a child, will take the child to their home to give the adoptive parents and the child some breathing space. There may be telephone hotlines for adoptive parents to talk with more experienced adoptive parents, as well as post-adoption workshops and discussion groups. Many groups try to bring in speakers from around the country to talk with their members on adoption-related issues, or hold annual daylong or weekend conferences that focus as much on how to raise an adopted child as on how to find one.

Some parent groups, such as COAC of Texas, also offer special support groups for grade-school-age children and teens. "The kids' support groups introduce them to other adopted kids, so they can learn that their particular situations are not as unique as they may seem in the community at large," reports one parent whose children participated. She also feels that the group provided "a sounding board—adults who are not 'parents' and other kids of about the same age who are safe to talk to about how they really feel." If you're interested in starting a group, the North American Council on Adoptable Children has developed a training program, "Family Preservation: The Second Time Around," that prepares mental health profession-als, adoptive parents, and adult adoptees for working with par-ents and children on adoption issues. The curriculum materials are available from NACAC; training sessions are provided to groups upon request and are also made available at NACAC's annual conference. Says NACAC Executive Director Joe Kroll, "People need to talk about adoption issues before they hit crisis situations and not wait until someone blows up."

The number of agencies that see adoption services as extend-ing through the lifetime of the adoptee is also growing as atti-tudes toward adoption continue to evolve and policies about disclosure change. The Children's Home Society of Minnesota, for example, has developed an extensive program for adoptive parents, adoptees, and birth parents. Special workshops have ranged from discussions of the questions children ask to the use of a positive adoption vocabulary. For the family with children adopted from South Korea there's everything from workshops ("Korea: Past and Present") to preteen and teen groups (to learn about Korea and to talk over their experiences of being adopted) to Korean Children's Day (a social event for children ages four to twelve and their parents that includes a Korean meal, arts and crafts, and storytelling). The agency also provides counseling services. The Post-Legal Adoption Services Department (Children's Home Society of Minnesota, 2230 Como Avenue, St. Paul, Minnesota 55108) also has booklets, including Marietta E. Spenser's *Understanding Adoption as a Family-Building Option* and Hyun Sook Han's *Understanding My Child's Korean Origins,* as well as videos you can rent or purchase.

You'll want to check with the agency that placed your child or another local agency about its postadoption services. Try also adoption umbrella organizations, particularly those that promote special-needs adoption. The Three Rivers Adoption Council in Pittsburgh, for example, operates an Adoption Support Network: Its programs include a therapist referral service, a twenty-four-hour hotline, and two newsletters—one for adults and the other for kids. Don't forget to call your state's adoption office. Some states are now underwriting—or even offering—postadoption support programs. Residents of New Jersey, for example, can turn to the state-supported postadoption counseling services provided through the Division of Youth and Family Services.

You can also check community centers and colleges for postadoption classes. In some communities there are also freestanding adoption support programs. Parenting Resources in Tustin, California, for example, is an educational and counseling firm specializing in the lifelong issues of adoption. Parenting Resources works with infertile families trying to decide their options, pregnant families in crisis, and families planning an open adoption. There are support groups for adoptees starting at age four, for adult adoptees, for birth grandparents, for birth parents, and for families involved with cooperative adoptions. The staff mediates between birth families and adoptive families working out their relationships. There's a range of classes: how to adopt, open adoption, transracial adoption, and lifelong issues. Some classes are geared to parents-in-waiting and new adoptive parents; others are for more experienced adoptive parents and their teenagers. Parenting Resources also stocks adoption-related books, audiotapes, and videotapes in their bookstore and sells them through the mail. Says executive director Sharon Kaplan: "We see ourselves as a neutral one-stop shop because we're not connected to a particular facility. That gives us a real opportunity to disseminate basic information."

You may also want to subscribe to *Adopted Child* (P.O. Box 9362, Moscow, Idaho), a monthly newsletter prepared by Lois Melina. *OURS*, the magazine of Adoptive Families of America, also has a strong focus on postadoption issues.

The goal of postadoption support is to forge links and to help people understand that their family situation is not unique. Says Reuben Pannor, coauthor of *The Adoption Triangle*, "I worry about the people who are out there on their own."

Disruption

By summertime, we hoped that a major adjustment time was past and that after six months our living pattern was familiar and secure to Ken. However, each day it was as though it was Ken's first day in our family routine.

It was one thing after another. Ken talked out loud to himself continuously at school, at home and everywhere. We talked about how to act every place we went. Ken could not seem to remember from one time to the next how to act, whether it was at the store, at church, or just visiting. Day after day, there was no significant change.

We became so disheartened, guilty, and frustrated. My life became a see-saw of hope and despair. I became very afraid of what would happen to us during those critical adolescent years. I began to realize that the uncertainty of Ken's behavior was more than I could cope with. I knew he needed time, but I had invested so much of my life and self in trying to help us make it so far, I had no further resources left to give him. This handsome, kind child whom we loved was so confused and fearful within himself. Could we finalize this adoption and make it?[19]

Ken's family chose to disrupt the adoption. His parents felt that the toll that the placement was taking on their family life and on their other children was more than they could handle. They had tried for a year and a half, had gone for counseling, but the family had still not begun to fit together. They talked with their social worker and their adoption counselor and learned that Ken, a seven-year-old boy, would be able to find another placement. A new adoption plan was made; Ken's new family met with him several times, and finally he left to begin another life. Ken's first adoptive mother continues: "We experienced a mixture of sadness and relief: sadness that our hopes for this adoption had not worked out; relief that Ken was moved and was settled with another family. We had come to realize that we were not a family who could survive the continuous emotional upheavals."

Not all adoptions proceed to finalization: Studies have shown that upwards of 10 percent of the adoptions of older children dissolve.[20] Research shows that older children are likely to have more problems, and the more problems children have and the more moves they have made, the greater the likelihood the adoption will disrupt. While thorough preparation of adoptive parents and the provision of postadoption services give families a better chance of success, adoption experts believe that there will always be some risky placements.

One failed adoptive placement does not mean, however, that a child is unadoptable or that the adoptive parents will be unsuccessful in their parenting of another child. "In view of the emotional baggage that children bring to a placement, the multiplicity of factors in the home environment, and the flaws in our ability to predict their interaction, it is inevitable that some disruption will occur," observes Trudy Festinger, author of *Necessary Risk: A Study of Adoptions and Disrupted Adoptive Placements.* "Disruptions do not end the hope for, nor likelihood of, a later successful adoption. In the process, children, families and workers can learn how to improve the chances that the next placement will hold."[21]

The challenges of adoptive parenthood are enormous, but so, potentially, are the emotional rewards. "I'm still 'hooked on adoption,'" concluded one adoptive parent after chronicling the rocky road she'd just gone down. "It's just that I'm learning that sometimes the joy takes a little longer to surface."[22] When that joy does, you'll be glad you are around.

12

Raising the Adopted Child

There is nowadays a substantial literature written by adult adoptees about growing up adopted: Florence Fisher's *The Search for Anna Fisher*, David Leitch's *Family Secrets*, Betty Jean Lifton's *Twice-Born* and *Lost and Found*, Doris McMillon's *Mixed Blessing*, and Katrina Maxtone-Graham's *An Adopted Woman*. These books convey the disconnectedness, the anomie felt by some adoptees, and they dramatize the strong need some adoptees feel to search for their biological roots. Some adoptive parents may have difficulty understanding or sympathizing with these books, for they touch on the issue of shared parenthood—one that many adoptive parents would like to forget.

Consider these books instead as ones that parents can use to help them understand some of their children's needs. Katrina Maxtone-Graham tells us in her memoir *An Adopted Woman* that she knew as a child that she had been adopted when she was three and a half. She knew that in those few years before her final placement she had lived in several foster homes and had had one adoption disrupted. What she could not integrate were her memories—a name by which she had previously been called, images and feelings from those early years that she could not pin down. She writes: "I thought of my origins as a vacuum.

I possessed a birthdate: March 9, 1935; a birthplace: Borough of Manhattan, New York City; and a beginning: July 1938."[1] For her, this information was not enough:

> I had thought of my loss at all times, and since as long ago as I can remember. Every moment, every breath, I was consumed with wondering, and longing and searching. Each stranger on the street, each house along the road, posed the same questions: Where? Why? Who? There were no answers; and so my yearnings were without resolution, a confirmation of my inadequacy.

At the age of thirty-eight Maxtone-Graham set out to fill that vacuum. Her story is of a long struggle for knowledge that begins with a search for basic information, that includes meeting her birth mother, learning about her deceased birth father, and visiting a foster parent. It is a struggle that pits her against the agency that once placed her as a toddler and now takes her to court. One of the first pieces of information she gains, on the day that she meets the agency's social worker, tells us exactly how isolated she has been:

> It is a remarkable experience to sit across from a person who knows who your parents are when you do not; to hear, at the age of thirty-eight, someone tell you simple facts about your own private spectres. "Your father was six foot one, brown hair, blue eyes, a college graduate."
> Just like that you *know* something. Not six foot two, not six foot even. Six foot one. "Brown hair." Your own hair is brown, too—what a glorious coincidence! You try to imagine what a man with brown hair and blue eyes and six foot one *looks* like. You had not even expected to hear anything about your father; you had not thought his identity was even known. And now, "six foot one." I could go home, mark a spot on the wall six feet and one inch from the floor and proclaim a victory, "There, there is my *father.*"

Many adult adoptees live with this thirst for knowledge. They are missing the "who, what, where, when, why, and how" about their lives that people born into a family take for granted. What prompts them to start pushing for the answers? One fifty-year-old adoptee says that his search started when he was sitting in a new doctor's office, confronted once again with a question-naire asking him for his family's medical history. As he kept writing "Don't know," he decided, "I want to know." Others say that it was the birth—or impending birth—of a child that made them wonder about their own genealogical history. Or a contemplated marriage and the fear of inadvertently marrying a birth sibling. Or the death of a parent.

But the need to know is not limited to the adult. Wondering about birth parents is a theme that echoes through Jill Krementz's interviews with youngsters in *How It Feels to Be Adopted.* Reports one twelve-year-old: "There is one time when I do always think about my biological mother, and that's on my birthday. How does she feel on this day? Does she think of me, or does she just pretend that I was never born and it's any other day? Is she sad, or is she happy?"[2] A five-year-old foreign-born adoptee, when asked by an adult who was travel-ing to his birth country what he wanted as a souvenir, requests: "Can you bring me a photo of the hospital where I was born?" And a seventeen-year-old adoptee reports:

> I think that I have always wanted to know about my roots but pushed it out of my mind. I became aware of this about two years ago when my grandfather was visiting. We had one of those big family dinners and he kept talking about relatives that did great things. Everyone started to trace our ancestry. It struck me then that I really needed to know about myself. I want to be able to tell my children and grandchildren about their ancestors. I don't want to leave my parents or go back to my natural parents. I just want to ask them a million questions.[3]

Sharing Information

All parents have to come to grips with some basic questions:

- When and what do you tell your child generally about adop-tion?
- How do you tell your child about adoption?

- If your child does not ask questions, do you initiate them?
- How much information do you share with your child about his past?
- How old should your child be when you tell him about his adoption?
- If there are unpleasant facts, do you reveal them? If so, when?
- How should you present the birth parents?
- Should you tell the whole truth and nothing but the truth?
- If your child has memories of his birth parents, do you encourage him to share them with you?

There are some other questions that parents will face—those that their children ask them:

- What is adoption? What does it mean that I was adopted?
- Why do some children need or want to be adopted?
- How do people go about adopting a baby?
- Why couldn't I be born to you?
- Why didn't my mother/father keep me?
- Where is my mother now? What about my father?
- What did my parents look like? What were their names? Were they married?
- Did I have another name when I was born?
- How do you know my birthday?
- Did I have any other brothers or sisters?
- Who is my *real* mother?
- Did you buy me?
- Why did you adopt me?
- What did the social worker, adoption agency, or lawyer do?

Not all the questions will be asked at one time. Rather, they are likely to come up at different times—sometimes at odd moments—and at different stages of development in your child's life.

Children must be told about adoption and must be helped to

understand it in order to grow. As a parent, you must be open and accepting of adoption. You must acknowledge that your family is built by adoption, and that the process of family building by adoption is different than building families by birth. You must also accept that you are involved in a shared parenthood experience. Your child has a set of parents, whether known or unknown to him and you, who gave him life. Your child may also have had foster parents to whom he formed attachments. Your child's interest in his other parents is natural. He will fantasize about them, and ask questions about them. Curiosity about one's origins is normal.

Recognize that children and parents have different tasks. *Yours* is to tell your child about adoption and the circumstances of his adoption; *his* is to understand. As your child grows up, he may ask the same questions again and again, plus many new ones, but what he needs and wants to know, and what he understands, will deepen with age. Make sure that openness and communication are an integral part of your adoption telling.

Telling a child about adoption is not something you save up until a child reaches a certain magical age. Nor is it something that you reveal in one fell swoop at a very young age, thereby getting the "telling" over with and behind you. You are involved in a lifetime process of sharing information about family building.

This chapter touches briefly on many of the basic issues parents confront in raising adopted children. For more in-depth discussions, you'll want to look at Lois Ruskai Melina's *Making Sense of Adoption* and *Raising Adopted Children,* Cheri Register's *Are Those Kids Yours?* and Judith Schaffer's and Christina Lindstrom's *How to Raise an Adopted Child.* A more scholarly book is *The Psychology of Adoption,* edited by David M. Brodzinsky and Marshall D. Schechter.

Children's Understanding of Adoption

Child: Adoption is when you are born.
Adult: What do you mean?
Child: You came out of a lady.
Adult: Tell me more about that.
Child: Well, then you go to live with your parents.
Adult: Which parents?
Child: Your adopted parents. You came out of one lady, but she's not your mommy.
Adult: Is that true for all children?
Child: Sure, that's how it is.
Adult: Are all children adopted?
Child: Of course they are.
Adult: You mean that all kids are born to one set of parents, but then are adopted by other parents?
Child: That's what I said, didn't I?[4]

Here's one precocious four-and-a-half-year-old adoptee's explanation of birth and adoption. "Too often we are fooled by the child's words," observes Rutgers University psychologist David Brodzinsky. "Children can talk to us about things that suggest they have a real understanding, having learned to apply a vocabulary to a particular topic. It's a working vocabulary without much substance behind it. The surface knowledge is there, but when you scratch the surface, the real understanding of what is going on is missing." Brodzinsky and other researchers have found that the depth of a young child's understanding of adoption parallels her understanding of birth and reproduction. Even if preschoolers can rattle off some of the facts of life, they actually have a very limited comprehension of where babies come from. Their concept of family, then, tends to be fairly simple: a group of people who live in the same place—whether they are biologically related or not.[5]

Not until the elementary school years, when children are ages six to eleven, do they begin to appreciate the genetic and kinship ties connecting families. As their understanding of the birth process comes into focus, their questions about adoption sharpen. They observe that most of their friends are not adopted and that they're different. It is the child of eight or ten—not the preschooler—who asks pointed, specific questions: Why couldn't my mother keep me? Was there something wrong with me? Was I so bad? These are the children who are grappling with the key issue: Why did my birth mother give me up?

As elementary-school-age children start problem solving and figuring out relationships, the questions multiply. They may be able to empathize with the birth parent but can't truly understand *why* a woman might choose not to parent. ("But Mommy, my friend Jane's mommy isn't married." "But Mommy, if she didn't have enough money to take care of a baby, couldn't somebody just give her some money?" "She couldn't take care of a baby; why didn't she get someone to teach her how to take care of a baby?") Equally hard to comprehend is why a birth parent might release one child for adoption and choose to raise another. Research has also shown that until children are about eleven years old, they do not understand how the legal system protects them from being taken away from their adoptive parents and ensures an adoption's permanency. Adopted children may need reassurance in the meantime that the adoptive parent is really the *forever* parent.

It's not uncommon for school-age children to fantasize about their birth parents. ("What's my birth mother like? Would life be better with her? Would she make me pick up my room and go to bed so early?") They may blame themselves for the adoption ("She didn't keep me because I have a crooked smile") and have a negative self-image. Comparing themselves with others, adopted youngsters realize that they have lost a set of birth parents (whom they very likely never met) and grieve for them.

Feelings of anger, directed at the birth parents and the adoptive parents, are not uncommon. Observed the researchers at the Rutgers Adoption Project:

> Many school-aged adopted children are actively struggling with issues of separation and loss. . . . Rather than representing emotional disturbance, or poor adjustment to adoption, *these attempts by school-aged children to understand the basis for their relinquishment—which often include overt displays of sadness and anger—actually are normal, age-appropriate, and probably inevitable components of the adoption experience.* Like reactions to parental death and divorce, they represent children's grief and bereavement in response to parental loss.[6]

As youngsters reach adolescence, their understanding of adoption broadens so that they know that adoption entails a legal transfer of rights and responsibilities between parents. They can understand why their birth parents chose to make an adoption plan, and why infertility or a desire to help children led their adoptive parents to adoption. Adolescence is a time for self-discovery and questioning, a time when youngsters contemplate who they are, who you are, what makes you alike and different, what others think of them, and what gives you authority. It is a time when they think about how life might have been different for them and when they attempt to put some distance between themselves and their parents, asserting their independence. Thus it is a time of emotional vulnerability and one when some youngsters will crave additional information and desire to search for their birth parents.

While we may fashion for our children a simple explanation of adoption, the concept itself is complex and difficult to comprehend. Children must come to understand birth and reproduction and what a family is. They must develop an awareness of, and sensitivity to, interpersonal motives. They must grasp why, for example, a parent chooses to place rather than parent a child. And they must comprehend the roles societal institutions, such as agencies and courts, play in the adoption process.

This information gathering and processing, begun when the child is a toddler, continues throughout the elementary school years. While the adoptive process was fuzzy to the four-year-old, it's crystal clear to the twelve-year-old:

Adult: Suppose an important decision had to be made about the child after it was adopted. Who should make that decision—the adoptive parents or the birth parents?

Child: The adoptive parents, of course.

Adult: Why?

Child: Once you give up a child and he's adopted, then he doesn't belong to you anymore. You don't have the right to say he should do this or that.

Adult: Why is that?

Child: It wouldn't be fair to the adoptive parents. The child is theirs and they have to take care of him. They're the ones who are responsible for how he should grow up. Besides it would really mix up the adopted kid if the other parents suddenly came back into his life.

Adult: But what if the birth parents really wanted the child back?

Child: No way. When they signed the adoption papers, that's that. The laws say it isn't their child anymore and they don't have the right to try and get him back and upset the whole family.[7]

Talking About Adoption

Adoptive parents often start talking about adoption long before their children are able to understand what it means. While there have been a few writers who argue that an early telling hinders attachment,[8] most adoption experts believe that adoptive parents should use the term *adopted* in their home from infancy on—but appropriately. Looking at photographs in a scrapbook that show your child's arrival, you can mention *adoption* just as you might use the word *born* when looking at a photo of your child at the hospital on the day he was born. Perhaps you've been told to look at your baby and say, "Oh, my beautiful adopted baby." Would you look at a birth child and say, "Oh, my beautiful birth baby"?

Recognizing that young children may not fully understand adoption, it's still important for parents to explain from the start that adopted children aren't different from anybody else: They are conceived and born the same way other children are, and don't come from adoption storks, adoption agencies, or airplanes. The preschool-age child needs to know how she came into the world ("You grew inside a woman, just like all babies do, but not inside me") and that she was adopted ("Sometimes people can't take care of the children they give birth to, so other parents raise them. That's how you came into our family.").

School-age children need to understand that birth parents are people who were in a difficult situation and had to think hard about their problem and come up with a solution that would give their child a fuller life. Be aware that your child must deal with rejection, since his birth parents, no matter how loving, chose not to raise him. Don't place the burden of the rejection on his shoulders, however; don't even unwittingly lead your child to believe that some flaw in him led his parents to decide on making an adoption plan. Saying "Your mother couldn't take care of *you*" suggests that he wasn't worthy of care. Better to say "Your mother couldn't take care of any child at that time."

Try to be honest, matter-of-fact, and nonjudgmental in your explanations, since you are also conveying your own attitudes about adoption. Steer clear of loaded words such as *abandoned, rejected, lucky, special,* and *chosen.* Avoid speaking in hushed tones that suggest secrecy or shame, and avoid implying that your child should feel sorry for being adopted. In your discussions you might also want to mention some of the different types of families your child knows, pointing out Aunt Sally's and Uncle Joe's blended family where there are stepchildren.

Always answer your child's questions. If he's capable of asking them, you're capable of answering them. "In talking with very young children," cautions Brodzinsky, "answer what they are asking. Most of the times parents overexplain and overinterpret the question." Give real answers to real questions, and don't make up stories. Don't tell your child that his mother made a loving "plan" for him if she abandoned him on an empty road in India. Telling a child that his birth parent gave him up because she loved him so much can also be problematic: Your child may get the idea that being loved leads to being given away. Be prepared that your child may ask questions when you least expect them. One parent tells the story of how she was driving on an interstate highway when her three-year-old son asked, "Did I grow in your tummy?" She answered "No" and waited for the next question. It was "Mommy, did you see that dump truck?"

Preserving Your Family Story

Families preserve their joint history through stories, photographs, videotapes, mementos, and traditions. If you have a camera, use it as your child joins your family. If you meet the birth parents or their extended family, photograph them with their child, with you, and by themselves. Ask for photographs from your agency or foster family. Keep drawings, mementos, or other keepsakes for your child. Perhaps the birth parents have written a letter—or letters—to their child that you can preserve and share.

You might want to buy one of the special memory books created for children. Traditional baby books work best for families who have adopted newborns. More adaptable are calendars that track a child's development over the first year (and can be started on the day of the baby's arrival into the family) or a memory book that asks the child to fill in basic birth data and also answer questions about himself (e.g., "The people who were in my family when I was first brought home . . ."). You can check *OURS* magazine and other adoption mail-order catalogs for alternative books.

When your child is school-age, consider making your own lifebook with your child. Lifebooks, which have traditionally been used to prepare older children for moving to a new family, reconstruct important instances in childhood. The book chronicles key events—birth, foster care, moving to a new house, starting school, vacations, adoption, getting a pet—and people. The child puts the book together, drawing pictures, writing, adding clippings, photographs, and mementos. Adults work with the child, filling in details and helping to ensure accuracy. You'll find that as your child works on his lifebook, it's a natural time to pull out those pictures, letters, and other items from his birth family you'd stashed away. All adopted children can gain from creating a lifebook, since it gives them a chance to talk about their past. Making the book also lets you talk about adoption and explore your child's knowledge and feelings.

What about commemorating the adoption? While baby showers are traditional, showers for expectant adoptive parents are not. In open adoptions, some agencies have held a birth parents' farewell/adoptive parents' welcoming ceremony at the agency, the hospital, or in a chapel or church. Some families will celebrate a child's joining their family with a party or a religious ceremony sometime after the child has settled in. Christians often baptize or rebaptize their children; some churches have a special adoption service. Jews may formally convert their children to Judaism if their mothers were gentile. Boys undergo a Brit Milah (circumcision) and a *tevilah* (immersion at a ritual bath); girls undergo a *tevilah* and a naming ceremony at the synagogue.[9] Ten-year-old Josh discusses the importance of his family's celebrations in *Growing Up Adopted*. "Mom says that they invited seventy people to this big party just to meet *me*.

Of course, I don't remember any of it, but I still like hearing the story."[10] These are all formal ways of linking the child with the family, and they are events that a family can remember and talk about in the future.

Some families also celebrate the anniversary of their child's arrival as a family holiday. That's what Josh's family has done each year: "Usually the four of us go out for dinner, and the child whose day it is gets to pick the place."

Parents of foreign-born children may want to commemorate their child's citizenship by asking their congressional representative or senator to arrange for a flag to be flown over the U.S. Capitol in the child's honor. (You pay for the flag and get it as a souvenir.) Later on your child can bring it to school for show-and-tell when the class talks about citizenship.

If you adopt an older child, you will want to involve her in the planning of any celebrations. Consider also the creation of new family rituals and the incorporation of her traditions into yours. Ask your child about the holiday traditions in her birth and foster families, or at the orphanage where she lived. You can then work some of her favorite practices into your family celebrations, linking her past with your present.

Family stories about the adoption itself are also to be cherished. Says one mother:

> The older they get, the more they want to hear their story. Thomas likes to hear about our going in a taxi to pick him up at the agency. We tell him how I held him in my lap and he smiled at me. It's important to Sandra that we changed her into certain clothing. That we painted her crib. She wants to know what people said about her when we first saw her. Each child has his own story. They hear their story. They are beginning to retell their story. It's folklore.

Folklore is important for families. But there's a side to the adoption folklore that parents must guard against. For as parents emphasize the adoption story, children may lose the sense that they were ever born. Betty Jean Lifton tells us:

Sometimes when I'm with nonadopted friends, I will spring the question, "Did you ever think you weren't born?" I get quizzical looks as to my seriousness or sanity, but always the reply, "Of course, I was born." For without knowing it, while they were growing up, they heard random fragments about how they kicked in the womb, how Mama almost didn't make it to the hospital, and without understanding it, they were receiving direct confirmation about their entrance into the universe and their place in the flow of generations.

But the Adoptee says: "I'm not sure I ever was born."[11]

The focus in adoption stories is on children's entering into their families, not on their entrance into the world. In order for children to understand how they entered the world, they need to know about their birth families. Chapter 10 discussed the importance of getting background information for your child. How can you respond to your child's questions if you have not tried to get the answers?

One mother decided to travel to South Korea to search for information about her children because "what would their chances be after almost twenty years had passed to find records, addresses, and people halfway around the world."[12] In the agency records, she found out more about her daughter's birth date and name. The agency also arranged for her to meet one of her children's foster mothers. But the high point of her trip came when, using her son's documents, which gave the names and addresses of the people who had signed his relinquishment, she located her son's grandmother (who had cared for the baby boy after his birth) and visited her at her house. She writes:

My son's grandmother told me that she had met him often in her dreams and that she worried about him greatly, even whether or not he had lived. She had told me he was so sick when she gave him away, she thought he would die. She lives in peace now, for she always had thought she would die not knowing if he was happy. When she got out the family album, there in a place of honor were pictures of our son. Mark, also, now has invaluable pictures of his grandparents, aunt, and father.

Jeannette Watkins had never met the birth mother of her son, but she did have her name. One night when her son was three years old, she called his birth mother. "She was just dumbfounded," Jeannette recalls. "She was really glad to hear about him. She asked questions about him. I sent her photos and then she sent photos."

As it turned out, the birth mother was about to get married and did not want to stay in touch. (She did, however, give Jeannette her new surname and address.) Jeannette learned how valuable that one contact had been, however, when her son, now nine years old, started asking questions about his adoption. "One day he was overwhelmingly possessed with it," she says, "whining, crying. I said, 'Let's go to the bank and see what's in the safe deposit box.' He studied the picture of his mother, we talked about it, and then we came out. He hasn't pushed the issue again." As Jeannette learned, the appropriate time to share photos and other documents with a school-age child is when the child *needs* it—not on a "special occasion" set aside to discuss adoption issues. Maintains Lois Melina: "This material belongs to the child—it is not a gift from you."[13] If you provide your school-age child with *copies* of letters, photographs, and other documents pertaining to his birth family (preserving the originals in a safe deposit box), your child can study them whenever he wishes.

For your child to build a strong identity, he needs to have the basic building blocks. In families formed through birth ties, children have a family and a genetic history to link up with. As they grow up, they may choose to affirm or deny that history. They have the knowledge, and thus can make the choice. Should not children of an adoptive family have the same opportunities? Writes Lifton: "Adoptive parents can help their children by returning to the agencies or professionals who arranged the adoption and requesting all missing information. By preparing in advance, they can give their children the feeling they are working on their side, not against them, that as parents they care about them in the deepest sense possible—which means having empathy for their needs."[14]

Updating Information

As your child grows, you may want to inform the agency, the intermediary, the birth parents directly, or the other people who were involved with your child's adoption about his development. You might want to send periodic letters describing your child, and photos. If you did not work out any arrangement for communication with the birth parents at the time of your child's placement but are now willing to have the updates shared, be sure you specify that these updates are to be placed in your child's file and that you give permission for them to be shared with the birth parents. (If you're willing for identifying information to be provided, ask the agency about its policy. Will the agency leave it in or insist on blacking it out?)

If your child develops a medical condition such as diabetes that has a possible genetic link, be sure to let people know and find out what the intermediary's or agency's policy is in relaying such information on to the birth family. Such information should be passed on to the birth parents, who might like to know this if they have other children. "We had a very sad situation where the child died at age seven," recalls Marlene Piasecki of the Golden Cradle agency. "The couple contacted us, and we tracked down the birth mother and told her. This wasn't an open adoption and there had been no contact, but our perspective on all the parties was that they have a continued interest in one another."

You should also let your agency or intermediary know that you would like any updated information provided by the birth parents. And you should be prepared that your child's birth parents, even if you participated in a closed or semi-open adoption, may request photographs and additional information from you. Reports Piasecki: "The woman who placed eight years ago is going to decide to ask for an update. We're seeing that all the time. Openness not only has an impact on new adoptions, but on adoptions that took place before."

If you are vacillating about whether to update information or request it, consider the story of adolescent Jane, in Jill Krementz's *How It Feels to Be Adopted:* [15]

> When I was five, I developed epilepsy and the specialists were always asking questions about my medical history. My father and my doctor both wrote to the adoption agency requesting additional medical data, but the agency people never responded. We had very little information and it was extremely frustrating.

Jane's birth mother, independent of the agency, later tracked her down. Jane reports:

> The most upsetting part of our conversations was learning that she had written to the adoption agency in Rochester several times asking if my parents wanted any more medical information. They always told her no, even though my doctors had been asking—and begging—for updates because of my epilepsy.

Try to put yourself also in the birth mother's shoes. One woman whose social worker contacted the adoptive parents of the girl that she had relinquished eighteen years earlier says: "Just knowing that she's alive and well and happy is quite a relief, but I shouldn't have had to wait eighteen years to find out so small a fact."

If your child is adopted from abroad, don't assume that there's no information available or that updating is not possible. Adoptive parents of South Korean children, for example, have found that even in circumstances where South Korean children are "abandoned," there may actually be some data in the Korean agency's files. Some children are "technically abandoned" (they do not have legal documents comparable to a birth certificate). Children's records coming out of South Korea in the late eighties and nineties have had more information about the birth parents than those provided in earlier years, although they still contain only nonidentifying information.

When Sarah obtained additional information about her daughter, she learned that Evelyn had been brought by her birth mother to the South Korean child welfare agency that arranged the adoption. Sarah's discovery came about after friends in Seoul carried a letter to the agency on her behalf. In her daughter's case file was the original intake file compiled eight years earlier. The documents revealed the birth mother's name and age, her education and employment, her reasons for placing the baby, and who joined her at the agency when she released the baby. A separate request for information, which Sarah had sent to the U.S. agency that handled Eveyln's adoption, belatedly led to a one-page confidential background information memo.

While the amount of information in your child's file may not be extensive, some may be forthcoming. If your child was born in a hospital, it's possible that there are separate birth records you can obtain. There may also be an intake worker's file that contains notes from an interview with the birth parents that was not put into your child's case history. "You play detective," says Sherry Simas, a social worker at Associated Catholic Charities in Baltimore. To get more information, you might be in touch with the U.S. agency that placed your child, or contact the agency, orphanage or intermediary in the foreign country directly. If you have friends in the foreign country, don't feel shy about asking them to help you find any additional records pertaining to your child. If you write, enclose a list of specific questions, a letter describing your child today, and some photographs of your child. Finally, keep in mind that at some agencies, it's possible that some information may be shared with the adoptee who visits the agency as an adult that was not provided to the adoptive parents.

A DUAL PERSPECTIVE:
BIRTH MOTHER AND ADOPTIVE MOTHER

Barbara North was nineteen when she gave birth to her son in December 1966. She didn't decide on adoption until her eighth month of pregnancy: "It was a very difficult decision. I knew that I couldn't provide for the child, and I didn't think it was fair to have my parents do it." She saw the baby in the hospital—"I walked down every day, but didn't want to hold him. I knew that I wouldn't be able to give him away"—and then went home. "I was told by the agency, 'Don't ask us any questions because we won't give you any answers.' That's the way it was back then, so I never asked any questions."

Within a year Barbara had met her husband-to-be and married. While many birth mothers have a replacement child soon after the surrender, she did not. Although she wanted a child, she discovered she suffered from secondary infertility. Finally she and her husband approached the agency through whom she'd made her adoption plans and inquired about adoption for themselves: "I was afraid that the agency wouldn't let us adopt because I had placed." Her fears were unfounded, however, and they ultimately adopted two children. When she expressed interest about her son, her social worker shared with her some nonidentifying information from the file about her son's adoptive parents.

Still, Barbara couldn't get her first child out of her mind: "I went through all the stages mentally with him that you do with your own children." She wondered what he was up to in school, whether he was playing sports, and later if he was attending college. "There were so many things that I thought I needed to know," she says, "but couldn't ask."

She also grew increasingly depressed: "Every birthday I was crying, and the holidays were really hard. I'd be a real crab throughout the Christmas season. No matter how hard I would try to be happy and make it a joyful event, I wasn't putting my heart into it. Every year it got worse. All I could think about was him."

She updated medical information about herself at the agency and left a letter in his agency file for him. When her son finally contacted the adoption agency asking for more information about his birth family, her letter was forwarded to him. The two did not get in touch, however, until he was twenty-two, when both listed information about themselves with an adoption registry. Her son has now visited her home; his family has given her a photo album of his childhood, and the families have vacationed together. "It makes me feel wonderful," says Barbara. "A two-ton weight has been lifted off my shoulders."

When it comes to her adopted children's birth parents, Barbara confesses, "I don't think we've acknowledged them like we should have. We've always talked to our children about being adopted. You would think that with me being a birth mother, I would have thought about their birth parents more than I have. I was so wrapped up in my feelings, I really didn't stop to think about how other birth parents may feel."

Barbara would be comfortable exchanging letters with her children's birth parents right now (they've told the agency about their willingness to correspond if the birth parents contact the agency) and would support her children if they want to meet their birth parents when they are older. "Birth mothers don't forget, and the unknown is always worse because you imagine things," says Barbara. "If I had been able to know every five years, I think that would have been plenty for me. To not know anything for so long was much worse."

Sharing Information Beyond the Nuclear Family

Dave and Katherine Wilcox happily announce the adoption of a baby daughter estimated to have been born on March 5, 1978 (she was discovered, abandoned, on a road in South Korea on March 8, 1978).

That arrival announcement was sent to friends of the joyful adoptive parents. How would they have felt several years later if the daughter of one of these friends, who was having a fight with their daughter, told her, "You were dumped in the street. My mommy told me."

Before your child arrives, you need to sit down and consider who should be informed about your child's adoption and exactly what details they should be given. The background information that you have about your child is his and yours. If there is information that you want to share with your child alone, don't discuss it with others. Even people with the best of intentions, including grandparents, aunts, and uncles, may later slip parts of your child's history to your child or others. "I'm quite willing to answer people's questions about the adoption process, the practices of different agencies, our reasons for adopting, and how my children reacted to what was a major change in their life," notes Melina in *Making Sense of Adoption*. "I consider information to be 'private' if it refers to a child's genetic and social history."[16] Her rule of thumb: Would you readily share that information about yourself?

In the beginning everyone who knew you before the adoption took place will know that you have adopted a child. But as time passes, as you meet new people, move, or enter new situations, not everyone will necessarily know that your child is adopted. You'll have to decide whom to tell, when, and for what reason. Does your baby-sitter need to know? Does your mailman need to know? When someone who doesn't know you well comments on your child's curly blond hair (and yours is straight and brown), what do you say? Do you automatically say, "That's because she's adopted"? Observes Melina: "The person who asks, 'Where did she get those blond curls?' probably has no interest in the child's heredity, but is merely remarking on the child's attractive hair. Parents should therefore respond to the remark in the way it was intended, saying, for example, 'Yes, isn't her hair lovely?' " In the same vein, the person who says "Oh, you have a new baby. What obstetrician did you use?" may be seeking a referral to a doctor rather than information about your adoption. Putting the question into context, therefore, is important. "Parents are under no social or moral obligation to reveal personal and potentially stigmatizing information about themselves to casual acquaintances or strangers," says Melina.[17]

The Adopted Child at School

What exactly do you tell the school? If you have adopted an older child, you have probably worked closely with the school in getting him established in your community. But if your child entered your family as an infant, the school may not know about his adoption. Parents may be reluctant to tell the school or an individual teacher because they feel that some people associate adopted children with problems. If openness is a part of your life, however, not telling the school will present you with quite a dilemma. What kind of message are you delivering to your child about adoption if you conceal it now?

"A child's adoptive status is part of his social history," counsels Melina in *Raising Adopted Children.* "And schools need to know the social histories of their students."[18] When you share any history, however, ask the school personnel to consider this as "privileged" information: It is not to be talked about with others. If you provide the teacher with any background details that you have not discussed with your child, be sure you make this known.

Try to meet with your child's teacher at the beginning of the school year. This gives you the chance to talk about his needs and to learn about the curriculum for the year, for there do seem to be certain universal school assignments that cause adoptive families discomfort. "Our son came home one day and said, 'How can I do my homework?' " reported one father. The assignment was to look at his parents and decide from which parent he inherited his eye and hair color, his height and other physical characteristics. What was he to do? Another child, adopted when she was older, had trouble when her teacher asked the class to bring in a baby picture for the bulletin board. Still another child balked when her teacher assigned reports on their families' countries of origin. She wanted to write about Poland or Germany—the countries from which her grandparents emigrated—but the teacher insisted that she study South Korea, her birth country.

Lessons about genetics and heredity, autobiographies, family trees, and ethnic origins are difficult for adopted children to do. Do they talk about their adoptive families, their birth families, or whom? Each family's—and child's—solution may be different. There will be times when your child will be very willing to share information about his adoption, and others when he just wants to blend in. Talk with your child about how he wants to handle a particular assignment. If he's uncomfortable adapting it to fit his particular situation, let him do it the way the other kids do. Give him the freedom to make that choice.

You can also help your child by helping his teachers learn more about adoption. You might share with them materials prepared by Lois Melina or articles that have appeared in *OURS* magazine.[19] Discuss some of the notorious curricular pitfalls with your child's teacher and explore ways that these lessons might be adapted. Talk about the materials and worksheets being dispensed. How would an adopted child, a foster child, a child of divorced parents, or a child of a single unmarried mother be able to complete the assignment? How could units on the family be used to talk about adoption? Are there books about foster care and adoption available in the class and school library that the teacher might like to highlight? (See the reference directory at the back of this book for some suggestions.) Perhaps these books might be grouped together permanently or displayed during National Adoption Week. You can also offer to be a resource to the classroom teacher and the school about adoption. But before you venture into the classroom for a presentation, check with your child about his feelings. If your discussion of adoption at school embarrasses him, you'll want to work behind the scenes only.

Prejudice

Another six-year-old said to Jason, "You don't have a mother; you're adopted." Jason did not say anything. His teacher overheard the conversation and said: "Why do you think he doesn't have a mother? Who do you think is standing outside waiting to take him home?"

Doesn't have a mother . . . adopted. The words ring in your ears. Jason's teacher handled the situation by stepping in and speaking out. She also called Jason's mother and asked her to bring in a book about adoption for the class to read. And Jason's mother also worked with him on a "cover story"—a simple basic explanation about adoption.

Your family is likely to have such experiences. Elementary-school-age children like Jason are often subjected to questions and outright teasing from their peers. After all, kids at this age are problem solving and figuring out relationships, thinking about what sets some children apart from others. As part of *their* development, they're checking out the idea of adoption.

H. David Kirk reports in *Shared Fate,* a provocative book published in 1964, that more than half of the adopters he surveyed had encountered the following statements:

- Isn't it wonderful of you to have taken this child? (92%)
- This child looks so much like you he (she) could be your own (92%)
- He (she) is certainly lucky to have you for parents (87%)
- Tell me, do you know anything about this child's background? (82%)
- He (she) is a darling baby, and after all, you never know for sure how even your own will turn out (55%)[20]

Kirk includes the story of one couple who returned their questionnaire with the note, "You will probably be amused to know that when I first scanned your questionnaire I found these questions anachronistic. Adoptions, I said to myself, are accepted in our community. Those questions are not in good taste or ever asked. Yet when my wife and I carefully reviewed them I was surprised that we had been asked at least five of them." These questions and others are still being asked.

Has someone referred to your child's birth parents as the "natural" parents or "real" parents? Does that make you "un-

natural" or "unreal" or "not his mother"? If you have children
by birth, how do people refer to them? Are they your "real"
children or "your own" as distinguished from your "adopted
children"? If people use phrases that you don't like about adoption, tell them. Often they are just repeating what they've
grown up hearing. They may not be aware of the implications
of their remarks, or the alternatives like "birth mother" and
"birth father."

In addition to coping with our society's sometimes thought-
less attitudes about adoption, some adoptees must also confront
the prejudices that people may hold against their ethnic group.
"I can recall being teased constantly about my slanted eyes and
flat little nose. I even heard the words 'chop chop' and 'aw so'
and all the degrading rhymes associated with Orientals," recalled one adult Korean adoptee.[21]

According to adoption therapist Holly van Gulden, parents of
transracially adopted children must be especially sensitive to
the racial prejudices that their children may encounter. Even
preschoolers, says van Gulden, "know that there are differences
and can tell the hierarchical differences in our society." Within
the community, school, and perhaps within their own family,
they may hear racial slurs, or at least unfeeling comments about
different groups. At school a child may refuse to play with your
child or even to hold your child's hand because he's been told
to stay away from those "chinks." One parent tells the story of
the day when her son, a black Amerasian, excitedly invited a
girl to his junior prom. The girl, a close school friend, eagerly
accepted. Three days later, however, she declined the invita-
tion because "my dad won't let me go out with blacks." Imagine
if this were your child. Or consider this letter sent to columnist
Eda LeShan: "My youngest son has been dating a Korean girl
for three years. She was adopted by Anglo parents and raised
in Iowa. She is a lovely girl in every sense of the word, but I
don't want her in my family. Perhaps I am very biased, but that
is how I feel."[22]

Helping Children Build Their Special Identities

I wish that I was white because everybody else in this family is white.

Barbara's four-year-old Korean daughter told her this as she stared at the white, blond, blue-eyed child on the Cheerios box. Had Barbara failed as a mother? Was her daughter seriously disturbed? If you look at the daughter's situation from her vantage point, her comment shouldn't stun you. Young children want to be like the adults around them, so it's natural for Barbara's daughter to wish that she looked like the rest of her family. Most of her friends probably look like their parents (and she's probably heard comments about her cousins like "Oh, he's got the Jones family nose"). Why shouldn't she want this? Children at whatever age do not like difference. Said one transracially adopted black youth: "It's hard enough growing up. Growing up as a Black child in a white family is harder. Being 'other' isn't funny."[23]

"The history of oppression and discrimination that black Americans have had to endure requires that white parents adopting a black American child must make sustained efforts to understand what their child may come up against outside the home," note Judith Schaffer and Christina Lindstrom in *How to Raise an Adopted Child.*[24] They must be prepared for racial slurs, stares from strangers when the family is out together, and shopkeepers who keep close tabs on them in stores. At the 1982 North American Conference on Adoptable Children, a panel of black adolescent adoptees who had been raised by white parents discussed their feelings about transracial adoption. They felt that families who chose to adopt transracially should live in integrated neighborhoods and participate in interracial groups. The parents should have black friends and help the child explore the richness of the black community and his black heritage. The adoptee should be able to spend time with other adopted children, particularly with others who are growing up in racially heterogeneous families. Parents and children must talk about how it feels to be black in a white family.

Families with children adopted from Asia or Latin America will also want to consider issues of identity. In one of its pre-adoption pamphlets Holt International Children's Services has touched on how children may feel growing up in an interracial home:[25]

> *Preschool Years:* The people he loves the most look different from him. It will be natural for him to want to resemble those he loves, or else understand why he is different, and to learn that difference is not a bad thing.
>
> *School Age:* The child will need help in understanding his heritage and background so he can explain and feel comfortable about his status with his pals. He needs to be able to answer their questions: "What are you?"
>
> *Adolescence:* This is the time he tries to figure out "Who am I?" Curiosity about his original parents or background may become stronger. We share with adoptive families everything that is known to us about the child. At best the information on family background is limited, and for abandoned children there is none. The child will need help in accepting this lack of factual information. Questions about dating arise, and you should look at your community and try to guess how many of your friends or neighbors would wholeheartedly accept their children dating your child. How would you feel if your child developed a special interest in his homeland, identified himself as a foreigner, and got involved in a group for Asian, Indian, black, or Latin American teens, or wanted to visit his original country?
>
> *Moving into Adulthood:* "Whom will I marry?" This is sometimes a different answer than "Whom will I date?" as dating is not seen as serious or permanent. Do you have an idea now that your child would probably marry a white person, or a person of his own background? Why? Would you recommend for or against an interracial marriage for your child?

Transracially adopted children who grow up in small communities can feel particularly isolated. "I spoke, ate, lived American," recalled a nineteen-year-old Californian who was adopted when she was two years old, "but I definitely looked Korean.

This had bothered me since I was a little girl."[26] To help their children feel less isolated, some parent groups around the United States hold summer culture camps for younger foreign-born adoptees. At these camps children can learn about their birth country and meet with other adoptees. Holt International Children's Services, for example, runs sleep-over Heritage Camps in Oregon and New Jersey for kids ages nine to fifteen years old. The counselors are older adoptees, and they share their experiences of growing up adopted. "At Holt Camp, adoptees learn to feel good about Korea," says Susan Cox, a Korean adoptee and the Director of Development at Holt who has served in the past as the camps' director. "They recognize how they are part of the global community." And what do the kids think? Camp, enthused one ten-year-old, "was a fun experience with lots of activities. Good food and nice counselors. You cook traditional Korean dishes and get to taste them. There's fan dancing and tae kwon do. You learn and sing songs. You learn Korean art and culture. You get to meet other children of your heritage."

If you're interested in having your child participate in a camp, or in starting one in your area, check with Adoptive Families of America for information on where camps are held. Several adoption agencies also sponsor homeland tours for older teens and adult adoptees and "family tours" for parents and younger adoptees. On Holt's Motherland Tour, for example, participants spend time in South Korea at Holt's Il San Center and also meet with Korean families. They sightsee around the country. "Everything I saw and experienced, heard and tasted, felt and smelled," wrote one adoptee afterward, "served to be the sources to gain the knowledge and pride I had so badly desired."[27] If you're interested in this type of travel experience, check with the intercountry adoption agency that placed your child, as well as Adoptive Families of America.

There are many other resources that your family can tap. Among them:

Information Center on Children's Cultures (United States Committee for UNI-CEF, 331 East 38 Street, New York, New York 10016; 212-686-5522). They will send you book lists, information sheets, and teaching units. There are bibliographies for various countries, as well as lists for a variety of other topics, including food and cookbooks, games from around the world, and sources of children's books from other countries. The U.S. Committee for UNICEF also sells books (including an excellent children's cookbook of recipes from around the world), games, puzzles, and records.

Organization of American States (19th Street and Constitution Avenue, Washington, D.C. 20006). Its illustrated magazine, *Americas* (Subscription Service Department, P.O. Box 973, Farmingdale, NY 11737; 800-227-7585), covers Latin America.

East Rock Institute (251 Dwight Street, New Haven, Connecticut 06511; 203-624-8619). As part of an annual conference that focuses on issues of concern to Koreans and Korean-Americans, there is usually a session that looks at Korean-American adoptees.

Adoptive Families of America. This parent-support group offers adult and children's books about Asia and Latin America, paper dolls, baby dolls, and videotapes.

Interracial Family Circle (P.O. Box 53290, Washington, D.C. 20009; 301-772-7718). This parent-support group focuses on the needs of the interracial/intercultural family.

Council on Interracial Books for Children (1841 Broadway, New York, New York 10023; 212-757-5339). The council compiles lists of books that have an interracial focus and publishes the *Interracial Books for Children Bulletin*.

How about an ethnic doll for your child? "When children are able to see dolls that have a similar ethnicity to them, or just see dolls of diverse ethnicity, they can identify a lot better," says Dr. Michael J. Barnes, a clinical psychologist at Hofstra University who has looked at the impact of white dolls on black children. "They are able to see the world in the pluralistic way it is."[28] You can find black, Hispanic, and Asian versions of dolls, including realistic-looking baby dolls. While many of the international dolls available at stores are of the "show doll" or "collectors" variety—delicate dolls dressed in elaborate costumes and so not intended for everyday play—some are meant to be handled by children. Check with your specialty toy store or with your department store about their selections. But don't be surprised if some of these specialty dolls carry a price tag upwards of $50. You might also enjoy looking at Loretta Holtz's *How-to Book of International Dolls.* This heavily illustrated book surveys dolls around the world and is filled with information about costumes, crafts, traditions, and holidays. Holtz discusses, for example, the bread-dough dolls of Ecuador and the chain-stitch dolls of Peru, and shows you how to create your own.

Search and Reunion

Some adoptees' need for information goes beyond their desire to know as much factual information as possible about their birth families. It evolves into a need to search out and arrange for a meeting with their birth parents, birth siblings, and other members of their birth families. Says Linda Yellin, project director of Post Adoption Resources at Lutheran Adoption Service in Oak Park, Michigan: "A lot of search is dealing with unfinished business. Reunion allows the reworking of many issues."

Although many adoptive parents are comfortable with their children's need to search, others fear that their children are seeking to forge new families centering on their birth parents. They may see the search as a rejection, as a symbol of their failure as parents. If those are your fears, consider the explanation of Jayne Askin, author of *Search:*

Adoptees have been taken as son or daughter by adoptive parents who provide them a home and family where they are loved. The adoptive families have loved and cared for the child they've adopted and have earned the right to be called Mother and Father. What many people do not understand is that adoptees aren't searching for new families. Adoptees already have one, thank you. All that an adoptee doesn't have is a complete sense of connectedness with the past.[29]

Birth parents, also, are clear that they don't seek to replace the adoptive parents. Says Diane Dauber, whose daughter, Laurie, found her twenty-five years after placement: "I'm coming in with a clean slate. I can talk to Laurie a lot more comfortably about things than the girls I raised because we didn't go through the traumatic high school years together. To come in and say to her adoptive mother 'You did a good job and now I want to be her mother' is very presumptuous." For Diane, Laurie "is this grown-up adult friend of mine, this really good friend."

Meeting birth parents may, in fact, lead to stronger bonds between the adoptee and his adoptive parents. Arthur D. Sorosky, Annette Baran, and Reuben Pannor reported in *The Adoption Triangle* that most adoptees emerged from the search and reunion experience with "a deeper sense of their love and appreciation for their adoptive parents, whom they viewed as their true 'psychological' parents."[30]

Just as there are adoptive parent groups, there are adoptee support groups. These groups provide both expertise and emotional support, and your family will want to link up with one of them. To find local groups, or to get more information about search issues, contact the **American Adoption Congress** (1000 Connecticut Avenue N.W., Washington, D.C. 20036; 800-274-6736) and the **Adoptee Liberty Movement Association** (P.O. Box 154, Washington Bridge Station, New York, New York 10033; 212-581-1568). The National Adoption Information Clearinghouse can also provide you with information. The **International Soundex Reunion Registry** (P.O. Box 2312, Carson City, Nevada 89702-2312) lists birth parents, adoptees, and other family members willing to exchange information. Write to them (enclosing a self-addressed, stamped envelope) to learn the details about registration. To help clarify issues, take a look at Jayne Askin's *Search,* Betty Jean Lifton's *Lost and Found,*

and Arthur D. Sorosky, Annette Baran, and Reuben Pannor's
The Adoption Triangle.

What should you do if your adult son or daughter expresses a desire to search? If honesty has been the cornerstone in building your family, you should share whatever information you have. If you have not previously contacted the agency or the person who handled the adoption, then you will want to help your son or daughter do so now. By writing to your state's bureau of vital statistics, you may be able to obtain additional birth data. If there is a state mutual consent adoption registry that matches identifying information of adoptee and birth parents, encourage your child to register. While these registries are not always effective, in some states they are one of the few routes available. If the state registry requires *your* signature to release records, be sure you give your permission.

Should your response be different if your school-age child or teenager asks to meet his birth parents? If you've had indirect contact through letter writing or an intermediary, or if you've updated information by recontacting the agency, it might be a natural step to move on to direct contact. If you are considering opening up an adoption, you will want to have some professional counseling. Cautions open adoption expert Sharon Kaplan: "The older children are, the more we have to keep in mind that they too have a need for control in their lives and need to be involved in the process carefully. It's different for children who grow up knowing their birth parents than for children who suddenly have to make a major right-hand shift in life. I'm not saying 'don't do it,' but we need to be much more aware of the therapeutic issues involved." You may want to proceed very gradually, communicating first by letter, then by telephone, and then finally arranging a face-to-face meeting after everyone is comfortable. Beatrice, a birth mother whose fifteen-year-old daughter's adoptive parents initiated the opening up of the adoption through a search counselor, describes how complicated a dance it was for her as well:

The easiest way for me to deal with Wendy all those years was to make her a closed chapter in my life. What's made this slightly awkward for me is how I've dealt with it all these years. She's known that she was adopted from the beginning. She's been raised knowing about the adoption—all her friends and all of her family know that. Whereas none of mine do. I'm opening a whole new door in my life to everyone who knows me.

I spent the year of 1987 getting to know the counselor, writing letters, and talking to Wendy's parents. Then I met Wendy. I didn't want my kids (who are younger than Wendy) to know anything about Wendy until I was sure that our relationship was going to grow rather than be a passing little thing. I didn't want to have *my* children get to know her and then be tossed aside. I didn't want my kids to be disappointed.

Keep in mind that there may be some rough patches ahead as you all work out a relationship that's comfortable. Professional counseling is likely to ease the transition. Advises Patricia Martinez Dorner, coauthor of *Children of Open Adoption:* "People are re-entering each other's lives without a previous history of contact. They may have different communication styles, different values, different ways of looking at the world. They need to learn about each other and build trust."[31]

This book began with information about how to get started on the road to adoptive parenthood and how to find the children who will complete your family. It has come full circle with information about seeking out birth parents.

Your family will have its own special history. As adoptive parents, we all share important rights and crucial responsibilities that we must exercise for the sake of our children. If this book has given you a clearer perspective on adoption today, and if it has set out some guideposts that will point you toward your own informed decisions, then it will have done its job.

Adoption Directory
A State-by-State Guide

This list gives basic information about adoption in each of the states and the District of Columbia. It includes information about agency adoption (public and private) and independent adoption. There is also a separate Intercountry Adoption Directory that follows this directory.

This directory starts with the state agency that oversees adoptions in your state. You'll probably want to begin, however, by contacting the county, district, regional, or city agency that is the local representative of the state office. This agency is usually listed under "Adoption" or "Child Welfare" or "Public Welfare" or "Social Services" in your telephone book and has children to place. Your state agency can answer your questions about adoption in your state and, in some states, may be eager to provide you with information. Its staff can also tell you about their state's adoption registry and what steps adult adoptees, adoptive parents, and birth parents must take to request information from adoption records.

The state adoption exchanges do not place children but do help waiting parents find waiting children. You, or your worker, can contact them. Check to see if you can list your family with them. The state exchanges often function as the "adoption information centers" for the state and will try to answer questions, even if you are not thinking about a special-needs adoption. Those states that do not have their own exchanges often list children with the regional exchanges (see Chapter 6). If you find that you are having trouble getting help at the state level, you may want to contact the regional exchange. Find out also if you can list your family with the regional exchange.

The directory also gives the names of state photolisting books. If you are hoping to adopt a waiting child, you will want to consult your state's photolisting book frequently and quite possibly the photolisting books of other states.

This directory also indicates whether independent adoption is permitted in a state, whether you can use an intermediary (a friend, doctor, or attorney, perhaps), and whether you can place a newspaper advertisement. In some states independent adoption is legal, but using an intermediary to make a link or to maintain confidentiality between the birth parents and the adoptive parents is not. Remember also that state regulations about independent adoption are often revised, so you'll want to check with local authorities. Many states will also permit identified adoption, also known as designated adoption, if independent adoptions are restricted or not permitted.

This directory also lists the state representatives of the **North American Council on Adoptable Children.** These volunteers are willing to answer many of your basic questions about adoption and will put you in contact with a local parent group. You can also contact **Adoptive Families of America** for help in locating a local group. See also the Getting Advice section later in this book.

Finally, this directory lists private agencies in each state that are involved in adoption. This list was compiled primarily from data provided by each of the states in a 1991 survey. Remember, some agencies place children of all ages; some have specialties. Some agencies will have geographic or religious restrictions; others will not. Start with your local or neighboring agencies, but if you need to, don't hesitate to check with other agencies in your state, or possibly out-of-state. If you are interested in an intercountry adoption, you'll want to study the Intercountry Adoption Directory that follows.

Although this directory strives to be comprehensive and up-to-date, keep in mind that state agencies frequently reorganize, shuffle personnel, and change their telephone numbers. Laws concerning adoption change, and local agencies may move or change their programs. Since the primary source for the data in this directory was derived from a survey sent to each state's adoption units in 1991, you may want to double-check the information with the appropriate telephone information service before you place your call or write your letter. Don't be surprised if you get a recording telling you that the number has been changed.

A little persistence usually pays off. If you call for information and are rebuffed, be persistent. Try again. Turn to others for advice.

ALABAMA
State Agency: State Department of Human Resources, 50 Ripley Street, Montgomery 36130; 205-242-9500
State Exchange: Alabama Adoption Resource Exchange
State Photolisting Book: Alabama Resource Book
Independent Adoption: Permitted/intermediaries allowed/no newspaper advertising
NACAC Representative: Jan Gentry, 601 Warwick Road, Birmingham 35209; 204-879-6455
Private Agencies
AGAPE of Central Alabama, P.O. Box 230472, 3118 Covered Bridge Road, Montgomery 36116; 205-272-9466
AGAPE of North Alabama, P.O. Box 3887, 2733 Mastin Lake Road, Huntsville 35810-0887; 205-859-4481
AGAPE of South Alabama, P.O. Box 850663, 6300 Airport Road, Mobile 36685-0663; 205-343-4875
Alabama Baptist Children's Home, P.O. Box 1805, 1404 16th Avenue S.E., Decatur 35602; 205-355-6893
Alabama Baptist Children's Home, P.O. Box 91294, 6512 Grelot Road, Mobile 36691; 205-639-1022
Alabama Baptist Children's Home, P.O. Box 429, 715 Elm Street, Troy 36081; 205-566-2840
Catholic Family Services, 2164 11 Avenue South, Birmingham 35205; 205-324-6561
Catholic Family Services, P.O. Box 724, 1010 Church Street, Huntsville 35801; 205-536-0041
Catholic Family Services, 733 37th Street East, Tuscaloosa 35405; 205-553-9045
Catholic Social Services, P.O. Box 759, 404 Government Street, Mobile 36601; 205-438-1603
Catholic Social Services, 137 Clayton Street, Montgomery 36104; 205-269-2387
Children's Aid Society, 3600 8th Avenue, South, Birmingham 35222; 205-251-7148.
Family Adoption Services, 631 Beacon Parkway West, Birmingham 35209; 205-290-0077
Lifeline Children's Services, 2809 Pumphouse Road, Birmingham 35233; 205-939-0302
New Woman Adoption Agency, 2700 Highway 280 East, Birmingham 35233; 205-879-1461
United Methodist Children's Home, 1712 Broad Street, Selma 36701; 205-875-7283
Villa Hope, P.O. Box 131267, Birmingham 35213; 205-870-7359

ALASKA
State Agency: Department of Health & Social Services, Division of Family and Youth Services, P.O. Box H, Juneau 99811-0630; 907-465-3633.
State Exchange: *See above*

State Photolisting Book: No

Independent Adoption: Permitted/intermediaries permitted/newspaper advertising allowed

NACAC Representative: Sue White, 1018 26th Avenue, Fairbanks 99701; 907-452-5397

Private Agencies

Adoption Advocates International (*see* Washington State)

Catholic Social Services, 225 Cordova Street, Anchorage; 99501; 907-277-2554.

Fairbanks CMHC, 1423 Peger Road, Fairbanks 99709; 907-452-1342

Fairbanks Counseling and Adoption, 753 Gaffney Road, Fairbanks 99701; 907-456-4729

Family Focus, 313 Seventh Avenue, Fairbanks 99701; 907-452-5802

Hope Cottages, 540 West International Airport Road, Anchorage 99519; 907-561-5335

LDS Social Services, 6901 DeBarr Road, Anchorage 99504; 907-337-6696. Serves state. Religious requirement.

New Hope (*see* Washington State)

WACAP (see Washington State)

ARIZONA

State Agency: Department of Economic Security, P.O. Box 6123, Site Code 940A, Phoenix 85005; 602-542-2362

State Exchange: Arizona Adoption Exchange, P.O. Box 17951, Tucson 85731; 602-327-3324 and also State Adoption Registry, P.O. Box 6123, Phoenix 85005

State Photolisting Book: *Arizona Adoption Exchange Book*

Independent Adoption: Permitted/no newspaper advertising

NACAC Representative: Rachel Oesterle, AASK-AZ, 234 North Central Avenue, Phoenix 85004; 602-254-2275

Private Agencies

AASK (Aid to the Adoption of Special Kids), 234 North Central Avenue, Phoenix 85004; 602-254-2275. Serves waiting children.

Arizona Children's Home, 2700 South 8th Avenue, Tucson 85725; 602-622-7611

Birth Hope Adoption Agency, 3225 North Central Avenue, Phoenix 85012; 602-277-2860

Black Family and Children's Services, 2323 North 3 Street, Phoenix 85004; 602-256-2948

Catholic Community Services of Cochise County, 19 Howell Avenue, Bisbee 85603; 602-458-3530

Catholic Community Services of Yuma, 1700 First Avenue, Yuma 85364; 602-783-3308

Catholic Social Service/East Valley, 325 East Southern Avenue, Tempe 85282; 602-894-1871

Catholic Social Service of Flagstaff, 201 West University Drive, Flagstaff 86001; 602-774-9125

Catholic Social Service of Phoenix, 1825 West Northern Avenue, Phoenix 85021; 602-997-6105

Catholic Social Service of Tucson, 155 West Helen Street, Tucson 85703; 602-623-0344

Catholic Social Services, Yavapai County, 116 North Summitt, Prescott 85301; 602-778-2531

Christian Family Care Agency, 1101 East Missouri, Phoenix 85014; 602-234-1935

Dillon Southwest, P.O. Box 3535, Scottsdale 85271-3535; 602-945-2221

Family Service Agency, 1530 East Flower Street, Phoenix 85014; 602-264-9891

Globe International, 6334 Villa Theresa Drive, Glendale 85308; 602-843-7276

House of Samuel, 2430 North Sycamore, Tucson 85712; 602-325-2662

LDS Social Services, 235 South El Dorado, Mesa 85202; 602-968-2995

LDS Social Services, P.O. Box 3544, Page 86040; 602-645-2489

LDS Social Services, P.O. Box 856, Snowflake 85937; 602-536-4118

LDS Social Services, 3535 South Richey, Tucson 85713; 602-745-6459

Southwest Adoption Center, 2999 North 44 Street, Phoenix 85018; 602-234-2229. Infant adoptions.

ARKANSAS

State Agency: Department of Human Services, Division of Children and Family Services, P.O. Box 1437, Little Rock 72203; 501-682-8345.

State Exchange: *See above*

State Photolisting Book: *Portfolio*

Independent Adoption: Permitted/intermediaries must be attorneys or physicians/no newspaper advertising

NACAC Representative: Jean Dahms, AFACT, 31 Brookway Lane, North Little Rock 72120; 501-372-3300

Private Agencies

Adoption Services, 2415 North Tyler, Little Rock 72207; 501-664-0340

Bethany Christian Services, 1100 North University Avenue, Little Rock 72207; 501-664-5729

The Edna Gladney Center (*see* Texas)

Highlands Child Placement Services (*see* Missouri)

LDS Social Services (see Oklahoma)

Searcy Children's Home, 900 North Main, Searcy 72143; 501-268-3243

Sellers Baptist Home and Adoption Center (*see* Louisiana)

Small Miracles International (*see* Oklahoma)

VOA Child Placing Agency (*see* Louisiana)

CALIFORNIA

State Agency: Adoptions Branch, Department of Social Services, 744 P Street, Sacramento 95814; 916-322-3778

State Exchange: Family Builders by Adoption, 1230 Second Avenue, Oakland 94606; 415-272-0204

State Photolisting Book: *California's Waiting Children*

Independent Adoption: Permitted/intermediaries allowed/no newspaper advertising

NACAC Representative: Katherine Miller, California Adoption Advocacy Network, 1214 South Gramercy Place, Los Angeles 90019; 213-731-3467

Private Agencies

AASK (Aid to Adoption of Special Kids), 3530 Grand Avenue, Oakland 94610; 415-451-1748 and 2081 Business Center Drive, Irvine 92715-1165; 714-752-8305. Statewide. Serves waiting children.

Adoption Horizons, 630 J Street, Eureka 95501; 707-444-9909

Adopt International, 3142 La Mesa Drive, San Carlos 94070; 415-593-1008

Adoption Services International, 4737 Ortega Drive, Ventura 93003; 805-644-3067

Adoptions Unlimited, Box 462, Chino 91708; 714-621-5819

Bal Jagat, 9311 Farralone Avenue, Chatsworth 91311; 818-709-4737

Bay Area Adoption Services, 20111 Stevens Creek Boulevard, Cupertino 95014; 408-446-2227

Bethany Christian Services, 2937 Veneman Avenue, Modesto 95356; 209-522-5121 and 9928 Flower Street, Bellflower 90706; 213-804-3448. Religious requirement.

Black Adoption Placement and Research Center, 506 15th Street, Oakland 94612; 415-839-3678

Catholic Charities, 2045 Lawton Street, San Francisco 94122; 415-665-5100

Catholic Charities Adoption Agency, 349 Cedar Street, San Diego 92101-3197; 619-231-2828. Infant adoptions.

Children's Bureau of Los Angeles, 2824 Hyans Street, Los Angeles 90026; 213-384-2515. Branch offices.

Children's Home Society of California, 2727 West 6 Street, Los Angeles 90057; 213-389-6750. Serves state. Branch offices.

Children's Services Center, 684 Pine Avenue, Pacific Grove 93950; 408-649-3033

Christian Adoption and Family Services, 2121 West Crescent Avenue, Anaheim 92801; 714-533-4302 and 213-860-3766

Christian Children's Services of California, 10016 Pioneer Boulevard, Santa Fe Springs 90670; 213-948-4441

Chrysalis House, 2134 West Alluvial Avenue, Fresno 93711; 209-432-7170

Family Builders by Adoption, 1230 Second Avenue, Oakland 94612; 415-272-0204. Serves waiting children.

Family Connections, 1528 Oakdale Road, Modesto 95355; 209-524-8844

The Family Network, 282 Sirena Del Mar Road, Marina 93933; 408-384-6101

Future Families, 3233 Valencia Avenue, Aptos 95003; 408-662-0202.

Help the Children, 2538 North West Lane, Stockton 95205; 209-547-0255

Hispanic Family Institute, 5701 South Eastern Avenue, City of Commerce 90040; 213-887-1573

Holt International Children's Services, 5230 Clark Avenue, Lakewood 90712; 213-925-0933. Intercountry adoptions.

Holy Family Services, 155 North Occidental Boulevard, Los Angeles 90026; 213-387-1600. Branch offices. Religious requirements.

Indian Child and Family Services, 736 North State Street, Hemet 92343; 714-929-3319

Infant of Prague, 149 North Fulton Street, Fresno 93701-1607; 209-737-3700

Institute for Black Parenting, 7100 South Western Avenue, Los Angeles 90047; 213-752-0223 and 800-367-8858

Jewish Family and Children Services, 1600 Scott Street, San Francisco 94115; 415-567-8860. Infant adoptions.

LDS Social Services, 5464 Grossmont Center Drive, La Mesa 92042; 619-466-5558. Branch offices. Serves state.

LDS Social Services, 3000 Auburn Boulevard, Sacramento 95821; 916-971-3555

Life Adoption Services, 440 West Main Street, Tustin 92680; 714-838-5433

Lilliput Homes, 548 East Park Street, Stockton 95202; 209-943-0530

Partners For Adoption, 3913 Mayette Avenue, Santa Rosa 95404; 707-578-0212

Sierra Adoption Agency, P.O. Box 361, Nevada City 95959; 916-265-6959

Vista Del Mar Child and Family Services, 3200 Motor Avenue, Los Angeles 90034; 213-836-1223

COLORADO

State Agency: Department of Social Services, 1575 Sherman Street, Denver 80203-1714; 303-866-3209 or 303-866-3228

State Exchange: No

State Photolisting Book: *Colorado Adoption Resource Registry* (CARR Book)

Independent Adoption: Permitted/no intermediaries/newspaper advertising not addressed in statutes

NACAC Representative: Violet Pierce, Adoptive Families of Denver, P.O. Box 3313, Littleton 80161; 303-289-2787

Private Agencies

Adoption Alliance, 2620 South Parker Road, Suite 165, Aurora 80114; 303-337-1731

Adoption Center, 6595 South Dayton, Englewood 80111; 303-799-6852

Adoption Center of America, 316 North Tejon Street, Colorado 80901; 719-473-4444

Adoption Connection, 650 South Cherry Street, Denver 80222; 303-321-3829

Adoption Consultants, 200 Union Boulevard, Lakewood 80228; 303-988-4226

Adoption Option, 2600 South Parker Road, Aurora 80014; 303-695-1601.

Adoptive Services, 2212 West Colorado Avenue, Colorado Springs 80904; 719-632-9941

Bethany Christian Services, 2140 South Ivanhoe, Denver 80222 303-758-4484. Serves state. Religious requirement.

Catholic Community Services of the Diocese of Colorado Springs, 29 West Kiowa, Colorado Springs 80903; 719-636-2345

Catholic Social Services, Family Counseling Center, 302 Jefferson, Pueblo 81005; 719-544-4234

Christian Family Services, 1399 South Havana Street, Aurora 80012; 303-337-6747. Religious requirement. Serves state.

Christian Home for Children, 6 West Cheyenne Road, Colorado Springs 80906; 719-632-4661. Religious requirements.

Colorado Adoption Center, 1136 East Stuart Street, Fort Collins 80525; 303-493-8116

Colorado Christian Services, 4796 South Broadway, Englewood 80110; 303-761-7236

Creative Adoptions, 2546 West Main Street, Littleton 80120; 303-730-7791

Denver Catholic Community Services, 1020 Upham Street, Lakewood 80215; 303-238-0521

Designated Adoption Services of Colorado, 1701 Washington Street, Golden 80401; 303-277-9249

Family Ties Adoption Agency, 7257 Rogers Street, Golden 80403; 303-420-3660

Friends of Children of Various Nations (FCVN), 1756 High Street, Denver 80218; 303-321-8251

Hand in Hand, 1617 West Colorado Avenue, Colorado Springs 80904; 719-473-8844

Hope's Promise, 3813 West Greenwood Road, Sedalia 80135; 303-660-9920

Innovative Adoptions, 1850 Race Street, Denver 80206; 303-355-2107

LDS Social Services, 3263 Fraser Street, Aurora 80011; 303-371-1000. Religious requirement. Serves state.

Loving Homes, 301 North Main, Pueblo 81003-3257; 719-545-6181

Lutheran Social Services, 363 South Harlan, Denver 80226; 303-922-3433. Serves state.

Lutheran Social Services of Colorado, 3707 Parkmoor Village, Colorado Springs 80917; 719-597-0700

Methodist Mission Home of Texas (*see* Texas)

Parent Resource Center, 7025 Tall Oak Drive, Colorado Springs 80919; 719-594-9987

The Whole Family, 2870 North Speer Boulevard, Denver 80211; 303-433-6886

The parent group, Colorado Parents For All Children, puts out an informative booklet, *How to Adopt in Colorado.* Copies may be ordered from Linda Reilly, 4491 West Lake Circle, Littleton 80123. Copies are also donated to all the library systems in the state.

CONNECTICUT
State Agency: Department of Children & Youth Services, Connecticut Adoption Resource Exchange, Whitehall Building 2, Undercliff Road, Meriden 06450; 203-238-6640
State Exchange: *See above*
State Photolisting Book: *CARE Book*
Independent Adoption: Not permitted; identified adoption permitted
NACAC Representative: Lynn Gabbard, Open Door Society of Connecticut, 1530 Ridge Road, North Haven 06473; 203-248-9937

Private Agencies

Adoption Services of Connecticut, 769 Newfield Street, Middletown 06457-1815; 203-635-0003

Bethany Christian Services of New England, 222 Lincoln Street, Kensington 06037; 203-223-0645

CARE, 31 Old Willimantic Road, P.O. Box 44, Columbia 06237; 203-228-1570

Casey Family Services, One Corporate Drive, Shelton 06484; 203-929-3837. Branch offices. Special-needs children.

Catholic Charities, Diocese of Norwich, 11 Bath Street, Norwich 06360; 203-889-8346

Catholic Family and Social Service of the Diocese of Bridgeport, 238 Jewett Avenue, Bridgeport 06606; 203-372-4301. Branch offices. Identified adoptions possible.

Catholic Family Services, Archdiocese of Hartford, 467 Bloomfield Avenue, Bloomfield 06002; 203-242-9577. Branch offices.

Child and Family Agency of Southeastern Connecticut, 255 Hempstead Street, New London 06320; 203-443-2896

Child and Family Services, 1680 Albany Avenue, Hartford 06105; 203-523-9259

The Children's Center, 1400 Whitney Avenue, Hamden 06514; 203-248-2116. Identified adoptions possible.

Community Children & Family Services, 226 Dixwell Avenue, New Haven 06511; 203-624-7993. Identified adoptions possible.

Downey Side, 75 Pratt Street, Hartford 06103; 203-560-7500

Family and Children's Aid of Greater Norwalk, 9 Mott Avenue, Norwalk 06850; 203-855-8765. Identified adoptions possible.

Family Life Center, Shady Brook Lane, Norwalk 06854; 203-838-1188. Identified adoptions possible.

Family Service, 92 Vine Street, New Britain 06052; 203-223-9291. Identified adoptions possible.

Franciscan Family Care Center, 267 Finch Avenue, Meriden 06450; 203-237-8084.

Hall Neighborhood House, 52 Green Street, Bridgeport 06608; 203-334-3900

Highland Heights, 651 Prospect Street, New Haven 06505; 203-777-5513. Serves Mormon children.

International Alliance for Children, 23 South Main Street, New Milford 06776; 203-354-3417

Jewish Family Service, 2370 Park Avenue, Bridgeport 06604; 203-366-5438

Jewish Family Service Infertility Center, 740 North Main Street, West Hartford 06117; 203-236-1927. Identified adoptions possible.

Jewish Family Service of New Haven, 152 Temple Street, New Haven 06510; 203-777-6641. Identified adoptions possible.

LDS Social Services, 1000 Mountain Road, Bloomfield 06002; 800-735-0149. Religious requirements.

Lutheran Child and Family Services of Connecticut, 74 Sherman Street, Hartford 06105; 203-236-0670. Identified adoptions possible.

Professional Counseling Center, One Eliot Place, Fairfield 06430; 203-259-5300. Identified adoptions possible.

Thursday's Child, 227 Tunxis Avenue, Bloomfield 06002; 203-242-5941

Wide Horizons for Children, 99 West Main Street, New Britain 06051; 203-223-6172

The Department of Children & Youth Services has a list of approved "Out-of-State Licensed Child-Placing Agencies." This includes agencies that place healthy infants out of their state and agencies that handle intercountry adoption placements. For this list, contact the state office.

DELAWARE

State Agency: Adoption Services, 1825 Faulkland Road, Wilmington 19805-1195; 302-633-2655

State Exchange: *See above*

State Photolisting Book: *Deladopt*

Independent Adoption: Not permitted

NACAC Representative: Nancy Czeiner, 8 Chadd Road, Newark 19711; 302-737-5530

Private Agencies

The Adoption Agency, 1308 Delaware Avenue, Wilmington 19806; 302-658-8883

Catholic Charities, 1200 North Broom Street, Wilmington 19806-4297; 302-655-9624. Serves state.

Catholic Charities, 442 South New Street, Dover 19901; 302-674-1600

Catholic Charities, 21 Chestnut Street, Georgetown 19947; 302-856-9578

Child and Home Study Associates, 101 Stonecrop Road, Wilmington 19801; 302-475-5433

Children's Bureau of Delaware, 2005 Baynard Boulevard, Wilmington 19802; 302-658-5177

Children's Bureau of Delaware, 1308 Delaware Avenue, Wilmington 19806; 302-422-8013

Welcome House, 2388 Brackenville Road, Hockessin 19707; 302-239-2102

DISTRICT OF COLUMBIA

Public Agency: Department of Human Services, 609 H Street N.E., Washington 20002; 202-727-7226

Exchange: No

Photolisting Book: No

Independent Adoption: Permitted

NACAC Representative: Karen Howze, Adoption Support Institute, 1319 Geranium Street N.W., 20012; 202-291-2290

Private Agencies

Adoption Service Information Agency (ASIA), 7720 Alaska Avenue N.W., Washington 20012; 202-726-7193

American Adoption Agency, 1228 M Street N.W., Washington 20005; 202-638-1543

Associated Catholic Charities, 1438 Rhode Island Avenue N.E., Washington 20018; 202-526-4100

Barker Foundation, 4114 River Road, Washington 20016; 202-363-7751

Catholic Charities of D.C., 1438 Rhode Island Avenue, Washington 20018; 202-526-4100

Children's Adoption Support Services, 3824 Legation Street N.W., Washington 20015; 202-966-5144

Cradle of Hope, 1815 H Street N.W., Washington 20006; 202-296-4700

Datz Foundation, 4545 42nd Street N.W., Washington 20016; 202-686-3400

Family & Child Services, 929 L Street N.W., Washington 20001; 202-289-1510

For Love of Children, 1711 14th Street N.W., Washington 20009; 202-462-8686

International Families, 5 Thomas Circle N.W., Washington 20005; 202-667-5779

Lutheran Social Services, 5121 Colorado Avenue N.W., Washington 20011; 202-829-7640

New Family Foundation, 3408 Wisconsin Avenue, Washington 20016; 202-244-1400

Pan American Adoption Agency, 503 11th Street S.E., Washington 20003; 202-690-3079

Progressive Life Center, 1123 11th Street N.W., Washington 20001; 202-842-4570

World Child, 4300 16th Street N.W., Washington 20011; 202-829-5244

The parent group Families Adopting Children Everywhere (P.O. Box 28058, Northwood Station, Baltimore 21239; 301-239-4252) has an excellent directory, *The FACE Adoption Resource Manual,* which provides detailed information.

FLORIDA

State Agency: Department of Health and Rehabilitative Services, Children, Youth and Families, 1317 Winewood Boulevard, Tallahassee 32399-0700; 904-488-8000. For special needs adoptions, 800-962-3678.

State Exchange: Florida Adoption Exchange *(see above)*

State Photolisting Book: *Florida's Waiting Children*

Independent Adoption: Permitted/intermediaries allowed/newspaper advertising by intermediaries only

NACAC Representative: Gail Kreitz, Lifeline for Children, 611 NW 45th Avenue, Coconut Creek 33066; 305-972-2735

Private Agencies

Adoption Centre, 500 North Maitland Avenue, Maitland 32751; 407-740-0044

Adoption Consultants, 6201 Presidential Court, Fort Myers 33919

Adoption Services (Chosen Children), 3767 Lake Worth Road, Lake Worth 33461; 407-969-0591

Advent Christian Home for Children, P.O. Box 4309, Dowling Park 32060; 904-658-3333

Baptist Home for Children, 2332 Bartram Road, Jacksonville 32207; 904-721-2711

Camelot Care Centers, 9160 Oakhurst Road, Seminole 34646; 813-596-9960

Career Parents (Daniel Memorial, Inc.), 3725 Belfort Road, Jacksonville 32216; 904-737-1677

Catholic Charities Bureau, 1717 N.E. 9th Street, Gainesville 32207; 904-372-0294

Catholic Charities Bureau, P.O. Box 1931, 700 Arlington Road, Jacksonville 32211; 904-354-3416

Catholic Charities Bureau, P.O. Box 543, St. Augustine 32084; 904-892-6300

Catholic Community Services, 1300 South Andrews Avenue, Fort Lauderdale 33316; 305-522-2513

Catholic Foster Care, 2700 S.W. 3rd Avenue, Miami 33133; 305-856-2257

Catholic Services Bureau, 3190 Davis Boulevard, Naples 33942; 813-774-6483

Catholic Social Services, 319 Riveredge Boulevard, Cocoa 32922; 305-636-6144

Catholic Social Services, Inc., 40 Beal Parkway S.W., Fort Walton Beach 32548; 904-244-2581

Catholic Social Services, 803 East Palmetto Street, Lakeland 33801; 813-686-7153

Catholic Social Services of Pasco County, 1810 South Boulevard, New Port Richey 34652; 813-596-3135

Catholic Social Services, 1771 North Semoran Boulevard, Orlando 32807; 407-658-1818

Catholic Social Services of Bay County, 3128 East 11th Street, Panama City 32404; 904-763-0475

Catholic Social Services, 222 East Government Street, P.O. Box 285, Pensacola 32501; 904-438-8564

Catholic Social Services, 6533 Ninth Avenue North, St. Petersburg 33710; 813-345-9126

Catholic Social Services, 2015 South Tuttle Avenue, Sarasota 33579; 813-957-4496

Catholic Social Services, 855 West Carolina Street, Tallahassee 32309; 904-222-2180

Catholic Social Services, 730 South Sterling Boulevard, Tampa 33505; 813-870-6220

Catholic Social Services, 900-54th Street, West Palm Beach 33407; 407-842-2406

The Children's Home, Inc., 10909 Memorial Highway, Tampa 33615; 813-855-4435

Children's Home Society, P.O. Box 10097, Jacksonville 32207; 904-396-4084. Serves state. Branch offices throughout the state.

Christian Family Services, 4001 Newberry Road, Gainesville 32601; 904-378-6202

Christian Home and Bible School, P.O. Box 32757, Mt. Dora 32757; 904-383-2155

Creative Adoptions, 10711 SW 104 Street, Miami 33176; 305-596-2211

Faith House, 602 East Palm Avenue, Tampa 33602; 813-229-0309

Family Services Center, 2960 Roosevelt Boulevard, Clearwater 33520; 813-536-9427. Serves waiting children.

Father Flanagan's Boys Town of Florida, 2516 A,B,C Hartsfield Road, Tallahassee 32303; 904-385-1074

Florida Baptist Children's Home, P.O. Box 1653, Lakeland 33802; 813-687-8811. Branch offices.

Florida United Methodist Children's Home, P.O. Box 8, Enterprise 32725; 305-668-4486

International Children's Foundation, 9260 N.E. 2nd Avenue, Miami Shores 33138; 305-751-9600

Jewish Family & Community Services, 3601 Cardinal Point Drive, Jacksonville 32257; 904-448-1933

Jewish Family Services of Broward County, 4517 Hollywood Boulevard, Hollywood 33021; 305-966-0956

LDS Social Services, 1020 North Orlando Avenue, Winter Park 32789; 407-628-8899

Lutheran Ministries of Florida, 5375 North Ninth Avenue, Pensacola 32504; 904-484-4205

Lutheran Ministries, 4015 South Westshore Boulevard, Tampa 33611; 813-831-4449

Parent Services, 3191 Coral Way, Miami 33145; 305-441-0223

St. Vincent Maternity & Adoption Center, 717 Ponce de Leon Boulevard, Coral Gables 33134; 305-445-5714

Seagrave, 212 East Colonial Drive, P.O. Box 536488, Orlando 32803; 305-425-4491

Shepherd Care Ministries, 5935 Taft Street, Hollywood 33021; 305-981-2060. Religious requirement.

Suncoast International Adoptions, 12800 Indian Rocks Road, Largo 34644; 813-596-3135

United Methodist Children's Home, 2824 Desert Street, P.O. Box 15310, Pensacola 32514; 904-478-8950

Universal Aid for Children, 8760 Northeast 15th Street, Miami Shores 33138; 305-754-4886

GEORGIA

State Agency: State Adoption Unit, 878 Peachtree Street N.E., Atlanta 30309; 404-894-4454

State Exchange: Adoption Exchange *(see above)*

State Photolisting Book: *My Turn Now*

Independent Adoption: Permitted/no intermediaries/no newspaper advertising

NACAC Representative: Kathyrn Karp, *My Turn Now,* P.O. Box 7727, Atlanta 30357; 404-894-3779

Private Agencies

Adoption Planning, 125 Clairmont Avenue, Decatur 30030; 404-373-2620

Adoption Services, 115 Harris Street, Pavo 31778; 912-859-2654

Bethany Christian Services, 1852 Century Place, Atlanta 30345; 404-320-1057

Catholic Social Services, 680 West Peachtree Street N.W., Atlanta 30308; 404-881-6571

Covenant Care Services, 682 Mulberry Street, Macon 31201; 912-741-9829

Families First, 1105 West Peachtree Street, Atlanta 30309; 404-853-2800

Family Counseling Center/CSRA, 1914 Central Avenue, Augusta 30904; 404-738-9750

Georgia AGAPE, 790 Church Street, Smyrna 30080; 404-432-0063

Georgia Baptist Children's Homes and Family Ministries, Route 2, Box 4, Palmetto 30268; 404-463-3344

Greater Chattanooga Christian Services (*see* Tennessee)

Homes for Children International, P.O. Box 8898, Atlanta 30306; 404-897-1766

Illien Adoptions International, 1250 Piedmont Avenue, Atlanta 30309; 404-872-6787.

Jewish Family Services, 1605 Peachtree Street N.E., Atlanta 30309; 404-873-2277

LDS Social Services, 4823 North Royal Atlanta Drive, Tucker 30084; 404-939-2121

Lifeline Children's Services of Georgia, 844 Second Street, Macon 31208-4786; 912-746-4969

Lutheran Ministries of Georgia, 756 West Peachtree Street N.W., Atlanta 30308; 404-875-0201

New Beginning Adoption and Counseling Agency, 3564 Forrest Road, Columbus 31907; 404-561-7954

Open Door Adoption Agency, P.O. Box 4, 116 East Monroe, Thomasville 31792; 912-228-6339

Parent and Child Development Services, 21 East Broad Street, Savannah 31401; 912-232-2390.

HAWAII

State Agency: Department of Human Services, Family and Adult Services Division, 420 Waiakamilo Business Center, Waiakamilo Road, Suite 113, Honolulu 96817; 808-832-5151

State Exchange: No

State Photolisting Book: No

Independent Adoption: Permitted

NACAC Representative: Darlene Ogata, 94-360 Hokuala Street #191, Mililani Town 96789; 808-623-8235

Private Agencies

Catholic Charities, 250 South Vineyard Street, Honolulu 96813; 808-537-6321

Child and Family Service, 200 North Vineyard Boulevard, Honolulu 96817; 808-521-2377

Christian Adoptions, 305 Hahani Street, Kailua 96834

Crown Child Placement International, 75-5851 Kuakini Highway, Kailua-Kona 96740; 808-326-4444

Hawaii International Child Placement, P.O. Box 13, Hawi 96719; 808-889-5122

LDS Social Services, 1500 South Beretania Street, Honolulu 96826; 808-942-0050

Queen Liliuokalani Children's Center, 1300 Halona Street, Honolulu 96817; 808-847-1302

Rainbow Families, 32 Kainehe Street, Kailua 96734; 808-262-2733

IDAHO

State Agency: Adoptions, Division of Family & Children's Services, Department of Health & Welfare, 450 West State Street, Boise 83720; 208-334-5700

State Exchange: No
Photolisting Book: No
Independent Adoption: Permitted/no newspaper advertising allowed
NACAC Representative: Susan Smith, 1301 Spokane Street, Post Falls 83854; 208-773-5629
Private Agencies
Christian Counseling Services, 545 Shoup Avenue, Idaho Falls 83402; 208-529-4673
Community Counseling and Adoption Services, 323 Allumbaugh Street, Boise 83704; 208-322-1262
Franciscan Family Care Center, 892 McKiney, Pocatello 83201; 208-233-7364
Idaho Youth Ranch Adoption Services, 1416 West Franklin Street, Boise 83702; 208-342-6805
LDS Social Services, 10740 Fairview, Boise 83704; 208-376-0191
LDS Social Services, 255 North Overland Avenue, Burley 83318; 208-678-8200
LDS Social Services, 1420 East 17th Street, Idaho Falls 83404; 208-529-5276
LDS Social Services, 1070 Hiline, Pocatello 83201; 208-232-7780
Lutheran Social Services (*see* Washington)
New Hope Child and Family Agency, 545 Shoup Avenue, Idaho Falls 83402; 208-522-7700
WACAP, 6968 Butte Court, Boise 83704; 208-322-7944

ILLINOIS
State Agency: Department of Children and Family Services, 406 East Monroe, Springfield 62701. However, for adoption resources and general information, contact the state exchange *(see below)*.
State Exchange: Adoption Information Center of Illinois, 201 North Wells Street, Chicago 60602; 312-346-1516 or in state 800-572-2390
State Photolisting Book: *Adoption Listing Service*
Independent Adoption: Permitted/intermediaries permitted/newspaper advertising allowed
NACAC Representative: Drucilla Fair, Illinois Parents for Black Adoptions, 7930 South Colfax, Chicago 60617; 312-734-2305
Private Agencies
Adoption World, One East Erie, Chicago 60611; 312-664-8933. Intercountry adoptions.
Aunt Martha's Youth Services, 233 Joe Orr Road, Chicago Heights 60411; 708-754-1044. Special needs adoptions.
The Baby Fold, 108 East Willow Street, Normal 61761; 309-452-1170. Branch offices.
Bensenville Home Society, 331 South York Road, Bensenville 60106; 708-766-5800
Bethany Christian Services, 9730 South Western Avenue, Evergreen Park 60642; 312-422-9626. Serves state.
Bethany Home, 220 Eleventh Avenue, Moline 61265; 309-797-7700

Casa Central, 1349 North California, Chicago 60622; 312-276-1902

Catholic Charities of Chicago, 126 North Desplaines, Chicago 60606; 312-236-5172. Branch offices.

Catholic Charities-Joliet Diocese, 411 Scott Street, Joliet 60432; 815-723-3405. Branch offices.

Catholic Charities of Lake County, 1 North Genesee, Waukegan 60085; 312-249-3500

Catholic Charities-Springfield Diocese, 800 South 5th Street, Springfield 62703; 217-523-9201. Branch offices.

Catholic Social Services, 617 South Belt West, Belleville 62220; 618-277-9200

Catholic Social Services, Peoria Diocese, 412 Northeast Monroe, Peoria 61603; 309-671-5720

Catholic Social Services, Rockford Diocese, 921 West State Street, Rockford 61102; 815-965-0623. Branch offices.

Central Baptist Family Services, 201 North Wells Street, Chicago 60606; 312-782-0874

Chicago Child Care Society, 5467 South University Avenue, Chicago 60615; 312-643-0452.

Chicago Youth Centers, 10 West 35th Street, Chicago 60616; 312-225-8200. Special needs adoptions.

Children's Home and Aid Society of Illinois, 1122 North Dearborn, Chicago 60610; 312-944-3313. Serves state. Branch offices.

Childserv, 1580 North Northwest Highway, Park Ridge 60068; 708-298-1610

Christian Family Services, 9955 Bunkham Road, Fairview Heights 62208; 618-397-7678. Serves state. Religious requirement.

Counseling and Family Service, 1821 North Knoxville Avenue, Peoria 61603; 309-685-5287.

Cradle Society, 2049 Ridge Avenue, Evanston 60201; 708-475-5800. Places infants.

Evangelical Child and Family Agency, 1530 North Main Street, Wheaton 60187; 312-653-6400

Family Care Services of Metropolitan Chicago, 234 South Wabash Avenue, Chicago 60604; 312-427-8790. Focus on waiting children.

Family Counseling Clinic, 19300 West Highway 120, Grayslake 60030; 312-223-8107.

Family Resources (*see* Iowa)

Family Service Agency, 915 Vermont, Quincy 62301; 217-222-8254

Family Service Center of Sangamon County, 1308 South Seventh Street, Springfield 62703; 217-528-8406

Family Service of Decatur, 151 East Decatur Street, Decatur 62521; 217-429-5216

Habilitative Systems, 415 South Kilpatrick, Chicago 60644; 312-261-2252. Special needs adoptions.

Hobby Horse House, 325 West State Street, Jacksonville 62651; 217-243-7708

Human Enrichment Development Association, 163½ East 154th Street, Harvey 60426; 708-333-6909

Illinois Baptist Maternity and Adoption Services, 601 South 21st Street, Mount Vernon 86864; 618-242-4944 or 800-458-BABY. Serves state. Religious requirement.

Jewish Children's Bureau of Chicago, 1 South Franklin, Chicago 60606; 312-444-2090. Serves state. Religious requirement.

LDS Social Services, 1813 North Mill Street, Naperville 60540; 312-369-0486. Serves state. Religious requirement.

Lutheran Child and Family Services, 7620 Madison Street, River Forest 60305; 312-771-7180. Serves state. Branch offices.

Lutheran Social Service of Illinois, 420 West Lawrence Avenue, Chicago 60630; 312-794-6500. Serves state. Branch offices.

St. Mary's Services, 717 West Kirchoff Road, Arlington Heights 60005; 708-870-8181. Places infants. Religious requirement.

Ada S. McKinley Foster Care Services, 11006 South Michigan Avenue, Chicago 60628; 312-568-0270.

Sunny Ridge Family Center, 2 South 426 Orchard Road, Wheaton 60187; 708-668-5117. Serves state. Branch offices. Places infants. Has done open adoptions.

Travelers and Immigrant's Aid, 327 South LaSalle Street, Room 1500, Chicago 60604; 312-435-4562. Serves state. Intercountry adoptions only.

Volunteers of America, 2100 South Indiana, Chicago 60616; 312-326-4916.

You can obtain from the Adoption Information Center of Illinois for a $5 donation the comprehensive book *Adoption: A Guide to Adoption in Illinois.*

INDIANA

State Agency: Department of Public Welfare, Children and Family Services Division, 402 West Washington Street, Room W364, Indianapolis 46204; 317-232-5613

State Exchange: Indiana Adoption Resource Exchange *(see above)*

State Photolisting Book: *Indiana Adoption Resource Exchange*

Independent Adoption: Permitted/intermediaries permitted/newspaper advertising allowed

NACAC Representative: Jeanine Jones, Adoptive Parents Together, 5320 Far Hill Road, Indianapolis 46226; 317-638-0965

Private Agencies

Adoption Alternatives, 116 South Taylor, South Bend 46601; 219-232-5843

Adoption Resources Services, 231 Airport North Office Park, Fort Wayne; 219-262-2499. Serves state.

Adoption Services, 3050 North Meridian Street, Indianapolis 46208; 317-926-6338

Adoption Support Center, 6331 North Carrollton Avenue, Indianapolis 46220; 317-255-5916

Americans for African Adoptions, 8910 Timberwood Drive, Indianapolis 46234; 317-271-4567

Baptist Children's Home, 354 West Street, Valparaiso 46383; 219-462-4111. Serves state.

Bethany Christian Services, 6144 North Hillside Avenue, Indianapolis 46220; 317-254-8479. Branch offices.

Catholic Charities Bureau, 603 Court Building, Evansville 47708; 812-423-5456

Catholic Charities, 315 East Washington, Fort Wayne 46802; 219-422-7511

Catholic Charities, 120 South Taylor Street, South Bend 46601; 219-234-3111

Catholic Family Services, 973 West 6th Avenue, Gary 46402; 219-882-2723

Catholic Family Services, 524 C Franklin Square, Michigan City 46360; 219-879-9312

Child Placement, Childplace, Inc., 2420 Highway 62, Jeffersonville 47130; 812-282-8248. Religious requirements.

Children of the Covenant, 2310 Chestnut Street, Columbus 47203; 812-372-9937

Children's Bureau of Indianapolis, 615 North Alabama Street, Indianapolis 46204; 317-634-6481

Chosen Children Adoption Services, 204 Pearl Street, New Albany 47150; 812-945-6021. Serves state.

Coleman Adoption Services, 615 North Alabama Street, Indianapolis 46203; 317-638-0965. Serves state.

Compassionate Care, 253 North Main Street, Oakland City 47660; 812-749-4152. Serves state.

Family and Children's Services, 305 South Third Street, Evansville 47708; 812-425-5181

G.L.A.D., 5000 First Avenue, Evansville 47711; 812-424-4523

Homes for Black Children, 3131 East 38 Street, Indianapolis 46218; 317-545-5281. Serves waiting children. Recruits black families.

Jeremiah Agency, 3021 Stella Drive, P.O. Box 864, Greenwood 46142-0864; 317-887-2433

Jewish Family and Children's Services, 9002 North Meridian Street, Indianapolis 46260; 317-573-9949. Serves state.

LDS Social Services, 5151 West 84th Street, Indianapolis 46268; 317-875-7066

Lutheran Child and Family Services, 1525 North Ritter Avenue, Indianapolis 46219; 317-359-5367. Serves state.

Lutheran Social Services, 60 West 67th Place, Merrillville 46420; 219-769-3521

St. Elizabeth's, 2500 Churchman Avenue, Indianapolis 46203; 317-787-3412. Serves state.

Shults-Lewis Child and Family Services, P.O. Box 471, Valparaiso 46383; 219-462-0513. Serves state. Religious requirement.

Sunny Ridge Family Center, 9105 A Indianapolis Boulevard, Highland 46322; 219-838-6611. Serves state.

The Villages, 2346 South Lynhurst Drive, Indianapolis 46241; 317-486-1474. Serves state.

IOWA

State Agency: Adoption Program, Department of Human Services, Hoover Building, Des Moines 50319; 515-281-5358

State Exchange: Iowa Adoption Exchange *(see above)*

State Photolisting Book: *Iowa's Waiting Children*
Independent Adoption: Permitted/intermediaries permitted/newspaper advertising allowed
NACAC Representative: Phyllis Nielsen, Iowa Foster/Adoptive Parents, R.R. 1, Box 89, Everly 51338; 712-834-2512
Private Agencies
American Home Finding Association, 217 East Fifth, Ottumwa 52501; 515-682-3449
Baptist Children's Home & Family Ministries, 224½ N.W. Abilene, Ankeny 50021; 515-964-0986
Bethany Home, 1606 Brady Street, Davenport 52803; 319-324-9169
Bethany Christian Services, 322 Central Avenue, Box 143, Orange City 51041; 712-737-4831. Serves state. Religious requirement.
Catholic Charities of Dubuque, 1229 Mt. Loretta Street, Box 1390, Dubuque 52001; 319-556-2580.
Catholic Charities of Sioux City, P.O. Box 2025, Sioux City 51104; 712-252-2701. Branch offices.
Catholic Council for Social Concern, Inc., 818 5th Avenue, Box 713, Des Moines 50303; 515-244-3761
Families of Northeast Iowa, 210A West Platt, Box 806, Maquoketa 52060
Family Resources, 115 West 6 Street, Davenport 52803; 319-323-1853. Branch offices.
Florence Crittenton Home, 1105 28th Street, Sioux City 51104; 712-255-4321
Four Oaks, 5400 Kirkwood Boulevard, Cedar Rapids 52404
Hillcrest Family Services, 1727 First Avenue S.E., Cedar Rapids 52404; 319-362-3149
Holt International Children's Services, 2200 Abbott Drive, Carter Lake 51510; 712-347-5911
Iowa Children's & Family Services, 1101 Walnut, Des Moines 50309; 515-288-1981
LDS Social Services, 3301 Ashworth Road, West Des Moines 50265
Lutheran Social Service, 230 Ninth Avenue North, Fort Dodge 50501; 515-573-3138
Lutheran Social Service of Iowa, 3116 University Avenue, Des Moines 50311; 515-277-4476. Serves state. Branch offices throughout state. Religious requirements.
Young House, 105 Valley Street, Burlington 52601; 319-752-4000

KANSAS
State Agency: Commission of Adult and Youth Services, Department of Social and Rehabilitation Services, 300 S.W. Oakley, Topeka 66606; 913-296-4661
State Exchange: *See above*
State Photolisting Book: *Kansas Adoption Resource Exchange Photo-Listing*
Independent Adoption: Permitted/intermediaries allowed/no newspaper advertising

NACAC Representative: Contact National Office
Private Agencies
Adams Center (*see* Missouri)
Adoption, Counseling & Training, 817 South Fourth Street, Leavenworth 66048;
    913-682-7914
Adoption & Counseling Services, 10045 Hemlock, Overland Park 66212; 816-753-
    4333
Baughmann, Powell and Stonestreet Independent Adoptions, 5847 S.W. 29th
    Street, Topeka 66614; 913-273-7524
Catholic Charities, Diocese of Dodge City, 2546 20th Street, Great Bend 67530;
    316-792-1393
Catholic Charities, 229 South 8th, Kansas City 66102; 913-621-1804. Branch
    offices.
Catholic Charities, 137 North Ninth, Salina 67401; 913-825-0208
Catholic Social Services, 2546 20th Street, Great Bend 67530; 316-792-1393
Child Placement Services, 7842 Mission Parkway, Prairie Village 66208; 913-648-
    7695. Branch offices.
Christian Family Services, 10901 Granada, Overland Park 66211; 913-491-6751
Family Life Services Adoption Agency, 115 Chestnut Avenue, Arkansas City
    67005; 316-442-1688
Gentle Shepherd Child Placement Services, 6310 Lamar Avenue, Overland Park
    66202; 913-764-3811. Infant adoptions.
Hagar Associates, 3601 West 29th Street, Topeka 66614; 913-271-6045
Heart of America Family & Children's Services, 6300 West 95th, Overland Park
    66214; 913-642-4300
Highlands Child Placement Service (*see* Missouri)
Inserco, 5120 East Central, Wichita 67208; 316-681-2129
Kansas Children's Service League, P.O. Box 517, Wichita 67201; 316-942-4261.
    Branch offices. Serves state. Focuses on special needs.
Lutheran Social Service, 1855 North Hillside, Wichita 67214; 316-686-6645.
    Serves state. Serves waiting children.
Maude Carpenter Children's Home, 1501 North Meridan, Wichita 67203; 316-942-
    3221
The Villages, P.O. Box 1695, Topeka 66601; 913-273-5900. Serves state.

KENTUCKY
State Agency: Cabinet for Human Resources, Department for Social Services,
    275 East Main Street, Frankfort 40621; 502-564-2136. SNAP (Special Needs
    Adoption Project), 710 West High Street, Lexington 40508; 606-252-1728 and
    908 West Broadway, Louisville 40263; 502-588-4303
State Exchange: KARE *(see above);* in state 800-432-9346
State Photolisting Book: *The SNAP Book*
Independent Adoption: Permitted/intermediaries allowed/no newspaper adver-
    tising

NACAC Representative: Virginia Sturgeon, SNAP, 710 West High Street, Lexington 40508; 606-252-1728
Private Agencies
Baptist Community Services, 10801 Shelbyville Road, Louisville 40243; 502-245-2101
Bluegrass Christian Adoption Service, 342 Waller Avenue, Lexington 40504; 606-276-2222
Catholic Charities Agency, 2911 South Fourth Street, Louisville 40208; 502-637-9786
Catholic Social Service Bureau, 3629 Church Street, Covington 41015; 606-581-8974
Catholic Social Service Bureau, 1310 Leestown Road, Lexington 40508; 606-253-1993
Childplace, 3248 Taylor Boulevard, Louisville 40215; 502-363-1633
Chosen Children Adoption Services, 5227 Bardstown Road, Louisville 40291; 502-491-6410. Places infants.
LDS Social Services, 1000 Hurstbourne Lane, Louisville 40224; 502-429-0077
Mary Kendall Home, 193 Phillys's Court, Owensboro 42301; 502-683-3723

LOUISIANA
State Agency: Office of Community Services/Children, Youth and Family, 1967 North Street, Baton Rouge 70821; 504-342-4086
State Exchange: Louisiana Adoption Resource Exchange (LARE) *(see above)*
State Photolisting Book: *The LARE Album*
Independent Adoption: Permitted/intermediaries allowed/newspaper advertising permitted
NACAC Representative: Cecile Tebo, Volunteers of America, 3900 North Causeway Boulevard, #700, Metairie 70002; 504-836-5225
Private Agencies
Adoption Options, 2332 Eastgate, Baton Rouge 70816; 504-291-4588
Associated Catholic Charities of New Orleans, 1231 Prytania Street, New Orleans 70130; 504-523-3755
Baptist Children's Home, 7200 DeSiard Road, Monroe 71203; 318-343-2244
Beacon House, 750 Louisiana Avenue, Port Allen 70767; 504-387-6365
Bethany Christian Services, 4854 Constitution Avenue, Baton Rouge 70808; 504-927-3235. Religious requirements.
Catholic Community Services, 4884 Constitution Avenue, Baton Rouge 70821; 504-927-4930
Catholic Social Services of Houma/Thibodaux, 1220 Aycock Street, Houma 70260; 504-876-0490
Catholic Social Services of Lafayette, 708 West University, Lafayette 70501; 318-235-5218
Children's Bureau of New Orleans, 921 Canal Street, Suite 840, New Orleans 70112; 504-525-2366. Serves state.
The Gail House, 10033 Mammoth Drive, Baton Rouge 70895; 504-926-2229

Edna Gladney Center (*see* Texas)

Holy Cross Child Placement Agency, 929 Olive Street, Shreveport 71104; 318-222-7892

Jewish Family Services of Greater New Orleans, 2026 St. Charles Avenue, New Orleans 70130; 504-524-8475

LDS Social Services, 2000 Old Spanish Trail, Slidell 70458; 504-649-2774

Louisiana Child Care and Placement Services, 9080 Southwood Drive, Shreveport 71118; 318-686-2243

New Family Adoption Services, 206B West Harrison Avenue, New Orleans 70124; 504-482-3653

St. Elizabeth Foundation, 8054 Summa Drive, Baton Rouge 70809; 504-769-8888

St. Gerard's Adoption Network, 100 South Vivan Street, Eunice 70535; 318-457-9048

Sellers Baptist Home and Adoption Center, 2010 Peniston Street, New Orleans 70115; 504-895-2088. Serves state.

Special Delivery Adoption Services, 7809 Jefferson Highway, Baton Rouge 70809; 504-924-2507

VOA Adoption Services, 3900 North Causeway Boulevard, Metairie 70002; 504-836-5225

VOA Child Placing Agency, 354 Jordan Street, Shreveport 71101; 318-221-2669

MAINE

State Agency: Department of Human Services, 221 State Street, Augusta 04333; 207-289-5060

State Exchange: The Maine-Vermont Exchange *(see above)*

State Photolisting Book: *The Maine-Vermont Exchange*

Independent Adoption: Permitted/no intermediaries/newspaper advertising allowed

NACAC Representative: Judy Collier, Adoptive Families of Maine, 156 Essex Street, Bangor 04401; 207-941-9500

Private Agencies

Community Counseling Center, 622 Congress Street, Portland 04101; 207-874-1030

Good Samaritan Agency, 450 Essex Street, Bangor 04444; 207-942-7211

Growing Thru Adoption, P.O. Box 7082, Lewiston 04243; 207-786-2597

Maine Adoption Placement Service, P.O. Box 772, Houlton 04730; 207-532-9358. Serves state.

Maine Children's Home for Little Wanderers, 34 Gilman Street, Waterville 04901; 207-873-4253. Serves state.

St. Andre's Home, 283 Elm Street, Biddeford 04005; 207-282-3351. Serves state. Places infants. No special-needs children.

Sharing in Adoption, 2 Springbrook Lane, Gorham 04038; 207-839-2934

MARYLAND

State Agency: Family and Children's Services, Social Services Administration, 311 West Saratoga Street, Baltimore 21201; 301-333-0236 or 800-492-1978

State Exchange: Maryland Adoption Resource Exchange *(see above)*
State Photolisting Book: *Maryland Adoption Resource Exchange*
Independent Adoption: Permitted/no paid intermediaries/newspaper advertising allowed
NACAC Representative: Clyde Tolley, Families Adopting Children Everywhere, P.O. Box 28058, Baltimore 21239; 301-239-4252
Private Agencies
Adoption Services Information Agency (*see* District of Columbia)
Adoptions Together, 5830 Hubbard Drive, Rockville 20852; 301-881-0033
American Adoption Agency (*see* District of Columbia)
Associated Catholic Charities of Baltimore, 320 Cathedral Street, Baltimore 21201; 301-547-1103. Serves state.
Associated Catholic Charities (*see* District of Columbia)
Barker Foundation (*see* District of Columbia)
Bethany Christian Services, 1641 Route 3 North, Crofton 21114; 301-721-2835. Religious requirements. Serves state.
Catholic Social Services, 1405 Wesley Drive, Salisbury 21801; 301-749-1121
Datz Foundation (*see* District of Columbia)
Family and Children's Services of Central Maryland, 204 West Lanvale Street, Baltimore 21217; 301-669-9000
Homes for Black Children (*see* District of Columbia)
Jewish Family Services, 5750 Park Heights Avenue, Baltimore 21215; 301-466-9200. Religious requirement.
Jewish Social Service Agency, 6123 Montrose Road, Rockville 20852; 301-881-3700. Religious requirement.
LDS Social Services, 198 Thomas Jefferson Drive, Frederick 21701; 202-829-7640. Serves state. Religious requirement.
Lutheran Social Services of National Capital Area (*see* District of Columbia)
Methodist Board of Child Care, 3300 Gaither Road, Baltimore 21207; 301-922-2100. Serves state.
New Family Foundation (*see* District of Columbia)

The parent group Families Adopting Children Everywhere produces *The FACE Adoption Resource Manual,* which provides detailed adoption information about the state. Contact them for details on how to obtain the booklet.

MASSACHUSETTS
State Agency: Department of Social Services, 24 Fannsworth Street, Boston 02110; 617-727-0900
State Exchange: Massachusetts Adoption Resource Exchange, 867 Boylston Street, Boston 02116; 617-536-0362
Photolisting Book: *MARE Manual*
Independent Adoption: Not permitted/identified adoption possible
NACAC Representative: Annette Lawson, Open Door Society of Massachusetts, P.O. Box 343, Hopedale 01747; 508-473-3400

Private Agencies

Adoption Center, 55 Wheeler Street, Cambridge 02138; 617-864-5437

Adoptions of New England, 190 High Street, Boston 02110; 617-739-2229

Adoptions with Love, 188 Needham Street, Newton 02164; 617-964-4357

Alliance For Children, 40 William Street, Wellesley Office Park 02181; 617-431-7148

Beacon Adoption Center, 66 Lake Buel Road, Great Barrington 02130; 413-528-2749

Berkshire Center for Families & Children, 472 West Street, Pittsfield 01201; 413-448-8281

Bethany Christian Services, 62 Foundry Street, Wakefield 01880; 508-246-1890

Boston Adoption Bureau, 14 Beacon Street, Boston 02108; 617-227-1336

Boston Children's Service, 867 Boylston Street, Boston 02116; 617-267-3700

Cambridge Adoption & Counseling Association, Box 190, Cambridge 02142; 617-923-0370

Cambridge Family & Children's Services, 99 Bishop Allen Drive, Cambridge 02139; 617-876-4210

Catholic Charitable Bureau of Boston, 10 Derne Street, Boston 02114; 617-523-5165

Catholic Charities Center, 686 North Main Street, Brockton 02401; 508-587-0815

Catholic Charities/North Suburban, 55 Lynn Shore Drive, Lynn 01902; 617-593-2312 and 3 Margin Street, Peabody 01960; 508-532-3600

Catholic Charities, 470 Washington Street, Somerville 02143; 617-625-1920

Catholic Charities, 15 Ripley Street, Worcester 01610; 508-798-0191

Catholic Social Services, 783 Slade Street, Fall River 02724; 508-674-4681

Children's Aid and Family Services, 8 Trumbull Road, Northampton 01060; 413-584-5690

Children's Services of Roxbury, 2406 Washington Street, Roxbury 02119; 617-445-6655

Concord Family Service, Community Agencies Building, Concord 01742; 508-259-8556

DARE Family Services, 55 Dimock Street, Boston 02119; 617-427-7346

DARE Family Services-North, 3 Monument Square, Beverly 01915; 508-927-1674

DARE Mentor Adoption, 32 Hampden Street, Springfield 01105; 413-787-9915

DARE Worcester, 22 Front Street, Worcester 01614; 508-755-7100

Downey Side, 999 Liberty Street, Springfield 01104; 413-781-2123. Places adolescents.

Florence Crittenton League, 119 Hall Street, Lowell 01854; 508-452-9671

Jewish Family and Children's Service, 31 New Chardon Street, Boston 02114; 617-227-6641

Jewish Family Service of Greater Springfield, 15 Lenox Street, Springfield 01108; 413-737-2601

Jewish Family Service of Metrowest, 14 Vernon Street, Framingham 01701; 508-875-3100

Jewish Family Service of the North Shore, 564 Loring Avenue, Salem 01970;
508-745-9760

Jewish Family Service of Worcester, 646 Salisbury Street, Worcester 01609; 508-
755-3101

La Alianza Hispana, 409 Dudley Street, Roxbury 02119; 617-427-7175

LDS Social Services of Massachusetts, 150 Brown Street, Weston 02193; 603-
889-0148

Love the Children of Massachusetts, 2 Perry Drive, Duxbury 02332; 617-934-0332

Lutheran Child and Family Service, 6 Dean Street, Worcester 01609; 508-791-
4488

Merrimack Valley Catholic Charities, 430 North Canal Street, Lawrence 01840;
508-685-5930

New Bedford Child & Family Service, 1061 Pleasant Street, New Bedford 02740;
508-996-8572

New England Home for Little Wanderers, 161 South Huntington Avenue, Boston
02130; 617-232-8610

Northeastern Family Institute, 31 Exchange Street, Lynn 01930; 617-231-2500

Our Lady of Providence Children's Center, 2112 Riverdale Street, West Springfield
01089; 413-788-7366

Parsons Child and Family Center, 66 Lake Buel Road, Great Barrington 01230;
413-528-2749

Project IMPACT, 25 West Street, Boston 02111; 617-451-1472. Serves waiting
children.

Protestant Social Service Bureau, 776 Hancock Street, Wollaston 02170; 617-773-
6203.

Southeastern Adoption Services, 585 Fron Street, Marion 02738; 617-748-2529.

United Homes for Children, 2297 Main Street, Tewksbury 01876; 508-657-8331

Wide Horizons for Children, 282 Moody Street, Waltham 02154; 617-894-5330

Worcester Children's Friend Society, 21 Cedar Street, Worcester 01609; 508-753-
5425

The Open Door Society of Massachusetts (P.O. Box 1158, Westboro, 01581;
800-932-3678) has produced an informative booklet, *Adoptions Today,* that
is a general guide to adoption.

MICHIGAN

State Agency: Department of Social Services, P.O. Box 30037, Lansing 48909;
517-373-3513. General inquiries may be directed to the state exchange *(see
below).*

State Exchange: Michigan Adoption Resource Exchange, P.O. Box 6128, Jackson 49204; 517-783-MARE or 800-589-MARE

State Photolisting Book: *Michigan Adoption Resource Exchange Photolisting
Book*

Independent Adoption: Not permitted/identified adoptions possible

NACAC Representative: Candee Bobalek, AASK Midwest, 3051 Siebert Road,
Midland 48640; 571-832-8117

Private Agencies

Adoption Associates, 5570 32nd Avenue, Hudsonville 49426

Adoption Cradle, 576 Capital S.W., Battle Creek 49017; 616-963-0794

Adventist Adoption Agency, 8903 U.S. Highway 31, Berrien Springs 49103; 616-471-2221

Alternative Adoption Advisors, 87 Lathrop, Battle Creek 49017; 616-629-4347

Alternatives for Children, 644 Harrison, Flint 48502; 313-235-0683

Americans for International Aid and Adoption, 877 South Adams, Birmingham 48011; 313-645-2211

Baptist Family Services, 214 North Mill Street, St. Louis 48880; 517-681-2171

Bethany Christian Services, 901 Eastern Avenue N.E., Grand Rapids 49503; 616-459-6273 or 800-BETHANY. Branch offices. Religious requirements for U.S. children. Intercountry adoptions have different requirements.

D. A. Blodgett Services for Children and Families, 805 Leonard Street N.E., Grand Rapids 49503; 616-451-2021.

Catholic Family Services, 1008 South Wenona Avenue, Bay City 48706; 517-892-2504

Catholic Family Services, 1819 Gull Road, Kalamazoo 49001; 616-381-9800

Catholic Social Services, 117 North Division, Ann Arbor 48104; 313-662-4534. Infants.

Catholic Social Services, 9851 Hamilton, Detroit 48202; 313-883-2100

Catholic Social Services, 202 East Boulevard Drive, Flint 48503; 313-232-9950

Catholic Social Services, 1152 Scribner N.W., Grand Rapids 49504; 616-456-1443

Catholic Social Services, 347 Rock Street, Marquette 49855; 906-228-8630

Catholic Social Services, 16 East Fifth, Monroe 48161; 313-242-3800

Catholic Social Services, 235 South Gratiot, Mount Clemons 48043; 313-468-2616

Catholic Social Services, 1095 Third, Muskegon 49440; 616-726-4735

Catholic Social Services, 50 Wayne Street, Pontiac 48058; 313-333-3700

Catholic Social Services, 2601 Thirteenth Street, Port Huron 48060; 313-987-9100

CFCS-Catholic Charities, 1000 Hastings Street, Traverse City 49684; 616-947-8110. Open adoptions.

Child and Family Services, P.O. Box 516, Alpena 49707; 517-356-4567

Child and Family Services, 904 Sixth Street, Bay City 48708; 517-895-5932

Child and Family Services, 412 Century, Holland 49423; 616-396-2301

Child and Family Services, 4801 Willoughby Road, Holt 48842; 517-699-1600

Child and Family Services, P.O. Box 706, Marquette 49855; 906-226-2516

Child and Family Services, 1352 Terrace Street, Muskegon 49442; 616-726-3582

Child and Family Services, 1002 Tenth Avenue, Port Huron 48060; 313-984-2627

Child and Family Services, 1226 North Michigan, Saginaw 48602; 517-753-8491

Child and Family Services, 2000 South State, St. Joseph 49085; 616-983-5545

Child and Family Services of Livingston, 3075 East Grand River Avenue, Howell 48843; 517-546-7530. Branch office.

Child and Family Services of Northwest Michigan, 3785 Townhall Road, Traverse City 49684; 616-946-8975

Child and Parent Services, 30600 Telegraph, Birmingham 48010; 313-646-7790

Children's Aid Society, 7700 Second Avenue, Detroit 48202; 313-875-0020

Children's Hope, 7823 South Whiteville Road, Shepherd 48883; 517-828-5842

Christian Cradle, 5303 South Cedar, Lansing 48912; 517-351-7500

Christian Family Services, 17105 West 12 Mile Road, Southfield 48076; 313-557-8390

Ennis Center for Children, 20100 Greenfield, Detroit 48235; 313-342-2699. Branch offices.

Evergreen Children's Services, 21590 Greenfield, Oak Park 48237; 313-968-1416

Family and Child Services of Calhoun, 182 West Van Buren Street, Battle Creek 49017; 616-965-3247

Family and Children's Services of the Kalamazoo Area, 1608 Lake Street, Kalamazoo 49001; 616-344-0202

Family and Children's Services of Midland, P.O. Box 2086, Midland 48641; 517-631-5390.

Family and Children's Services, 114 Orchard Lake Road, Pontiac 48053; 313-332-8352

Family Service and Children's Aid of Jackson County, 906 West Monroe Avenue, Jackson 49204; 517-787-2738

Foreign Adoption Consultants, 421 West Crosstown Parkway, P.O. Box 489, Kalamazoo 49005; 616-343-3316

Golden Cradle International, 1660 Cliffs Landing, Ypsilanti 48198; 313-485-0902

Homes for Black Children, 2340 Calvert, Detroit 48206; 313-869-2316

Jewish Family Services, 24123 Greenfield, Southfield 48075; 313-559-1500

Judson Center, 23077 Greenfield, Royal Oak 48072; 313-443-5000

Keane Center for Adoption, 930 Mason, Dearborn 48124; 313-277-4664

LDS Social Services, 37634 Enterprise Court, Farmington 48018; 313-553-0902

Lutheran Adoption Service, 20700 Greenfield, Oak Park 48237; 313-968-1700

Lutheran Social Services, 135 West Washington, Marquette 49855; 906-226-7410

Methodist Children's Home Society, 26645 West 6 Mile Road, Detroit 48240; 313-531-4060

Morning Star Adoption Resource Services, 2300 North Woodward, Royal Oak 48073; 313-399-2740

Northern Michigan Adoption Services, 701 South Elmwood Street, Traverse City 49684; 616-941-1300

Orchards Children's Services, 30233 Southfield Road, Southfield 48076; 313-258-0440

St. Vincent Home, 2800 West Willow Street, Lansing 48917; 517-323-4734

Spaulding for Children, 17390 West 8 Mile Road, Southfield 48075; 313-443-0300. Serves waiting children.

Spectrum Human Services, 17000 West 8 Mile Road, Southfield 48075; 313-552-8020

Teen Ranch, 24331 West 8 Mile Road, Detroit 48219; 313-255-9770

Touch of Hope Adoption Center, 8 West Main Street, Hartford 49057; 616-621-2411

Whaley Children's Center, 1201 North Grand Traverse, Flint 48503; 313-234-3603
Youth Living Centers, 30000 Hively, Inkster 48141; 313-563-5005

MINNESOTA

State Agency: Department of Human Services, 444 Lafayette Road, St. Paul
   55155-3831; 612-296-0584
State Exchange: *See above*
State Photolisting Book: *Minnesota's Waiting Children*
Independent Adoption: Yes/intermediaries permitted if licensed/newspaper ad-
   vertising permitted
NACAC Representative: Contact National Office
Private Agencies
Bethany Christian Services (*see* Iowa).
Caritas Family Services, 305 7th Avenue North, St. Cloud 56301; 612-252-
   4121
Catholic Charities, 1200 Memorial Drive, Crookston 56716; 218-281-4224
Catholic Charities, Diocese of Winona, 111 Riverfront, Winona 55987; 507-454-
   2270
Catholic Charities of the Archdiocese of Minneapolis/St. Paul, 1600 University
   Avenue, St. Paul 55104; 612-641-1180
Children's Home Society of Minnesota, 2230 Como Avenue, St. Paul 55108; 612-
   646-6393. Serves state.
Christian Family Services (*see* North Dakota)
Crossroads Adoption Services, 4640 West 77th Street, Minneapolis 55435; 612-
   831-5707. Serves state.
Families for Children, 1566 Sumter Avenue North, Golden Valley 55427; 612-545-
   1750. Serves state.
Forever Families International Adoption Agency, 2004 Highway 37, Eveleth 55734;
   218-744-4734. Serves state.
Hope International Family Services, 421 South Main Street, Stillwater 55082;
   612-439-2446
Jewish Family Services of St. Paul, 1546 St. Clair Avenue, St. Paul 55105; 612-
   698-8081. Serves state.
LDS Social Services (*see* Illinois)
The Lutheran Home, 611 West Main Street, Belle Plain 56011; 612-873-2215.
   Serves state. Religious requirement.
Lutheran Social Service of Minnesota, 2414 Park Avenue, Minneapolis 55404;
   612-871-0221. Serves state.
New Horizons International Family Services, P.O. Box 623, Frost-Benico Building,
   Highway 254, Frost 56033; 507-878-3200
New Life Family Service, 3361 Republic Avenue, St. Louis Park 55426; 612-920-
   8117. Religious requirement.
Wellspring Adoption Agency, 1219 University Avenue S.E., Minneapolis 55414;
   612-333-0489

MISSISSIPPI
State Agency: Department of Human Services, Adoption Unit, P.O. Box 352, Jackson 39205; 601-354-0341
State Exchange: Mississippi Adoption Resource Exchange *(see above)*
State Photolisting Book: Mississippi Adoption Resource Exchange
Independent Adoption: Permitted/intermediaries allowed/newspaper advertising permitted
NACAC Representative: Linda West, Ministers for Adoption, P.O. Box 1078, Jackson 39205; 601-352-7784
Private Agencies
Adoption Ministries of Mississippi, P.O. Box 20346, Jackson 39289-0346; 601-352-7888
Bethany Christian Services, 3000 Old Canton Road, Room 360, Jackson 39216; 601-366-4282
Catholic Charities, 748 North President Street, P.O. Box 2248, Jackson 39205; 601-355-8634
Catholic Social and Community Services, P.O. Box 1457, Biloxi 39530-1457; 601-374-8316
Latter Day Saints Social Services (*see* Louisiana)
Mississippi Children's Home Society, P.O. Box 1078, 1801 North West Street, Jackson 39205; 601-352-7784. Serves state.
New Beginnings of Tupelo, P.O. Box 7055, Tupelo 38802; 601-841-5341
West Tennessee AGAPE (*see* Tennessee)

MISSOURI
State Agency: Division of Family Services, Department of Social Services, P.O. Box 88, Jefferson City 65103; 314-751-2882; Foster/Adopt Hotline 800-554-2222
State Exchange: No
State Photolisting Book: *Missouri Adoption Photo-listing*
Independent Adoption: Permitted/certain intermediaries permitted
NACAC Representative: Lauren Johnson, Open Door Society of Missouri, 9417 Pine, St. Louis 63144; 314-968-5239
Private Agencies
ACT Adoption Services, 7600 N.W. Barry Road, Kansas City 64111; 913-682-7914
Adams Center, 9200 Ward Parkway, Kansas City 64114; 816-444-4545
Adoption & Counseling Services for Families, 4320 Wornall Road, Kansas City 64111; 816-753-4333
Adoption Associates, 100 North Euclid, St. Louis 63108; 314-367-1557
Adoption Option, 1215 S.E. 6th Street, Lee's Summit 64063; 816-224-1525
Adoption Resource Center, 1903 Lafayette Avenue, St. Louis 63104-2525; 314-928-9090
APLACE, 7721 Delmar, P.O. Box 28036, St. Louis 63130; 314-721-3917
Associates in Adoption Counseling, 3820 North Cherry Lane, P.O. Box 1523, Kansas City 64106; 816-452-0139

Bethany Christian Services, 7750 Clayton Road, St. Louis 63117; 314-644-3535

Boys Town of Missouri, P.O. Box 189, St. James 65559; 314-265-3251

Catholic Charities of Kansas City, 1112 Broadway, Kansas City 64111; 816-221-4377

Catholic Services for Children and Youth, 4140 Lindell Boulevard, St. Louis 63108; 314-371-4980

Central Baptist Family Services, 7700 Clayton Road, St. Louis 63117; 314-644-4548

Child Placement Services, 221 West Lexington, Independence 64050; 816-461-3488

Children's Foundation—Adoption and Counseling, 8301 State Line, Kansas City 64114; 816-822-8333

Children's Home Society of Missouri, 9445 Litzsinger Road, Brentwood 63144; 314-968-2350

Christian Family Life Center, 7700 Clayton Road, St. Louis 63117; 314-367-7070

Christian Family Services, 8039 Watson Road, Webster Groves 63119; 314-968-2216

Christian Family Services, 6000 Blue Ridge Boulevard, Raytown 64133; 913-491-6751

Evangelical Children's Home, 8240 St. Charles Rock Road, St. Louis 63114; 314-427-3755

Family Network, 811 Cherry Street, Columbia 65201; 314-449-3231

Family Network, 9378 Olive Street Road, St. Louis 63122; 314-567-0707

Family Therapy Center of the Ozarks, 1345 East Sunshine, Springfield 65804; 417-882-7700

Gentle Shepherd Child Placement Agency, P.O. Box 30341, Kansas City 64112; 913-764-3811

Good Samaritan Boy's Ranch, P.O. Box 617, Brighton 65617; 417-756-2238

Heart of America Family Services, 3217 Broadway, Kansas City 64111; 816-753-5280

Highlands Child Placement Services, 5506 Cambridge Avenue, P.O. Box 5040, Kansas City 64129; 816-924-6565. Serves state.

Jewish Family & Children's Services, 9385 Olive Boulevard, Olivette 63044; 314-933-1000

Kansas Children's Service League, 3200 Wayne, Kansas City 64109; 913-621-2016

LDS Social Services, 517 West Walnut, Independence 64050; 816-461-5512. Religious requirement.

The Light House, 1409 East Meyer Boulevard, Kansas City 64131; 816-361-2233

Love Basket, 4472 Goldman Road, Hillsboro 63050; 314-789-4100. Religious requirement.

Lutheran Family & Children's Services, 4625 Lindell Blvd., St. Louis 63108; 314-361-2121. Religious requirement. Serves state.

Missouri Baptist Children's Home, 11300 St. Charles Rock Road, Bridgeton 63044; 314-739-6811

Presbyterian Home for Children, P.O. Box 31, Farmington 63640; 314-756-6744

Provident Counseling, 2650 Olive Street, St. Louis 63103; 314-371-6500

James A. Roberts Agency, 8301 State Line Road, Kansas City 64114; 816-523-4440

Salvation Army Hope Center, 3740 Marine Avenue, St. Louis 63118; 314-773-0980

United Methodist Children's & Family Services, 110 North Elm, Webster Groves 63119; 314-961-5718

Universal Adoption Services, 124 High Street, Jefferson City 65101; 314-635-6362

Worldwide Love for Children, 1221 East Republic Road, Springfield 65807; 417-881-1044

Youth Emergency Services, P.O. Box 24260, St. Louis 63130; 314-862-1334

MONTANA

State Agency: Department of Family Services, Box 8005, Helena 59604; 406-444-5900

State Exchange: No

State Photolisting Book: No

Independent Adoption: Permitted/no intermediaries/no newspaper advertising

NACAC Representative: Lois Jones, Families for Adoptable Children, P.O. Box 485, Anaconda 59711; 406-563-5077

Private Agencies

Catholic Social Services, 530 North Ewing, Box 907, Helena 59601; 406-442-4130. Serves state.

Florence Crittenton, 846 Fifth Avenue, Helena 59604; 406-442-6950

LDS Social Services, 2001 11 Avenue, Helena 59601; 406-443-1660. Religious requirements.

Lutheran Social Services, P.O. Box 1345, Great Falls 59403; 406-761-4341. Serves state.

Montana Intercountry Adoption, 109 South 8th Avenue, Bozeman 59715; 406-587-5101

Montana Post Adoption Center, 25 South Ewing, P.O. Box 634, Helena 59624; 406-449-3266

Shodair, 840 Helena Avenue, Helena; 406-444-7500

NEBRASKA

State Agency: Department of Social Services, 301 Centennial Mall South, Lincoln 68509; 402-471-9331

State Exchange: *See above*

State Photolisting Book: *Nebraska Adoption Exchange*

Independent Adoption: Permitted/no intermediaries but counsel from attorney possible/newspaper advertising allowed

NACAC Representative: Kathy Moore, Voices for Children in Nebraska, 5005 South 181 Plaza, Omaha 68135; 402-896-4536

Private Agencies

Catholic Social Service Bureau, 215 Centennial Mall South, Lincoln 68508; 402-474-1600. Serves state.

Child Saving Institute, 115 South 46 Street, Omaha 68132; 402-553-6000. Serves state. Has done open adoptions. Has special program for black applicants, Black Homes for Black Children; 402-595-2912

Holt International Children's Services (*see* Iowa)

Jewish Family Services, 333 South 132 Street, Omaha 68154; 402-330-2024. Religious requirements.

Kids Each Served in Love, P.O. Box 12175, Omaha 68112; 402-457-6408

LDS Social Services (*see* Missouri). Serves state.

Lutheran Family and Social Services, 120 South 24 Street, Omaha 68102; 402-342-7007. Serves state. Branch offices.

Nebraska Children's Home Society, 3549 Fontenelle Boulevard, Omaha 68104; 402-451-0787. Serves state. Branch offices.

Nebraska Christian Services, 11600 West Center Road, Omaha 68144; 402-334-3278

United Catholic Social Services, 3300 North 60th Street, Omaha 68106; 402-554-0520

NEVADA

State Agency: Division of Child and Family Services, 700 Belrose Street, Las Vegas 89158; 702-486-5270

State Exchange: *See above*

State Photolisting Book: No

Independent Adoption: Permitted/no compensation for intermediaries/no newspaper advertising

NACAC Representative: Margaret Dunn, Southern Nevada Adoption Association, 2300 Theresa Avenue, Las Vegas 89101; 702-649-8464

Private Agencies

Catholic Community Services of Nevada, 808 South Main Street, Las Vegas 89101; 702-385-2662

Catholic Community Services, P.O. Box 5415, Reno 89513; 702-385-2662

Jewish Family Services, 1555 East Flamingo Road, Las Vegas 89119; 702-732-0304

LDS Social Services, 1906 Santa Paula Drive, Las Vegas 89105; 702-735-1072. Serves state. Religious requirement.

NEW HAMPSHIRE

State Agency: Division for Children and Youth Services, 6 Hazen Drive, Concord 03301; 603-271-4721

State Exchange: No

State Photolisting Book: No

Independent Adoption: Permitted/intermediaries allowed/newspaper advertising permitted

NACAC Representative: Karen Needham, OURS of New England, 347 Candia Road, Chester 03036; 603-887-3293

Private Agencies

Adoptive Families for Children, 26 Fairview Street, Keene 03431; 603-357-4456. Serves state.

Bethany Christian Services (*see* Massachusetts)

Child & Family Services of New Hampshire, 99 Hanover Street, Manchester 03105; 603-668-1920 or in New Hampshire 800-640-6486. Serves state.

LDS Social Services, 131 Route 101A, Amherst Plaza, Amherst 03031. Serves state. Religious requirement.

Lutheran Child and Family Services of New Hampshire, 244 North Main Street, Concord 03301; 603-224-8111. Serves state.

New Hampshire Adoption Bureau, 71 West Merrimack Street, Manchester 03103; 800-338-2224. Infant adoptions.

New Hampshire Catholic Charities, 215 Myrtle Street, P.O. Box 686, Manchester 03105; 800-562-5249. Serves state.

Vermont Children's Aid Society (*see* Vermont). Serves border towns.

Wide Horizons for Children (*see* Massachusetts)

NEW JERSEY

State Agency: Division of Youth and Family Services, Adoption Unit, CN 717, 1 South Montgomery Street, Trenton 08625-0717; 609-633-6902

State Exchange: New Jersey Adoption Resource Exchange

State Photolisting Book: *New Jersey Adoption Photolisting Book*

Independent Adoption: Permitted/no intermediaries/newspaper advertising allowed

NACAC Representative: Lois Cowen, SNAP, 8 North Whittesbog Road, Browns Mills 08015; 609-893-7875

Private Agencies

Adopt A Miracle, 15 Quill Pen Way, Warren 07059-5517; 908-596-3958 or 800-423-6784

The Adoption Agency, 18 Washington Avenue, Haddonfield 08033; 609-795-5400

Adoption and Infertility Services, P.O. Box 447, Lincroft 07748; 201-671-8959

Adoption Service Associates (*see* Texas)

Adoptions International (*see* Pennsylvania)

A.M.O.R., 12 Grenoble Court, Matawan 07747; 908-583-0174

Associated Catholic Charities, 17 Mulberry Street, Newark 07102; 201-596-3958

Bethany Christian Services, 475 High Mountain Road, North Haledon 07508; 201-427-2566. Religious requirement.

Bethany Christian Services (*see* Pennsylvania)

Better Living Services, 1975 Saint Georges Avenue, Rahway 07065; 908-388-1880

Brookwood Child Care (*see* New York)

Casa del Mundo, 44 Main Street, Flemington 08822; 908-782-9393

Catholic Charities, Diocese of Metuchen, 288 Rues Lane, East Brunswick 08816; 908-257-6100

Catholic Family & Community Services, 476-17th Avenue, Paterson 07504; 201-523-2666

Catholic Home Bureau (*see* New York)

Catholic Social Services (*see* Pennsylvania)

Catholic Social Services, 1845 Haddon Avenue, Camden 08103; 609-756-7945. Religious requirement.

Catholic Welfare Bureau, 47 North Clinton Avenue, Trenton 08607; 609-394-5181

Child and Home Study Associates (*see* Pennsylvania)

Children of the World, 855 Bloomfield Avenue, Glen Ridge 07028; 201-429-0045. Serves state.

Children's Aid Society (*see* New York)

Children's Aid and Adoption Society of New Jersey, 575 Main Street, Hackensack 07601; 201-487-2022. Branch offices.

Children's Home Society of New Jersey, 929 Parkside Avenue, Trenton 08618; 609-695-6274. Serves state.

Choices (*see* Pennsylvania)

Chosen Children Adoption Services (*see* Kentucky)

Christian Homes for Children, 272 State Street, Hackensack 07601; 201-343-4235. Religious requirement. Serves state.

Downeyside (*see* New York)

Edna Gladney Center (*see* Texas)

Family and Children's Counseling and Testing Center, 40-52 North Avenue, Elizabeth 07207; 908-352-7474. Serves state. Branch offices.

Golden Cradle, 2201 Route 38, Cherry Hill 08002; 609-667-2229

Graham-Windham Child Care (*see* New York)

Growing Families, 1 Tall Timber Drive, Morristown 07960; 201-984-7875

Harlem-Dowling Children's Service (*see* New York)

Holt International Children's Services, 2490 Pennington Road, Trenton 08638; 609-737-7710. Intercountry adoptions. Serves state.

Homestudies, 1182 Teaneck Road, Teaneck 07666; 201-833-9030

International Adoption League, 55 Schanck Road, Freehold 07728; 908-409-6285

Jewish Child Care Association (*see* New York)

Jewish Family & Children's Services (see Pennsylvania)

LDS Social Services (*see* New York)

Little Flower Children's Services (*see* New York)

Louise Wise Services (*see* New York)

Love the Children (*see* Pennsylvania)

Lutheran Social Ministries of New Jersey, 120 Route 156, Yardville 08620; 609-585-0400. Serves state.

Mission of the Immaculate Virgin (*see* New York)

New Beginnings Family and Children Services (*see* New York)

New York Catholic Guardian Society (*see* New York)

New York Foundling Hospital (*see* New York)

Sheltering Arms Childrens Services (*see* New York)

Small World Agency (*see* Tennessee)

Spaulding for Children, 36 Prospect Street, Westfield 07090; 908-233-2282. Serves state. Serves waiting children. Branch offices.

Spence-Chapin Adoption Services (*see* New York)

Tabor Childrens Services (*see* Pennsylvania)

Talbot-Perkins Children's Services (*see* New York)
Texas Cradle Society (*see* Texas)
Todays Adoption Agency (*see* Pennsylvania)
United Family and Children's Society, 305 West Seventh Street, Plainfield 07060; 908-755-4848
Voice for International and Domestic Adoptions (*see* New York)
Welcome House (*see* Pennsylvania)
Women's Christian Alliance (*see* Pennsylvania)

The New Jersey Division of Youth and Family Services has produced an informative booklet, *Directory of Adoption Agencies Serving New Jersey,* that outlines each agency's eligibility requirements.

NEW MEXICO
State Agency: Department of Human Services, P.O. Box 2348, Santa Fe 87504; 505-827-8423 or in New Mexico 800-432-2075
State Exchange: New Mexico Adoption Exchange *(see above)*
State Photolisting Book: *New Mexico Adoption Exchange*
Independent Adoption: Permitted/intermediaries allowed/newspaper advertising allowed
NACAC Representative: Carol Schreiber, Child-Rite, P.O. Box 1448, Taos 87571; 505-758-0343
Private Agencies
Catholic Social Services, P.O. Box 443, 839 Paseo de Peralta, Santa Fe 87504; 505-982-0441
Chaparral Maternity & Adoption Division, 1503 University N.E., Albuquerque 87102; 505-266-5837. Serves state.
Christian Child Placement Services, HC69, Box 48, Portales 88130; 505-356-4232
Families for Children, 920 Ortiz N.E., Albuquerque 87108; 505-266-8282
La Familia Placement, 4600 B. Montgomery N.E., Albuquerque 87109; 505-292-3678
LDS Social Services, 3811 Atrisco N.W., Albuquerque 87120; 505-836-5947
LDS Farmington, 925 West Lee Murray Thruway, Farmington 87401; 505-327-6123
New Mexico Christian Children's Home, West Star Route, Box 48, Portales 88130; 505-356-8414
Rainbow House International, 19676 Highway 85, Belen 87002; 505-865-5550
Triad Adoption Services, 2811 Indian School Road NE, Albuquerque 87106; 505-266-0456

NEW YORK
State Agency: Department of Social Services, Adoption Services, 40 North Pearl Street, Albany 12243; 800-345-KIDS
State Exchange: No

State Photolisting Book: *New York State's Waiting Children* (often referred to as the "Blue Books")

Independent Adoption: Permitted/intermediaries allowed/newspaper advertising permitted

NACAC Representatives: Judith Ashton, New York State Citizens' Coalition for Children, 614 West State Street, Ithaca 14850; 607-272-0034; You can also contact the Council on Adoptable Children, 666 Broadway, New York 100121; 212-475-0222. The New York State Citizens' Coalition for Children can give you information about the more than 80 adoptive parent groups in the state.

Private Agencies

Abbott House, 100 North Broadway, Irvington 10533; 914-591-7300. The overwhelming majority of the children served are minority.

Adoption & Counseling Services, One Fayette Park, Syracuse 13202; 315-471-0109

Americans for International Aid and Adoption, P.O. Box 290, Plainville 13137; 315-638-9449

Angel Guardian Home, 6301 12 Avenue, Brooklyn 11219; 718-232-1500

Brookwood Child Care, 25 Washington Street, Brooklyn 11201; 718-596-5555. Places primarily black children.

Cardinal McCloskey School/Home, 2 Holland Avenue, White Plains 10603; 914-997-8000

Catholic Charities of Buffalo, 525 Washington Street, Buffalo 14203; 716-856-4494

Catholic Charities of Ogdensburg, P.O. Box 296, Ogdensburg 13669-0296; 315-393-2660. Branch offices.

Catholic Charities of Ogdensburg/Plattsburgh, 151 South Catherine Street, Plattsburgh 12901; 518-561-0470

Catholic Charities of Oswego, 181 West 2nd Street, Oswego 13126; 315-343-9540

Catholic Charities of Syracuse, 1654 West Onondaga Street, Syracuse 13204; 315-424-1871

Catholic Charities of Syracuse/Rome, 212 West Liberty Street, Rome 13440; 315-337-8600

Catholic Family Center, 50 Chestnut Street, Rochester 14604; 716-546-7220

Catholic Guardian Society of Brooklyn, 191 Joralemon Street, Brooklyn 11201; 718-330-0638

Catholic Guardian Society of New York, 1011 First Avenue, New York 10022; 212-371-1000

Catholic Home Bureau, 1011 First Avenue, New York 10022; 212-371-1000

Catholic Social Services of Broome County, 232 Main Street, Binghamton 13905; 607-729-9166

Catholic Social Services of Utica/Syracuse, 1408 Genessee Street, Utica 13502; 315-724-2158

Cayuga Counseling Service, 46 South Street, Auburn 13021; 315-253-9795

Child & Family Services of Erie, 330 Delaware Avenue, Buffalo 14202; 716-856-3802

Child & Family Services, 678 West Onondaga Street, Syracuse 13204; 315-474-4291

Children's Aid Society, 150 East 45 Street, New York 10017; 212-949-4836

Children's Home of Kingston, 26 Grove Street, Kingston 12401; 914-331-1448

Children's Home of Poughkeepsie, 91 Fulton Street, Poughkeepsie 12601; 914-452-1420

Children's Village, Dobbs Ferry 10522; 914-693-0600

Community Maternity Services, 27 North Main Avenue, Albany 12203; 518-438-2322

Downey Side Families for Youth, 371 Seventh Avenue, New York 10001-3984; 212-629-8599

Edwin Gould Services for Children, 41 East 11 Street, New York 10003; 212-598-0051

Episcopal Mission Society, 1331 Franklin Avenue, Bronx 10456; 212-589-1434

Evangelical Family Services, 119 Church Street, North Syracuse 13212; 315-458-1415

Family and Children's Services of Albany, 12 South Lake Avenue, Albany 12203; 518-462-6531

Family and Children's Services of Ithaca, 204 North Cayuga Street, Ithaca 14850; 607-273-7494

Family and Children's Services of Broome County, 257 Main Street, Binghamton 13905; 607-729-6206

Family and Children's Services of Schenectady, 246 Union Street, Schenectady 12305; 518-393-1369

Family Focus, 54-40 Little Neck Parkway, Little Neck 11362; 718-224-1919

Family Service of Utica, 401 Columbia Street, Utica 13502; 315-735-2236

Family Service of Westchester, 470 Mamaroneck Avenue, White Plains 10605; 914-948-9004

Forestdale, 67-35 112 Street, Forest Hills 11375; 718-263-0740

Friendship House of Western New York, 264 Ridge Road, Lackawanna 14218; 716-826-1500

Graham-Windham, 33 Irving Place, New York 10003; 212-529-6445

Green Chimneys, Putnam Lake Road, Brewster 10509; 212-892-6810

Greer-Woodycrest Services, Hope Farm, Millbrook 12545; 914-354-0214

Harlem-Dowling Children's Services, 2090 Seventh Avenue, New York 10027; 212-749-3656. Places primarily black children.

Hillside Children's Center, 1337 East Main Street, Rochester 14609; 716-654-4529

Jewish Board of Family and Children Services, 120 West 57 Street, New York 10019; 212-582-9100

Jewish Child Care Association, 575 Lexington Avenue, New York 10022; 212-371-1313. Will do identified adoptions.

Jewish Family Services of Erie County, 70 Barker Street, Buffalo 14209; 716-883-1914

Jewish Family Service of Rochester, 441 East Avenue, Rochester 14607; 716-461-0110

LDS Social Services of New York, 105 Main Street, Fishkill 12524; 914-896-8266. Religious requirement.

Leake & Watts Childrens Home, 463 Hawthorne Avenue, Yonkers 10705; 914-963-5220. Places black children.

Little Flower Children's Service, 186 Joralemon Street, Brooklyn 11201; 718-875-3500

Louise Wise Services, 12 East 94 Street, New York 10028; 212-876-3050

Love the Children, 28 Foxboro Lane, Fairport 14450; 716-223-1868

Lutheran Community Services, 27 Park Place, New York 10007; 212-406-9110

Lutheran Service Society, 2500 Kensington Avenue, Buffalo 14226; 716-839-3391

Malone Catholic Charities, 105 West Main Street, Malone 19253; 518-483-1460

McMahon Services for Children, 225 East 45 Street, New York 10017; 212-972-7070

Mercy Home for Children, 273 Willoughby Avenue, Brooklyn 11205; 718-622-5842

Miracle Makers, 33 Somers Street, Brooklyn 11233; 718-385-CARE

Mission of the Immaculate Virgin, 6581 Hylan Boulevard, Staten Island 10309; 718-317-2605. Serves waiting children.

New Alternatives for Children, 37 West 26th Street, New York 10010; 212-696-1550

New Beginnings Family and Children's Services, 141 Willis Avenue, Mineola 11501; 516-747-2204

New York Foundling Hospital, 590 Avenue of the Americas, New York 10011; 212-727-6828

Ohel Children's Home, 4423 16 Avenue, Brooklyn 11204; 212-851-6300. Religious requirements.

Our Lady of Victory, 790 Ridge Road, Lackawanna 14218; 716-827-9611

Parsons Child & Family Center, 60 Academy Road, Albany 12208; 518-426-2600

Pius XII Youth/Family Services, 369 East 149 Street, New York 10455; 212-993-3650

Praca Child Care, 853 Broadway, New York 10003; 212-673-7320

St. Augustine Center, 1600 Fillmore, Buffalo 14211; 716-897-4110

St. Christopher Ottilie, 570 Fulton Street, Brooklyn 11217; 718-855-0330. Branch offices.

St. Christophers/Jennie Clarkson, 71 South Broadway, Dobbs Ferry 10522; 914-693-3030

St. Dominics, 535 East 138 Street, Bronx 10454; 212-402-5900

St. Josephs Children's Services, 345 Adams Street, Brooklyn 11201; 718-858-8700

St. Mary's of the Angels, Convent Road, Syosset 11791; 516-921-0808

St. Vincent's Services, 66 Boerum Place, Brooklyn 11202; 718-522-3700

Salvation Army Foster Home Services, 132 West 14 Street, New York 10011; 212-807-4200

Sheltering Arms Childrens Service, 122 East 29 Street, New York 10016; 212-679-4242

Society for Seamen's Children, 26 Bay Street, Staten Island 10301; 718-447-7740

Spence-Chapin Adoption Services, 6 East 94 Street, New York 10028; 212-369-0300

Talbot Perkins Children's Services, 116 West 32 Street, New York 10001; 212-736-2510

Voice for International and Domestic Adoptions (VIDA), 354 Allen Street, Hudson 12534; 518-828-4527

Wide Horizons for Children, 22 Yerk Avenue, Ronkonkoma 11779; 515-585-1008

The Interstate Compact Office in the New York State Department of Social Services also approves out-of-state agencies to do fee-based adoptive placements in New York state. For a list of approved out-of-state agencies, contact the Interstate Compact Office (518-474-9582 or 800-342-3715).

NORTH CAROLINA

State Agency: Division of Social Services, 325 North Salisbury Street, Raleigh 27603; 919-733-3801

State Exchange: North Carolina Adoption Resource Exchange *(see above)*

State Photolisting Book: *PALS (Photo Adoption Listing Service)*

Independent Adoption: Permitted/no intermediaries/no advertising

NACAC Representative: Liz Grimes, Triad Adoptive Parent Support Group, 133 Penny Road, High Point 27260; 819-886-8230

Private Agencies

AGAPE of North Carolina, 302 College Road, Greensboro 27410; 919-855-7107

Bethany Christian Services, 25 Reed Street, Asheville 28813; 704-274-7146. Serves state. Religious requirement.

Catholic Social Ministries, 400 Oberlin Road, Raleigh 27605; 919-832-0225

Catholic Social Services, 116 East First Street, Charlotte 28235; 704-333-9954

The Children's Home Society of North Carolina, 740 Chestnut Street, Greensboro 27415; 919-274-1538. Serves state. Branch offices.

Christian Adoption Services, 624 Matthews-Mint Hill Road, Matthews 28105; 704-847-0038

Family Resources, 1521 Foxhollow Road, Greensboro 27410; 919-852-5357

Family Services, 610 Coliseum Drive, Winston-Salem 27106-5393; 919-722-8173

LDS Social Services, 5624 Executive Center Drive, Charlotte 28212; 704-535-2436. Religious requirement.

Lutheran Family Services, P.O. Box 12287, Raleigh 27605; 919-832-2620

NORTH DAKOTA

State Agency: Children and Family Services, Department of Human Services, 600 East Boulevard Avenue, Bismarck 58505-0250; 701-224-4811

State Exchange: No

State Photolisting Book: No

Independent Adoption: Not permitted
NACAC Representative: Contact National Office
Private Agencies
Catholic Family Service, 2537 South University, Fargo 58103; 701-235-4457
Christian Family Life Services, 15 South 10th Street, Fargo 58102; 701-237-9247.
    Infant adoptions.
LDS Social Services, P.O. Box 3100, Bismarck 58502; 605-342-3500
Lutheran Social Services of North Dakota, 1325 South 11 Street, Fargo 58107;
    701-235-7341
New Horizons Foreign Adoption Service, 2876 Woodland Place, Bismarck 58504;
    701-258-8650
Professional Christian Resource Center, 1501 North 12th Street, Bismarck 58501;
    701-255-3325. Infant adoptions.
The Village Family Service Center, 1201-25 Street South, P.O. Box 9859, Fargo
    58106-9859; 701-235-6433

OHIO
State Agency: Department of Human Services, Adoptions, 65 East State Street,
    Columbus 43266; 800-686-1581 or 614-466-9274
State Exchange: Ohio Adoption Resource Exchange *(see above)*
State Photolisting Book: *Photolisting of Ohio*
Independent Adoption: Permitted/no newspaper advertising
NACAC Representative: Oliva Simpson, Group of Black Adoptive Parents, 1055
    Grayview Court, Cincinnati 45224; 513-541-4166
Private Agencies
Agape for Youth, 906 Senate Drive, Dayton 45459; 513-223-7217
The Bair Foundation, 325 North State Street, Girard 44420; 216-545-0435
Baptist Children's Home and Family Ministries, 1934 South Limestone Street,
    Springfield 45505; 513-322-0006
Berea Children's Home, 202 East Bagley Road, Berea 44017; 216-234-2006
Bethany International Adoptions/Bethany Christian Services, 1655 West Market
    Street, Akron 44313; 216-867-2362
Black Family Connections, 562 East Main Street, Columbus 43215; 614-341-6015
Catholic Community League, 625 Cleveland Avenue N.W., Canton 44702; 216-
    455-0374
Catholic Community Services, 2932 Youngstown Road S.E., Warren 44484; 216-
    369-4254
Catholic Service Bureau of Lake County, 8 North State Street, Painesville 44077;
    216-946-7264
Catholic Service League of Summit County, 640 North Main Street, Akron 44310;
    216-762-7481
Catholic Service League of Ashtabula County, 4436 Main Avenue, Ashtabula
    44004; 216-992-2121
Catholic Service League of Western Stark County, 1807 Lincoln Way East, Massil-
    lon 44646; 216-833-8516

Catholic Service League of Youngstown, 5385 Market Street, Youngstown 44512; 216-788-8726

Catholic Social Services (*see* Kentucky)

Catholic Social Services Bureau, 2136 North Ridge Road, Elyria 44035; 216-277-7228

Catholic Social Services of Cuyahoga County, 3409 Woodland Avenue, Cleveland 44115; 216-881-1600

Catholic Social Services, 1933 Spiebusch Avenue, Toledo 43624; 419-244-6711

Catholic Social Services, 197 East Gay Street, Columbus 43215; 614-221-5891

Catholic Social Services of the Miami Valley, 922 West Riverview Avenue, Dayton 45407; 513-223-7217

Catholic Social Service of Southwest Ohio, 100 East 8 Street, Cincinnati 45202; 513-241-7745

Children's Home of Cincinnati, 5051 Duck Creek, Cincinnati 45227; 513-272-2800

Children's Services, 1001 Euclid Avenue, Cleveland 44115; 216-781-2043

Family and Community Services of Catholic Charities, Columbiana County, 966½ North Market Street, Lisbon 44432; 216-424-9509

Family and Community Services of Catholic Charities, 302 North Depeyster Street, Kent 44240; 216-678-3911

Family Counseling & Crittenton Services, 1229 Sunbury Road, Columbus 43219; 614-252-5229

Family Counseling Services of Central Stark County, 618 Second Street N.W., Canton 44703; 216-454-7066

Family Counseling Services of Western Stark County, 51 North Avenue N.E., Massillon 44646; 216-832-5043

Family Service Agency, 535 Marmion Avenue, Youngstown 45502; 216-782-5664

Family Service Association, P.O. Box 1027, Steubenville 43952; 614-283-4763

Family Service Association, 1704 North Road S.E., Warren 44484; 216-856-2907

Family Services of Summit County, 212 East Exchange Street, Akron 44304; 216-376-9494

Foreign Adoption Consultants, 8536 Crow Drive, Macedonia 44056; 216-468-0673

General Protestant Orphan Home, 6881 Beechmont Avenue, Cincinnati 45230; 513-231-6630

Gentle Care Adoption Services, 243 East Livingston Avenue, Columbus 43215; 614-469-0007

Hannah Neil Center for Children, 301 Obetz Road, Columbus 43207; 614-491-5784

HARAMBEE: Services for Black Families, 1468 East 55 Street, Cleveland 44103; 216-391-7044

Jewish Children's Bureau, 22001 Fairmount Boulevard, Cleveland 44118; 216-932-2800

Jewish Family Service, 3085 West Market Street, Akron 44320; 216-867-3388

Jewish Family Service, 2831 East Main Street, Columbus 43209; 614-231-1890

Jewish Family Service, 1710 Section Road, Cincinnati 45237; 513-351-3680

Jewish Family Services, 4501 Denlinger Road, Dayton 45426; 513-854-2944

Jewish Family Service, 6525 Sylvania Avenue, Toledo 43560; 419-885-2561
Jewish Family & Children's Service, 505 Gypsy Lane, Youngstown 44501; 216-746-3251
KARE, Inc., 5055 North Main Street, Dayton 45405; 513-275-5715
Lake/Geauga Adoption Services, 8 North State Street, Painesville 44077; 216-946-7264
LDS Social Services, 4431 Marketing Place, Groveport 43125; 614-836-2466
Lutheran Children's Aid and Family Services, 4100 Franklin Boulevard, Cleveland 44113; 216-281-2500
Lutheran Social Services of Central Ohio, 57 East Main Street, Columbus 43215; 614-228-5209
Lutheran Social Services of the Miami Valley, 3304 North Main Street, Dayton 45405; 513-278-9617
Lutheran Social Services of Northwestern Ohio, 2149 Collingwood Boulevard, Toledo 43620; 419-243-9178
Midwestern Children's Home, 4581 Long Spurling Road, Pleasant Plain 45162; 513-877-2141
Northeast Ohio Adoption Services, 8029 East Market Street, Warren 44484; 216-856-5582. Serves waiting children.
Ohio Youth Advocate Program, 1460 West Lane Avenue, Columbus 43221; 614-221-0895
Regional Family Counseling, 635 West Spring Street, Lima 45801; 419-225-1040
Spaulding for Children-Beech Brook, 3737 Lander Road, Cleveland 44124; 216-464-4445. Serves waiting children.
United Methodist Children's Home, 1033 High Street, Worthington 43085; 614-885-5020

The Ohio Department of Human Services can send you an interesting booklet, *Epilogue: Post Adoption Services in Ohio.*

OKLAHOMA
State Agency: Department of Human Services, P.O. Box 25352, Oklahoma City 73125; 405-521-2475
State Exchange: No
State Photolisting Book: *OKCARE* (inactive)
Independent Adoption: Permitted/intermediaries allowed/newspaper advertising permitted
NACAC Representative: Dwe Williams, Oklahoma COAC, 2609 NW 38th Street, Oklahoma City 73112; 405-942-0810
Private Agencies
Adoption Center, P.O. Box 595, Bartlesville 74005; 918-336-1827
Adoption Affiliates, 6136 East 32nd Place, Tulsa 74135; 918-665-6400
Associated Catholic Charities, 516 Northwest Seventh Street, Oklahoma City 73101; 405-232-8512
Bethany Adoption Services, 3940 North College, Bethany 73008; 405-787-6913

Catholic Social Services, 739 North Denver, Tulsa 74106; 918-585-8167

Chosen Child, 10759 East Admiral, Tulsa 74116; 918-250-6837

Cradle of Lawton, 7901 Terrace Hills, Lawton 73505; 405-353-8897

Deaconness Home, 5401 North Portland, Oklahoma City 73112; 405-942-5001. Religious requirement. Infants.

Department of Child Care Baptist, 1141 North Robinson, Oklahoma City 73103; 405-236-4341

Dillon International, 7615 East 63 Place South, Tulsa 74133; 918-250-1561. Religious requirement.

Hannah's Prayer, 2651 East 21st, Tulsa 74114; 918-743-5400

Kalamazoo & Baby Too, 6506 South Lewis, Tulsa 74105; 918-747-9998

LDS Social Services of Oklahoma, 2005 South Elm Place, Broken Arrow 74012; 918-451-0342

Lutheran Social Services, 2901 North Classen, Oklahoma City 73103; 405-528-3124

MetroCenter for Family Ministries, P.O. Box 2380, Edmond 73083; 405-359-1400

Neighborhood Services, 613 North Broadway, Oklahoma City 73102; 405-236-1839

Small Miracles International, 1380 South Douglas Boulevard, Midwest City 73130; 405-732-7295

United Methodist Counseling Services, 2617 North Douglas, Oklahoma City 73106; 405-528-1906

OREGON

State Agency: Adoption Services, Children's Services Division, 198 Commercial Street S.E., Salem 97310; 503-378-4121

State Exchange: No

State Photolisting Book: *CSD Special Needs Bulletin*

Independent Adoption: Permitted/intermediaries allowed/newspaper advertising allowed

NACAC Representative: Harriet Gahr, 18605 S.W. Massonville Roads, McMinnville 97128; 503-472-6960

Private Agencies

Adventist Adoption & Family Services Program, 6040 S.E. Belmont Street, Portland 97215; 503-232-1211. Serves state.

Albertina Kerr Center for Children, 722 N.E. 162nd, Portland 97230; 503-255-4205. Serves state.

Boys & Girls Aid Society of Oregon, 18 S.W. Boundary Court, Portland 97201-3985; 503-222-9661 or 800-342-6688. Serves state.

Caring Connections, 5439 S.E. Bantam Court, Milwaukee 97267; 503-282-3663

Catholic Community Services, 231 S.E. 12th Avenue, Portland 97214; 503-231-4866

Columbia Counseling, 1445 Rosemont Road, West Linn 97068; 503-655-9470

First American's Adoptions, 4820 S.W. Barbur, P.O. Box 69622, Portland 97201; 503-243-5576

Give Us This Day, P.O. Box 11611, Portland 97211; 503-288-4335

Holt International Children's Services, P.O. Box 2880, Eugene 97402; 503-687-2202

Hope Services (*see* Washington state)

LDS Social Services, 3000 Market Street, Salem 97304; 503-581-6652. Serves state. Religious requirements.

Northwest Adoption and Family Services, 2695 Spring Valley Lane NW, Salem 97304; 503-224-4974

Open Adoptions and Family Services, 529 S.E. Grand, Portland 97214; 503-233-9660

PLAN International Adoption Services, P.O. Box 667, McMinnville 97128; 503-472-8452. Serves state.

PENNSYLVANIA

State Agency: Department of Public Welfare, Office of Children, Youth and Families, P.O. Box 2675, Harrisburg 17105-2675; 717-257-7003

State Exchange: Pennsylvania Adoption Exchange, Lanco Lodge, Second Floor, P.O. Box 2675, Harrisburg 17105-2675; 717-257-7105 or 800-227-0225

State Photolisting Book: *Pennsylvania Adoption Exchange Photolisting Service (P.A.C.E.)*

Independent Adoption: Permitted/intermediaries allowed/advertising permitted

NACAC Representatives: Phyllis Stevens, Tabor Adoptive Parents, 1801 Maple Circle, Lansdale 19446; 215-699-8546, and Sherry Anderson, COAC of SW Pennsylvania, P.O. Box 81044, Pittsburgh 15217; 412-361-4419

Private Agencies

The Adoption Agency, 76 Rittenhouse Place, Ardmore 19003; 215-642-7200

Adoption Alliance, 859 Stirrup Lane, Warrington 18976; 215-343-0758

Adoption Horizons, 403 Roxbury Road, Shippensburg 17257; 717-249-8850

Adoption Services, 115 South St. Johns Drive, Camp Hill 17011; 717-737-3960

Adoption Unlimited, 2770 Weston Road, Lancaster 17603; 717-872-1340

Adoptions International, 125 South 9th Street, Philadelphia 19107; 215-627-6313

Aid for Children International, 118 West Walnut Street, Marietta 17547; 717-426-2948

The Bair Foundation, 241 High Street, New Wilmington 16142; 412-946-2220

Bethanna, 1030 Second Street Pike, Southampton 18901; 215-345-0430

Bethany Christian Services of Western Pennsylvania, 694 Lincoln Avenue, Pittsburgh 15202; 412-734-2666

Pearl S. Buck Foundation, Green Hill Farms, Perkasie 18944; 215-249-0100

Catholic Charities, 15 Washington Street, New Castle 16101; 412-658-5526

Catholic Charities of the Diocese of Greensburg, 115 Vannear Avenue, Greensburg 15601; 412-837-1840

Catholic Charities of the Diocese of Harrisburg, 4800 Union Deposit Road, P.O. Box 3551, Harrisburg 17105; 717-657-4804

Catholic Charities of the Diocese of Pittsburgh, 300 South Washington Street, Butler 16001; 412-287-4011

Catholic Social Agency, 928 Union Boulevard, Allentown 18103; 215-435-1541

Catholic Social Agency, 138 North Ninth Street, Reading 19601; 215-374-4891

Catholic Social Services, 1300 12th Avenue, P.O. Box 1349, Altoona 16603; 814-944-9388

Catholic Social Services, 81 South Church Street, Hazelton 18201; 717-455-1521

Catholic Social Services, 232 Walnut Street, Johnstown 15901; 814-535-6538

Catholic Social Services of the Archdiocese of Philadelphia, 222 North 17th Street, Philadelphia 19103; 215-587-3500

Catholic Social Services of Luzerne County, 33 East Northampton Street, Wilkes-Barre 18701-2406; 717-822-7118

Catholic Social Services, 400 Wyoming Avenue, Scranton 18503; 717-346-8936

Catholic Social Services of Shenango Valley, 786 East State Street, Sharon 16146; 412-346-4142

Catholic Social Services of the Diocese of Erie, 329 West 10th Street, Erie 16502; 814-465-2091

Child and Home Study Associates, 1029 North Providence Road, Media 19063; 215-565-1544

Children's Aid Society, 1004 South Second Street, Clearfield 16830; 814-765-2685

Children's Aid Society of Franklin County, 255 Miller Street, P.O. Box 353, Chambersburg 17201-0353; 717-263-4159

Children's Aid Society of Mercer County, 350 West Market Street, Mercer 16137; 412-662-4730

Children's Aid Society of Montgomery County, 1314 DeKalb Street, Norristown 19401; 215-279-2755

Children's Aid Society of Somerset County, 574 East Main Street, Somerset 15501; 814-445-2009

Children's Home of Pittsburgh, 5618 Kentucky Avenue, Pittsburgh 15232; 412-441-4884

Choices—An Adoption Agency, 115 East Glenside Avenue, Glenside 19038; 215-884-1414

Common Sense Associates, 208 West Main Street, Mechanicsburg 17055; 717-766-6449

Concern, 1 East Main Street, Fleetwood 19522; 215-944-0445

Council of Three Rivers American Indian Center, 200 Charles Street, Pittsburgh 15238; 412-782-4457

Eckels Adoption Agency, 915 Fifth Avenue (Rear), Williamsport 17701; 717-323-2520

Family and Child Services, 670 West 36 Street, Erie 16508; 814-864-0605

Family and Children's Service, 630 Janet Avenue, Lancaster 17601; 717-397-5241

Family Services of Beaver County, 1260 North Brodhead, Monaca 15061; 412-775-8390

Family Services and Children's Aid Society of Venango County, 716 East 2nd Street, Oil City 16301; 814-677-4005

Jewish Family and Children's Services, 10125 Verree Road, Philadelphia 19116; 215-698-9950

Jewish Family & Children's Service, 234 McKee Place, Pittsburgh 15213; 412-683-4900

Love the Children, 221 West Broad Street, Quakertown 18951; 215-536-4180

Lutheran Children and Family Service, 2900 Queen Lane, Philadelphia 19120; 215-276-2800

The Lutheran Home at Topton, One Home Avenue, Topton 19562; 215-682-1504

Lutheran Service Society of Western Pennsylvania, 11 Garden Center Drive, Greensburg 15601; 412-837-9385

National Adoption Network, 223 Gypsy Lane, Wynnewood 19096; 215-649-5046

Option of Adoption, 504 East Haines Street, Philadelphia 19144-1215; 215-742-7423

Project STAR, 6301 Northumberland Street, Pittsburgh 15217; 412-521-9000. Serves waiting children.

St. Joseph's Center, 2010 Adams Avenue, Scranton 18509; 717-342-8379

Small Miracles, 3246 Birch Road, Philadelphia 19154; 215-632-8630

Tabor Children's Services, 601 New Britain Road, Doylestown 18901; 215-348-4071

Three Rivers Adoption Council, 307 Fourth Avenue, Pittsburgh 15222; 412-471-8722

Thy Kingdom Come, Orwigsburg 17961; 717-366-1108

Today's Adoption Agency, P.O. Box G, Hawley 18428; 717-226-4258

Tressler-Lutheran Services, 836 South George Street, York 17403; 717-845-9113. Serves waiting children.

Welcome House, P.O. Box 836, Doylestown 18901; 215-345-0430

Wiley House, 1650 Broadway, Bethlehem 18015; 215-867-5051

Women's Christian Alliance, 1610-12 North Broad Street, Philadelphia 19121; 215-236-9911. Serves waiting children.

RHODE ISLAND
State Agency: Department for Children & Their Families, 610 Mt. Pleasant Avenue, Providence 02908; 401-457-4654

State Exchange: Ocean State Adoption Resource Exchange, 500 Prospect Street, Pawtucket 02860; 401-724-1910

State Photolisting Book: *Ocean State Adoption Resource Exchange Manual*

Independent Adoption: Permitted/no intermediaries/no newspaper advertising

NACAC Representative: Donna Caldwell, Adoption Rhode Island, P.O. Box 1495, Kingston 02881; 401-792-3240

Private Agencies
Alliance for Children, 509 Armistice Boulevard, Pawtucket 02881; 401-725-9555

Bethany Christian Services, P.O. Box 29, East Greenwich 02818; 401-885-7655

Catholic Social Services, 433 Elmwood Avenue, Providence 02907; 401-467-7200

Children's Friend and Service, 153 Summer Street, Providence 02903; 401-331-2900

Jewish Family Services, 229 Waterman Street, Providence 02906; 401-331-1244

Wide Horizons for Children (*see* Massachusetts)

SOUTH CAROLINA

State Agency: Department of Social Services, Division of Adoption and Birth
  Parent Services, P.O. Box 1520, Columbia 29202; 803-734-6095 or in South
  Carolina 800-922-2504

State Exchange: Utilizes SEEUS (Southeastern Exchange of the United States)

State Photolisting Book: *South Carolina Seedlings,* Route 13, Box 298, Easley
  29640; 803-269-7713

Independent Adoption: Permitted/intermediaries allowed/newspaper advertising
  permitted

NACAC Representative: Jennifer Mayo, South Carolina COAC, 421 Brook Hollow
  Drive, Columbia 29223; 803-736-3822

Private Agencies

Bethany Christian Services, 300 University Ridge, Greenville 29601; 803-235-
  2273. Serves state. Religious restriction.

Catholic Charities of Charleston, 119 Broad Street, Charleston 29401; 803-724-
  8360. Serves state. Religious restriction.

Children Unlimited, P.O. Box 11463, Columbia 29211; 803-799-8311. Part of Family
  Builders Agency Network. Serves waiting children.

Christian World Adoption, 171 Church Street, Charleston 29401; 803-723-2188

Connie Maxwell Children's Home, P.O. Box 1178, Greenwood 29646; 803-942-
  1400. Serves state. Focuses on special needs.

LDS Social Services (*see* North Carolina)

Love Life Ministries, P.O. Box 247, Florence 29503; 803-665-8473

Shekinah Life House, Heritage USA-Business Highway 21, Fort Mill 29715; 803-
  548-6630

Southeastern Children's Home, 825 Woods Chapel Duncan Road, Duncan 29334;
  803-439-0259

SOUTH DAKOTA

State Agency: Child Protection Services, Department of Social Services, 700
  Governors Drive, Pierre 57501; 605-773-3227

State Exchange: No

State Photolisting Book: No

Independent Adoption: Permitted/intermediaries allowed/newspaper advertising
  permitted

NACAC Representative: Carol Heltzel, State Adoption Council, Box 105, Philip
  57567; 605-859-2039

Private Agencies

Bethany Christian Services, 2100 South Seventh Street, Rapid City 57701; 605-
  343-7196

Catholic Family Services, 3100 West 41 Street, Sioux Falls 57105; 605-333-3375.
  Another office is in Aberdeen. Religious requirement.

Catholic Social Services, 918 Fifth Avenue, Rapid City 57701; 605-348-6086
Christian Counseling Service, 350 Boyce Greeley Building, 231 South Phillips
    Avenue, Sioux Falls 57102; 605-336-6999
Holt International Children's Services (*see* Iowa)
Lutheran Social Services of South Dakota, 600 West 12 Street, Sioux Falls 57104;
    605-336-3367. Serves state. Religious requirement.

TENNESSEE
State Agency: Department of Human Services, 400 Deaderick Street, Nashville
    37248-9000; 615-741-5935
State Exchange: Tennessee Adoption Resource Exchange *(see above)*
State Photolisting Book: *TAP (Tennessee Adoption Profiles)*
Independent Adoption: Permitted/intermediaries allowed/newspaper advertis-
    ing permitted
NACAC Representative: Joyce Maxey, Knoxville Council on Adoptable Children,
    P.O. Box 1787, Knoxville 37901; 615-577-1187
Private Agencies
Adoptions International, 2714 Union Avenue Extended, Memphis 38112
AGAPE, 2702 Nolensville Road, Nashville 37211; 615-256-0575
Associated Catholic Charities of the Diocese of Memphis, 1805 Poplar Avenue,
    Memphis 38104; 901-725-8240
Associated Catholic Charities of East Tennessee, 119 Dameron Avenue, Knoxville
    37917; 615-524-9896
Bethany Christian Services, 4719 Brainerd Road, Chattanooga 37411; 615-622-
    7360. Religious requirement.
Catholic Charities of Tennessee, 30 White Bridge Road, Nashville 37205; 615-352-
    3087
Child and Family Services of Knox County, 114 Dameron Avenue, Knoxville 37917;
    615-524-7483
Christian Counseling Services, 515 Woodland Street, Nashville 37206; 615-254-
    8336
Church of God Home for Children, 435 Park Road, Sevierville 37864; 615-453-
    4644
East Tennessee Christian Services, P.O. Box 22816, Knoxville 37933-0816; 615-
    584-0841
Family & Children's Service, 210 23rd Avenue North, Nashville 37203; 615-320-
    0591
Family & Children's Services of Chattanooga, 300 East 8 Street, Chattanooga
    37403; 615-755-2822
Greater Chattanooga Christian Services & Children's Home, 400 Vine Street,
    Chattanooga 37403; 615-756-0281
Holston United Methodist Home for Children, P.O. Box 188, Holston Drive,
    Greeneville 37743; 615-638-4172
Jewish Family Service, P.O. Box 38268, 6560 Poplar Street, Memphis 38138;
    901-767-8511

Life Choices, 3297 Park Avenue, P.O. Box 11245, Memphis 38111; 901-323-5433

Madison Children's Home, 106 Gallatin Road North, Madison 37115; 615-860-3240

Mid-Cumberland Children's Services, 106 North Mountain Street, Smithville 37166; 615-597-7134

Mid-South Christian Services, 3100 Walnut Grove Road, Memphis 38111; 901-454-1401

Porter-Leath Children's Center, 868 North Manassas Street, P.O. Box 111229, Memphis 38111-1229; 901-577-2500

Small World Ministries, 105 Bonnabrook, Hermitage 37076; 615-883-4372. Religious requirement.

Tennessee Baptist Children's Home, P.O. Box 728, Brentwood 37024-0728; 615-371-2000. Branch offices.

Tennessee Children's Home, P.O. Box 10, Spring Hill 37174; 615-486-2274. Branch offices.

Tennessee Conference Adoption Services, 900 Glendale Lane, Nashville 37204; 615-292-3500

West Tennessee AGAPE, 1881 Union Avenue, P.O. Box 1141, Memphis 38104; 901-272-7339

TEXAS

State Agency: Department of Human Services, P.O. Box 149030, Austin 78714-9030; 512-450-3302

State Exchange: Texas Adoption Resource Exchange, P.O. Box 2960, Mail Code 538-W, Austin 78769

State Photolisting Book: *Texas Adoption Resource Exchange*

Independent Adoption: Permitted/no intermediaries/newspaper advertising allowed

NACAC Representative: Margie Hoelscher, COAC of Texas, 304 Monaco Drive, Cedar Park 78613; 512-258-6791, and Marye Lou Mauldin, Adopting Children Together, 2111 North Cooper Street, Arlington 76011; 817-265-3496

Private Agencies

AAA-Alamo Adoption Agency, 1222 North Main, San Antonio 78212; 512-226-4124

AASK/Texas, 3500 Overton Park West, Fort Worth 76109; 817-927-8135. Serves waiting children.

ABC Adoption Agency, 417 San Pedro Avenue, San Antonio 78212; 512-227-7820

Adoption Advisory, 3607 Fairmount, Dallas 75219; 214-520-0004

Adoption Advocates, 800 N.W. Loop 410, San Antonio 78216; 512-344-4838

Adoption Alliance, 7303 Blanco Road, San Antonio 78216; 512-349-3991

Adoption Affiliates, 215 West Olmos Drive, San Antonio 78212; 512-824-9939. Infant adoptions.

Adoption, Inc., 3519 Cedar Springs Road, Dallas 75219; 214-520-1700

Adoption Information and Counseling, 2020 Southwest Freeway, Houston 77098; 713-529-5125

Adoption Resource Consultants, P.O. Box 1224, Richardson 75083; 214-517-4119 or 800-673-4371

Adoption Services Associates, 8703 Wurzbach Road, San Antonio 78240; 512-699-6088. Infant adoptions.

Adoption Services, 3500 Overton Park West, Fort Worth 76109; 817-921-0718

Adoption Services Unlimited, P.O. Box 644, De Soto 75115; 214-223-3887

AGAPE Social Services, 7929 Brookriver Drive, Dallas 75247; 214-631-6784

All-Church Home for Children, 1424 Summit Avenue, Fort Worth 76102; 817-335-4041

Bair Foundation of Texas, 8840 Business Park Drive, Austin 78759; 512-346-3555

Blessed Trinity Adoptions, 7062A Lakeview Haven, Houston 77095; 713-855-0137

Buckner Baptist Benevolences, P.O. Box 271189, Dallas 75227; 214-328-3141

Casa de Esperanza de Los Ninos, 2607 Hopkins, Houston 77006; 713-529-0639

The Care Connection, 400 Harvey Street, San Marcos 78666; 512-396-8111

Catholic Charities of the Diocese of Galveston-Houston, 3520 Montrose, Houston 77066; 713-526-4611

Catholic Counseling Services, 3845 Oak Lawn, Dallas 75219; 214-526-2772

Catholic Family Service, P.O. Box 15127, Amarillo 79102; 806-376-4571

Catholic Family and Children Services, 2903 West Salinas, San Antonio 78207; 512-433-3256

Catholic Social Service, 1300 South Lake, Fort Worth 76104; 817-926-1231

Catholic Social Services of Laredo, P.O. Box 3305, Laredo 78044; 512-724-5051

Child Placement Center, 2212 Sunny Lane, Killeen 76541; 817-690-5959

Children's Home of Lubbock, P.O. Box 2824, Lubbock 79408; 806-762-0481

Children's Service Bureau, 625 North Alamo Street, San Antonio 78215; 512-223-6281

Christian Child Help Foundation, 4219 Richmond, Houston 77027; 713-850-9703

Christian Counseling Associates, 4001 West Airport Freeway, Bedford 76021; 817-283-6000

Christian Homes of Abilene, 242 Beech Street, Abilene 79604; 915-677-2205

Christian Services of the Southwest, 8510 Military Parkway, Dallas 75227; 214-381-8265

Christ's Haven for Children, P.O. Box 467, Keller 76248; 817-431-1544

Covenant Children, P.O. Box 1656, Rockwall 75087; 214-637-2229

Cradle of Life Adoption Agency, 245 North Fourth Street, Beaumont 77701; 409-832-3000

DePelchin Children's Center, 100 Sandman Street, Houston 77007; 713-861-8136

Dillon International (see Oklahoma)

Edna Gladney Center, 2300 Hemphill, Fort Worth 76110; 817-926-3307. Places infants.

Family Counseling and Children's Services, 5020A Lakeland Circle, Waco 76710; 817-751-1777

Hendrick Home for Children, P.O. Box 5195, Abilene 79608; 915-692-0112

High Plains Children's Home, P.O. Box 7448, Amarillo 79114; 806-355-6588. Serves state.

Homes of St. Mark, 1302 Marshall, Houston 77006; 713-522-2800. Serves state. Places infants. Has served out-of-state military applicants who are Texas residents.

Hope Cottage, 4209 McKinney Avenue, Dallas 75205; 214-526-8721. Serves state. Places infants.

International Child Placing Agency, Route 3, Los Fresnos 78566; 512-233-5705

Jester Adoption Services, P.O. Box 280, Denton 76202; 817-387-7585

Jewish Family Service, 7800 Northaven Road, Dallas 75230; 214-696-6400

Jewish Family Service, P.O. Box 20548, Houston 77225; 713-667-9336

LDS Social Services, 1100 West Jackson Road, Carrolton 75006; 214-242-2182. Religious requirement.

Lee and Beulah Moor Children's Home, 1100 Cliff Drive, El Paso 79902; 915-544-8777. Infant adoptions.

Life Anew, 2635 Loop 286 N.E., Paris 75460; 214-785-7701. Infant adoptions.

Los Ninos International, 25231 Grogans Mill, The Woodlands 77380; 713-363-2892

Loving Alternatives Adoptions, P.O. Box 131466, Tyler 75713; 214-581-2891

Lutheran Social Services of Texas, P.O. Box 49589, Austin 78765; 512-459-1000. Branch offices. Lutheran Social Service in San Antonio (4203 Woodcock Drive, San Antonio 78228; 512-734-0012) was one of the first agencies to open up infant adoptions.

Lutheran Social Services of Texas, One Medical Plaza, Dallas 75234; 214-620-0581

Lutheran Social Service of Texas, 3131 West Alabama, Houston 77098; 713-521-0110

Marywood Maternity and Adoption Services, 510 West 26 Street, Austin 78705; 512-472-9251

Methodist Home, 1111 Herring Avenue, Waco 76708; 817-753-0181

New Life Children's Services, 19911 SH 249, Houston 77070; 713-955-1001. Religious requirement. Infant adoptions.

Pleasant Hills Children's Home, Route 2, Box 770, Fairfield 75840; 214-389-2641

Presbyterian Children's Home and Service Agency, 274 South Treadway Plaza, Dallas 75235; 214-352-7662

Presbyterian Home for Children, 3400 South Bowie, Amarillo 79109; 806-352-5771

Prince of Peace Adoption Service, 10114 Miller Road, Houston 77086; 713-580-1001

Quality of Life, P.O. Box 781382, Dallas 75378; 214-350-1637. Religious requirement. Infant adoptions.

Read Adoption Agency, 718 Myrtle, El Paso 79901; 915-533-3697

Sherwood-Myrtie Foster Home for Children, P.O. Box 978, Stephenville 76401; 817-968-2143

Smithlawn Maternity Home and Adoption Agency, P.O. Box 6451, Lubbock 79413; 806-745-2574

South Texas Children's Home, 6040 SPID #6, Corpus Christi 78404; 512-994-0940

Southwest Maternity Center, 6487 Whitby Road, San Antonio 78240; 512-696-
2410. Has placed black and infants of mixed ethnic heritage out-of-state.
Spaulding for Children, 4219 Richmond Avenue, Houston 77027; 713-850-9707.
Serves waiting children.
Texas Adoption Service, P.O. Box 743443, Dallas 75374; 214-553-1485
Texas Baptist Children's Home, P.O. Box 7, Round Rock 78664; 512-255-3668
Texas Cradle Society, 221 West Poplar, San Antonio 78212; 512-225-5151.
Serves state. Has placed infants of mixed ethnic background (e.g., Mexican/
black) out-of-state.
Therapeikos, 2817 North Second, Abilene 79603; 915-677-2216
West Texas Adoption Agency, 331 West Avenue B, San Angelo 76903; 915-655-
3563

UTAH
State Agency: Division of Family Services, 120 North 200 West, Salt Lake City
84103; 801-538-4080
State Exchange: No
State Photolisting Book: No
Independent Adoption: Permitted/intermediaries allowed/newspaper advertis-
ing permitted
NACAC Representative: Suzanne Stott, FIA & FFC, 1219 Windsor Street, Salt
Lake City 84105; 801-487-3916
Private Agencies
Catholic Community Services of Salt Lake City, 333 East South Temple, Salt Lake
City 84111; 801-328-8641
Children's Aid Society of Utah, 652 26 Street, Ogden 84401; 801-393-8671
Children's House International, P.O. Box 2321, Salt Lake City 84110; 801-272-
4822
Children's Service Society, 576 East South Temple, Salt Lake City 84102; 801-
355-7444
LDS Social Services, 50 East North Temple, Salt Lake City 84150; 801-531-2848.
Branch offices.

VERMONT
State Agency: Social and Rehabilitation Services, 103 South Main Street, Water-
bury 05676; 802-241-2131
State Exchange: Maine-Vermont Adoption Exchange, 221 State Street, Augusta
04333; 207-289-5060
State Photolisting Book: *Maine-Vermont Adoption Exchange*
Independent Adoption: Permitted/intermediaries allowed/newspaper advertis-
ing permitted
NACAC Representative: Hector Badeau, Rootwings, P.O. Box 96, Barre 05641;
802-479-7944
Private Agencies
Adoption Centre, 278 Pearl Street, Burlington 05401; 802-862-5855

Adoption Resource Services, 1904 North Avenue, Burlington 05401; 802-863-5368

Bethany Christian Services (*see* Massachusetts)

Casey Family Services, 7 Palmer Court, White River Junction 05001-3323; 802-649-1400

Friends in Adoption, South Street, R.R. #1, Box 7102, Middletown Springs 05757; 802-235-2312. Open infant adoptions.

LDS Social Services (*see* New Hampshire)

Lund Family Center, P.O. Box 4009, Burlington 05401; 802-864-7467

Parsons Child & Family Center (*see* New York)

Vermont Catholic Charities, 351 North Avenue, Burlington 05401; 802-658-6110. Serves state.

Vermont Children's Aid Society, P.O. Box 127, Winooski 05404; 802-655-0006. Serves state.

Wide Horizons for Children (*see* Massachusetts)

VIRGINIA

State Agency: Department of Social Services, Bureau of Child Welfare Services, 8007 Discovery Drive, Richmond 23229; 804-662-9025 or 800-DO-ADOPT

State Exchange: Adoption Resource Exchange of Virginia (AREVA)

State Photolisting Book: *Adoption Resource Exchange of Virginia Child Photolisting Book*

Independent Adoption: Permitted/intermediaries allowed/newspaper advertising by birth parents or adoptive parents allowed

NACAC Representative: Sharon DeButts Richardson, Virginia Citizens for Children, 3407 Hawthrone Avenue, Richmond 23222; 804-321-5336

Private Agencies

Adoption Service Information Agency, 7659 Leesburg Pike, Falls Church 22043; 202-726-7193

American Adoption Agency, 3600 West Broad Street, Richmond 23230; 804-342-0411

Barker Foundation, c/o McLean Professional Park Family Counseling Center, 1495 Chainbridge Road, McLean 22101; 703-536-1827

Bethany Christian Services, 10523 Main Street, Fairfax 22030; 703-385-5440

Catholic Charities, 3838 North Cathedral Lane, Arlington 22203; 703-841-2531. Branch offices.

Catholic Charities of Hampton Roads, 4855 Princess Anne Road, Virginia Beach 23462; 804-467-7707. Branch offices.

Catholic Charities of Richmond, 1010 North Thompson Street, Richmond 23230; 804-354-0720. Branch offices.

Catholic Charities of Southwestern Virginia, 820 Campbell Avenue S.W., Roanoke 24016; 703-344-5107. Branch offices.

Children's Home Society of Virginia, 4200 Fitzhugh Avenue, Richmond 23230; 804-353-0191. Serves state.

Coordinators/2, 5001 West Broad Street, Richmond 23290; 804-288-0442

Datz Foundation, 404 Pine Street, Vienna 22180; 703-242-8800

Family Life Services, 1000 Villa Road, Lynchburg 24503; 804-384-3043. Infant adoptions.

Family and Child Services of Washington, D.C., 3321 Duke Street, Alexandria 22314; 703-823-2656

Family Services of Tidewater, 222-19th Street West, Norfolk 23517; 804-622-7017

Holston Methodist Home, 300 Moore Street, Bristol 24201; 703-466-3883

Jewish Family Services, 6718 Patterson Avenue, Richmond 23226; 804-282-5644

Jewish Family Service of Tidewater, P.O. Box 9305, Norfolk 23505; 804-489-3111. Branch offices.

Jewish Social Service Agency, 7345 McWhorter Place, Annandale 22003; 703-750-5400

LDS Social Services of Virginia, 8110 Virginia Pine Court, Chesterfield 23832; 804-743-0727

Lutheran Social Services of the National Capital Area, 7401 Leesburg Pike, Falls Church 22043; 703-698-5026

New Family Foundation, 11350 Random Hills Road, Fairfax 22030; 703-273-5960

Pan American Adoption Agency, 12604 Kahns Road, Manassas 22111; 703-791-3260

Rainbow Christian Services, P.O. Box 9, 6400 Artemus Road, Gainesville 22065; 703-754-8516

United Methodist Family Services of Virginia, 3900 West Broad Street, Richmond 23230; 804-353-4461. Branch offices.

Virginia Baptist Children's Home, & Family Service, Mount Vernon Avenue, Box 849, Salem 24153; 703-389-5468. Branch offices.

Welcome House, 5905 West Broad Street, Richmond 23230; 804-288-3920

WASHINGTON

State Agency: Division of Children and Family Services, P.O. Box 45713/OB41, Olympia 98504; 206-753-2178

State Exchange: Washington Adoption Resource Exchange or WARE *(see above)*

State Photolisting Book: No

Independent Adoption: Permitted/intermediaries allowed/newspaper advertising permitted with verification of completed home study

NACAC Representative: Jackie Erholm, The Family Foundation, 1229 Cornwall Avenue #206, Bellingham 98225; 206-676-5437

Private Agencies

Adoption Advocates International, 136 Old Black Diamond Road, Port Angeles 98362; 206-452-4777

Adventist Adoption and Family Services, 1207 East Reserve Street, Vancouver 98661; 206-693-2110. Religious requirement.

Americans for International Aid and Adoption, P.O. Box 6051, Spokane 99207; 509-489-2015

Bethany Christian Services, 103 East Holly Street, Bellingham 98225; 206-733-6042

Black Child Adoption Program, 123-16th Avenue, P.O. Box 22638, Seattle 98122; 206-329-3933

Catholic Children and Family Services of Pasco, 611 West Columbia, Pasco 99301; 509-547-0521

Catholic Children & Family Service, 418 Drumheller Building, Walla Walla 99362; 206-525-0572

Catholic Children's Services of Skagit Island, San Juan and Whatcom Counties, 207 Kentucky, Bellingham 98225; 206-733-5800

Catholic Community Services, 5410 North 44th, Tacoma 98407; 206-752-2455

Catholic Community Services, King County, 1715 Cherry Street, Seattle 98122; 206-323-6336

Catholic Community Services-Snohomish, Commerce Building, Everett 98201; 206-622-8905

Catholic Family and Child Services of Ephrata, 121 Basin N.W., Ephrata 98823; 206-754-2211

Catholic Family and Child Service, 302 Division Street, Grandview 98930; 206-882-3050

Catholic Family and Child Service, 1329 George Washington Way, Richland 99352; 206-946-4645

Catholic Family and Child Service of Wenatchee, 5 North Wenatchee Avenue, Wenatchee 98801; 206-662-6761

Catholic Family and Child Service of Yakima, 5301-C Tieton Drive, Yakima 98908; 509-882-3050

Catholic Family Counseling Center, 410 West 12th, Vancouver 98860; 206-696-0379

Children's Home Society of Washington, 201 South 34 Street, Tacoma 98408; 206-472-3355. Serves state. Branch offices.

Church of Christ Homes for Children, 30012 Military Road South, Federal Way 98003; 206-839-2755

The Family Foundation, 1229 Cornwall Avenue, Bellingham 98225; 206-676-5437

Hope Services, 424 North 130th Street, Seattle 98133; 206-367-4606 or 800-922-HOPE

International Children's Services of Washington, 3251 107th S.E., Bellevue 98004; 206-451-9370

Jewish Family Services, 1214 Boylston Avenue, Seattle 98101; 206-447-3240

LDS Social Services, 220 South Third Place, Renton 98055; 206-624-3393

Lutheran Social Services, 6920 220th Street S.W., Mountlake Terrace 98043; 206-672-6009. Serves state. Branch offices.

Medina Children's Services, P.O. Box 22638, Seattle 98111; 206-461-4520. Serves waiting children.

New Hope of Washington, 2611 N.E. 125th, Seattle 98125; 206-363-1800

Regular Baptist Child Placement Agency, P.O. Box 16353, Seattle 98116; 206-938-1487

Seattle Indian Center, 121 Stewart Street, Seattle 98101; 206-447-9191

TASC, The Adoption of Special Children, 123 16th Avenue, Seattle 98122; 206-324-9473

Travelers Aid Adoption Services, 909 Fourth Avenue, Seattle 98104; 206-447-3888

WACAP, P.O. Box 88948, Seattle 98188; 206-575-4550

WEST VIRGINIA

State Agency: Department of Health and Human Resources, Bureau of Human Resources, Office of Social Services, State Capitol Complex, Building 6, Charleston 25305; 304-348-7980

State Exchange: West Virginia Adoption Exchange, P.O. Box 2942, Charleston 25330

State Photolisting Book: *West Virginia Adoption Exchange (WVAE)*

Independent Adoption: Permitted/intermediaries allowed/newspaper advertising permitted

NACAC Representative: Judith Dyer, AFFA, 1511 Byng Drive South, Charleston 25303; 304-744-9602

Private Agencies

Burlington United Methodist Home, 3963 Teays Valley Road, Scott Depot 25560; 304-757-9127

Catholic Charities of Southwestern Virginia (*see* Virginia)

Childplace (*see* Indiana)

Children's Home Society of West Virginia, 1422 Kanawha Boulevard East, Charleston 25301; 304-346-0795

Comprehensive Studies, 111 Patterson Street, Charleston 25302; 304-343-7084. Home studies and placement reports only.

Family Services Association (*see* Ohio)

LDS Social Services (*see* Ohio)

Northern Tier Youth Services, 105 Pennsylvania Avenue, South Charleston 25302; 304-345-6897

Shenandoah Adoption & Maternity Services, 101 Clifton Square II, Suite 108, Martinsburg 25401; 304-267-2223

Voice for International and Domestic Adoptions (*see* New York)

WISCONSIN

State Agency: Department of Health & Social Services, Division of Community Services, P.O. Box 7851, Madison 53707-7851; 608-266-0690. State also funds *Adoption Information Center,* 1212 South 70th Street, West Allis 53214; 800-522-6882. Brochures available.

State Exchange: Special Needs Adoption Network, P.O. Box 10176, Milwaukee 53210; 414-475-1246

State Photolisting Book: *ADOPT!*

Independent Adoption: Identified adoptions permitted/newspaper advertising permitted

NACAC Representative: Colleen Ellingson, P.O. Box 10176, Milwaukee 53210; 414-475-1246

Private Agencies

Adoption Advocates, 1310 Mendota Street, Madison 53714; 608-246-2844. Serves state.

Adoption Choice, 815 North Cass Street, Milwaukee 53202; 414-276-3262

Adoption Option, 1804 Chapman Drive, Waukesha 53186; 414-544-4278

Adoption Services of Green Bay, 529 South Jefferson, Green Bay 54301; 414-432-2030. Open adoption possible.

Bethany Christian Services of Wisconsin, W255 N477 Grandview Boulevard, Waukesha 53188; 414-547-6557. Serves state. Religious requirement.

Catholic Charities, Inc., 128 South Sixth Street, LaCrosse 54601; 608-782-0704. Branch offices. Religious requirement.

Catholic Social Services, Diocese of Green Bay, P.O. Box 1825, Green Bay; 414-437-6541. Religious requirement.

Catholic Social Service, Madison, 4905 Schofield Street, Monona 53716; 608-221-2000

Catholic Social Services, Milwaukee, 2021 North 60th Street, Milwaukee 53208; 414-771-2881. Branch offices. Religious requirement.

Children's Service Society of Wisconsin, 1212 South 70 Street, West Allis 53214; 414-453-1400. Serves state. Branch offices.

Community Adoption Center, 101 East Milwaukee, Janesville 53545; 608-756-0405. Serves state.

Evangelical Child & Family Agency, 2401 North Mayfair Road, Milwaukee 53226; 414-476-9550. Religious requirement.

Family Service Association of Sheboygan, 2020 Erie Avenue, Sheboygan 53081; 414-458-3784

Focus on Families, P.O. Box 2121, Appleton 54915; 414-739-8878

Homes Open Wide, 208 State Street, Oshkosh 54901-4839; 414-235-6239

Hope International Family Services (*see* Minnesota)

Institute for Child and Family Development, 4222 West Capitol Drive, Milwaukee 53216; 414-449-2274

LDS Social Services, 5651 Broad Street, Greendale 53129; 414-421-7506. Religious requirement.

Lutheran Counseling and Family Services, 3800 North Mayfair Road, Wauwatosa 53222; 414-536-8333. Serves state. Branch offices. Religious requirement.

Lutheran Social Services, 3200 West Highland Boulevard, Milwaukee 53208; 414-342-7175. Serves state. Branch offices. Religious requirement.

Northern Family Services, 1835 North Stevens Street, P.O. Box 237, Rhinelander 54501; 715-369-1554

Pauquette Children's Services, 304 West Conant Street, Portage 53901; 608-742-8004. Serves state. Branch offices.

Seven Sorrows of our Sorrowful Mothers Infants' Home, Route 2 Box 905, Necedah 608-565-2417. Serves state. Religious requirement.

Sunny Ridge Family Center, 414 East Walnut, Green Bay 54301; 414-437-4437. Religious requirement.

Wisconsin Lutheran Child & Family Services, 6800 North 76th Street, P.O. Box 23980, Milwaukee 53223; 414-353-5000. Serves state.

Families thinking about intercountry adoption might want to obtain from the state's Adoption Information Center the informative booklet *Handbook for Persons Thinking About International Adoption.*

WYOMING

State Agency: Department of Family Services, 319 Hathaway Building, 2300 Capitol Avenue, Cheyenne 82002; 307-777-7561

State Exchange: No

State Photolisting Book: No

Independent Adoption: Permitted/intermediaries allowed/newspaper advertising permitted

NACAC Representative: Irene Tate, Northern Wyoming Adoptive Parents, P.O. Box 788, Basin 82410; 307-568-2729

Private Agencies

Catholic Social Services, 2121 Capitol Avenue, P.O. Box 1026, Cheyenne 82003; 307-638-1530 or 800-734-2379. Branch offices.

LDS Social Services, P.O. Box 2805, Cody 82414-2805; 307-587-3607. Religious requirement.

Wyoming Children's Society, P.O. Box 105, 716 Randall Avenue, Cheyenne 82003-0105; 307-632-7619. Serves state.

Wyoming Parenting Society, P.O. Box 4120, Jackson 83001; 307-733-6357

Intercountry Adoption
A Guide to U.S. Agencies

Many agencies in the United States have developed intercountry adoption programs. Some place only within a particular metropolitan area or state. Others have programs that will accept applicants from several states or even around the country. Some agencies do not have their own programs but network with agencies that specialize in intercountry adoption.

This list is *not* all-inclusive, although it lists many agencies with intercountry programs. To compile this list I have drawn upon fact sheets from parent groups, information provided by state departments of social services, the *Report on Foreign Adoption,* and the *Adoptive Families of America 1992 Adoption Agency Listing.*

This list is intended solely as a guide, giving you many places to start. I have marked with an asterisk (*) those agencies that have extensive intercountry adoption programs and are known for their networking with other agencies around the country. Remember that some agencies use the interstate compact to place children out of state or have branch offices in other states. You may want to contact these agencies as well as adoption agencies listed for your state. For the addresses and telephone numbers of the agencies listed, see the previous state-by-state adoption directory.

For the most up-to-date information, contact parent groups, the NACAC representative for a state, Adoptive Families of America, or the **International Concerns Committee for Children** (911 Cypress Drive, Boulder, Colorado 80303; 303-494-8333), which publishes the *Report on Foreign Adoption.* Singles will want to check with the

Committee for Single Adoptive Parents (P.O. Box 15084, Chevy Chase, Maryland 20815), which compiles its own specialized list of resources.

If you write to an agency, be sure to include a stamped, self-addressed envelope. If you ask staff members to call you, say that they can call collect.

ALABAMA
Villa Hope

ALASKA
Adoption Advocates International
WACAP

ARIZONA
Dillon Southwest
Globe International
House of Samuel

ARKANSAS
Small Miracles International

CALIFORNIA
Adoption Horizons
Adopt International
Adoption Services International
Adoptions Unlimited
Bal Jagat
Bay Area Adoption Services
Catholic Charities, San Francisco
Children's Home Society of California
Children's Services Center
Chrysalis House
Family Connections
The Family Network*
Help the Children*
Holt International Children's Services
Holy Family Services
Life Adoption Services
Partners for Adoption
Sierra Adoption Agency
Vista Del Mar Child and Family Services

COLORADO
Adoption Alliance
Bethany Christian Services
Friends of Children of Various Nations*
Hand in Hand*
Loving Homes

CONNECTICUT
Catholic Family Services (Bloomfield)
Catholic Family and Social Service (Bridgeport)
International Alliance for Children
Jewish Family Service of New Haven
Wide Horizons for Children

DELAWARE
Child and Home Study Associates
Welcome House

DISTRICT OF COLUMBIA
Adoption Service Information Agency
American Adoption Agency*
Associated Catholic Charities of Baltimore
Barker Foundation
Cradle of Hope
Datz Foundation
International Families
New Family Foundation
Pan American Adoption Agency
World Child*

FLORIDA
The Adoption Centre
Creative Adoptions*
Jewish Family & Community Services
St. Vincent Maternity & Adoption Center
Suncoast International Adoptions*
Universal Aid for Children

GEORGIA
Homes for Children International
Illien Adoptions International*
Lutheran Ministries of Georgia

HAWAII
Hawaii International Child Placement
Rainbow Families

IDAHO
WACAP

ILLINOIS
Adoption World
Bensenville Home Society
Bethany Christian Services
Counseling and Family Service
Family Service Agency
Family Service of Decatur
Lutheran Child and Family Services
Lutheran Social Services of Illinois
Travelers and Immigrants Aid

INDIANA
Americans for African Adoptions*
Bethany Christian Services
Sunny Ridge Family Center

IOWA
Hillcrest Family Services
Holt International Children's Services

KANSAS
Inserco

KENTUCKY
Mary Kendall Home

LOUISIANA
Adoption Options
Children's Bureau of New Orleans

MAINE
Growing Thru Adoption
Maine Adoptive Placement Service
Sharing in Adoption

MARYLAND
Adoptions Together
American Adoption Agency

Associated Catholic Charities of Baltimore
Barker Foundation
Datz Foundation
Family and Children's Services of Central Maryland

MASSACHUSETTS
Alliance for Children
Beacon Adoption Center
Cambridge Adoption & Counseling Association
Florence Crittenton League
Love the Children of Massachusetts
Wide Horizons for Children*

MICHIGAN
Americans for International Aid and Adoption*
Bethany Christian Services*
Children's Hope*
Foreign Adoption Consultants
Jewish Family Services
Morning Star Adoption Resource Services

MINNESOTA
Children's Home Society of Minnesota*
Crossroads Adoption Services
Families for Children*
Forever Families International Adoption Agency
Hope International Family Services
Lutheran Social Service of Minnesota
New Horizons International Family Services
Wellspring Adoption Agency*

MISSOURI
Adoption Resource Center
Children's Foundation—Adoption and Counseling*
Family Network
Love Basket

MONTANA
Montana Intercountry Adoption

NEBRASKA
Holt International Children's Services (see Iowa)
Kids Each Served in Love
Nebraska Children's Home Society

NEW HAMPSHIRE
Lutheran Child and Family Services of New Hampshire
Wide Horizons for Children

NEW JERSEY
The Adoption Agency
A.M.O.R.*
Casa del Mundo
Children of the World
Growing Families
Holt International Children's Services
International Adoption League*
Love the Children (*see* Pennsylvania)
New Beginnings Family and Children's Services (*see* New York)
Spence-Chapin Adoption Services (*see* New York)
Voice for International and Domestic Adoption (*see* New York)
Welcome House (*see* Pennsylvania)

NEW MEXICO
Rainbow House International

NEW YORK
Americans for International Aid and Adoption
New Beginnings Family and Children's Services
Parsons Child & Family Center
Spence-Chapin Adoption Services
Voice for International and Domestic Adoption*
Wide Horizons for Children

NORTH CAROLINA
Bethany Christian Services
Christian Adoption Services
Lutheran Family Services

NORTH DAKOTA
New Horizons Foreign Adoption Service

OHIO
Foreign Adoption Consultants
Gentle Care Adoption Services
Lutheran Social Services of the Miami Valley

OKLAHOMA
Dillon International*
Small Miracles International*
United Methodist Counseling Services

OREGON
Holt International Children's Services*
Plan International Adoption Services*

PENNSYLVANIA
The Adoption Agency
Adoption Unlimited
Adoptions International
Child and Home Study Associates
Concern
Love the Children
Lutheran Children and Family Service
Pearl S. Buck Foundation
Today's Adoption Agency
Welcome House*

RHODE ISLAND
Alliance for Children
Wide Horizons for Children

SOUTH CAROLINA
Bethany Christian Services
Christian World Adoption*

SOUTH DAKOTA
Holt International Children's Services (*see* Iowa)
Lutheran Social Services of South Dakota

TENNESSEE
Associated Catholic Charities of East Tennessee
Holston United Methodist Home for Children

TEXAS
Adoption Resource Consultants
Adoption Services Associates
Dillon International
Los Ninos International*
Quality of Life

UTAH
Children's House International

VERMONT
Lund Family Center
Wide Horizons for Children (*see* Massachusetts)

VIRGINIA
Adoption Service Information Agency
American Adoption Agency
Barker Foundation
Catholic Charities of Richmond
Coordinators/2
Datz Foundation
Pan American Adoption Agency
Welcome House

WASHINGTON
Adoption Advocates International*
Catholic Community Services, King County
Children's Home Society of Washington
International Children's Services of Washington
Travelers Aid Adoption Services
WACAP*

WEST VIRGINIA
Associated Catholic Charities (*see* Maryland)
Voice for International and Domestic Adoptions (*see* New York)

WISCONSIN
Adoption Services of Green Bay
Bethany Christian Services of Wisconsin
Children's Service Society of Wisconsin
Community Adoption Center
Hope International Family Services (*see* Minnesota)
Lutheran Social Services of Wisconsin & Upper Michigan
Pauquette Children's Services
Sunny Ridge Family Center

Getting Advice

The following organizations can answer questions about adoption and put you in touch with adoption agencies, parent groups, and other experts. Keep in mind that there are several hundred parent groups in the country.

Adoptive Families of America, 3333 Highway 100 North, Minneapolis, Minnesota 55422; 612-535-4829

Adoption support organization, with headquarters in Minneapolis and member groups scattered throughout the United States. Provides counseling and referral. You may want to subscribe to the bimonthly magazine *OURS* or purchase books, cassettes, and other resource materials.

Adoptees Liberty Movement Association, P.O. Box 154, Washington Bridge Station, New York, New York 10033; 212-581-1568

Search and support organization for adult adoptees and birth parents.

American Adoption Congress, 1000 Connecticut Avenue N.W., Washington, D.C. 20036; 800-274-6736

Educational network concerned with openness and honesty in adoption. Advocates for adoption reform, including the opening of records, and educating the public. Particularly focused on the needs of adult adoptees and can direct you to local organizations.

Child Welfare League of America, 440 First Street N.W., Washington, D.C. 20001; 202-638-2952

Social-welfare organization concerned with setting standards for agencies in the field, pushing for research on all aspects of adoption, and strengthening services. Publishes books, the journal *Child Welfare,* and several newsletters.

Committee for Single Adoptive Parents, P.O. Box 15084, Chevy Chase, Maryland 20815

> Clearinghouse for information for singles interested in adopting. Can refer you to local parent support groups and direct you to agencies that will work with singles.

Concerned United Birthparents (CUB), 2000 Walker Street, Des Moines, Iowa 50317; 800-822-2777 or 515-263-9558

> Nationwide system of mutual help, with a special focus on birth mothers and birth fathers. CUB has educational materials that adoptive parents and social workers will find enlightening.

Families Adopting Children Everywhere (FACE), P.O. Box 28058, Northwood Station, Baltimore, Maryland 21239; 410-488-2656

> Although this parent group is centered in Maryland, it publishes an informative newsletter and tries to stay informed about events around the United States. Runs adoption information classes in the District of Columbia, Maryland, and Virginia.

International Soundex Reunion Registry, P.O. Box 2312, Carson City, Nevada 89702; 702-882-7755

> Links adoptees with birth parents and other family members. Designed to match people who are searching for each other.

National Adoption Center, 1218 Chestnut Street, Philadelphia, Pennsylvania 19107; 215-925-0200

> Promoting special-needs adoption is a fundamental concern of the center. Can also provide you with general adoption information and specialized resource materials. Will make referrals to local organizations and agencies.

National Adoption Information Clearinghouse, 11426 Rockville Pike, Rockville, Maryland 20852; 301-231-6510

> Just what the name says—a clearinghouse providing free adoption publications and other services. Can refer you to adoption agencies, parent support groups, and experts nationwide. For adoption-related research there's a computerized information data base containing the titles and abstracts of books, articles, and program reports. You can ask for a computer search and receive a printout of relevant titles. The clearinghouse also has full text listings of state and federal laws related to adoption.

National Committee for Adoption, 1930 17th Street N.W., Washington, D.C. 20009-6207; 202-328-1200

> Lobbies actively on adoption issues. Can refer you to member agencies and affiliated local groups. Generates adoption information materials.

National Resource Center for Special Needs Adoption, 16250 Northland Drive, Suite 120, Southfield, Michigan 48075; 313-443-7080

Offers advice on special-needs adoption, runs training workshops, and disseminates resource materials. You can receive its free newsletter, *The Roundtable*.

North American Council on Adoptable Children (NACAC), 1821 University Avenue, St. Paul, Minnesota 55104; 612-644-3036

This adoption advocacy organization, composed of parent groups and individuals, keeps track of adoption activities in each of the states through its volunteer representatives and member parent groups. Dedicated to promoting special-needs adoption and pushing for reform in adoption policies. See the state-by-state directory in this book for information about NACAC's local representatives.

Resolve, 1310 Broadway, Somerville, Massachusetts 02144; 617-623-0744

Provides infertility counseling and referral services. Some members are adoptive parents. A good resource for information about infant adoption. The national headquarters can refer you to the nearest local chapter.

For Further Reference

There is a vast and constantly growing literature about adoption and infertility. For an overview of adoption literature, see Lois Ruskai Melina, *Adoption: An Annotated Bibliography and Guide* (New York: Garland Publishing, 1987), which is a library reference book. The **National Adoption Information Clearinghouse** in Rockville, Maryland, will do a customized search for you on a particular adoption topic.

For a listing of children's books about adoption and foster care, see Lois Melina's *Making Sense of Adoption.* Paulette Bochnig Sharkey also detailed "Adoption in Fiction for Teens and Preteens: Best of the 1980s" in the March/April 1991 issue of *OURS* magazine. You'll find that the preponderance of the children's books are fiction. One perennial problem with them: The adoption message may be so overlaid that the story itself is secondary.

There are several mail-order sources for books. Adoptive Families of America in Minneapolis, Minnesota, has a large collection of current literature and is constantly adding to its list. Families Adopting Children Everywhere, in Maryland; Wallmark Associates (P.O. Box 173, Ringoes, New Jersey 08551; 800-765-ADOPT); and Parenting Resources (250 El Camino Real, Suite 111, Tustin, California 92680; 714-669-8100) also sell books by mail. The Child Welfare League of America sells its own publications as well as a select list from other publishers, while the National Resource Center for Special Needs Adoption in Michigan sells books, materials, and videotapes that concentrate on special-needs and waiting children.

If you're interested in subscribing to an adoption magazine, *OURS,* published by Adoptive Families of America, is excellent. As the magazine has evolved in recent years, it has carried fewer personal tales and focused more on issue-oriented articles. Lois Melina's *Adopted Child* (P.O. Box 9362, Moscow, Idaho 83843) is a monthly newsletter that focuses on raising adopted children.

If you prefer to get your information by listening to audiocassettes or watching videotapes, there is a growing number of choices. You can request a free copy of the *Catalogue of Audiovisual Materials on Adoption* (CAMA), a comprehensive listing of films, videotapes, audiocassettes, and multimedia presentations, from the National Adoption Information Clearinghouse in Rockville, Maryland. Lois Melina has developed a series of audiotapes, available through *Adopted Child,* that touch on such issues as *While You Wait to Adopt* and *Introduction to Adoption for Family and Friends.* Adoptive Families of America has sold the videotape *American Eyes,* which presents the story of a Korean-American adoptee who has identity and adoption questions as a teen. This video first aired on CBS as a Schoolbreak Special. Sharon Kaplan and Carol Land have produced the video and audio collection *Winning at Adoption* (The Family Network, P.O. Box 1995F, Studio City, California 91614-0995; 800-456-4056), which is designed to serve as a preadoption course. Keep in mind that many parent groups and agencies now purchase audiocassettes and videotapes and lend them out to interested families.

Don't forget to check out your local video store: There's *Immediate Family,* for example, which chronicles an open, independent adoption, with Glenn Close and James Woods as the prospective adoptive parents.

You may find the following books and pamphlets stimulating reading. These materials focus on a variety of subjects related to adoption. The list that follows, comprised primarily of books in print, is not comprehensive, but singles out current interesting books for adults and children. You'll want to update this list as you discover new works.

Adoption: Information and Issues

Christine A. Adamec, *There ARE Babies to Adopt* (New York: Pinnacle Books, 1991). Basic how-to information for adopting an infant.

Adoption Factbook: United States Data, Issues, Regulations and Resources (Washington, D.C.: National Committee for Adoption, 1989). A compendium about adoption designed to fill in information gaps.

Jayne Askin with Bob Oskam, *Search: A Handbook for Adoptees and Birthparents* (New York: Harper & Row, 1982). A resource book that takes interested people through the stages of the search— what's involved and how to go about it. A state-by-state compilation of information including inheritance, the sealing and opening of records, state agencies connected to adoption, and where records are held.

Edmund Blair Bolles, *The Penguin Adoption Handbook: A Guide to Creating Your New Family* (New York: Penguin Books, 1984). Observes Bolles: "Forget the rumors and the scary headlines. You can adopt a child." Look to this book for details about how to adopt rather than issues of child-rearing.

Linda Bothun, *When Friends Ask About Adoption: Question & Answer Guide for Non-Adoptive Parents and Other Caring Adults* (Chevy Chase, Maryland: Swan Publications, 1987). Answers to "Do you love her like your own?" and the other questions that adoptive parents inevitably hear.

David Brodzinsky and Marshall D. Schechter, eds., *The Psychology of Adoption* (New York: Oxford University Press, 1990). This scholarly collection of essays by well-known adoption researchers highlights the problems facing adoptees, adoptive parents, and birth parents. Note the editors: "Our goal was to provide an overview of current work in adoption, with a focus primarily on mental health issues."

Linda Cannon Burgess, *The Art of Adoption* (New York: Norton, 1981). Focuses on the feelings of birth parents, adoptees, and adoptive parents. Grapples with questions of raising children.

Charlene Canape, *Adoption: Parenthood Without Pregnancy* (New York: Avon Books, 1988). A how-to-adopt book that skims the surface of basic issues. One feature: a list of adoption agencies and parent groups state by state. Canape has clearly written this book with infertile couples in mind. Her subtitle reveals a lot.

Arty Elgart with Claire Berman, *The Golden Cradle: How the Adoption Establishment Works and How to Make It Work for You* (New York: Citadel Press, 1991). Elgart's autobiography and the story of the founding of the adoption agency Golden Cradle inserted into a how-to-adopt book.

William Feigelman and Arnold R. Silverman, *Chosen Children* (New York: Praeger, 1983). A research study that examines new patterns of adoptive relationships. Among its subjects: the differences in attitudes between infertile couples and "preferential adopters" (fertile couples, singles), adjustments of black children adopted by white families, adaptation of transracially adopted Korean-born adolescents, and adjustment of Colombian-born children adopted by white families.

Carol Hallenbeck, *Our Child: Preparation for Parenting in Adoption* (Wayne, Pa.: Our Child Press, 1988). An instructor's guide to creating a class for adoptive parents.

Claudia Jewett, *Adopting the Older Child* (Harvard: Harvard Common Press, 1978). A landmark book that introduces people to the adoption of older children. Jewett follows the history of several children and their adoptive families, starting before the adoption and continuing through to the postplacement period.

Patricia Irwin Johnston, *An Adoptor's Advocate* (Fort Wayne, Ind.: Perspectives Press, 1984; to order books, write Perspectives Press, P.O. Box 90318, Indianapolis, Ind. 46290-0318). Linking infertility and adoption, the book seeks to "bring out into the open some of those most carefully concealed fears and doubts that preadoptive parents experience, to help couples and counselors understand the emotional processes that connect infertility and adoption, and to offer some suggestions for improving the system for the benefit of all concerned."

H. David Kirk, *Adoptive Kinship: A Modern Institution in Need of Reform* (Toronto: Butterworth, 1981). This book extends the argument that Kirk set forth in his *Shared Fate: A Theory and Method of Adoptive Relationships,* that the adoptive situation is different from the family whose bonds are based on birth. People involved in adoption must acknowledge the differences as they build their family relationships.

Miriam Komar, *Communicating with the Adopted Child* (New York: Walker and Company, 1991). How to talk with your adopted child, including sample conversations.

Betty Jean Lifton, *Lost and Found: The Adoption Experience,* rev. ed. (New York: Harper & Row, 1988). Focuses on the adoptee's struggle for a sense of identity using extensive interviews with members of the adoption triangle. Her chapter "Rights and Responsibilities for Everyone in the Adoption Circle" is one of the most cogent statements I have seen.

Hope Marindin, ed., *The Handbook for Single Adoptive Parents* (Available from Committee for Single Adoptive Parents, P.O. Box 15084, Chevy Chase, Maryland, 20815). Although written for the single considering adoption, this book contains much valuable information for anyone contemplating adoption. There is a nice mix of practical information (the mechanics of adoption and managing single parenthood) with adoption experiences.

Cynthia D. Martin, *Beating the Adoption Game* (New York: Harcourt Brace Jovanovich, 1988). "This book is written for the potential losers in the adoption agency game who want to know the rules before they start, in order to increase their chances of winning," says Martin. The how-to is refracted through the glass darkly.

Lois Ruskai Melina, *Making Sense of Adoption* (New York: Harper & Row, 1989). Through sample conversations, this book covers the questions adoptees ask and provides answers that adoptive parents may use. There are also sample activities, such as making your own adoption storybook.

Lois Ruskai Melina, *Raising Adopted Children: A Manual for Adoptive Parents* (New York: Harper & Row, 1986). A comprehensive guide that looks at the special circumstances of adoptive parenting. Melina begins with the "instant family" and takes you through the teenage years. Topics covered in the book include adjustment of the family, bonding and attachment, talking to your child about adoption, sexuality, behavior problems, and the importance of family history.

Stanley B. Michelman and Meg Schneider with Antonia van der Meer, *The Private Adoption Handbook: A Step-by-Step Guide to the Legal, Emotional, and Practical Demands of Adopting a Baby* (New York: Villard Books, 1988). Written by an attorney who has specialized in independent adoptions and an adoptive mother who used him for her attorney, the book provides an overview of the process. There's a heavy emphasis on the role that the attorney plays, how newspaper advertising works, installing a baby phone, and the other methods that Michelman's clients have used. If you're considering a private adoption, this book lays out many of the steps.

National Adoption Information Clearinghouse, *National Adoption Directory* (available from the Clearinghouse). Comprehensive state-by-state listings of adoption agencies, parent support groups, and postadoption services.

Jacqueline Plumez, *Successful Adoption: A Guide to Finding a Child and Raising a Family,* rev. ed. (New York: Harmony, 1987). A realistic, helpful book that takes you from the initial stages of thinking about adoption through extended discussions of raising adopted children. Valuable state-by-state information.

Julia L. Posner with James Guilianelli, *CWLA's Guide to Adoption Agencies and Adoption Resources* (Washington, D.C.: Child Welfare League of America, 1990). A state-by-state listing of agencies and their services, including the wait, the children, the requirements, and the costs. For some states there's a 100% response by agencies; for others, much less.

Fred Powledge, *The New Adoption Maze* (St. Louis: C. V. Mosby, 1985). Well-written, readable account of how to adopt that is better at highlighting the maze than in getting you through it. One strong point: the discussion of open adoption. Powledge's technique relies on extended interviews.

Judith Schaffer and Christina Lindstrom, *How to Raise an Adopted Child* (New York: Crown, 1989). The authors see their book as the adoptive parents' Dr. Spock: Adoption information is grafted onto general parenting information. Helpful questions and answers, modeled on an advice column, accompany each chapter.

Dorothy W. Smith and Laurie Nehls Sherwen, *Mothers and Their Adopted Children—The Bonding Process* (New York: Tiresias Press, 1983). Based on a survey and interviews, the book looks at how bonding takes place.

Jerome Smith, *You're Our Child: A Social/Psychological Approach to Adoption* (Washington, D.C.: University Press of America, 1981). Looks at the psychological tasks faced by adoptive parents and adoptees.

Michael Sullivan with Susan Shultz, *Adopt the Baby You Want* (New York: Simon & Schuster, 1990). A step-by-step guide, with a focus on how agencies work, written by an attorney who founded the Southwest Adoption Center in Phoenix. The sample home study at the back of the book and the discussion of agency fees are instructive.

Arthur D. Sorosky, Annette Baran, and Reuben Pannor, *The Adoption Triangle: Sealed or Open Records: How They Affect Adoptees, Birth Parents, and Adoptive Parents*, rev. ed. (New York: Anchor Press/Doubleday, 1984). Examines the effect of the sealed record on adoptees, birth parents, and adoptive parents and sets forth the belief that adoption is a lifelong process. The authors call for reevaluation of current adoption practices toward more openness.

For Children and Adolescents

Nina Bawden, *The Finding* (New York: Lothrop, Lee and Shepard, 1985). A young boy inherits a fortune; the event leads to questions about his adoption. Fiction.

Suzanne Bloom, *A Family for Jamie* (New York: Clarkson Potter, 1991). A simple picture book that describes how a family waited to adopt a baby. Fiction.

Anne Braff Brodzinsky, *The Mulberry Bird* (Fort Wayne, Ind.: Perspectives Press, 1986). How a mother bird realizes that she cannot raise her baby bird and finds a new family for her child. Fiction.

Catherine and Sherry Bunin, *Is That Your Sister? A True Story of Adoption* (New York: Pantheon Books, 1976). Illustrated with photographs of her family and narrated by six-year-old Catherine, this book tells her family's adoption story—the building of a transracial family. Presents questions that children may hear from others. Nonfiction.

Betsy Byars, *The Pinballs* (New York: Harper & Row, 1977). The tale of three children who find themselves in foster care and how they build a friendship. Fiction.

Jeannette Caines, *Abby* (New York: Harper & Row, 1973). Picture book for preschoolers. Abby, who was adopted when she was an infant, likes to look at her baby book and hear the story of her arrival in her family. Fiction.

Iris L. Fisher, *Katie-Bo: An Adoption Story* (New York: Adama Books, 1987). Charming story recounted by older brother of how his Korean sister Katie-Bo comes into the family. Fiction.

Susan Gabel, *Filling in the Blanks: A Guided Look at Growing Up Adopted* (Indianapolis, Ind.: Perspectives Press, 1988). A workbook, designed for children ages ten to fourteen, with pages to fill in about "My Birth Family," "My Adoption Process," "My Adoptive Family," and "My Self." Nonfiction.

Susan Gabel, *Where the Sun Kisses the Sea* (Indianapolis, Ind.: Perspectives Press, 1989). Picture book story of a young boy in a Korean orphanage and his joining a family in the United States. Fiction.

Shirley Gordon, *The Boy Who Wanted a Family* (New York: Harper & Row, 1980). The fears, hopes, and experiences of seven-year-old Michael during the one-year waiting period before the finalization of his adoption. The account takes him from his foster home, the last of many, to his home with his single adoptive mother. Fiction.

Phoebe Koehler, *The Day We Met You* (New York: Bradbury Press,

1990). Simple picture book with lush illustrations about the activities and feelings of a couple on the day they first saw their baby. Fiction.

Irina Korschunow, *The Foundling Fox* (New York: Harper & Row, 1984). Charming picture book telling how a young fox, whose mother had been killed by hunters, got a new mother. Fiction.

Jill Krementz, *How It Feels to be Adopted* (New York: Knopf, 1982). Nineteen children, ages eight to sixteen, shared their feelings with Krementz. Photographs of the children, alone and with their parents and family, are an integral part of the book. A book for parents of young children to read and think about, for older children to read, and for families to share together. Nonfiction.

Betty Jean Lifton, *I'm Still Me* (New York: Knopf, 1981). The book starts out: "It may sound weird to say that your whole life changed because of an American history assignment. But that's the way it was. . . ." When teenager Lori Elkins is asked to prepare a family tree, she has to deal with the issues of adoption, origins, and feelings. In this engrossing novel, Lori Elkins decides to search. A book that's not for teenagers only. Fiction.

Carole Livingston, *Why Was I Adopted?* (Secaucus, N.J.: Lyle Stuart, 1978). Some people like this book; others don't. The message is forthright and clear, the drawings less so. Nonfiction.

Lois Lowry, *Find a Stranger, Say Goodbye* (Boston: Houghton Mifflin, 1978). A teenager seeks out her birth mother. The book explores her complex emotions. Fiction.

Patricia MacLachlan, *Mama One, Mama Two* (New York: Harper & Row, 1982). Simple children's picture book that tells the story of a little girl's entry into foster care. Fiction.

Joyce McDonald, *Mail-Order Kid* (New York: Putnam, 1988). Ten-year-old Flip purchases a fox through a mail-order catalog. As he tries to tame it, he comes to understand the process of acculturation that his newly adopted brother Todd, age six, has been going through. Fiction.

Elisabet McHugh, *Raising a Mother Isn't Easy* (New York: Greenwillow Books, 1983), *Karen's Sister* (New York: Greenwillow Books, 1983), and *Karen and Vicki* (New York: Greenwillow Books, 1984). Tales told by Korean adoptee Karen about her family. *Karen's Sister* highlights adoption issues, since it recounts the arrival and adjustment of five-year-old Meghan from South Korea. Fiction.

Claudia Mills, *Boardwalk with Hotel* (New York: Macmillan, 1985).

Eleven-year-old adoptee Jessica Jarrell is convinced that her parents love her brother and sister, their children by birth, more. Fiction.

Steven L. Nickman, *The Adoption Experience: Stories and Commentaries* (New York: Julian Messner, 1985). Seven short stories on adoption-related themes: from the search, to the "assignment," to the most harrowing—a failed adoption years later. Accompanying the stories are Nickman's commentaries. Fiction.

Joan Lowery Nixon, *A Family Apart, Caught in the Act, In the Face of Danger, A Place to Belong* (New York: Bantam Books, 1987–1989). The "Orphan Train Quartet" chronicles the adventures of the Kelly children, who are sent on an orphan train in the nineteenth century to begin new lives in the American West. Fiction.

Jean Davies Okimoto, *Molly by Any Other Name* (New York: Scholastic, 1990). In this sensitively written story, teenager Molly, with the support of her parents, initiates a search for her birth mother. The author tells the story from both Molly's and her birth mother's perspective. Fiction.

Katherine Paterson, *The Great Gilly Hopkins* (New York: Thomas Y. Crowell, 1978). Eleven-year old Gilly has been shuffled around. When she lands in her latest foster home, she schemes against everyone who tries to befriend her. Fiction.

Fred Powledge, *So You're Adopted* (New York: Scribner's, 1982). A straightforward discussion for adolescents about the feelings of being adopted. Powledge is an adult adoptee and shares his own experiences as part of the narrative. Nonfiction.

Maxine B. Rosenberg, *Being Adopted* (New York: Lothrop, Lee & Shephard, 1984). Using the photographs of George Ancona, Rosenberg profiles a few youngsters: Rebecca, seven, who is part black; Karin, eight, who is Korean; and Andrei, ten, who is Indian. This team has produced other books you might want to look at: *My Friend Leslie*, about a handicapped child; *Living in Two Worlds*, about biracial children; and *Making a New Home in America*, which focuses on the experience of children who have moved from their native countries to the United States. Nonfiction.

Maxine B. Rosenberg, *Growing Up Adopted* (New York: Bradbury Press, 1989). The author asked fourteen adoptees—older children and adults—to talk about their experiences being adopted. Nonfiction.

Jane T. Schnitter, *William Is My Brother* (Indianapolis, Ind.: Perspectives Press, 1991). A picture book whose message is: "Some people tell William that he is special because he was adopted. William is not special because he was adopted. William is special because he is William." Fiction.

Harriet Langsam Sobol, *We Don't Look Like Our Mom and Dad* (New York: Coward-McCann, 1984). Photo essay about two Korean adoptees and their family. Nonfiction.

Susan and Gordon Adopt a Baby (New York: Random House/Children's Television Workshop, 1986). For those who missed the big day on Sesame Street when Susan and Gordon adopted baby Miles, here's a book chronicling the event. Big Bird is jealous, and herein lies the tale. A picture book for Sesame Street aficionados without a preachy adoption message. Fiction.

Theodore Taylor, *Tuck Triumphant* (New York: Doubleday, 1991). Part of a series of stories about Helen and her Labrador Friar Tuck Golden Boy. In this book Helen's parents adopt a six-year-old boy, Chok-Do, from South Korea and discover that he is deaf. How the family deals with his disability is the book's focus. Fiction.

Ann Turner, *Through Moon and Stars and Night Skies* (New York: HarperCollins, 1990). A young Korean boy tells the story of his adoption from South Korea, his flight to the United States, and his meeting with his adoptive parents in this handsomely illustrated picture book. Fiction.

Valentina Wasson, *The Chosen Baby* (New York: Lippincott, 1977). The classic adoption story with updated pictures and text. Fiction.

Marjorie Ann Waybill, *Chinese Eyes* (Scottdale, Penn.: Herald Press, 1974). A picture book that tells the story of a first-grade Korean adoptee's encounter with prejudice—"There's little Chinese eyes!" The book looks at her feelings and her mother's explanation of differences and similarities. Fiction.

Infertility

Gay Becker, *Healing the Infertile Family: Strengthening Your Relationship in the Search for Parenthood* (New York: Bantam Books, 1990). A look at how men and women react—what happens to their identities and their relationship—when confronted with impaired fertility and guidance on coping.

Dr. Joseph H. Bellina and Josleen Wilson, *You Can Have a Baby: Everything You Need to Know About Fertility* (New York: Bantam Books, 1985). A primer of the nuts and bolts of male and female

infertility, providing a rundown of how the body works, the necessary workups and tests, causes, and treatment.

Gary S. Berger, M.D., Marc Goldstein, M.D., and Mark Fuerst, *The
Couple's Guide to Fertility: How New Medical Advances Can Help
You Have A Baby* (New York: Doubleday, 1989). A rundown of the
medical facts of infertility and the various treatments, including
the new reproductive technologies. One distinctive feature: lists
of questions throughout the book that you should be asking yourself and your physician.

Gena Corea, *The Mother Machine: Reproductive Technologies from
Artificial Insemination to Artificial Wombs* (New York: Harper &
Row, 1985). Feminist Corea's stridency may be off-putting, but her
investigation of the "new" reproductive methods—artificial insemination, embryo transfer, *in vitro* fertilization, sex predetermi-
nation—raises questions that people grappling with infertility
should consider.

Stephen L. Corson, M.D., *Conquering Infertility: A Guide for Couples*
(New York: Prentice-Hall, 1990). Detailed medical explanations,
with an emphasis on female fertility problems.

Robert R. Franklin, M.D., and Dorothy Kay Brockman, *In Pursuit of
Fertility: A Consultation with a Specialist* (New York: Holt, 1990).
Written by an infertility specialist, a detailed overview of the
causes of infertility and an explanation of the popular treatments.
There's a look at "infertility breakthroughs" such as IVF, GIFT
and ZIFT, AID, and surrogate motherhood.

Rochelle Friedman and Bonnie Gradstein, *Surviving Pregnancy Loss*
(Boston: Little, Brown, 1982). A sensitive discussion of miscarriage,
stillbirth, ectopic pregnancy, and multiple losses.

Ellen S. Glazer, *The Long-Awaited Stork: A Guide to Parenting After
Infertility* (Lexington, Mass.: Lexington Books, 1990). People's
feelings of loss and of being different do not vanish because of a
successful pregnancy or adoption. How the emotional impact of
infertility spills over into parenting is at the heart of this book.

Ellen Sarasohn Glazer and Susan Lewis Cooper, *Without Child: Experiencing and Resolving Infertility* (Lexington, Mass.: Lexington
Books, 1988). A collection of essays, many of them firsthand accounts, and poems about infertility, pregnancy loss, the new reproductive technologies, adoption, child-free living, and parenting after infertility.

Michael Gold, *And Hannah Wept: Infertility, Adoption, and the Jewish Couple* (Philadelphia: Jewish Publication Society, 1988). Using

Jewish texts, Rabbi Gold explores infertility and adoption from the Jewish point of view. The book is intended as a resource for rabbis, social workers, and other professionals as well as Jewish families.

Joan Liebmann-Smith, *In Pursuit of Pregnancy: How Couples Discover, Cope With and Resolve Their Fertility Problems* (New York: Newmarket Press, 1987). Using three couples, the book highlights through their personal stories how infertility affects the individual. You'll find it hard to put the book down, since it captures the basic, raw emotions.

James McGuirk and Mary Elizabeth McGuirk, *For Want of a Child: A Psychologist and His Wife Explore the Emotional Effects and Challenges of Infertility* (New York: Continuum, 1991). Infertility from the man's and the woman's perspective, with advice offered to counselors as well.

Barbara Eck Menning, *Infertility: A Guide for the Childless Couple* (Englewood Cliffs, N.J.: Prentice-Hall, 1988). Focuses on the experience of infertility and how it affects people. Written by the founder of Resolve, this book looks at the psychological and social toll that infertility takes.

Linda P. Salzer, *Surviving Infertility: A Compassionate Guide Through the Emotional Crisis of Infertility* (New York: Harper-Collins, 1991). While most other books give lip service to the emotional pressure that infertility places on a relationship, Salzer attacks the issue head-on. Writes Salzer: " 'Do you have children?' Such an ordinary question—but for the couple facing infertility, it brings thoughts of temperature charts, doctors' appointments, marital conflict, and sex on schedule. The struggle to have a child can turn your life on end and change a calm, well-adjusted person into a bundle of nerves. I know—I've been there." There's a resonance in this book that makes it required reading if you're in pain.

Sherman J. Silber, *How to Get Pregnant* (New York: Warner, 1991). A basic guide discussing infertility, particularly strong in explaining the reproductive system. Silber emphasizes that infertility is a problem shared by a couple, hence treatment must be directed at both husband and wife.

John J. Stangel, M.D., *The New Fertility and Conception: The Essential Guide for Childless Couples* (New York: Plume Books, 1988). The medical aspects of infertility, from the workup through the new technologies.

Lynne Rutledge Stephenson, *Give Us a Child: Coping with the Personal Crisis of Infertility* (San Francisco: Harper & Row, 1987).

Mixes autobiography with infertility explanation and Christian issues.

Intercountry Adoption

Howard Altstein and Rita J. Simon, eds., *Intercountry Adoption: A Multinational Perspective* (New York: Praeger, 1991). A research volume with essays that describe the experiences of foreign-born adoptees in the United States, Canada, Norway, The Netherlands, Denmark, West Germany, and Israel.

Hyun Sook Han, *Understanding My Child's Korean Origins* (St. Paul, Minn.: Children's Home Society of Minnesota, 1980). Focuses on child care customs.

Frances M. Koh, *Oriental Children in American Homes: How Do They Adjust?* (Minneapolis: East-West Press, 1981). A study of culture and adoption. Koh analyzes the differences between Asian and American society in social relations, methods of discipline, education, and personality development, and discusses their effects on the adjustment of Asian children in American homes.

Jean Nelson-Erichsen and Heino R. Erichsen, *Gamines: How to Adopt from Latin America* (Minneapolis: Dillon Press, 1981). A general overview.

James A. Pahz, *Adopting from Latin America: An Agency Perspective* (Springfield, Illinois: Charles C. Thomas, 1988). The director of Children's Hope in Michigan offers advice, and his perspective, on how intercountry adoption works.

Cheri Register, *Are Those Kids Yours?: American Families with Children Adopted from Other Countries* (New York: Free Press, 1991). Any parent of a child adopted from abroad has heard that question. A broad-ranging book on the issue of international adoption that asks and answers many questions. Says Register: "My intention in writing this book is to identify some of the ethical issues raised by international adoption and to show how they are played out in the actual day-to-day experience of adoptive families."

Report on Foreign Adoption (International Concerns Committee for Children, 911 Cypress Drive, Boulder, Colo. 80303). Issued annually, this report takes a country-by-country, agency-by-agency look at intercountry adoption. Updated during the year.

Hei Sook Park Wilkinson, *Birth is More Than Once: The Inner World of Adopted Korean Children* (Bloomfield Hills, Mich.: Sunrise

Ventures, 1985). In this brief study, Wilkinson reports on her observations of eight young children.

Legal Concerns

Adoption Law and Practice (Albany, N.Y.: Matthew Bender, 1988). A basic textbook for attorneys written by experts in the field.

Open Adoption

Suzanne Arms, *To Love and Let Go* (New York: Knopf, 1983.) A group of profiles: birth mothers who relinquished their children, an adult adoptee's search, an adoption attorney, and prospective adoptive families. Arms vividly describes several open infant adoptions, including one in which the parents were present at the child's birth. The adoptions that she witnessed occurred through independent placement, and the book is a strong plea for more openness in adoption. In 1990 Celestial Arts in Berkeley issued a revised, updated, and expanded edition, *Adoption: A Handful of Hope*. I prefer the first edition and suggest you check for it at your local library.

Lincoln Caplan, *An Open Adoption* (New York: Farrar, Straus & Giroux, 1990). A close-up, engrossing account of how twenty-year-old Peggy Bass in Maryland chose Dan and Lee Stone in Massachusetts as the adoptive parents of her child. Interwoven with this is a more general account of open adoption.

James L. Gritter, ed., *Adoption without Fear* (San Antonio: Corona, 1989). Seventeen couples who adopted through Community, Family and Children's Services in Traverse City, Michigan, tell their story. You'll get a sense of how adoptive parents and birth parents feel when they first meet.

Jeanne Warren Lindsay, *Open Adoption: A Caring Option* (Buena Park, Calif.: Morning Glory Press, 1987). An extensive discussion of open adoption. Lindsay shares the experiences of birth parents and adoptive parents and describes a variety of programs.

Bruce Rappaport, *The Open Adoption Book: A Guide to Adoption Without Tears* (New York: Macmillan, 1992). Written by the director of the Independent Adoption Center, the book focuses on people's fears of open adoption and the realities they will encounter.

Mary Jo Rillera and Sharon Kaplan, *Cooperative Adoption: A Hand-*

book (Westminster, Calif.: Triadoption Publications, 1985). Describes open adoption, setting out guidelines for birth parents and adoptive parents.

Kathleen Silber and Patricia Martinez Dorner, *Children of Open Adoption* (San Antonio: Corona, 1990). A chronicling, based on case studies, of the effect that open adoption has on children from infancy through the teen years. While there's some how-to information, the book is primarily anecdotal.

Kathleen Silber and Phylis Speedlin, *Dear Birthmother* (San Antonio: Corona, 1983). The letters exchanged between adoptive parents and birth parents as well as the letters sent from birth parents to their children form the backbone of this book. The letters are used to hammer away at four myths: (1) that birth parents don't care about their children, (2) that adoption must be a strictly confidential matter, (3) that birth parents will forget about their children, and (4) that if the adoptee loved her parents, she would not have to search for her birth parents.

Mary Stephenson, *My Child Is a Mother* (San Antonio: Corona, 1991). A birth grandmother offers her account of her daughter's unplanned pregnancy and the open adoption that followed.

Personal Accounts/Family Profiles

Barbara J. Berg, *Nothing to Cry About* (New York: Bantam Books, 1983). A moving account of the author's experiences (she suffered two late miscarriages before successfully giving birth). One chapter chronicles her daughter's adoption through an independent placement. Berg's technique involved spreading the word through résumés.

Joseph Blank, *Nineteen Steps Up the Mountain: The Story of the De-Bolt Family* (New York: Lippincott, 1976). Biography of the De-Bolts, who built a large family of special-needs children and later founded Aask America.

Mary Earle Chase, *Waiting for Baby: One Couple's Journey Through Infertility to Adoption* (New York: McGraw Hill, 1990). From infertility and inseminations and psychics to a successful private adoption. And some how-to-adopt information appended for good measure.

Michael Dorris, *The Broken Cord* (New York: HarperCollins, 1989). The chronicle of a single adoptive father's day-to-day experience raising a son affected by Fetal Alcohol Syndrome. You'll understand why this eloquent, absorbing book was a best-seller.

Lorraine Dusky, *Birthmark.* (New York: M. Evans, 1979). Birth mother's account of her pregnancy, her relinquishment of her child, and her postpartum feelings. The book appeared some thirteen years after the birth of her child. Dusky searched for—and eventually found—her daughter.

Florence Fisher, *The Search for Anna Fisher* (New York: Arthur Fields, 1973). A landmark personal chronicle of an adoptee's search for her birth family. Fisher was instrumental in the creation of the adoptee group Adoptees' Liberty Movement Association (ALMA).

Bertha Holt, *The Seed from the East* and *Outstretched Arms* (Eugene, Or.: Reprinted by Industrial Publishing Company, 1983). The story of the development of the Holt adoption program in South Korea. If you're the parent of a child from South Korea, particularly if your child came from the Holt agency in the United States or in South Korea, you'll enjoy reading this family's story. Check with Holt International Children's Services about availability.

Barbara Holtan and Laurel Strassberger, eds., *They Became Part of Us: The Experiences of Families Adopting Children Everywhere* (Maple Grove, Minn.: Mini-World, 1985). A compilation of family chronicles that first appeared in *FACE Facts.*

Betsy Israel, *Grown-Up Fast* (New York: Pocket Books, 1988). The publisher billed this book as "a stark, moving portrait of teenage life in America." It's also the autobiography of a young woman in the 1970s who became pregnant in 1973 and then chose adoption for her baby.

Carolyn Koons, *Tony: Our Journey Together* (San Francisco: Harper & Row, 1984). The saga of the adoption by a single mother of a Mexican youth who had spent years in a boys' prison. A candid chronicle of their adjustment process written in a religious spirit.

Tony Kornheiser, *The Baby Chase* (New York: Atheneum, 1983). What's it like to find yourself involved in an independent placement adoption where the go-between wants $15,000 in cash? Kornheiser describes the difficulties he and his wife encountered in dealing with their infertility, their wanting to adopt a child, and their temptation to pursue this opportunity. The book is strong in conveying their pain and anguish and also their lack of support and basic information.

David Leitch, *Family Secrets: A Writer's Search for His Parents and*

His Past (New York: Delacorte Press, 1984). British journalist Leitch recounts what happens after he meets the birth mother he's spent a lifetime fantasizing.

Betty Jean Lifton, *Twice-Born* (New York: McGraw-Hill, 1975). An autobiography focusing on how Lifton felt as an adoptee, her search and meeting with her birth mother, and the relationship that developed following her search. The emotional complexities of adoption, rather than any legal barriers set up in Lifton's path, form the heart of the book.

Doris Lund, *Patchwork Clan: How the Sweeny Family Grew* (Boston: Little, Brown, 1982). Portrait of John and Ann Sweeny and their seventeen children. The book is particularly good in its description of the adjustment processes of the children in this multiracial family.

Katrina Maxtone-Graham, *An Adopted Woman* (New York: Remi Books, 1983). An autobiography describing the author's search and the many barriers thrown up in her path. Her account raises questions about the policy of closed records and particularly the reluctance of one agency to provide even nonidentifying information.

Tolbert McCarroll, *Morning Glory Babies: Children with AIDS and the Celebration of Life.* The inspirational story of Melissa, Aaron, and Marti, babies with AIDS, who come to live at the Starcross Community in California.

Doris McMillon with Michelle Sherman, *Mixed Blessing: The Dramatic True Story of a Woman's Search for Her Real Mother* (New York: St. Martin's, 1985). Black newscaster Doris McMillon's roots go back to West Germany. Confusion, fantasy, parental tension, child abuse, and adolescent rebellion are central themes in this book.

Jacquelyn Mitchard, *Mother Less Child: The Love Story of a Family* (New York: Norton, 1985). The pace of this book is quite dizzying: from an ectopic pregnancy in the summer of 1982, through infertility and psychological and marital crises, to tubal surgery, to choosing not to parent one newborn through a private adoption and accepting another by January 1984.

Marguerite Ryan, *Adoption Story: A Son Is Given* (New York: Rawson Associates, 1989). How one independent adoption ended up in a bitter court battle for several years.

Carol Schaefer, *The Other Mother: A Woman's Love for the Child She Gave Up for Adoption* (New York: Soho, 1991). Secrecy, shame, guilt, and pain are key ingredients in the moving chronicle of this birth mother. You'll cringe when you read her account of the months spent in a Catholic home for unwed mothers in the 1960s.

Gail Sheehy, *Spirit of Survival* (New York: Morrow, 1986). The story of how the child Phat Mohm survived Pol Pot's Cambodia and came to live in America as Sheehy's adopted daughter. A fascinating chronicle of the day-to-day building of a relationship and how the survivor must come to terms with her past.

Susan T. Viguers, *With Child: One Couple's Journey to Their Adopted Children* (San Diego: Harcourt Brace Jovanovich, 1986). You share this couple's slow, painful coming to grips with infertility, complete with a failed pregnancy and a miscarried private adoption, capped finally with the adoption of two infants.

Marion Lee Wasserman, *Searching for the Stork: One Couple's Struggle to Start a Family* (New York: New American Library, 1988). The author's problem pregnancies are at the heart of this book. At the end of the tale, the couple adopts a baby girl through an agency.

Poetry

Patricia Irwin Johnston, comp., *Perspectives on a Grafted Tree: Thoughts for Those Touched by Adoption* (Fort Wayne, Ind.: Perspectives Press, 1983). Poetry written by adoptive parents and birth parents that touches on parts of the adoption process—"beginnings and endings," "the grafting," "reactions," "attachments," "motherspeakings," "identities," and "reflections."

Special-Needs Adoption

Linda Dunn, ed., *Adopting Children with Special Needs: A Sequel* (Washington, D.C.: NACAC, 1983). Stories by adoptive and foster parents describing their experiences.

Bernard McNamara and Joan McNamara, *The SAFE-TEAM Parenting Workbook* (Greensboro, N.C.: Family Resources, 1990). A workbook for adoptive families with sexually abused children.

Bernard McNamara and Joan McNamara, eds., *Adoption and the Sexually Abused Child* (Portland, Me.: University of Southern Maine, 1990). An anthology of essays that examine adoption and the sexually abused child.

Deborah H. Minshew and Chrisan Hooper, *The Adoptive Family as a Healing Resource for the Sexually Abused Child* (Washington, D.C.: Child Welfare League of America, 1990). A training manual for professionals.

Katherine Nelson, *On The Frontier of Adoption: A Study of Special-Needs Adoptive Families* (New York: Child Welfare League of America, 1985). Examines the experiences of 177 families and the types of services they needed. The book is designed to help adoption professionals and families understand the problems they will face.

John Y. Powell, *Whose Child Am I? Adults' Recollections of Being Adopted* (New York: Tiresias Press, 1985). Adults reflect with Powell about their experiences as older children joining new families. Echoing through the book are the words of Peter: "If you're older, even if you're adopted, you don't give up that feeling of where you first belonged. You can't lose that. I couldn't lose the feeling that—even as bad as my real father was—he existed."

Notes

1. Learning About Adoption

1. This section comes from interviews with adoptive parents and birth parents. For a more extended discussion of Sara's and Matt's experience, see Lois Gilman, "I Gave Up My Baby," *YM,* November 1990.
2. William D. Mosher and William F. Pratt, *Fecundity and Infertility in the United States, 1965–88* (Advance Data from Vital and Health Statistics, no. 192). Hyattsville, Md.: National Center for Health Statistics, 1990.
3. Linda P. Salzer, *Surviving Infertility* (New York: HarperCollins, 1991), p. 7.
4. Sherman J. Silber, *How To Get Pregnant* (New York: Scribner's, 1980), p. 5.
5. Salzer, p. 360
6. Marcia Stamell, "Infertility: Fighting Back," *New York,* March 21, 1983.
7. These questions are based on an interview with Salzer. For a fuller discussion, see her chapter "The Crossroads of Infertility" in Salzer, *Surviving Infertility.* There is also a similar set of questions.

2. Exploring Adoption Through an Agency

1. Barbara Joe, "Singles: Adopting the Family Way," *Washington Post,* Jan. 25, 1982.
2. Barbara Joe, "Black Children Waiting," *Metropolitan Washington Magazine,* Dec. 1982–Jan. 1983, reprinted in the newsletter of the International Concerns Committee for Children.
3. Peter Slavin, "So You Want To Adopt," *Air Force Times,* Feb. 13, 1989.

3. The Home Study

1. Thomas D. Morton, "Practice Issue: The Home Study," *Adoption Report,* 1982.

2. Morton, *Adoption Report,* p. 5.
3. Pat Shirley, *FACE Facts,* Nov. 1982.
4. I have drawn from on a fact sheet prepared in the early 1980s by the now-defunct Sonoma County, Calif., chapter of OURS, *What to Do If You Get Stuck.*
5. Pat Shirley, *FACE Facts,* Nov. 1982.
6. Based on Kenneth J. Hermann, Jr., *Adoption: Questions, Resources and Readings* (OURS of Western New York, Feb. 1983), *What to Do If You Get Stuck,* and interviews I conducted in 1990.

4. Searching for a Baby Independently

1. Bonnie D. Gradstein, Marc Gradstein, and Robert H. Glass, "Private Adoption," *Fertility and Sterility* 37, no. 4 (April 1982), pp. 548–51. Gradstein et al. also state that half of their clients had personal meetings with the mother, and nineteen attended the birth.
2. Lois Gilman, "Adoption: How to Do It on Your Own," *Money,* Oct. 1985, pp. 161–68.
3. Gradstein et al., p. 549. Cynthia White Hecker tells how she successfully used this approach in "Wanted: A Baby to Love," *Wellesley,* Summer 1983. Hecker and her husband met with success within a few months; in fact, they met with two birth mothers and ended up the parents of two infants. For a fuller discussion of the various alternatives, see Cynthia D. Martin, *Beating the Adoption Game* (New York: Harcourt Brace Jovanovich, 1988).
4. I have drawn my examples from the section "Financial Considerations," in the handbook *Successful Private Adoption!* (Washington, D.C.: Families for Private Adoption, 1989). The examples of fifteen families are given, as well as a helpful discussion, "Guidelines for Financing a Private Adoption."
5. I have relied on the section "Obtaining Background and Medical Information" in *Successful Private Adoption!* There are sample forms that you can use.

5. Understanding Open Adoption

1. There are many definitions of open adoption today, and the definitions keep changing. When *Dear Birthmother* by Kathleen Silber and Phylis Speedlin first appeared in 1982, the authors talked about the "process of accepting the responsibility of raising an individual who has two sets of parents"—and called for different practices: sharing names, sharing letters, sharing photographs, meeting face-to-face. As this chapter shows, open adoption has moved beyond that. I have relied on experts such as Kathleen Silber, Jim Gritter, and Sharon Kaplan and on my interviews with adoptive parents and birth parents who have been participating in open adoptions to help me more fully understand what they are experiencing. I have tried to read the currently available literature and attended adoptive parents' preparation sessions offered by Lutheran Social Services of Colorado in 1990.

Finally, it should be noted that, with the cooperation of Catholic Social
Services of Green Bay, Wisconsin, I first conducted extensive telephone
interviews with birth mothers and with adoptive parents in 1983 for the
first edition of *The Adoption Resource Book*. While the names Joan Smith,
Sharon Blair, and Donna King are pseudonyms, these three women have
kept in touch with me since then and updated their stories over the years.
This book is the beneficiary.

2. *Cooperative adoption* is a trademark term developed by Sharon Kaplan and
Mary Jo Rillera. You can find a fuller description in their book *Cooperative
Adoption* (Westminster, Calif.: Triadoption Publications, 1985).
3. Beverly Fritz, "Healing the Past," *OURS,* Nov.–Dec. 1989.
4. Kathleen Silber and Patricia Martinez Dorner, *Children of Open Adoption*
(San Antonio: Corona, 1990), pp. 85–6.
5. *Ibid.,* p. 15.
6. *Ibid.,* p. 15.
7. Jeanne Warren Lindsay, *Open Adoption: A Caring Option* (Buena Park,
Calif.: Morning Glory Press, 1987), p. 180.
8. Lois Gilman, "I Gave Up My Baby," *YM,* Nov. 1990. I have quoted from
the article as well as drawn from unpublished sections of the interview with
Sara and from an unpublished interview with the adoptive mother Becky
Miller. The names used are pseudonyms.
9. Professor Grotevant discussed preliminary observations at the 1991 Adoptive Families of America conference in Chicago in June 1991 in the workshop "Research on the Continuum on Open Adoption." Other quotes from
Professor Grotevant come from this session.
10. Sharon Harrigan, "Problems You May Face," *OURS,* Nov.–Dec. 1989.
11. This list is derived from my interviews concerning open adoption and my
participation in the orientation process at Lutheran Social Services in Denver. You'll find a similar list in the personal workbook accompanying the
video/audiotape collection *Winning at Adoption* (The Family Network,
P.O. Box 1995, Studio City, Calif. 91614-0995).
12. While I interviewed Kathleen Silber for this book, this opinion was expressed in *Open Adoption: The Experts Speak Out,* produced by Carol
Land and Sharon Kaplan. This videotape and its accompanying booklet can
be obtained from Children's Services Center in Pacific Grove, Calif.

6. Searching for a Waiting Child in the United States

1. These anecdotes come from the *Growing with FAS* newsletter, January
1990, p. 3, and Sandra Blakeslee's, "Child-Rearing Is Stormy When Drugs
Cloud Birth," *New York Times,* May 19, 1990. For a subscription to the
newsletter, contact Pamela Groves, ed., *Growing with FAS,* 7802 S.E. Taylor, Portland, Or. 97215.
2. This anecdote comes from an unpublished manuscript of the Jenkinses,
"Koko, an AIDS Baby's Story," that the family generously shared with me.
3. Elizabeth Bartholet, "Where Do Black Children Belong: The Politics of

402
NOTES

Race Matching in Adoption," *University of Pennsylvania Law Review* 139, 5, May 1991, pp. 1183–4.
4. Based on material in the newsletter of Alabama Friends of Adoption (Birmingham) in 1982.
5. Connecticut Adoption Resource Exchange, *Second Annual Report,* July 1, 1981–June 30, 1982, p. 30.

7. Pursuing an Intercountry Adoption

1. The Immigration and Naturalization Service keeps track of the number of "immigrant orphans" admitted annually and does a country-by-country breakdown. Figures given here were provided by the statistics office.
   Meetings were held in 1990 and 1991 under the auspices of the Hague Conference on Private International Law to develop a convention on international cooperation in the intercountry adoption of children. Noted Peter H. Pfund of the U.S. State Department in a May 1990 memorandum to members of a study group: "The convention may well come to be seen as establishing an authoritative international standard or norm for the intercountry adoption of children."
2. From *Adoption—A Family Affair,* prepared by Holt International Children's Services, Eugene, Or.
3. This was originally published in *FACE Facts.* Reprinted in Barbara Holtan and Laurel Strassberger, eds., *They Became Part of Us* (Maple Grove, Minn.: Mini-World, 1985), p. 180.
4. *GIFT,* Summer 1982.
5. Margeret K. Hostetter, M.D., Sandra Iverson, R.N., Kathryn Dole, O.T.R., and Dana Johnson, M.D., Ph.D., "Unsuspected Infectious Diseases and Other Medical Diagnoses in the Evaluation of Internationally Adopted Children," *Pediatrics* 83, no. 4, April 1989, p. 559.
6. James A. Pahz, *Adopting from Latin America* (Springfield, Ill.: Charles C. Thomas, 1988), pp. 47–8.
7. Article by Dr. Jerri Jenista in *ICCC Newsletter,* 1988. Dr. Jenista shared the manuscript with me.
8. *Ibid.*

8. Paperwork

1. Based on information in *Where to Write for Vital Records* (U.S. Department of Health and Human Services, National Center for Health Statistics, June 1990, August 1990 update, and July 1991 update).
2. A detailed, current book, written for use by attorneys, is *Adoption Law and Practice* (Albany, N.Y.: Matthew Bender, 1988). The National Adoption Information Clearinghouse in Rockville, Maryland, will provide individuals with information about their state adoption law.

9. The Special Paperwork of an Intercountry Adoption

1. This list is based on information in *The Immigration of Adopted and Prospective Adoptive Children* (U.S. Immigration and Naturalization Service, revised 1990) and the fact sheet "Ask Immigration" (Rev. Sept. 13, 1990).

10. Preparing for Your Child

1. From the newsletter of New York Singles Adopting Children, Dec. 1990.
2. Claudia L. Jewett, *Adopting the Older Child* (Harvard, Mass.: Harvard Common Press, 1978), p. 53.
3. *New York Times,* Nov. 2, 1983.
4. *State Laws and Regulations Guaranteeing Employees Their Jobs After Family and Medical Leave,* Women's Legal Defense Fund brochure, 1990.
5. Hewitt Associates, *Adoption Benefits,* Jan. 1991
6. U.S. General Accounting Office, "Adoption: Assistance Provided by Selected Employers to Adopting Parents," Dec. 1989.
7. Margaret Hostetter, M.D., and Dana E. Johnson, M.D., Ph.D., "International Adoption: An Introduction for Physicians," *American Journal of Diseases of Children,* 143, March 1989.
8. Among the specialized literature addressed to physicians about adopted children are: Hostetter and Johnson *(see above);* Margaret K. Hostetter, M.D., Sandra Iverson, R.N., Kathryn Dole, O.T.R., and Dana Johnson, M.D., PhD., "Unsuspected Infectious Diseases and Other Medical Diagnoses in the Evaluation of Internationally Adopted Children," *Pediatrics* 83, no. 4, April 1989; Jerri Ann Jenista, M.D., and Daniel Chapman, M.D., "Medical Problems of Foreign-Born Adopted Children," *American Journal of Diseases of Children,* 141, March 1987; Carl M. Melina, M.D., and Lois Melina, M.A., "The Family Physician and Adoption," *American Family Physician,* February 1985; and Carl M. Melina, M.D., and Lois Melina, M.A., "The Physician's Responsibility in Adoption, Part II: Caring for the Adoptive Family," *Journal of the American Board of Family Practice* 1, no. 2, 1988.
9. Jewett, *Adopting the Older Child,* p. 99.
10. *Ibid.,* pp. 99–100. Jewett also spoke with me in 1991 and reviewed portions of the manuscript. Some of these questions, as well as additional comments from her, come from our discussions.
11. For a discussion of breast-feeding adopted children, see Lois Ruskai Melina, *Raising Adopted Children: A Manual for Adoptive Parents* (New York: Harper & Row, 1986); Vicki Yeager Patton; "Breastfeeding Your Adopted Baby," *Open Adoption,* June/July 1990; and Judith Gelman, "Breast or Bottle," *FACE Facts,* Nov.–Dec. 1987.
12. Lois Melina, "Cocaine and Alcohol Affect Unborn Babies," *Adopted Child,* Nov. 1988; and Judith Schaffer, *Cocaine Use During Pregnancy: Its Effects on Infant Development and Implications for Adoptive Parents* (New York State Citizens' Coalition for Children [614 West State Street, Ithaca, New

York 14850], 1989). The National Association for Perinatal Addiction Research and Education has prepared a special Adoptive Parents' packet that you can order.

13. Cheri Register, *Are Those Kids Yours?: American Families with Children Adopted from Other Countries* (New York: Free Press, 1991), pp. 78, 79.
14. Comments made by Jack Frank at the Adoptive Parents Committee adoption conference, "Adoption: Directions for the 80s," Nov. 20, 1983.
15. Jewett, p. 81.
16. James L. Gritter, ed., *"Adoption Without Fear"* (San Antonio: Corona, 1989), pp. 138, 145.
17. *PLAN,* July–Aug. 1984. Reprinted in *FAIR,* Oct. 1982, p. 11.
18. Melina, *Raising Adopted Children,* p. 12.
19. Lois Melina, "Don't Re-name Even a Young Child," *Adopted Child,* July 1982, pp. 1, 4. Another interesting article on the subject is Joyce S. Kaser and R. Kent Boesdorfer, "What Should We Name This Child? The Difficulties of Naming Older Adopted Children," *Children Today,* Nov.–Dec. 1981, p. 8.
20. Gloria Petersen, ed., *The Special Student* (Illinois Council on Adoptable Children, 1982), p. 1.
21. Comments made by Jack Frank at the Adoptive Parents Committee adoption conference, "Adoption: Directions for the '80s," Nov. 20, 1983.
22. For a discussion of how grandparents feel about adoption, see Lois Gilman, "A Special Kind of Love," *New Choices,* Feb. 1990.
23. Melina, *Raising Adopted Children,* p. 35.

11. Adjustments

1. *Buena Vista,* May 1983. Many adoptive parents talked with me about their adjustment experiences. Where the anecdote is based on a published source, I have footnoted the source. Otherwise the information comes from my interviews.
2. David M. Brodzinsky, "Adjustment to Adoption: A Psychological Perspective," *Clinical Psychology Review* 7, 1987, p. 32.
3. Barbara J. Berg, *Nothing to Cry About* (New York: Bantam Books, 1983), p. 199.
4. Originally printed in *FACE Facts,* April 1983. Reprinted in Holtan and Strassberger.
5. *Clark Adoption Resources Newsletter,* June 1983.
6. Dorothy W. Smith and Laurie Nehls Sherwen, *Mothers and Their Adopted Children: The Bonding Process* (New York: Tiresias Press, 1983), p. 102.
7. *Ibid.,* p. 103.
8. Register, p. 111.
9. Jill Krementz, *How It Feels to Be Adopted* (New York: Knopf, 1982), p. 16.
10. Maxine B. Rosenberg, *Growing Up Adopted* (New York: Bradbury Press), pp. 91–5.

11. "Infant Adoption: Two Family Experiences with Intercountry Adoption," *Children Today,* Nov.–Dec. 1980, pp. 2–5. All quotations about Jane are taken from this article.
12. Brazelton is quoted in Lois Gilman, "Adoption—Big Adjustments, Big Rewards," *Mothers Today,* Sept.–Oct. 1984, p. 31.
13. Barbara Holtan, "Are We Having Fun Yet?" *Report on Foreign Adoption,* 1991, p. 34.
14. Ibid.
15. Laurie Flynn, "Why Would Anyone Adopt a Teenager?" *Change,* Fall 1980, pp. 7–8. All quotations from Flynn are from this article.
16. When discussing the grieving process, experts often refer to Elisabeth Kübler-Ross, *On Death and Dying* (New York: Macmillan, 1969). You might also want to read Claudia L. Jewett's *Helping Children Cope with Separation and Loss* (Harvard, Mass.: Harvard Common Press, 1982).
17. Claudia Jewett, *A Parent's Guide to Adopting an Older Child,* p. 21. (pamphlet available from the Open Door Society of Massachusetts).
18. Jewett, *Adopting the Older Child,* p. 288.
19. "Looking Back at Disruption." Materials developed at a 1975 "Disruption" workshop in conjunction with the annual meeting of Spaulding for Children. The quoted material is excerpted from a section entitled "Disruption."
20. See Trudy Festinger, "Adoption Disruption: Rates and Correlates," in David Brodzinsky and Marshall D. Schechter, eds., *The Psychology of Adoption* (New York: Oxford University Press, 1990) and Richard P. Barth and Marianne Berry, *Adoption and Disruption—Rates, Risks, and Responses* (Hawthorne, N.Y.: Aldine de Gruyter, 1988).
21. Festinger, p. 217.
22. *Clark Adoption Resources Newsletter,* June 1983.

12. Raising the Adopted Child

1. All quotations are from Katrina Maxtone-Graham, *An Adopted Woman* (New York: Remi Books, 1983).
2. Krementz, p. 8.
3. Betty Jean Lifton, *Lost and Found* (New York: Harper & Row, 1988), pp. 205–6.
4. David H. Brodzinsky, Dianne Schechter, and Anne Braff Brodzinsky, "Children's Knowledge of Adoption: Developmental Changes and Implications for Adjustment," in R. Ashmore and D. Brodzinsky, eds., *Thinking About the Family: Views of Parents and Children* (Hillsdale, N.J.: Erlbaum, 1986), p. 212.
5. Some of this material originally appeared in Lois Gilman, "Adoption: Tackling the Tough Questions," *Parenting,* November 1990. I interviewed both David Brodzinsky and Lois Melina for this article.
6. Brodzinsky et al., pp. 227–8.

7. *Ibid.*, pp. 213–14.

8. See, for example, Miriam Komar, *Communicating with the Adopted Child* (New York: Walker, 1991).

9. For a discussion of Judaism and adoption, see Michael Gold, *And Hannah Wept: Infertility, Adoption and the Jewish Couple* (Philadelphia: Jewish Publication Society, 1988).

10. Rosenberg, *Growing Up Adopted*, p. 8. For a discussion of the importance of rituals in adoption, see Lois Melina, "Adoption Rituals Needed to Enhance Sense of Family," *Adopted Child*, March 1990.

11. Lifton, p. 20.

12. Pat Tobin, "Blessing in a Back Street," in FACE booklet, *Family Building Through Adoption.*

13. Lois Melina, *Making Sense of Adoption: A Parent's Guide* (New York: Harper & Row, 1989), p. 113.

14. Lifton, pp. 205–6.

15. Krementz, pp. 79–80.

16. Melina, *Making Sense of Adoption*, p. 37.

17. Excerpted from Lois Melina, "Even Well Adjusted Parents Can Be Uneasy Disclosing Adoption," *Adopted Child*, Jan. 1991. For a more complete discussion, see the article.

18. Melina, *Raising Adopted Children*, p. 81.

19. In addition to the discussions in Melina's books, there is her "Teachers Need to Be More Sensitive to Adoption Issues," *Adopted Child*, Aug. 1990, and her audiotape, *The Adopted Child in the Classroom.* Contact Adoptive Families of America in Minnesota for reprints of articles that have appeared in *OURS* magazine.

20. H. David Kirk, *Shared Fate* (New York: Free Press, 1964), pp. 30, 35.

21. Article in the newsletter of Holt International Children's Services, Jan.–March 1982.

22. *Woman's Day*, Sept. 13, 1983, p. 12.

23. Ruth Chamberlin, "Conference Review: Adoptees Talk About Transracial Adoption," *Adoptalk*, Oct. 1982.

24. Judith Schaffer and Christina Lindstrom, *How To Raise an Adopted Child* (New York: Crown, 1989), pp. 280–81.

25. Holt International Children's Services, *Adoption–A Family Affair.*

26. Holt newsletter, 1982.

27. Holt newsletter, 1982.

28. *New York Times*, Nov. 1, 1990.

29. Jayne Askin with Bob Oskam, *Search* (New York: Harper & Row, 1982), p. xiv.

30. Arthur D. Sorosky, Annette Baran, and Reuben Pannor, *The Adoption Triangle: Sealed or Open Records: How They Affect Adoptees, Birth Parents, and Adoptive Parents*, rev. ed. (Garden City, N.J.: Anchor Press/Doubleday, 1984), p. 201.

31. Lois Melina, "Middle Childhood May Be Time to Contact Birth Parents," *Adopted Child*, Dec. 1990, p. 4.

Index